TIGERS O...

COVER PICTURES

Front Cover: Irish champion jump jockey, Charlie Swan, returns to the winner's enclosure to a tremendous reception on Montelado after his pulverising 12-lengths win in the Supreme Novices Hurdle at the 1993 Cheltenham Festival meeting (successful trainer, Pat Flynn, is on right). And (inset), left, Adrian Maguire in triumphant mood after winning the Gold Cup on Cool Ground in 1992 and (inset), right, Michael Kinane gives a thumbs up victory sign after his brilliant win on Carroll House in the 1989 Prix de l'Arc de Triomphe (main picture: Caroline Norris).

Back Cover: THE DAY ST. JOVITE SWAMPED DR DEVIOUS . . . Christy Roche shows his delight after winning the 1992 Budweiser Irish Derby in breathtaking style, beating the Epsom Derby winner, Dr. Devious by twelve lengths in record time and (inset), left, Jim Bolger, trainer of St. Jovite and (inset), right, Dermot Weld, who made history in 1993 by sending Dr Michael Smurfit's Vintage Crop to become the first horse from the Northern Hemisphere to win the Melbourne Cup (main picture: Caroline Norris).

Other books by Raymond Smith include:

Under the Blue Flag (1980)
The Poker Kings of Las Vegas (1982)
Charles J. Haughey: The Survivor (1983)
Garret: the Enigma (1985)
Haughey and O'Malley: The Quest for Power (1986)
Vincent O'Brien: The Master of Ballydoyle (1990)
The High Rollers of the Turf (1992)
The Complete Handbook of Gaelic Football (1993)

TIGERS OF THE TURF

By

RAYMOND SMITH

Sporting Books Publishers
Dublin
1994

TIGERS OF THE TURF

First published 1994

Copyright © Raymond Smith 1994

Published by Sporting Books Publishers, Dublin.
Cover origination and colour section by
Impress Communications Group Ltd., 14 Fitzwilliam Place, Dublin 2.
Printed by Leinster Leader Ltd., Naas, Co. Kildare.

CONTENTS

Author's Note

My book, *The High Rollers Of The Turf*, put the spotlight firmly on the big-time gamblers, of whom it has been said that they have ice water in the veins instead of blood.

I felt compelled to follow that book with another that would concentrate on outstanding personalities in the riding and training spheres, whose exploits in recent times have caught the imagination of the public. The milestones they have created will endure long beyond the point when they decide to step down.

I have been attracted especially by the singular achievements of Adrian Maguire, Michael Kinane, Jim Bolger and Dermot Weld, while I have no hesitation in saying that it would be possible to write a book on each, I hope I have done the next best thing by endeavouring to distil between the covers of one work the moments of greatest significance in their careers to date, with new insights into their backgrounds, methods and motivations and the professionalism that has been paramount to their success.

Through the chapters on this quartet you touch the very heart of much that is racing on the Flat and over the jumps. But there are others too who have co-operated fully with me and whose stories will be read avidly – Charlie Swan, Christy Roche, Tommy Stack and Aidan O'Brien to name another handful of real achievers.

Not overlooked are the small men – Tom Foley, Sirrell Griffiths, the O'Sullivans of Lombardstown, near Mallow, County Cork, and the Prices from Herefordshire. Tom Foley's triumph with Dan O'Neill's Danoli in the Sun Alliance Novices' Hurdle at the 1994 Cheltenham Festival meeting belonged to The Field of Dreams. From the same Field of Dreams scenario was Flakey Dove's victory in the Smurfit Champion Hurdle. The mare who shares a field with a flock of sheep gave her farmer-trainer, Richard Price, a moment that caused him to explain: 'Tell me that this is not all a dream.' His 70-year-old father, in whose colours the mare ran, had gone hunting that morning, not travellng to Cheltenham because he didn't like crowds. However, he joined with all the others in the celebration in 'The Lamb' (one of Stoke Prior's two pubs) that same evening.

In contrast you have big-name trainers from Newmarket, like Henry Cecil, who ride the High Sierras and who train for oil-rich Arab Sheikhs and you have National Hunt trainers like David 'The Duke' Nicholson and Martin Pipe who have the fire-power to turn out a constant stream of winners as they battle for the Trainers' crown in Britain. The big and the small, they all have a place.

I wish to extend a special word of thanks to Stephen Pepper and Maurice Moore for their work on the design of the cover jacket of this book.

My thanks also to Impress Communications Group Ltd. of 14, Fitzwilliam Place, Dublin, who were responsible for print originations of the cover and the colour section; to racing photographers, Caroline Norris, Peter Mooney, Ed Byrne, Colin Turner, Bernard Parkin and Liam Healy who provided the bulk of the pictures and also Michael Daly of the Photographic Library of Independent Newspapers; Eugene Webber of the Associated Press Library, Fleet Street, who again so readily and so quickly facilitated me with essential cuttings and the staff of Independent Newspapers cuttings' library, who, as always, were so co-operative.

My deep appreciation is expressed to Tony Sweeney for his work in checking dates and data relevant to races past and to Tom Brady for his assistance with the Shergar chapter. My thanks also to the papers in Ireland and Britain that allowed me to quote from various articles and news features.

The book would not have met the launching deadline but for the magnificent work of the Leinster Leader, who have printed all my recent books. A special word of thanks to my friend, Michael Kane, who like a good general in the field saw to it that everything went smoothly and that there were no hitches.

The grind of intensive writing over many long weeks from early Spring, through Summer days into the changing colours of Autumn was made easier by the conducive atmosphere and the friendship I found in favoured centres of mine, like the thatched cottages in Ballyvaughan (my thanks to my friends McNeill O'Loughlin and Jim Hyland for making my sojourns in the village so pleasant) and Corofin (again not forgetting Neil and Trish Cleary of Bofey Quinn's for all their kindness) and the happy times in Rosslare Strand (my deep appreciation and thanks to my friends, Terence and Annette Sweeney and not overlooking either Peter and Noreen Fox), while I must not forget to put on record once again my appreciation of the courtesy I experienced at all times from the staff of Kelly's Strand Hotel, while I must add that I derived much pleasure in playing Rosslare Golf Links on days when the typewriter was set aside.

RAYMOND SMITH

Dublin
September 1994

Introduction

"Thank you, Lord, for Giving us a Horse like Danoli"

Fr Seán Breen – known as "The Breener" to the regulars who patronise Irish racecourses – lifted his hands to heaven and thanked the Lord for giving Ireland a horse like Danoli.

He didn't have to interject at that moment of prayer that this one had rescued many an Irish punter who was facing extinction after the whitewash of the opening day of the '94 Festival meeting.

It was St Patrick's Day in the Golden Valley Hotel – Gold Cup Day – and, after collecting our winnings on Danoli from a bookmaker who had given us 2/1 a few nights previously, we were ready to "go to war" again with plenty of ammunition for the job in hand. I had a brandy and port (for the sake of a delicate stomach!) as I chatted with my good friend and Cheltenham regular, Liam Dillon. We both lifted our glasses to the memory of the incomparable Con Carroll, who hailed originally from Dungourney, West Cork, and who had been "Mein Host" in The Cotswold Pub through long, memorable Fridays. He had passed away in retirement since the last Festival meeting. And in this shared moment of remembrance of times past, Liam Dillon and I recalled how Con would cut the succulent slices of beef on the bar counter (one Cheltenham from the Tuesday to the Friday he served no less than thirty sides of beef, the equivalent of fifteen animals) while Jimmy Whelan, a true Dubliner, regaled us with stories of pigeon racing and how he was having an ante-post bet on a "dark one" to win the Blue Riband of that particular sport!

Now the management kindly closed the bar temporarily while Fr Breen was saying Mass. They left up on the spot behind his head the price-list for the drinks, including the champagne. He wore the shamrock over his priestly clothes. We all wore our shamrocks proudly.

I found myself part of a congregation that included three trainers – Arthur Moore, Michael Hourigan and Homer Scott – and one of the leading "rails" bookies on Irish racecourses, Dick Power, also well-known Dublin owner and hotelier, Paddy Fitzpatrick and familiar hard-bitten faces from the betting ring, veterans who would be back in the trenches that same afternoon in hand-to-hand combat with the "enemy" (bookies to the uninitiated) and, after Charlie Swan's treble on the Wednesday, especially Danoli's unforgettable triumph in the Sun Alliance Hurdle, they now had the fire-power to really go over the top with a vengeance.

Fr Breen had done a head-count beforehand of the number of people likely to partake of Holy Communion. He did another quick head-count during Mass itself. But he under-estimated the last-minute rush, like the rush of the prevous day to get on Danoli despite the restricted odds of 7/4. He actually ran out of consecrated hosts, having already split half of his supply.

We understood fully his sentiments as he said in the audible silence of the bar-turned-chapel "Thank you Lord for giving us a horse like Danoli' and we appreciated his gesture when he prayed that the Irish punters would be guided from on high in their battle with the bookies – and that they would hit more good winners.

Standing at the back of the congregation, I could not but smile at the incongruity of the champagne prices over-shadowing the bowed head of the priest sporting his shamrock at Mass, of the prayerful appeals to the good Lord to lend us wisdom on this day and the truly cosmopolitan nature of the congregation itself. But nothing surprises us anymore where Cheltenham is concerned.

To miss Cheltenham on a Friday, to rush home, I mean, on the Thursday night if you have no pressing engagements next day, is akin to leaving undrunk a bottle of a rare vintage wine. There are men, I know, who would be happy to have their ashes spread at the point at the winning post where Jonjo O'Neill's arm-aloft gesture to the heavens, as Dawn Run won the 1986 Gold Cup, was the signal for the most emotive victory scenes ever witnessed in the shadow of the Cotswolds. Others reflecting on the '94 Festival meeting would be quite happy to leave their ashes at the last flight – the one Danoli cleared as another great "Irish roar" rocked the stands and enclosures and the amphitheatre of the winner's enclosure erupted into a crescendo of sound as Tom Foley and Dan O'Neill, pride written all over their faces, came back in with the gelding who had restored Irish pride after the hammer-blows of the previous day.

The Friday of the '94 Festival meeting became for me a long day of "crack" that has rarely been equalled at any Festival meeting. It was a Happening in the bar of the Queen's Hotel, created out of a spontaneous gathering of characters, who would have done credit to the philosophy and outlook of my late Texan friend, Jack (Treetop) Straus, one of the most feared of all the High Rollers of the poker world that I came to know in Las Vagas, whose motto was "Better one day as a lion than a hundred years as a lamb."

Jimmy (The Buck) Ryan from Fethard, from the county that harbours the world-renowned Coolmore Stud complex and the stables of "Mouse" Morris, was telling us over the bucks fizz of the ingenuity of a guy who did the rounds exclaiming: "Roll up, roll up and see the dancin' duck."

"He had an old bit of galvanised sheeting with an oilburner under it," said Jimmy, "and you can bet that the goddam duck danced and danced like Fred Astaire or Gene Kelly as he felt his feet burning."

When one duck had had enough of the dancing, he was replaced by another. "Roll up, roll up and see the dancin' duck . . ."

Meanwhile, the guy's wife was on the other side of the makeshift tent exclaiming: "Roll up, roll up and see the Holy Fryer."

The Holy Fryer happened to be a frying pan with a hole in it.

And then the three Irish nuns who went to London to attend the International Convention of the good sisters. At the luncheon break they go into Hyde Park to partake of their sandwiches and the flask of tea. They happen to take a seat right next to one occupied by three ladies of easy virtue.

Anyway, one of the ladies of the night had been out with a Greek shipping tycoon who had given her an island and an oil tanker; the second had been out with a German who presented her with a factory and a diamond as big as the Ritz while the third had met a Japanese tycoon who left the other two completely in the shade as the yen showered on her like confetti in addition to a plethora of gifts.

One of the nuns was heard to remark quietly, as she finished her ham sandwich: "To hell with the parish priest and his Mars bar!"

Fr Phil Noonan of Fethard was a born character, an enthusiastic racegoer who never missed a meeting, especially during the jumping season, if he could manage it but yet at the same time he was a priest renowned for his charity and his rejection of the pomp and circumstance that creates barriers between people and can lead to judgements based on the money a person amasses in life.

When he died in a Dublin hospital, his remains were brought back to Fethard for burial. They stopped the hearse at the Curragh – "so that Fr Phil could bid a last farewell to a racecourse where he had a lot of enjoyment, especially on Derby day," according to Jimmy Ryan.

They buried him, at his own request, among the very poor in the local cemetery. He had been true in death to the outlook he held in life. "One of our own, our very own," as Jimmy Ryan put it.

Brian Geraghty of Bord Fáilte (the Irish Tourist Board), who wore the colours of his county at senior level in gaelic football, tells the story of the undertaker who liked his drop of the hard stuff. He had gone to Shannon Airport to collect a coffin that had arrived on a plane from England. A man from the West of Ireland who had taken no part in the War of Independence and expected no honours at his funeral. The undertaker, as he dropped into various establishments on the road, eventually cut things rather too finely and realised that he would have to put the boot down if he was to make it in time.

The coffin rolled off the hearse and hit the road with a bang. Fortunately, the lid did not come off but the coffin was dinged all the same.

Our man was worried. A damaged coffin being carried shoulder-high into the church. He couldn't have that.

He searched around the back of the hearse and found an Irish Tricolour. "'Twill do the job," he said to himself with his hand on his heart.

As these two old farmers, who had known the deceased in his youth, before he took the emigrant ship to England, watched the coffin being borne past them with the Tricolour covering it, one remarked to the other: "Sure, Mick, I never knew that Dan was out in the Troubles. God rest his soul."

And so it went through the Long Day and the popping champagne corks and all the laughter and the "crack" until we caught the last flight out of Birmingham.

We carried home with us too the memory of Ted Walsh at a Bord Fáilte dinner during the week, attended by quite a number of British racing writers and television personalities, bringing the house down with his story of the three Irishmen at the World Cup finals in Italy in 1990. They are travelling in a car outside Rome when they come upon the Popemobile overturned on the side of the road. They recognise it from the time of the Pope's visit to Ireland. Inside is the Pope – dead at the wheel. He had slipped out of the Vatican for a quiet afternoon's drive on his own just to enjoy the country-side.

Soon the three boys are surrounded by police cars, the sirens blaring, the Vatican dignitaries looking grave and solemn. It is impressed upon them that the announcement of the Pope's sudden death cannot be made until the following Monday, as the world will have to be told that he fell seriously ill and passed away peacefully in his sleep some days later. Nothing about this unfortunate accident. Not a word. The boys, like good Catholics, agree not to tell the proverbial sinner.

On the plane home the next day they hit upon a plan to make a "killing" out of the secret they were holding. Each will ring his bookmaker and ask for the odds on the announcement of the Pope's death being made the following Monday.

Naturally, the bookies thought they were facilitating mug punters in a league of their own. Betting on two flies going up a wall had nothing on this.

After events transpired as the Vatican officials had promised, the Kerryman rang the Galwayman and asked him how he had fared. He was smiling all the way to the bank. And likewise the cute Kerryman was already in the process of finalising the deal on buying a farm. A call was put through to the Dubliner. His amazing response was that he had won nothing – not a brass farthing.

Why? "I doubled it with the death of the Queen Mother," he said ruefully.

And Ted Walsh's addendum to the story was: "You will always come upon a chap in a Dublin betting office and if you give him a certainty, he will immediately ask: 'What will I put it in with?'"

❊　❊　❊　❊

Cheltenham '94 was everything – indeed, more – than we expected of this great Festival meeting. It had successes, like those of Danoli and Flakey Dove, that were right out of the Field of Dreams. It had proved once again, if there was any danger we would begin to doubt it, that the small man will always have a place here.

Edward Gillespie has gone on record to state that "Cheltenham without the Irish would be nothing."

That, of course, is true. At the same time it has got to be acknowledged that it is the mix of the English and Irish together over the three days, the relaxed togetherness in the bars, on the course and in the hotels and hostelries in town and its environs that contribute so much to making it all so different.

"It's the chemistry which makes it special," said Edward Gillespie, adding that "the mix of people from all walks of life is almost unique at this level."

The ring at Cheltenham is one of the strongest that you can get at any racecourse in any part of the world that you care to choose.

Why? "Because it's about class in every sense of the word," was how J. P. McManus put it to me for my book *The High Rollers of the Turf.* "It is about quality. Nothing can take the place of quality. You get the best horses from Britain locked in contention against the best from Ireland and nowadays also the best that France can send over, like The Fellow."

$$\maltese \quad \maltese \quad \maltese \quad \maltese$$

"The Sundance Kid" showed amazing discipline after a disastrous opening day at the 1994 Festival meeting. It was revealed most of all in the way he spurned backing one of his own horses because he didn't get the price he sought. But then, as he observed himself, if you have certain ground rules you must stick to them, come what may.

Racecourse rumour had it that he backed his own Deep Run gelding, Gimme Five, to win £1m in the last race on the Tuesday afternoon. There was pandemonium in the ring as the word got out that J.P. was on the warpath.

It took some money, believe me, to bring Gimme Five crashing from 10/1 to 4/1 favourite in a field of twenty-three for a 3m 2f handicap hurdle.

"It's not even half-true," McManus told Hugh McIlvanney of the *Sunday Times*, dismissing the suggestion that he stood to win a cool £1m if Gimme Five had obliged instead of finishing twentieth.

But, all the same, he did have a major lunge at Gimme Five. "It started when Stephen Little, in a single bet, laid him £250,000 to £30,000 – and there were other spectacular onslaughts," reported McIlvanney.

Many a punter would have folded his tent after suffering a hammer-blow like that and slipped quietly away into the night.

But resilience is J.P.'s middle name. And always has been from the time he first started backing horses as a schoolboy in Limerick.

Next day came "the emerald revenge, with McManus riding shotgun," as Mick Cleary described it so colourfully and Mickey "Asparagus Kid" Fletcher bemoaned to *The Observer* writer "I've done my cobblers" after "The Sundance Kid" had hit town with a vengeance.

He had told me before he left Ireland for Cheltenham that Danoli was the Irish banker of the meeting. All he wanted was a price commensurate with his estimation of what was a certainty on the book.

His bombardment of the rails bookies included bets of £155,000 to £80,000 and £60,000 to £30,000.

His winnings on Danoli were enough to restore the balance. "That put the wheel back on the bike," he told Hugh McIlvanney.

It could have been a day when "The Kid" could have written a special chapter in the history of Cheltenham gambling that would have emulated the flurry caused by Noel Furlong when he stood to win £4m in double bets had The Illiad won the 1991 Champion Hurdle.

Back ahead in his battle with the books, he was ready to go for the juggler on his own horse, Time For A Run in the Coral Cup Handicap Hurdle. He sent his trusted lieutenants to look for 10/1 or better. If Danoli had failed, the men J.P. did business with would have been only too willing to oblige him at 10/1 and maybe even slightly better odds. But now the shutters were up against any display of generosity and they knew from experience the scale of the bets he would have if he got the price he sought.

He told me himself that the best price on offer to him on the rails was 7/1 Time For A Run. You might ask why didn't he take the 10/1 that was going elsewhere to cash but J.P. is not the kind of man who carries around bundles of notes when he "goes to war" at Cheltenham. It's on credit and strictly on credit.

You can imagine his feelings when the starting price was announced as 11/1. I have no doubt that if he had got those odds he would have taken a cool £1 million or more out of the ring that day.

PART ONE

ADRIAN MAGUIRE

A Tiger in the Saddle

1

"The Best Since Martin Molony"

At the tender age of 12 Adrian Maguire was already revealing budding genius in the saddle. Much earlier than that, his mother Phyllis recalls, when he was only four or five, he would sit on the floor in front of the television set in the Maguire home in Kilmessan, County Meath, with his younger brother, Vinny and as they watched the field approach Becher's Brook in the Aintree Grand National, Adrian would exclaim: "That will be me, Vinny and that will be you some day", as he pointed his finger towards two of the runners right in contention. "He never wanted to be anything else in life only a jockey", said Mrs. Maguire.

Adrian and Vinny, two years his junior, were stone-mad about horses from the time they could walk, according to Mrs. Maguire. They had this favourite pony named Charlie. "Adrian would bring the pony right into the house and jump down the step into the kitchen right before my eyes. I was supposed to get cross at that but I couldn't, Vinny and himself were having such fun doing it in turns. I just turned a blind eye to it all".

"He was a spoilt brat, Adrian was, you know", she added, laughing with unmistakable affection in her voice.

Alan Sweeney of Moyehill, Milford, who keeps racing ponies as a hobby on his 300-acre farm in County Donegal, learned that there was going to be a race at Kingscourt in County Cavan that would enable him to enter his 13.2 hands pony. He rang the local Garda station and inquired if this was so. They told him there was a race in this category.

But on arriving at the course, he was informed that it was confined to local ponies. "So I had no option but to put my pony into the 14-hands race which was an open event", Sweeney recalled. "I had an announcement made over the public address system that I was seeking a jockey who could do 5st 7lbs.

"Michael Maguire, Adrian's brother, approached me. He offered the services of Adrian, who was only 12 at the time. I knew my pony – Misty Dawn – was probably the best in Ireland in the 13.2 hands category but she was very temperamental. I pointed this out to Michael Maguire. He responded 'Adrian will handle her; you need have no doubts at all about that'.

"The prize for the winning owner was £200. All Adrian was entitled to get for riding Misty Dawn was £1.50 but I remarked to him just before we reached the start: 'If you win this race for me, you can have half the prizemoney'.

"I didn't back the pony as it was hard to believe that she could win out of her own category. Adrian rode a truly brilliant race in winning by a short head.

"To put that victory in true perspective, you have got to remember that he had been thrown in at the deep end against bigger lads riding bigger ponies and yet such was his control in the saddle that he made light of it all. I knew then that he was something special."

Alan Sweeney was introduced to Adrian's parents and struck up an immediate accord with them. "I invited Adrian to join me in Donegal. He spent three years there altogether during the summer months. He not alone rode the ponies for me but trained them as well. You could say that he was my 'stable jockey'.

"He rode all around the Donegal circuit, at pony races in Rathmullen, Letterkenny, Convoy, Donegal town itself and in Derry.

"He lived in the house with us. My wife Mary was exceptionally fond of him. He almost became one of the family.

4

He had a very charming personality, was always well-mannered, though he did not talk a lot and could, I felt, be quick-tempered if roused.

"He would go to discos with my nephews and their friends. In that way he was like any other lad of his age. Where he differed was that he was a natural with horses – a pure natural, uncanny almost.

"I remember the day he rode Glenside for my brother Ronan in the Dingle Derby, the biggest annual event of its kind on the Southern circuit. Again he emerged the winner. Brilliant he was that day. Absolutely brilliant.

"I paid him a small weekly salary and also gave him £20 a ride. He was doing extremely well by the standards of other riders on the pony circuit."

Adrian Maguire didn't keep an exact count of all the winners he rode in pony races but he told me he reckoned the total could have reached 250.

He was only nine when he first rode the family's Shetland pony, Cresta by name. He would ride bareback in those days.

He recalled with a smile for me falling off and getting up on the pony and falling off and repeating the act until riding a pony was like a duck taking to water.

Michael Maguire, a professional jockey for a few years until he got too heavy, would instruct Adrian in the garden at the back of the house. He had the patience to spend hours with his brother. Perhaps he recognised the immense budding talent waiting to burst forth in full flower some day. When Adrian took a tumble he would be made get back up and do it all over again.

Adrian Maguire loved that little grey pony, Cresta. He graduated to hunting with her. He broke his collarbone twice in falls but, as his father Joe noted – "he came up the hard way; it was all part of the learning process".

Then one day Cresta caught his hind leg in the bull wire when jumping a fence following the hunt. The fall broke the pony's back.

"Adrian came home and went straight to bed. He cried for hours that same evening", said Mrs. Maguire. "In fact, he cried for almost a week he was so upset at the death of the pony."

Adrian and Vinny rode with the Tara Harriers and between hunter trials and county shows they collected a dresser-full of rosettes.

Eventualy it began to pall for Adrian and it was then that he hit the pony circuit, Vinny following suit.

So it was through the ponies – as it was with his youthful idol Tommy Carmody – that Adrian Maguire initially developed his talent as a rider and it would be burnished further on the point-to-point circuit to the stage where his exploits simply forced him to the notice of those who had the contacts to open an entire new world for him.

In 1992 – the year he rode Cool Ground to a famous victory in the Gold Cup – legendary bloodstock agent, Jack Doyle would say to me outside the weighroom in Cheltenham: "He is the best I have seen since Martin Molony".

High praise indeed. In the count-down to Cheltenham '94 Richard Pitman of the BBC, so agonisingly beaten on Crisp in the 1973 Aintree Grand National, would say of Maguire that "he is part – almost an extension – of any horse he is riding. He transmits incredible confidence. Horses feel it and respond to it".

Jockey-cum-racing writer, Marcus Armytage said of him: "He rides with a youthful exuberance combined with an old man's experience. They say fear runs through the reins but the opposite is also true. His confident invincibility in the saddle gets through to his mounts. They stand off an extra stride from the fence, they run an extra stride faster for him, stay a furlong further. Like an artist who can paint without being taught, it is one of those mystical qualities that you are born with".

And fellow Irish-born jockey, Norman Williamson, who hit a century of winners in the 1993-'94 season, paid him this tribute: "He's good fun. There's not a bother on him. It's probably why he rides so well and yet in a race he knows business is business".

"I have not seen any better", was the cryptic summing-up of Toby Balding, who was the first to employ Adrian in Britain while "The Duke" Nicholson, who succeeded Balding by making Maguire his No. 1 stable jockey after Richard Dunwoody had teamed up with Martin Pipe on the retirement of Peter Scudamore said that "Maguire is unquestionably the best to hit the scene since the Second World War".

6

You come upon the neat Maguire bungalow beyond the village of Kilmessan – a typical rural village with its pub, its foodstores and picturesque church.

The rolling country-side of the Royal County of Meath. A football and hurling area but steeped in the lore of horses also, as Garrison Savannah, the 1991 Cheltenham Gold Cup winner and runner-up the same year in the Aintree Grand National was "bred just down the road from this house", according to Joe Maguire.

You ask if Adrian Maguire was bred to be a jockey and a horseman and you find that, while none of his antecedents set the heather ablaze in the amateur or professional sphere over the jumps, you discover an understanding and love of horses and an instinct for horsemanship.

Joe Maguire, who works as a greenkeeper at the Royal Tara golf course, recalled that during the Second World War he would travel with friends on a turf-burning train the fifteen miles from Kilmessan to Fairyhouse for the Easter Irish Grand National meeting. "From that time I was hooked on horses", he admitted.

During the shooting of the American adventure film, *Captain Lightfoot* (starring Rock Hudson, and also including in the cast, Barbara Rush, Jeff Morrow, Kathleen Ryan and Denis O'Dea) in the West of Ireland in the mid-fifties, a man from the Kilmessan area, Ralph O'Brien, rode one of the horses in the film. Later when this horse and the others used in the film sequence went up for auction, Samuel McCabe purchased the animal that Joe Maguire used ride bareback at the age of 14 across-country. "I got a great feeling of exhilaration jumping ditches and hedges and crossing rivers on him", said Joe. "I just did it for recreation".

Joe Maguire will tell you proudly that the Maguire name has been part and parcel of the Kilmessan area for 300 years. "This is the patch of ground where I have spent my life", he adds.

His father James worked on the land and there is a picture of him extant – executed by Michael O'Brien, brother of Ralph (Captain Lightfoot) O'Brien – depicting him grubbing potato drills.

Phyllis Maguire grew up on a farm where stables had to be mucked out and her nephew became a jockey.

Like any couple who reared a large family, Joe and Phyllis Maguire had no pretensions to wealth and yet you cannot mistake the exceptionally close bonds between them and between all the members of the family. Mrs. Maguire was nursing at St. Joseph's Hospital in Trim throughout her ten pregnancies.

She reels off for me the names of the eight boys and two girls in the family – Seamus, David, John, Anne, Michael, Pauline, Adrian, Vinny (R.I.P.), Declan and Trevor.

Phyllis is unquestionably the extrovert by nature of the two parents, happily relaxed as she reveals her knowledge of horses and form and, while she never places a bet, she enjoys relating how on one visit to Huntingdon she picked out six winners. Joe found that hard to credit as he likes to have a bet – nothing serious – and would obviously regard himself as a shrewder judge than his wife (and no anti-feminism in that!).

Joe is happy to allow Phyllis to take centre-stage as you delve into the childhood and youthful days of Adrian and the others in the family who made their mark in the sporting arena. She becomes emotional and cannot constrain the tears that well up suddenly in her eyes anytime Vinny is mentioned. Vinny, who was Adrian's soulmate, was killed in a hit-and-run accident at the age of 17.

It touched all the members of this close-knit family very deeply, none more so than Adrian himself.

In the lead-up to Cheltenham '94 he told me that every time he rides a winner now, when he experiences a moment of high acclaim, he thinks of Vinny.

"I feel he is looking down on me, willing me on. Vinny could have been a better jockey than myself. We rode together on the pony circuit."

Adrian's brother Declan was a member of the Meath squad that won the All-Ireland Minor Football Championship crown in 1992, getting a coveted medal though he did not make the actual fifteen that beat Armagh by a point (2-5 to 0-10) in the final.

There is a coloured print of the squad occupying a proud place in the Maguire home and also a memento from the Kilmessan Club inscribed: "Presented to Declan Maguire for

8

his achievement in winning the All-Ireland Minor Football Championship with Meath in 1992".

Declan, although he still plays hurling and football for the local club, decided to concentrate on his studies to become a marine engineer rather than give the time that would be needed if he aimed to try and make it to the County senior panel.

Adrian himself played both hurling and football for Kilmessan and is actually the possessor of a Meath County Minor Hurling Championship medal. He normally played in the half-back line. During his summers in Donegal with Alan Sweeney he threw in his lot with the local club.

We can only speculate if he would have ended up wearing the Meath colours had he the same burning ambition to be a footballer as he had a jockey.

But then to be realistic about it, he was really cut out to be a jockey from the outset as in stature (5ft 6ins), he certainly didn't dwarf Anne who is only 5ft 1in tall.

The call of the saddle saw him leave the Vocational School in Trim when he was fifteen.

And he headed for England to join the stable of Con Horgan who has Meath connections on his father's side.

His mother recalled, "It was one of the worst winters imaginable and certainly not one to be remembered by a young lad who was away from home for the first time. He was riding out for Con for about seven months and I must say he was well looked after but eventually I think he got home-sick and when he returned he was with Johanna Morgan for a time".

Again it was all part of the learning process but he took the decisive step on the ladder that would in time lead to his first big break when he joined Michael Hourigan's establishment at Lisaleen, Patrickswell, County Limerick.

It was John Egan's father who asked Michael Hourigan to take on Adrian. "He must have asked me four or five times before I found a place for him", the trainer recalled in the course of a *Racing Post* interview with Tony O'Hehir.

"Adrian wanted to try and make a go of it as a professional but I advised him that he would have a better chance, and would gain more experience, if he started off with me as an amateur. I had John Kavanagh as a claimer at the time and Adrian got his grounding in the point-to-point fields."

Yet while Maguire quickly excelled in those fields, his relationship with Hourigan wasn't always plain-sailing.

"He was always a determined young man and he was prepared to listen – sometimes! He always thought he was right and during the season when he was point-to-point champion he told Ros Easom (Hourigan's long-serving assistant) that he was leaving as I was an impossible man to satisfy!

"In those days he could get a bit sour if we had an argument and he mightn't look at you for a day or two."

No doubt having been so prominent on the pony circuit and having known nothing but success all the way, Adrian naturally believed he already knew most of what needed to be learned but Michael Hourigan knew otherwise. There was a world of difference between the pony circuit and becoming a top National Hunt jockey in time.

Hourigan is one of Adrian Maguire's biggest fans and follows his career with deep interest. "Adrian is a seriously good rider but how he reacts to all the pressures he has known during the 1993-'94 season will be the making or breaking of him.

"He has a great eye for a stride and if a horse is half a stride wrong, he gives him so much courage that he will get there. He rode six winners for me at Dromahane one day and four of them were never heard of before or after."

❦ ❦ ❦ ❦

The 1990-'91 point-to-point season and his turbo-powered end-of-season blitz at Dromahane put a spotlight on Adrian Maguire's talent that catapulted him on to a new pedestal and created the sequence of events that resulted in his joining the Toby Balding stable. In a way it had elements of the romantic in it that made it something of a fairytale story in itself.

In a cliffhanger finish to the Riders' Championship on the point-to-point circuit Adrian Maguire and John Berry dominated the last couple of week-ends. Maguire had ridden 26 winners for his mentor Michael Hourigan and then sealed the title with that incredible six-timer at Dromahane (compared to Berry's Castletown-Geoghegan treble that same day), followed by another half dozen at the two-day Kinsale meeting with Berry only able to reply with two winners.

The final score: Adrian Maguire – 38 winners; John Berry – 34 winners.

Maguire's 38 winners from 94 rides represented an exceptional ratio of performance over fences, a 40% level of success. John Berry, five years Maguire's senior, produced a 37% ratio.

But before he was crowned champion, Maguire had already ridden his first Cheltenham winner at the age of 19, following it up by winning the Jameson Irish Grand National.

How he came to ride Omerta for Martin Pipe in the Fulke Walwyn Kim Muir Challenge Cup at the 1991 Festival meeting is an extraordinary story in itself.

Adrian had taken a fall on one of Michael Hourigan's horses – Lisnadee Miss – and spent a number of days in Limerick Regional Hospital with a leg injury.

He was back in the Patrickswell stable when the fateful call came that was to change his life overnight. "Paul Hourigan, Michael's son, came looking for me in the yard and told me I was wanted on the phone", Adrian recalled, "It was Homer Scott ringing on behalf of the McMorrows, the owners of Omerta.

"Homer started by saying, would I go to Cheltenham to ride Omerta. I thought at first that he was joking. In fact, I was certain it was a bit of a leg-pull.

"But then I realised that Homer Scott meant it and that they really wanted me to go to the Festival meeting. I dashed from the Hourigans' yard and put a call through to home asking that someone meet me off the train from Limerick."

Mrs. Maguire takes up the story: "I had made up my mind to buy Adrian a car. I went into Navan and got a second-hand one from Joe Norris. Adrian's leg was still hurting him after the fall he had taken at the point-to-point meeting. I remember him saying to me: 'I don't care if the leg falls off, I'm going to ride Omerta at Cheltenham'."

After getting a night's sleep at home, he met Jim McMorrow at Dublin Airport next morning and they travelled over together.

11

Adrian had heard a lot, of course, about the Cheltenham Festival meeting. He knew that it was part of Irish racing lore – something else entirely.

But, accustomed as he was to riding at tight point-to-point courses, he wasn't prepared for the impact his first sight of the historic Cheltenham racecourse would make on him. He actually stood in awe momentarily as his eyes took in the sweep of the green amphitheatre, the hurdles and fences stretching towards Cleve Hill in the background, timeless in its beauty, unmatched in the traditions it had created since the days of Golden Miller and Prince Regent's victory in the first Gold Cup (1946) after the Second World War, Cottage Rake's three-timer (1949-'51) for Vincent O'Brien, who won a fourth with Knock Hard in 1953 and then that first epic battle between the incomparable Arkle and England's pride, the Irish-bred Mill House; Arkle creating a thunderous "Irish roar" as Pat Taaffe swept to a never-to-be-forgotten victory that was only surpassed when Dawn Run and Jonjo O'Neill came from a seemingly impossible position after the last to snatch victory on the line in the 1986 Gold Cup and Jonjo raised his arm aloft in that memorable salute to the heavens.

"It was the size of the course itself that hit me", Adrian told Tim Richards of the *Racing Post* in a contribution for the official 1994 Cheltenham Festival magazine. "It was much more spread out than I expected. As I stood there, it was difficult to grasp just how big the place was. It's a marvellous sight. The lay-out of the whole place is amazing".

Then he walked the course. "I was immediately struck by how much bigger the fences were than the point-to-point fences I had been used to back home".

He had arrived at what was Mecca for jumping aficionados. "There are people in Ireland who will save all the year to be sure they can get to Cheltenham. I mean people who don't have good jobs and have to make sacrifices. When you see the place for yourself you understand why. To a lot of Irish people there is no meeting in the world to compare with the Cheltenham Festival meeting.

"For jump jockeys too it is special. Every jockey wants to win during the three days. It is a very fair track but a testing one. You have every chance to ride a race on this course.

12

"Nowhere else do you get a roar like you get at Cheltenham. And you don't find those sort of crowds anywhere else."

He heard the roar rise as he started the run for home on Omerta. There had been men who had seen in the racecard the name "Mr. A. Maguire" as the rider of the Martin Pipe-trained contender and it meant nothing to them, if they didn't follow happenings on the point-to-point circuit. To many then he was simply an unknown, one of those gangling amateurs plucked out of the backwoods, maybe a guy who would give his right hand to say that he had ridden over the Cheltenham fences, who was willing to take a tumble in the cause of savouring the praise of his friends for his courage in a social gathering that same evening in a hotel in Cheltenham town or out in the Cotswolds.

But shrewder punters, who had spotted the talent – indeed, the blossoming genius – of young Maguire as he booted home a succession of winners for Michael Hourigan and who knew that Homer Scott wouldn't contact a rookie with no ability for the McMorrows and Martin Pipe stepped in and made a "killing".

"It was only when we were heading towards the last fence that I suddenly thought to myself, 'I'm actually going to win' ", Adrian recalled.

It had been like a dream, a whirlwind unfolding in the crowded hours of a few days – from the moment the fateful call came from Homer Scott to Adrian Maguire now riding Omerta back into the winner's enclosure.

March 12, 1991 was the day that Adrian Maguire made a winning debut at Cheltenham – on his very first visit to the course. And it didn't end there. He went on to win the Jameson Irish Grand National on Omerta, wearing the colours of Mrs. McMorrow and starting at 6/1 in a field of 22.

Adrian Maguire had come a long way in a very short time from riding his first point-to-point winner – Equinoctial – at Askeaton on 11 February 1990 to his first win under Rules – Gladtogetit – for Michael Hourigan in a bumper at Sligo on 23 April 1990.

Hourigan wisely sought to keep Adrian's feet firmly on the ground while he was attached to his stable. The day after that red-letter day when he had his six-timer at Dromahane, Hourigan had him sweeping the yard and pushing the wheelbarrow.

Hourigan rightly feared that his protege might be travelling too fast. "It's a tough ladder to climb and it's how you handle the setbacks that can be the making of you in the end", is how he put it. "You have got to prove that you have the character to overcome adversity".

That was said with the wisdom of years by a man who knew how to take the knocks and still show he was a winner.

From the time he moved to England, Adrian Maguire's rise to the top was meteoric but at moments of singular triumph he found himself in trouble with the stewards for his use of the whip. But not even the suspensions he suffered could break the indomitable spirit in that stocky frame of his or dampen the fierce hunger for winners that burned in his heart.

In her bungalow home in Kilmessan, Phyllis Maguire was shocked and deeply hurt when one English scribe dubbed her son the "butcher boy".

She was recalling how he went to bed and cried the day his beloved pony broke his back under him out hunting. "He would never deliberately hurt an animal."

2

"Hunger For Winners Drives Me On"

Talking to me at "The Duke" Nicholson's Jackdaws establishment in the Cotswolds on the Monday morning of Cheltenham Festival Week '94, Adrian Maguire mused aloud about the whirlwind surge he had experienced in the space of three short years.

"It's all like a dream", he said. "Sometimes I almost have to pinch myself and say: 'Can it all have happened so quickly?'."

That whirlwind surge to the top of the ladder had seen Adrian – following his 1991 Kim Muir Chase and Jameson Irish Grand National triumphs on Omerta – win the 1992 Gold Cup on Cool Ground – his first ride in the race – the Cathcart Chase on Second Schedual and the Grand Annual Chase on Space Fair at the '93 Festival meeting, the Triumph Hurdle on Mysilv and the Queen Mother Champion Chase on Viking Flagship in 1994 and the 1993 King George VI Chase on Barton Bank to supplement the Hennessy Cognac Cup he had won on Sibton Abbey in 1992. Add to these victories the successive Digital Galway Plate wins on The Gooser in 1992 and General Idea in 1993 and you get some idea of the impact he had made on the National Hunt scene before he celebrated his 23rd birthday on 29 April 1994.

The two really big races that remained to be won were the Champion Hurdle and the Aintree Grand National. He

15

finished third on the David Nicholson-trained Moorcroft Boy in the '94 National, having been in the lead two out but relinquishing it at the last to the eventual winner, Miinnehoma, who was ridden to victory for his retaining Martin Pipe stable by Richard Dunwoody.

Adrian Maguire is not a man of many words but when he talks you listen. Drawing back the veil momentarily, he revealed to me what it is that has made him the most talked-of and sought-after jockey of the current era: "The hunger to ride more winners drives me on, spurs me to even greater endeavour".

I put to him the question that diplomatically, I suppose, I should never have broached but I had put it at one stage to Martin Molony, so I felt I had to pose it to Adrian.

Supposing someone came to him and offered him a five-figure or six-figure sum to stop a horse, how would he react? "I ride to win. I am always trying my best to win. The thought that I might do otherwise has never even entered my head".

No one had ever even dared to hint to Martin Molony that he might give a horse an easy race that he felt had the ability to win. Those who saw him at the peak of his powers have talked to me almost in awe of his ability and the power he could generate in a finish.

Nat McNabb, who with Bob Mulrooney, used do the commissions for Vincent O'Brien when Vincent – in the era when, on his own admission, he had to gamble to survive – repeatedly took the bookies to the cleaners, said to me unhesitatingly one day: "Martin Molony was without question the best jockey I ever saw. I would even put him ahead of Lester Piggott when it came to his finest performances on the Flat. He had strength, he had judgement of pace and horses ran for him in an uncanny manner. I believe that if he was riding today and concentrating totally on the Flat, he would be snapped up by one of the Arab Sheikhs and would be earning even more than Pat Eddery".

Therefore, when Jack Doyle said that Adrian Maguire was "the best I have seen since Martin Molony", it represented the highest praise that the legendary bloodstock agent could proffer.

For Doyle, like Nat McNabb, had seen the best over a span of half a century and more.

Adrian Maguire can now pick and choose when there are bigger plums to be won by avoiding taking risks on horses that give you a bad fall. He made the point to me that in the lead-up to a meeting like Cheltenham and the Liverpool Grand National meeting also, owners don't want you to take undue risks. They want you, if at all possible, to be there to bid for the top prizes and that meant, in effect, that they didn't want to be calling to see you in hospital or sending flowers when you could be up on their particular horses. Success then brought its own demands, its own priorities.

One of the most significant moves that Maguire had made when he moved to England was to appoint – on the recommendation of Toby Balding – an agent and the man he chose, Dave Roberts, is recognised as one of the best in the business.

Roberts, whose "stable" also includes Michael Hourigan (son of the Limerick trainer), Norman Williamson, Mick Fitzgerald and Brian Clifford, lives true to the old adage that the early bird catches the worm. Generally his day starts at 5 a.m. as he gets on the phone seeking out the winners for Adrian Maguire. These are the mounts outside his retaining stable that can make all the difference to his strike rate.

Maguire will go anywhere that Roberts arranges that he should go. It can mean a criss-crossing schedule taking in a variety of different tracks and it can mean also – as the season peters out – riding in the afternoon at one meeting and heading by helicopter to catch a few more rides at an evening meeting. In fact, Maguire was hoping to ride on the Wednesday at the 1994 Punchestown Festival meeting and get over in time for the Cheltenham evening meeting on the same day but because he had one to ride for "The Duke" Nicholson in the first at Cheltenham the plan fell through. Ironically, he had no winner that same evening at Cheltenham.

Maguire has complete faith in Dave Roberts. Acknowledging that "he is the best agent in Britain", he told me that he leaves everything to Dave and doesn't question his judgment in the arrangements he makes.

Roberts himself is proud of the rapport he has built up with Adrian and, apart from it being a business arrangement, they have also become very close friends. "Even if I sent him to Cartmel or to Fakenham and he came away empty-handed after a number of rides, he wouldn't complain", laughed Dave. "Even if he knew in his heart that it meant that he had probably missed a winner somewhere else".

Agents were an unheard-of luxury back in Martin Molony's time. But now they are an integral part of the National Hunt arena, as they have been a dominant feature of the Flat scene for much longer.

Allied to the agents, the jockey's life has also been made easier by the introduction of car phones. I remember once trying to get Lester Piggott's tip for the Epsom Derby for the *Sunday Independent* and talking to him on the car phone as he returned from Brighton.

But jockeys of an earlier era did not have to worry about the machinations of the British tabloids. Adrian Maguire must keep his guard constantly up. He knows that he must be extremely careful of what he says when they are on the prowl for scoops.

He knows, for example, that if he were to say one word that might be construed by them to mean that all was not well in relations between him and Richard Dunwoody, they would go to town in creating an "open war" situation.

He stressed to me that Dunwoody and himself are, in fact, good friends – very good friends and he added: "I have no problems whatsoever with Richard".

He has learned to handle the media – both the television and print. He draws a sharp dividing line between what he terms the recognised racing writers, who adopt a professional approach to their work and know the score when it comes to on-the-record and off-the-record comments and those others who are after the sensational and don't care one iota if they drop you in boiling hot water.

Richard Pitman of the BBC says that Maguire is much more at ease now in front of the cameras than was the case when he first arrived in Britain and because of his sensational start, he was rocketed immediately into centre stage. Then his responses were an interviewer's nightmare. Now it's all very different.

18

As Adrian put it to me: "I know I have to live now in the constant glare of the media. I know I have to face the media every day".

✼ ✼ ✼ ✼

I had journeyed out to "The Duke" Nicholson's stable near the village of Temple Guiting on a lovely Spring morning in the company of my very good friend, John McKenna, a leading Cheltenham-based veterinary surgeon with an immense knowledge and love of horses and National Hunt racing and Dubliner, Martin Purcell, boxing aficionado, raconteur and wit who had come down from Aberdeen for the Festival meeting (in Scotland he had been one of the guiding lights in directing the UCD boxing team to a famous seventh consecutive win in the British and Irish Universities Boxing Championship for the Harry Preston trophy). We pass the Foxhill Inn and other landmarks and soon hit the Nicholson "spread", almost breath-taking in how it was conceived as a perfect example of THE modern training establishment.

On this morning Adrian Maguire was up at 6.00 a.m. and on the gallops before 7.00 a.m. and that part of the day was over by 8.15 a.m.

I met him coming in with the rest of the string to the magnificent new circular yard and modern boxes that make Jackdaws Castle a model of its kind.

"The Duke" Nicholson, who hails from one of the most respected families in Britain, is simply "The Guv'nor" to him. You cannot mistake the respect between the trainer and the jockey he has praised so highly.

Nicholson had moved into Jackdaws Castle at the beginning of October, 1992 after spending twenty-four years down the road at Condicote House, from where he had sent out 799 winners.

The 250-acre purpose built training complex, set in a glorious sweep of country-side in the British Midlands, was the product of a pub lunch with the owner of the land, Colin Smith three years earlier.

It unquestionably offered a new challenge to Nicholson, who confessed in the course of an interview with Richard

Evans of *The Times*, carried in the 1993-'94 edition of the *Irish Racing Annual*, that he would have felt happy if he had finished the 1992-'93 National Hunt season with 55 winners. To have sent out 100 winners was "phenomenal".

Richard Dunwoody had retainers with both Nicholson and Nicky Henderson but in February, '93, Nicholson told him that he wanted to have a sole retainer on his services – and gave him until the end of the Aintree Grand National meeting to decide if that was acceptable.

No sooner had Aintree passed than Peter Scudamore, stable jockey to Martin Pipe, announced his retirement.

That changed the whole situation overnight and brought a new urgency as far as "The Duke" Nicholson was concerned to what he was demanding of Richard Dunwoody.

"It appeared that until Punchestown, Martin Pipe hadn't made up his mind whom he was going to go for", said Nicholson. "I told Richard (Dunwoody) that he had to make up his mind if he was offered the job and I wanted to know.

"I believe it caused Richard a lot of heartache to decide to leave me. From my point of view the split was very amicable.

"Richard and I had seven marvellous seasons. He came to me having just turned professional and he left me as champion jockey. That was the same route followed by Peter Scudamore. He came to me as an amateur and left me as champion jockey!"

Nicholson in the summer of 1993, as he talked to Richard Evans, was hoping that Adrian Maguire could complete an unique treble. "I have watched Adrian very closely over the last three years, especially when he rode the treble that got disqualified at Sandown, when he really hit the headlines.

"I think he is a very good horseman. To do what he has done in that space of time is phenomenal – better than any recent jockey, be it Francome, Scudamore or Dunwoody. None of them had ridden 125 winners in their third or fourth seasons."

When David Nicholson was considering a replacement for Dunwoody, Maguire and Charlie Swan were the only contenders. "I never got around to asking Charlie because I could not see him leaving Ireland given the situation he has over there. He rides 100 winners a year, gets a lot of spare rides in England, so he didn't really come into the equation".

Did Maguire have to think for long before accepting the job as No. 1 jockey at Jackdaws Castle? "Yes", said Nicholson, his blue eyes twinkling. "Five seconds!"

"I went to him at the Cheltenham April meeting. I said if the situation arises, would you? He said 'yes'. He came here in the third week of May and met Colin Smith. He was offered a retainer and he signed on the spot. No ifs, no buts.

"All I want to see him do is, as we did with Scu and Richard, riding the best horses on the day and finish up champion jockey sooner rather than later.

"All the people he rode for during the 1992-'93 season are keen that he rides for them again when he is not required for one of my horses. I have spoken to a majority of them. There is John White, Toby Balding, Ferdie Murphy, Mark Tomkins and Richard Lee. The most winners he had for any individual trainer in the 1992-'93 season was 18 for Toby. Richard Dunwoody rode 74 for me."

In throwing in his lot with "The Duke" Nicholson, Adrian Maguire was joining possibly the most powerful jump stable after Martin Pipe's – a stable in which quality mattered for everything. Apart from the established stars, Nicholson started off the 1993-'94 season with 34 unraced three, four and five-year-olds – most of them bought in Ireland. That Monday morning of the '94 Cheltenham Festival week, he proudly pointed out to me another acquisition to the stable purchased in Ireland a few weeks earlier after it had won a point-to-point in the South.

"I think over the years the Irish store horse has proved the most successful. They hopefully last until they are 10 or 12-year-olds."

Nicholson usually visits Ireland for a long week-end in late January or early February, attends point-to-points on the Southern circuit and casts an eye over young horses spotted by a handful of trusted spies, before stepping in to buy privately or at the Derby sales. He was, for example, tipped off on a visit to the Cork area about the potential of Danny Connors but J. P. McManus was already aware of it also and stepped in to acquire him for a whopping six-figure sum. It's history how he was sent to Jonjo O'Neill and landed a major gamble when winning the Coral Golden Handicap Hurdle (Final) at the 1991 Cheltenham Festival meeting.

"I always look for athleticism in a horse. If it has got a pedigree as well, all well and good", said Nicholson.

For a quarter of a century now "The Duke" Nicholson has been the very embodiment of the traditions and spirit of the National Hunt game – a man who does not hide his pride at the fact that his great great grandfather, one William Holman, "was Cheltenham", to use his own words. Nicholson cherishes a plaque on which the faded gold lettering, above the shape of eight horse-shoes, reads: "Horses owned or trained by William Holman, Cheltenham, 1843-'46".

It was fortuitous for Adrian Maguire that he should team up with a man for whom the three days of the Cheltenham Festival meeting stir him in a manner each year that no words can express. For Cheltenham has always been an integral part of the Nicholson family tradition.

His father, the famous "Frenchie" Nicholson lived just a few hundred yards from Prestbury Park and "The Duke" had his first taste of what the Festival meeting had to offer to the real aficionados of the winter game and of the bonds it helps to cement between those of similar outlook in Ireland and Britain when he watched Tim Hyde win the Gold Cup in 1946 on the mighty Prince Regent, regarded for a long time by Tom Dreaper as the greatest chaser he had trained until untimately he had to agree that there was only one Arkle after all and that we shall never see his like again.

When eventually he was training on his own he remembered his father's maxim: "Give a horse good hay, good oats and plenty of work".

There was another maxim too that the game had taught him: "When you stop learning, you stop winning. You are finished".

Amazingly, Nicholson was dogged by a Cheltenham hoodoo for eighteen years – broken at last when Solar Cloud won the 1986 Triumph Hurdle and then two years later Charter Party landed the Gold Cup.

Adrian Maguire was to win the 1994 Triumph Hurdle on Mysilv and the Queen Mother Champion Chase on Viking

Flagship and Nakir thwarted him from making it a three-timer for his retaining stable when beating Baydon Star into second place in the Guinness Arkle Challenge Trophy. Maguire had high hopes of winning the Gold Cup on Barton Bank but, unfortunately, he had to be pulled out of the event.

Maguire was seen at his brilliant best on Viking Flagship as he won an epic three-way battle with Travado (Jamie Osborne) and the 1993 winner, Deep Sensation (Declan Murphy).

"I knew he wasn't going to give up when we touched down after the last", said Maguire of Viking Flagship. "I knew the hill was ahead and he would fight all the way home. And I knew I wasn't going to give up".

There were gasps of admiration as he conjured an extra big leap from Viking Flagship at the second-last fence and another equally-fine jump at the last. "He met the second-last so long that he only just managed to get his toes over the top", said Adrian. "I think this win is the one I am most delighted with this season. The Cheltenham reception seems to get louder and louder each year".

Maguire had certainly every reason to be delighted for in that pulsating contest from the last, man and horse fought every inch of the way to the line, Viking Flagship eventually finishing with a neck to spare over Trevado with Deep Sensation, who looked to be going best when jumping the last in unison with the other two, finishing just another length away third. The 1992 champion and favourite, Remittance Man fell at the third last and we were left to ponder how greater still the climax of the race would have been if he had remained on his feet.

David Nicholson, so near in the past with Waterloo Boy and Very Promising, was deeply moved by the occasion. "Going to the last I thought 'I've got beat again'.

"But this is a very, very tough horse and you don't win these sort of contests without going for broke and Adrian went for broke and it came off.

They were both very brave and earned their reward. A great race we were lucky enough to be part of and they were brave enough to win."

The numerical firepower of Martin Pipe had prevented David Nicholson from being crowned National Hunt champion trainer in Britain season after season but as the 1993-'94 season left the milestones of Cheltenham and Aintree behind and moved into May, Nicholson was ahead of his great rival in win and place prizemoney, though, as might be expected, Pipe had turned out more winners from far more runners. And the bulk of Nicholson's winners had been ridden by Adrian Maguire.

The final statistics for the season showed that "The Duke" Nicholson had won his first Trainers' Championship crown by landing £754,069 sterling in prizemoney (win and place) – £34,462 more than Martin Pipe, who thus missed out on a sixth sucessive title.

Nicholson notched 81 winners, 46 less than Pipe but, unlike the Jockeys' Championship, the top trainer is decided on money won.

Nicholson, now 55, confessed on his arrival back from a safari holiday in South Africa with his wife Dinah that when the 1993-'94 season opened in July '93 he didn't think frankly that he could land the title. "I didn't think we had the horsepower", he said. "We had a lot of backward horses."

Asked whether he felt it was refreshing for the sport to have a new champion trainer, he replied diplomatically: "Let's just say I've had a lot of encouragement from a lot of people".

❀　❀　❀　❀

It was Adrian Maguire's great friend and mentor, Tom O'Mahoney, a farmer and horse-dealer from Youghal, County Cork, who was instrumental in advising the budding young star from Kilmessan to join the Toby Balding stable at the start of the 1991-'92 National Hunt season as second jockey rather than accept a more lucrative offer from Martin Pipe.

O'Mahony knew what he was doing. Balding, who was christened Gerald Barnard, was born to National Hunt racing, just like "The Duke" Nicholson. O'Mahony was only too well aware that when Vincent O'Brien was training in Churchtown, County Cork, and indeed, later, when he was still training jumpers at Ballydoyle, he used always lodge his Cheltenham horses with Toby Balding's father, Gerard, when the latter was based at Bishops Canning, not far from Prestbury Park.

Vincent was a great friend of the Balding family. Indeed, when Cottage Rake, winner of three successive Gold Cups (1948-'50), started to decline he spent the evening of his racing days with Balding snr.

Toby has always enjoyed a close affinity with Ireland and the Irish. He makes no secret of the fact that when he is seeking a potential equine champion, it is in Ireland he does his shopping.

"I always have and I always will", he told Geoff Lester of the *Sporting Life* in a special feature for the *Irish Racing Annual*. "It is the perfect scenario for breeding and bringing up young horses, while the Irish have blood lines that we know so well.

"The Irish breeding industry has seen off New Zealand, Poland and even America as far as jumpers are concerned and I like to see horses go through the Derby Sale and then follow their progress in the point-to-point world before making my move."

Balding has also bought some bumper horses in Ireland.

He gets a particular pleasure out of his trips to Ireland, combining business with relaxation. For example, during a trip he made in the summer of 1992, he journeyed to Wexford and met Michael Hickey who stands Over The River, sire of Cool Ground, who gave Adrian Maguire his first Gold Cup winner that same year.

When Adrian Maguire arrived at the multi-million pound 120-box Whitcombe Manor complex in Dorset, where Balding was training at the time – before returning to his old base at Fyfield – he was joining a stable that had built an impressive Cheltenham Festival record and indeed an impressive record overall in key races in the National Hunt sphere.

Balding's Festival winners, apart from Cool Ground's '92 Gold Cup triumph, included Beech Road (1989 Champion Hurdle) and Morley Street (1992 Champion Hurdle),

Kildimo (1987 Sun Alliance Chase), Boraceva (1989 National Hunt Chase) and Forest Sun (1990 Supreme Novices' Hurdle).

He had won the Aintree Grand National twice with Highland Wedding (1969) and Little Polveir (1989) and in addition his Decent Fellow was victorious in the 1977 Sweeps Hurdle, Heblin won the 1987 Tote Gold Trophy, Bishop's Yarn the 1987 Glen International Gold Cup while Morley Street won the Breeders' Cup Chase in 1990 and '91.

Toby Balding's record then spoke for itself. But he was more than just one of the long-established name players on the National Hunt scene. He has that gift of being able to put people completely at ease no matter from what walk of life they come. And like others born into the National Hunt game, his philosophy of life can be summed up in one sentence – "you must not only be a winner but you must also get fun out of life."

Balding has no doubt that the best thing that ever happened to Maguire was "coming to Whitcombe".

"Wonder boy", as he was known in the yard, had a great advantage over "stable-mates", Richard Guest and Jimmy Frost in that he was a natural lightweight. And, as Balding noted, he was fortunate in that "he has never ridden anything but 'live' horses".

He went on: "Being here at Whitcombe has meant that Adrian has had no time to get used to the adulation. He rides out for me in the morning, drives to the races and by the time he gets back to the yard he is knackered and just wants to climb into bed. If he were based in Lambourn the likelihood of him falling into bad habits would be that much greater."

And Tom O'Mahony would say later: "Adrian matured a lot under the eye of Toby, who has been an outstanding asset and a tremendous back-up at all times. Not everyone would let such a young boy ride Cool Ground, would they? And look what that did for Adrian – and Toby, come to that."

❃ ❃ ❃ ❃

His girl-friend Sabrina Winters, to whom he was to become engaged before Cheltenham '94, accompanied

Adrian to England and she played a key role also in keeping his feet firmly on the ground at a crucial stage in his career.

Sabrina, who hails from Kanturk, County Cork, met Adrian when he was attached to Michael Hourigan's stable and riding the point-to-point circuit, principally in the South.

She is of similar background, coming from a large family also, who are into sport, horse racing, greyhound racing and coursing.

Sabrina has that jovial outlook that Adrian loves when the pressure is really on.

When he and Sabrina arrived in England, life was a difficult grind during the National Hunt season as he travelled the length and breath of the country in search of winners.

Always Sabrina would be by his side, sharing the driving and helping him through the good times and the bad. She provided the base he needed in the evenings. Thus he was able to avoid the bright lights and the champagne flowing circuit that can so easily catch out the unwary.

Although Adrian was a natural star, he could easily have fallen victim to the many temptations of the racing world.

At first Adrian lived in a Portacabin. Then Sabrina and he acquired a flat in Whitcombe. They now live in a lovely modern house in the small town of Faringdon on the Berkshire-Oxfordshire border and it puts Adrian within striking distance of "The Duke" Nicholson's stable.

Putting on weight is not a problem to Adrian. He is small and stockily built, but because of that same build he is able to generate a power in the saddle that has led to the comparisons being drawn between him and Martin Molony.

"I can eat anything", Adrian told me. "And I love to eat well when I come home in the evening."

Tom O'Mahony paid this tribute to Sabrina: "She is a level-headed girl who likes to stay in the background. But when it is required, she will make Adrian toe the line, not that he would want to do otherwise.

"She is very much her own person. Overall she is a great levelling influence. They work as a team and that is of immense benefit to Adrian, as success has followed success for him. You can be at your most vulnerable at the top. Yes, Sabrina is a prize asset."

27

Tom O'Mahony was perfectly correct when he said that Sabrina likes to stay in the background. She understands the talent – call it genius – of the man she loves.

What struck me immediately about Sabrina when first I met her was her naturalness and the way her femininity and appealing personality shine through without any effort to impress. She is herself totally. And these very characteristics have created very close bonds between Adrian and herself. They are two people very happily in love.

Sabrina keeps out of the limelight knowing that Adrian wants their relationship to be one of complete understanding and not one that is pressurised day-after-day by the antics of the British tabloids.

When you come from a big family, you learn from an early age to live with reality, to know the basics of life.

Both Adrian and Sabrina have that going for them. They have known reality from the outset.

Adrian cemented his commitment to Sabrina when he slipped a sparkling engagement ring on her finger in the count-down to Cheltenham '94.

They had come a long way since the Autumn of '91. . . .

❦ ❦ ❦ ❦

Toby Balding has generously acknowledged that Cool Ground would never have won the 1992 Cheltenham Gold Cup had not Adrian Maguire given him such a forceful ride – "and I am sure if the jockeys were reversed he would probably have won on The Fellow too. He made Monsieur Kondrat look very ordinary".

Balding has gone further, in fact, and concedes that after Cool Ground's first two runs in the 1991-'92 season, which he described as "abysmal", he was given no encouragement to even dream of Gold Cups. "But he was a transformed character after the turn of the year and Adrian Maguire can take much of the credit for the improvement".

The fact of the matter was that Cool Ground was a horse who knew his own mind. He hated being organised. Maguire discovered that the way to induce him to give of his best was to let him do his own thing.

The partnership clicked immediately in the John Hughes Trophy at Chepstow and later in the Greenhills Gold Cup at Haydock Park, Cool Ground, with Maguire again in the saddle, gave 15lbs to Kildimo and beat him a length and a half.

"Hindsight is a great thing, but, I, more than anybody, should have known that giving Kildimo so much weight was a Gold Cup-winning performance", said Balding.

"Remember, when I had Kildimo, he beat Desert Orchid at levels at Wincanton and also ran him to two and a half lengths, giving him weight, in the Whitbred, so the form was there for all to see."

Peter Bolton, who was the boss of Whitcombe Manor, the man who paid the bills for the imposing complex set deep in Dorset and dubbed simply "Le Patron" by Balding, was always keen on the Gold Cup as the target for Cool Ground.

Balding himself would admit later that he believed that the Form Book showed Cool Ground to be 10lbs below Gold Cup standard.

But after the Greenhills Gold Cup success he came round to Bolton's way of thinking, especially too when he saw the Gold Cup cutting up. And yet he admitted that while – at best – he could not visualise Cool Ground being out of the frame, he could not see him beating The Fellow while Carvill's Hill was the unknown quantity, who certainly had the ability if he jumped the course.

⌘ ⌘ ⌘ ⌘

The 1992 Gold Cup will be remembered for the much-publicised alleged spoiling tactics adopted by the Jenny Pitman-trained Golden Freeze (Michael Bowlby) in order to enhance the victory prospects of stable-companion, Toby Tobias and at the same time disrupt the rhythm and composure of the favourite, the Martin Pipe-trained Carvill's Hill.

Brough Scott would write in *The Independent On Sunday* that Cheltenham takes no prisoners and Carvill's Hill was exposed as a "glass jaw" heavyweight, found out by the fences of the Gold Cup journey, especially the 9th, the 12th and 16th and "a final ghastly blunder at the second-last brought Carvill's to a ruined, trotting apology for a racehorse at the line".

And Hugh McIlvanney wrote in *The Observer* that Carvill's Hill's inadequacies under pressure were betrayed as early as the first fence which he ploughed through with a frightening exhibition of self-destructive clumsiness that one expert defined as "an absolutely ignorant jump". He made the point that Arkle would not have been affected by "a little awkward company" in any of his three Gold Cup triumphs.

And then he added: "Just as the best footballers must rise above the spoiling attentions of cynical opponents, so the best horses should cope with everything short of direct physical interference".

Toby Balding summed up: "In my view Carvill's Hill did himself with that first-fence blunder.

"He was never going from that point, and the controversy which surrounded his duel with Golden Freeze took something away from three very good performances from Cool Ground, The Fellow and Docklands Express. It was a shame."

"I've always looked on Carvill's Hill as a great galloper but he was a non-athlete", Balding went on. "He was never a natural jumper and, basically, when he met a fence right he was fine, but when he didn't he was useless.

"He was never any different. I have got tremendous admiration for Martin Pipe but he is no better a trainer than Jim Dreaper."

In a word, Balding was saying that Pipe wasn't going to turn Carvill's Hill into a Gold Cup winner if Dreaper couldn't do so.

When Carvill's Hill had matters much his own way as in the Welsh Grand National and in the Hennessy Cognac Gold Cup, he could look a world-beater when not making the odd bad error. But once he was taken on by horses competing at Gold Cup pace, he folded under pressure and that had to be seen as the chink in his armour.

Personally, I have no doubt that if Carvill's Hill was in the Arkle mould – and there were those prepared to hail him as such before the 1992 Gold Cup – he would have dismissed

Golden Freeze as Muhammed Ali dismissed Al Blue Lewis on a famous night in Dublin's Croke Park in the early seventies.

To all the lobbies that filled columns about "stalking" and "spoiling" tactics, one had only one word to say – just play the video of Arkle and Mill House locked in battle in that memorable 1964 Gold Cup and you will realise what it really means when two great chasers take each other on.

The Fellow could easily have gone into the record books as the winner of three Gold Cups if not four-in-a-row. He had the misfortune to be beaten in a photo finish by Garrison Savannah in 1991 and again in a photo finish by Cool Ground in 1992.

"Change jockeys and we'll fight you all over again", might well have been the Gallic cry as Adam Kondrat was clearly outpointed by Adrian Maguire in the drama-laden finish to the '92 Gold Cup.

There were two occasions, should I even say three, when I thought there was no way I could be denied collecting on the ante-post dockets I held on the French horse at nice odds (though, fortunately, on the course on the day I had a saver on Cool Ground at 30/1).

First, there was the moment when Carvill's Hill finally cracked and it looked a formality then for The Fellow. Coming to the last he was still in command but Kondrat took it in measured fashion (a few cynics remarked that it was as if he was ensuring he would have a clear round in the Aga Khan Cup at the RDS!) whereas Adrian Maguire drove Cool Ground into the fence with the fearlessness and panache of a Martin Molony.

Yet, The Fellow succumbed by only the narrowest of margins and trainer, Francois Doumen could rightly argue afterwards that if his jockey had used the whip in the same manner as Adrian Maguire then the result might well have been different. Was it a case of the French trainer not wanting his rider to incur the wrath of the English stewards while young Maguire, with glory beckoning, was willing to take the rap? And was Toby Balding going to scold him for suffering a four-day suspension for excessive use of the whip?

Not on your life!

As Balding would ask later in his capacity as the then Chairman of the National Trainers Federation: "Are we running the show for the onlooker? Or are we actually trying to win the races?"

"Obviously, we need to find a happy medium, but artistry is of paramount importance and jockeys will learn to be more artistic in their delivery.

"The bad old days of Fred Archer have long since gone, and we have virtually got rid of the cowboys out the back, who, despite being clearly well-beaten, persist in flogging their horses simply because they are angry at having been asked to ride such a moderate animal or just to show the stewards that they are trying their best."

Adrian Maguire was quite frank about it all after the four-day suspension was imposed on him by the Cheltenham stewards. "There's no denying I was hard on the horse. But if I hadn't been hard on him I wouldn't have won. And it wasn't as if I was beating a 'dead' horse or anything like that; he was responding the whole time."

He added: "In a seller you'd be conscious of how many times you were after hitting a horse. But not when you land over the last in the Gold Cup and with a chance of winning it."

Maguire was concussed in a fall 48 hours before the Grand National and missed the ride on Cool Ground at Aintree. Connections had no option but to go for the prize off a mark of 10st 12lbs. "We knew we would never be so well handi-capped again", said Toby Balding.

The mount fell to another Irishman Martin Lynch, but there was to be little joy for him either. With the ground drying out, the scales started to swing against Cool Ground. By the time of the "off", he had weakened to third favourite behind Docklands Express and Twin Oaks and in the end could finish only tenth to Party Politics, the hard race he had at Cheltenham probably affecting him more than the going. "He gave me a beautiful ride and jumped brilliantly, but he's had a tough season", said Lynch.

The suspension he incurred at Cheltenham '92 was not the last brush Adrian Maguire would have with the English stewards.

The 1993-'94 season would see him make the kind of headlines that he certainly had no wish to make, as he was suspended and fined and was even put under the spotlight by the Jockey Club as it introduced more stringent guidelines on the use of the whip.

You could even argue that the winners he missed on the days he was suspended may have made all the difference in the end to his wrestling the British National Hunt Jockey's crown from the reigning champion, Richard Dunwoody.

The ups-and-downs of that 1993-'94 season deserve a chapter to themselves. . . .

3

When "The Duke" said "It's A Scandal"

After Adrian Maguire had powered Barton Bank to a head victory over Bradbury Star and Declan Murphy in a titanic battle for the 1993 King George VI Chase before 24,000 cheering race-fans at Kempton Park, he found himself – along with Murphy – incurring there and then a suspension for two days (January 5 and 6, '94).

Barton Bank's trainer, David "The Duke" Nicholson was fuming afterwards and described the stewards' decision as "totally scandalous".

Nicholson said: "It is a great shame that a marvellous race was spoilt by a stupid and scandalous decision from the stewards. That applies not only to Adrian but also to Declan Murphy."

Yes, it was a pity really that the whip controversy should have marred what was a truly unforgettable occasion – a race that will always be remembered by those who had the privilege of being present for the brilliant riding performances of both Adrian Maguire and Declan Murphy.

"The Duke" Nicholson was in no doubt about the credit that Maguire deserved: "Some top-class jockeys have ridden for me, not least Peter Scudamore and Richard Dunwoody. And there's no doubt I have another champion in the yard in Adrian. I have only been racing since 1946 but he's the best I've seen. That's not an accolade – it's the truth."

Jeremy Ker, the Senior Stewards' Secretary, was at pains to point out that irrespective of whether it be a King George or a Kelso claimer, all cases must be treated the same.

The video showed Maguire had hit Barton Bank ten times, while Murphy picked up his whip half-way up the run-in and used it seven times.

Maguire, who was reluctant to attack the stewards, said: "We would have been fully aware of the (whip) rule if it had been a seller or claimer but this was the King George. And we did not abuse our horses."

Murphy said: "They told me I didn't give my horse enough time to respond, but I didn't pick my whip up until half-way up the run-in."

Jeremy Ker confirmed the stewards' attitude: "The stewards felt that both jockeys did not give their mounts time to respond between each stroke. It was an open-and-shut case."

Adrian Maguire who was reaching his 100th winner of the season with the victory of Barton Bank – the third fastest ton in jumping history – punched the air in jubilation as he passed the winning post.

Barton Bank's jumping had not always been without blemish. When he hit the fourth from home, Young Hustler tried to take advantage of the blunder. However, Declan Murphy on Bradbury Star and Adam Kondrat on The Fellow were content to bide their time.

At the second last there were five still in with a chance. Zeta's Lad belted that fence hard – and it was curtains for him.

The curtains were also coming down on Young Hustler's bid for glory. While The Fellow was hanging in their grimly, his chance was not helped when he got sandwiched, forcing Kondrat to switch lanes. He was always going to be third at best.

Adrian Maguire launched Barton Bank at the last fence with breath-taking panache and now the artistic Declan Murphy was moving ominously right on his heels and it had come down to a rare tussle between two outstanding horsemen.

In the lung-bursting battle to the finishing post, Maguire threw everything into his effort to keep Barton Bank in front.

Bradbury Star's doubtful stamina ebbed away in the dying strides and Declan Murphy would acknowledge later that his one was outstayed at the death.

You knew, however, that victory would have been his if he was facing any other jockey but Maguire of whom Nicholas Godfrey would write in the *Racing Post* the next day: "It is perhaps tempting fate to burden one so young with the mantle of greatness, but Adrian Maguire long ago used up the other superlatives" and Tim Richards noted in the same paper that the meteoric rise of Maguire hit a new peak with Barton Bank's memorable victory.

Reflecting on Barton Bank's one serious error at the fourth from home, Adrian Maguire said: "I knew he was going to hit that fourth last and I tried to pull him back a stride, but in the end I had to sit and pray. It looks a lot worse than it feels and, once we landed over the last, he stuck his head out and kept galloping. He is a very good horse with a serious engine."

Declan Murphy said: "You might have to wait a long time to see a better King George. Bradbury Star has never run a better race and I felt the whole way round that I would win but it got into a battle of stamina from the last and Barton Bank just outstayed me."

The Fellow, attempting a hat-trick of King George victories, was an honourable third, ten lengths behind Bradbury Star.

Francois Doumen, as ever gracious in defeat, said: "He might not have won, but he got sandwiched at the second last and that forced Adam (Kondrat) to pull back and change direction. It cost him a couple of lengths, but we'll be back for the Gold Cup."

Quietly accepting his fate, Adrian Maguire did not appeal the ban imposed on him by the Kempton stewards. Declan Murphy, one of the most articulate of the present-day crop of jockeys, fought the verdict with no legal representation at Portman Square. He won on appeal.

At the time the Kempton ban seemed but a mere hiccup in Adrian Maguire's relentless surge towards the British National Hunt Championship title. But, in fact, Kempton was to herald the beginning of a very turbulent period in this gifted jockey's professional life and it could well be argued that the "Ramstar Affair" and its consequences may have cost him his first championship crown.

For when it came down to the wire on the very last day of the season, there were only four between them (198 to 194) and Dunwoody's total was expected to be reduced by one with the probable disqualification of one of his winners, All For Luck at Newbury in March.

⌘ ⌘ ⌘ ⌘

Fourteen days after the King George, Adrian Maguire found himself in the middle of a raging storm over a televised race at Warwick in which he rode a horse named Ramstar in a relatively insignificant race – the Westminster-Motor Taxi Insurances Novices' Chase (£3,824.50) – for his retaining stable. Ramstar started joint 7/2 favourite with the Jenny Pitman-trained Don Valentino.

That name Ramstar was to haunt him for weeks.

Ironically, it should have been a day to remember for Maguire as he rode the David Nicholson-trained Moorcroft Boy to a brilliant three-lengths win in the Warwick National and found himself that same evening aboard the favourites for the Aintree Grand National (Moorcroft Boy) and Champion Hurdle (Fortune And Fame) and the second favourite for the Cheltenham Gold Cup (Barton Bank).

Richard Dunwoody, riding the 14/1 shot Castle Diamond, repelled Maguire's frenzied finish on Ramstar by the width of a nostril – the official verdict being a short head.

"The only question seemed to be not so much whether Maguire would be banned, but for how long", wrote John Karter next day in the *Sunday Times*. "He had been suspended for his winning ride aboard Barton Bank in the King George VI Chase at Kempton on Boxing Day and his use of the whip on Ramstar seemed far more wild than that."

The media reported that the film showed that Maguire appeared to bring his whip down at least 20 times from the last fence.

Chaseform Note-Book entered an "In-Focus" comment: "Adrian Maguire appeared to hit Ramstar at lest twenty times in what looked a clear breach of the whip guidelines, yet the Warwick stewards chose not to take any action, despite the advice of their secretaries. Following Declan Murphy's successful appeal against his whip ban imposed after the King George, it appeared that, at last, commonsense would prevail, but this incident had clouded the whole picture. The need for consistency of stewarding would appear stronger than ever."

Adrian Maguire said in the immediate aftermath of the race that during the final stages he had merely been waving his whip rather than connecting with it.

The Warwick stewards supported his view in imposing no ban.

But it didn't end there. A veritable witch-hunt began and Adrian found himself being dubbed "The Butcher Boy" by one scribe, who was later to get a verbal dressing-down from Ted Walsh when he came across for a meeting at Leopardstown.

Maguire's family and close friends were deeply hurt over Adrian being described as a "butcher" and none more so than his mother, who said to me: "How could they write such things about Adrian?"

The armchair racing followers, among them the little old dears caught up with the problems of their beloved pets and how the vets were resolving them and thinking primarily of their own agenda rather than the thrill to be derived from National Hunt racing when top horsemen become locked in battle from the last, joined in the hue and cry.

It was obvious that the Jockey Club would have to bow to the media campaign and the pressure from the public in Britain, irrespective of the attitude of the Warwick stewards.

Anthony Mildmay-White, chairman of the Jockey Club's Disciplinary Committee called for video evidence of the "Ramstar Affair" to be sent to Portman Square. The Jockey Club stewards considered there was a case to answer after all.

On the eve of the hearing, Maguire was suspended for four days, this time for careless riding at Folkstone on Tuesday, January 19.

His mount Spikey was demoted from second to third place for hampering Bollinger, ridden by Declan Murphy.

As Julian Muscat reported in *The Times*: "This was a classic case of Maguire's conmpetitive instinct landing him in trouble. Locked in a thrilling duel with Mailcom (Jamie Osborne), the eventual winner after the last fence, he knew the act of changing his whip hand would cost him any chance of victory, so he persevered, right-handed as Spikey veered to his left.

"Declan Murphy had no choice but to switch Bollinger, although it was doubtful that his progress was much impeded.

"Maguire would not comment on the verdict, which seemed fair on the evidence of the head-on camera. He said very little to the stewards, too, with their Secretary, Geoff Forster reporting: 'He kept his head down, bit his lip and walked out at the end'."

The decision of the Warwick stewards in the "Ramstar Affair" was overturned at Portman Square and Maguire was handed a six-day ban. So in total he was stood down for ten days.

Yet on the day of the Folkstone ban Maguire was 31 winners ahead of Richard Dunwoody. He was still odds-on to land the Jockeys' crown, though William Hill now made him 4/9 from 1/4 and reduced Richard Dunwoody from 5/2 to 13/8.

In the space of two weeks Dunwoody had ridden thirteen winners to Maguire's three.

Where he got brickbats from certain representatives of the British media, echoing the sentiments of a nation where the pet dog and the cat are "King" and to eat a hamster would only be for those with cannibalistic instincts – he had the satisfaction at least of seeing Irish racing writers moving to his defence.

On the Sunday – January 23 – that he rode Fortune And Fame to victory over Danoli in the A.I.G. Europe Champion Hurle at Leopardstown he would have read an article by Brian O'Connor in the *Sunday Press*, under the heading "Maguire a Victim of his own Talent and Determination", which made this very relevant point: "For the administration, so concerned with racing's image, Maguire is a problem. The British rule means stewards must look at a riding performance, if the jockey hits, or appears to hit, a horse six times or more, and the whip must not go over shoulder height.

"But how do those rules contain a blazing talent like Maguire's. By these guidelines Maguire broke the rules at Warwick . . . giving him another ban solves nothing in a sport where such an imprecise word as 'appear' has such influence.

"In a way, Maguire is a victim of his own talent and determination. Twenty years ago, and the ride he produced on Ramstar would have been acclaimed, but now, the welfare of horses is a priority; or it would be if the suspicion didn't persist that the British authorities' main aim is to pander to a largely ignorant section of the public. There is little doubt but that Maguire got carried away at Warwick, but the furore has more to do with the Jockey Club rules than with Maguire himself. He is the unfortunate catalyst."

A number of Irish trainers were asked for their views and Dermot Weld, one of Adrian Maguire's most fervent admirers, made the point that Lester Piggott had to go through the same thing when he was starting off. "As a person, Adrian is a determined character, highly intelligent and very fair, so I think he'll be fine."

"The whole stick issue is an emotive topic at the moment", Weld went on. "I've never been an advocate of the stick, and, when I was riding myself, I was known as a hand and heels rider. Mick Kinane it not noted as a whip rider, either, but you can't generalise.

"There's a big difference between a two-year-old filly, first time out over five furlongs and an old, hardened gelding in a three-mile chase. There are different individuals. Every horse is different, and every horse can take a different amount of pressure, depending on its age and sex."

"There's a lack of clarification in the whip rule in England", added Dermot Weld. "The stewards have gone a bit overboard and become too restrictive."

Paddy Mullins, the veteran Kilkenny trainer, who has seen more jockeys come and go than most, summed up: "I think it's a shame that a jockey of Adrian Maguire's ability should be put through such hassle. Some of it may be his own fault and he may have to adjust his style a little, but a little leniency should be shown.

"Some of the media aren't helping. The media do like to sensationalise things, and Adrian does get hassle from some of them. It's difficult to say why this should be so."

And Michael Hourigan, the man who started the Maguire phenomenon: "He's old enough now to get on with it. Maybe a year ago I'd have been worried how he'd react, but not now. He's got a good boss in David Nicholson who'll help him. I don't think he'll be turned off."

Hourigan recalled that the only time Maguire was suspended when riding for him was at Sligo one day. "It happened when a mare he was riding came off the bend, got unbalanced, and he didn't give her time to get balanced again. That was inexperience. It wouldn't happen now."

⌘ ⌘ ⌘ ⌘

Hassle. It didn't end for Adrian Maguire when he came back from the ten days suspension.

On the eve of his return he said: "I just want to get back and start riding winners. I'm not worried if I don't land the title. It's not something I'm setting out to win."

He was totally sincere in saying that, for he knew that he had time on his side as Richard Dunwoody, who celebrated his 30th birthday on 18 January '94, would relinquish his crown some day to a younger man, even if he were to farm it for a succession of seasons with the power of the Pipe stable behind him, as it was very difficult to dislodge Peter Scudamore from the top perch while he was No. 1 to Pipe.

Maguire was very philosophical and equally pragmatic when questioned about his prospects of staying ahead of Dunwoody in the battle for the title. "Martin Pipe has an enormous string and he will probably have runners right up until the end of the season, unlike David Nicholson", he said.

Agent Dave Roberts reckoned that it would go right down to the wire. "Adrian will always be in demand. Everyone knows that he tries to win on everything he sits on. He always gives it his best."

And then he added: "Adrian should never have been punished in the first place. He was only trying to win and what they did was very harsh.

"But he is a calm and intelligent person. He'll take everything that's happened on the chin and go out and do what he does best – ride winners."

During the period of suspension Maguire continued to school horses at Nicholson's yard every morning but he also practised his new riding style.

"I have been taking a close look at it and have concentrated on keeping the whip low", he said.

✳ ✳ ✳ ✳

On his return at Fontwell on Monday, February 7, he was in trouble again with the stewards – not for a whip offence this time but he was fined £400 for riding a finish a circuit too early.

His latest horror moment came in the Arundal Handicap Hurdle – the last race on the card.

He was riding the 10/1 shot, the Jeff King-trained Access Sun at the end of another winnerless day. He astonished everyone by riding his finish as the field was about to set out on the final circuit of the 2¾-mile race.

Here is how George Ennor described it in the *Racing Post*: "Access Sun was in second place behind Masai Mara when Maguire rode his mount out vigorously to keep second – thinking the third time the field passed the winning post was the final one, as is the case in 2¼-mile hurdles at the tight Fontwell track.

"Having ridden his finish, Maguire pulled up, only to look sideways in horror and see the rest of the field go past him and set out on the final circuit.

"By the time he realised his error it was too late to continue in the race. Instead, he rode Access Sun back to the unsaddling area and apologised to the horse's connections."

Called in immediately by the stewards, Maguire quickly acknowledged his error and had no complaints about the fine imposed on him.

"I totally misjudged it", he said. "It was very embarrassing but when I apologised to Jeff King he said that he'd also made the same mistake at one time."

Richard Dunwoody was quick to sympathise: "Adrian isn't the first to do this at Fontwell and he won't be the last."

Ten weeks after the Fontwell embarrassment, the Jockey Club's Disciplinary Committee produced a series of videos to outline the type of riding offences it was seeking to outlaw. Adrian Maguire featured prominently in these.

He was actually put under the spotlight as the Jockey Club, at a special seminar, presented to the media examples of the stringent new guidelines on the use of the whip and these included the outlawing of hitting a horse down the shoulder with the whip in the forehand position and reducing the number of strikes to six, at which time an automatic inquiry would be announced, it was stressed.

Maguire figured in four specific examples.

Highlighted was the fact that he allegedly hit Sibton Abbey, winner of the Hennessy Gold Cup, thirteen times – "using a high slashing action which was delivered with a considerable amount of force".

The Jockey Club emphasised to the media that the new guidelines were "a package designed to clamp down on the hard men who abuse both the whip and the horse".

Anthony Mildmay-White, Chairman of the Disciplinary Committee, said: "We do not have a personal vendetta against Adrian Maguire. We do not like the way his whip is used. He will have to change his style – and I am sure he will."

But, while Maguire was keeping his thoughts to himself, Toby Balding immediately rallied to his defence, urging the Jockey Club to issue a public apology to Adrian Maguire and describing comments about the Irish jockey as "an unfounded and totally unjustified attack".

"What happened at the Jockey Club seminar makes Adrian look a horse-hating vandal", said Balding. "He is entitled to feel aggrieved by such treatment. He has still not reached his 22nd birthday and it's very tough on him.

"I rang Anthony Mildmay-White and told him it was a personal vendetta against Adrian. He was adamant it wasn't.

"This is another classic case of racing shooting itself in the foot. The sport didn't need the publicity that suggested there was an element of thuggery in race riding. That is certainly not the case. Adrian is not hard on horses and it was most unfair to single him out.

"The first Adrian knew of the onslaught was when he picked up his morning paper. He has never abused a horse of mine. We all know of jockeys who hit them a lot harder."

Maguire's agent, Dave Roberts, said: "We are very upset that Adrian has been made the No. 1 target. It appears he has been publicly singled out.

"Adrian has ridden for over 140 different trainers this year and has had winners for more than 40 of them. None of these trainers has ever complained to me or Adrian about his style and that is surely the answer.

"All he wants to do is ride winners. He always does his best and there have been several instances where he hasn't used his whip at all. This seems like a personal attack on him."

Jockey Club spokesman, David Pipe commented: "The Disciplinary Committee certainly was not picking on Adrian Maguire. They merely used his riding to illustrate certain offences.

"Anthony Mildmay-White made the point that his style will have to change, which we are certain he is able to do. We have a lot of time to talk to him and show what is required."

✖ ✖ ✖ ✖

The season moved on and the furore abated.

The Dunwoody/Maguire roadshow had now developed into the most intense, longest-running duel in the history of National Hunt racing. And in its climactic stage it captured the imagination of the public to such an extent that bumper crowds were being attracted to the venues where they were throwing down the gauntlet to one another and the last grand-stand battle for the crown.

More than 7,000 people turned up at Market Rasen on Saturday evening, June 4, to witness the final scene of the final act of the drama. Normally they would have expected 5,000 paying customers at this meeting.

It was a battle of wits between the agents – a case of who would be in first to catch the early worm, who would come up with the best mounts outside of the retaining stables and other normal commitments. Maguire's agent, Dave Roberts, ended up with a phone bill of £8,000 for the season.

Roberts' total dedication was revealed when he took his mobile phone to the hospital when daughter Beth was born three weeks before the end of the season. And while helping Maguire ride 70 more winners than the previous season, he also steered Norman Williamson to his first century (at the end of it all, his holiday was spent with his family in Ireland and Scotland).

Dunwoody's agent, Robert Parsons (a 32-year-old former stable lad at Henry Candy's, who was recruited in early January) had a telephone bill for the last quarter that showed he made 2,751 calls and he was credited with playing a vital role in the champion's Houdini act in coming from 42 behind at one stage. The success that Parsons helped to mastermind was all the more remarkable as he had to learn the job of agent.

"I was determined to help make Richard champion again", he told Graham Green of the *Racing Post*. "I never lost faith we could do it, even though we were so far behind. There were plenty of anxious moments. I was on the phone to trainers morning, noon and night. I was analysing the form of all the races everywhere to see where we had the best chances. It was pressure all the way. It was just as bad when we did get it in front of Adrian trying to stay there."

The *Racing Post* added flavour and spice to the contest by publishing a "Title Fight" panel each day showing the state of the battle and listing the rides that Dunwoody and Maguire would have and which of their mounts would start favourite. The *Sporting Life* took a somewhat similar approach. Finally, the trade papers published detailed graphs of the Championship fluctuations when it was all over.

⌘ ⌘ ⌘ ⌘

When the 1993-'94 season started on 30 July '93 Richard Dunwoody was installed 1/4 favourite to retain his title with Adrian Maguire at 5/2. But the challenger got off to a flyer with a double at Bangor and, with John White providing the bulk of his ammunition at that stage, he took a lead of six (17-11) by the end of August. This was increased to 12 by the end of the following month as Maguire's total of winners reached 34.

He passed the century mark by the end of December and on January 8 was actually 42 winners ahead of Dunwoody, who had now gone out to 3/1 in the betting while Maguire was as low as 1/5 in some lists.

At the point it seemed that Adrian was heading to become the new champion in Britain.

But it all went wrong in January and the ten-day ban inflicted on him over the "Ramstar Affair" plus the careless riding at Folkestone allowed Dunwoody to close the gap between the two in double-quick fashion.

By January 29 – the day Dunwoody gained his 1,000th victory in Britain on Flakey Dove during a four-timer at Cheltenham – there were now only 20 winners separating the two rivals. Dunwoody's price was cut to evens while Maguire's eased to 8/11. Soon the gap was only two.

Then Richard Dunwoody himself was in the wars with the stewards over an incident in a race at Nottingham on Tuesday, March 1, when he was found guilty of intentional interference when Maguire was nearly put through the rails.

Dunwoody said in a *Daily Mail* interview: "Guilty – that was me at Nottingham and that's why I am not going to appeal against the ban the stewards there gave me for doing a Vinny Jones job on Adrian Maguire.

"I made a mistake and I'm going to pay for it. I pushed Adrian out, but I wasn't trying to kill my pal as some people are trying to make out – the idea that we are out to get one another is just ridiculous.

"When we are not racing we are big mates – we had a drink together on the way home from Nottingham, hardly the behaviour of two people who have go it in for one another."

Dunwoody cited Maguire's attempts to steal up on his inner as the catalyst for his actions.

He said: "I didn't think he had any right to try to challenge on the inside and, even though my horse moved away from him a bit, I pushed him back to threaten Adrian.

"It was a bit like Vinny Jones going in hard on Eric Cantona – Vinny was just letting Eric know he was around and I was doing the same.

"I thought I had left him enough room to jump the second-last hurdle, but his horse didn't have the nerve to go through with it and ran out. I was relieved to see that they were both OK.

"There is an unwritten law in this game that you don't try to come through on anyone's inside. Adrian was testing his luck and I felt I was in the right to stop him."

The axe came down heavily. Dunwoody was suspended for two weeks, the period of suspension taking in the Cheltenham Festival meeting. He took himself off on a skiing holiday and would say later: "I suppose my two-week break did me good, because it gave me time to recharge the batteries."

Meanwhile the bookies shortened the odds on Maguire on the assumption that he would clinch the title while his great rival was in the Alps.

Maguire went to Plumpton on the Monday of Festival week and drew a blank there. Cheltenham is a meeting where four winners will normally win you the Ritz Club trophy. Maguire actually came up with two winners (Viking Flagship and Mysilv) over the three days, had a second in Baydon Star, a third in Smarties, three fourths (Belvederian, Force Seven and Hawthorn Blaze) and a fifth (Kadi). But Triple Witching, a well-backed 6/1 shot for the Bonusprint Stayers' Hurdle was unplaced and so also the Dermot Weld-trained Judicial Field, who started 9/2 favourite for the County Handicap Hurdle, and Miinnehoma who would win the Aintree Grand National on his next outing.

The withdrawal of Fortune And Fame from the Champion Hurdle may well have cost Maguire a third winner at the meeting.

Still Maguire re-established a lead of 20. Ten more winners and he would have been certain of lifting the William Hill trophy. One had got to reckon with the late-season surge of the Martin Pipe stable and the fact that most of "The Duke" Nicholson's horses would be out on grass after Aintree. My own feeling at the time was that Adrian was just not far enough ahead to be certain.

And ultimately the "Pipe Factor" was to be the deciding one, for the statistics showed that in the last fortnight Pipe provided Dunwoody with a non-stop flow of "ammunition" represented by 31 runners and the champion won on eight of them. "The Duke" Nicholson in contrast supplied Maguire with two runners and one of these won.

Dunwoody pulled out all the stops on his return. Having ridden a winner at Wincanton on the Thursday, March 24, he followed up with a double at Ludlow on the Friday and a four-timer at Newbury on the Saturday as Maguire drew a blank. He would keep up his remorseless strike rate in the following week, landing a treble at Newton Abbot, another double at Ascot and a treble again at Newton Abbot.

The Pipe stable, as was anticipated, had clicked into top gear. Smaller stables that had provided Maguire with a flow of winners earlier in the season could not match Pipe's superiority in numbers and you felt that this could ultimately be the deciding factor in the race for the title. Dunwoody himself would pay tribute to Martin Pipe and his team on the day he retained his crown. "Without their help I wouldn't be in this position", he readily acknowledged.

Dunwoody finally overtook Maguire on May 14 and was long odds-on to retain the championship crown when bookmakers suspended betting. The amazing feature about it was that Hills had made over 70 price changes during the fluctuations in the fortunes of the two combatants. You could have backed each of them at 7/2 – and not lost a penny!

When Dunwoody went nine clear on May 25 (it was actually 190 to 180 ahead at that stage but it was reckoned he would lose one on a disqualification), the battle looked all over.

⌘ ⌘ ⌘ ⌘

Then began Maguire's great fight-back. His remarkable treble at Uttoxeter changed the entire picture dramatically and piled on the pressure on Dunwoody. The excitement generated during the last week became white-hot. There were effectively but two winners between them as they entered the final day of the season – Saturday, June 4 – with an afternoon meeting scheduled at Stratford and an evening meeting at Market Rasen.

There was everything to play for and with Maguire exclaiming to the world "I am on a roll", it was a brave man

THE VICTOR'S SMILE: A delighted Adrian Maguire holds the Gold Cup trophy high in triumph after his memorable win on the Toby Balding-trained Cool Ground in 1992.

COOL HAND ADRIAN: Adrian Maguire gives an arm-aloft salute to the cheering crowds thronging the amphitheatre of the winner's enclosure as he is led in on Cool Ground and (inset) the legendary Martin Molony with whom Maguire has been rightly compared.

Adrian Maguire comes with a powerful surge on the inside on Cool Ground (No. 2) at the last to beat Docklands Express (Mark Perrett) and The Fellow (Adam Kondrat) in the 1992 Gold Cup, the victory that confirmed him as a rider of genius.

The brilliance of Maguire was seen again in all its glory in the 1994 Queen Mother Champion Chase as he came on the inside on Viking Flagship to win an epic battle from the last with Jamie Osborne on Travado (left) and Declan Murphy on the '93 winner, Deep Sensation (centre).

Adrian Maguire on his way to victory in the 1991 Jameson Irish Grand National on the Martin Pipe-trained Omerta and (inset) a delighted Mrs. Eitne McMorrow with the trophy.
Before he left for England to join Toby Balding's stable, Maguire made his mark on the point-to-point circuit. Here he displays all his budding talent on Indian Tonic at Nenagh.

John Berry (top left) congratulates Adrian Maguire on winning the 1990-'91 Irish point-to-point Riders' Championship, Maguire sealing the title with an incredible six-timer at Dromahane; Michael Hourigan (top right), who was Maguire's Guv'nor when he was riding the point-to-point circuit; Toby Balding (bottom left), whose stable Adrian joined when he moved to England and (bottom right) ''The Duke'' Nicholson who appointed Maguire his No. 1 stable jockey when Richard Dunwoody joined Martin Pipe.

Adrian Maguire's parents, Phyllis and Joe outside the family home at Kilmessan, County Meath and (inset) how the signpost reads in Irish and English at the outskirts of the village.

THE BOY WONDER: On the pony circuit, Adrian Maguire was unbeatable, notching up a total of 250 winners. Here he displays all the intensity of a budding champion as he goes out on Salmon Leap to score another victory.

Adrian Maguire (left) in triumphant mood after winning the 1993 Digital Galway Plate on Dr. Michael Smurfit's General Idea and (right) jumping the last on Second Schedual earlier that same year to take the Cathcart Challenge Cup Chase by a head in a pulsating finish with General Idea.

Adrian Maguire on Omerta (left) comes from behind to catch the blinkered Master Bob and Golden Minstrel in the 1991 Fulke Walwyn Kim Muir Cup, his first Cheltenham Festival success and the one that catapulted him on to a new plane overnight.

ADRIAN MAGUIRE (above, right) powers the Pat Flynn-trained For Reg to victory over Land Afar in the Cordon Bleu Handicap Hurdle at the 1994 Aintree Grand National meeting and (right) with the charming Sabrina Winters from Kanturk, County Cork, to whom he became engaged in 1994.

who would have bet his house on "The Kid" not pulling it off.

On the face of it Dunwoody killed Maguire's challenge stone dead when he rode a treble at Stratford – all three provided by Martin Pipe.

So with Dunwoody five ahead Maguire knew as he left Stratford early on the forty-minute helicopter flight to Market Rasen that he would have to go through the card to become champion and win five races to share the title. An enormous task, a superhuman one really.

However, hope still flickered. His entry to the track was like that of Alex "Hurricane" Higgins entering The Crucible in his prime – the embodiment of charisma, the champion maybe not in name but surely the "people's champion". Surrounded by young autograph hunters as he made his way to the weighroom, unperturbed now by the clicking cameras.

The news filtered through from Stratford that Dunwoody had gone four up and then five and Dave Roberts summed it up in one six-word sentence: "He'll have to ride all six."

The course commentator set the pitch as the horses left the parade ring for the start of the first race, noting that Maguire was setting out towards "this impossible miracle".

He won that first race on Wayward Wind and then the second on a horse aptly named It's Unbelievable. The crowd had gone wild and, as Alan Lee noted in his report for *The Times*, "the roof of the stand was almost raised by a crowd revelling in the theatre". The excitement was heightened as they saw the helicopter bearing Richard Dunwoody landing at that very moment.

Bobby Socks was the Great White Hope in the third, the handicap chase. Maguire looked poised for victory as they approached the last fence and 7,000 throats were willing him on in the crescendo that 7,000 people out of their skins with excitement can create. But Bobby Socks went down by two lengths in a driving finish.

Then, at 8.09 p.m. as the evening shadows lengthened over Market Rasen and the great admiring roar, deep and sustained, echoing from the stands and enclosures at Cheltenham during the Festival meeting when he won the Queen Mother Champion Chase in unforgettable fashion on

Viking Flagship seemed a long time ago now, the curtain came down on the impossible dream as Logical Fun failed to win the Newark Storage Handicap Hurdle. That meant that Maguire was three winners behind with only two rides to come.

The young challenger was still the Young Pretender.

Ironically, Dunwoody failed to add to his total but Stratford and his afternoon treble had been the knock-out blow to Maguire's aspirations.

⌘ ⌘ ⌘ ⌘

While Dunwoody finally emerged triumphant from this prolonged and fascinating contest, it was Adrian Maguire who in the words of his agent was the "moral victor".

He set three new records – all captured from his rival.

Firstly, as John Randall revealed in a very well-researched article in the *Racing Post*, he attained the best-ever total by a non-champion, the previous record being 137 by Dunwoody in 1991/'92.

Secondly, Maguire rode in more races than any jump jockey had ever done in one season, and with 915 mounts he beat the old record of 740 set by Dunwoody the previous season.

Thirdly, he won the most prizemoney in a season in the history of National Hunt racing – his £1,193,917 sterling beating the total of £1,101,876 set by Dunwoody's mounts the previous season.

The totals achieved by Dunwoody and Maguire were respectively the second and third-highest scores by a jump jockey, surpassed only by the record of 221 by Peter Scudamore in 1988/'89.

If jockeys, like trainers, had their championship decided on prizemoney, Adrian Maguire would have emerged, like his Guv'nor David Nicholson, as the title-winner for 1993/'94.

John Randall noted that the climax to the 1993-'94 championship battle was the most exciting since Bob Davies (90), Stan Mellor (89) and Terry Biddlecombe (89) went into the final card at Stratford in the 1969-'70 season. Davies and Mellor each rode a winner, so the former prevailed in what might easily have been a triple dead-heat.

Mellor had won the title by default in 1959-'60 when Fred Winter, one in front with a day to go, went on holiday with his wife and children. Mellor had a double on the last day at Uttoxetter and prevailed 68-67.

"Mellor, young and seeking his first title, was hungrier than the four-times champion, Winter, but in any case jump jockeys at that time were cavalier in their attitude towards championships and records. Racing was still a sport, not a business, and agents were unheard of", noted Randall.

Jamie Osborne, who had watched the great ten-months battle from the saddle was more qualified than anyone else to put it into true perspective. And in a very perceptive piece in *The Times* on the eve of the last day of the season he wrote that Maguire and Dunwoody had maintained an unbelievable pace in their quest for winners – "their drive and commitment has been relentless, their dedication almost an obsession. Those looking on could feel nothing but admiration for what they achieved."

Then he went on to put his finger on what was entailed: "My 500 rides pale into insignificance in comparison to their totals (at the end of the final day 915 in Adrian Maguire's case and 891 in Richard Dunwoody's).

"To put this figure into context, Peter Scudamore was champion jockey eight times – the most rides he had in any one season was 663. John Francome was champion seven times, never having more than 570 rides. As for the number of winners, whoever loses this year's protracted battle will have ridden enough winners to be champion jockey in any year since the war, with the exception of 1989, when Scudamore rode 221.

"As ever, the season will be recorded statistically, but figures will not tell the whole story. Maguire and Dunwoody have suffered some deep lows and incredible highs.

"Adrian and I have had adjacent pegs in the changing room since he arrived in England three years ago and I have known Richard well since I started riding. While we are competitors, we are also colleagues and friends. I have therefore witnessed closely how the events of this season have affected them.

51

"Richard is intense. When things get tough, he becomes more inward; one would never know exactly what was going on in his head. Adrian is more open. There are times when he would volunteer his thoughts to spark a discussion – not that he would be looking for reassurance as confidence is something he has never lacked.

"In a way, their characters are mirrored in their race riding. With Richard, one gets the impression he is oblivious to what is happening around him. This is not the case: it is just that he tries hard not to allow anybody to get in the way of what he wants to do. He is aggressive and yet still very neat. He is somebody who always seems in control. Adrian is very natural. He has no set way of doing things, dealing with situations as they occur. At times, he may appear not to have Richard's composure, but he has an overriding will to win.

"Their season-long conflict has remained enacted on the course. They have the utmost respect for one another and I can guarantee that the victor will feel a tinge of sadness for the runner-up, each knowing what the other has gone through in order to ride almost 200 winners. Whatever the outcome, Dunwoody and Maguire have managed to add another dimension to the National Hunt season, maintaining its profile and adding interest in what is normally a low-key finale."

"No one has ever ridden 194 winners and not been champion jump jockey", wrote jockey-cum-journalist, Marcus Armytage in the *Daily Telegraph*.

Alan Lee quoted Richard Dunwoody in *The Times* as stating "I don't want to go through this again", Lee himself adding: "One look at the pale, emaciated features betraying ten months of pain and strain was sufficient to understand why Dunwoody had retained his title but the single-mindedness, stamina and sacrifice demanded of him to see off Adrian Maguire had been so severe that even he hardly knew how he had done it."

In fact, Dunwoody confessed: "I have been going to bed every night worrying about the next day and whether Adrian will ride a winner. It puts a lot of pressure on those closest to you – just ask my wife, Carol."

Marcus Armytage reported Dunwoody as making it clear that the emphasis in the 1994-'95 National Hunt season, as far as he was concerned, would not be on quantity, that he would "not be going to the extremes" he went to in the course of the 1993-'94 season, adding: "If Adrian wants to, he can, but I'm not chasing my tail around the country. I don't intend to have as many rides. Going to Sedgefield for one is a lot of driving and not much riding. I've enjoyed it this season, but it's been very, very busy."

Armytage then made this very significant point: "It will probably be a couple of days before either winds down enough to feel tired. The thing about Dunwoody, though, is that he doesn't like being second and statements made before the smoke has cleared from the battlefield are always going to be open to change when the adrenalin flows again.

"It will not be lost on Dunwoody either that while Peter Scudamore won championship after championship with Martin Pipe, it was he, as David Nicholson's jockey, who was winning in financial terms.

"Nicholson's jockey has again collected more in prizemoney. Maguire won £90,000 more than Dunwoody at £1,185,000 and that is on top of a retainer – which Dunwoody does not have with Pipe. What is more, Nicholson is leading trainer for the first time, with 81 winners which earned £754,481."

Dunwoody was quoted by other journalists as emphasising that he had five or six more seasons riding in him – "and I want to enjoy them".

He cited the Grand National win on Miinnehoma as the highlight of his season, especially as at that stage of the season he thought that the championship looked out of his reach. "To win it again still looked very hard, but then we've had a good couple of months and Adrian hit a slack time and it all changed."

In a way, perhaps, the National finish with Maguire clearing the last fence narrowly ahead only to find that Dunwoody's mount, Miinnehoma had the greater resources of stamina in the long run to the line capsulated the season itself and the battle for the jockey's crown. In the final analysis, as we have indicated already, it was the fire-power of the Pipe stable that provided Richard Dunwoody with the momentum as he made his final onslaught.

⌘ ⌘ ⌘ ⌘

In the moment of defeat Adrian Maguire put on a brave face and he was pictured smiling broadly as Dunwoody and himself were raised high by fellow-jockeys.

"I'm here in one piece, it's been a terrific battle, and I've ridden some good horses," he said. "It has been stressful getting so close, but I'm looking forward to my holiday now and I'll be trying even harder next season."

"It is only a matter of time before Maguire wins his first championship and he is sure to set many more records before he retires", concluded John Randall in the *Racing Post.*

Dunwoody and Maguire, the two dominant forces in the jumping game, headed away for their exotic holidays in the sun after Brendan Powell's wedding, neither worried about any communications from their bank managers. They were right at the top of the pile.

But Marcus Armytage noted that the new season was a Costa del Sol holiday away for the middle men of the game – "and a weekend at Blackpool away for those at the bottom of the pile".

When Adrian Maguire was riding the pony circuit and later the point-to-point circuit, he could never have dreamed of the fame and wealth that was in store for him.

But from the outset he had talent way beyond the ordinary and it was only a question of time as to when that genius would blossom in all its glory.

The full flowering of a Martin Molony-like talent was greater than the winning of any title.

[*Footnote: Adrian Maguire lit up a Bank Holiday Monday by riding the first five winners at Plumpton on Monday, 29 August 1994. He brought his winners total to 21 for the 1994-'95 season by scoring a near 63/1 nap hand with Sharp Spring (11/8), Crews Castle (6/4), Safety (21/20), Heretical Miss (1/2), and Wayward Wind (5/2). His bid to become the first jockey to go through the card in Britain since Alec Russell in 1957 was thwarted when newcomer, Drama Critic, after trailing the field, was pulled up by Maguire with a circuit to go in the last race. Incidentally, Peter Niven was the last jump jockey to ride five consecutive winners at a meeting, at Kelso on 5 October 1992.*]

PART TWO

CHARLIE SWAN

Bringing home the Ritz Club
Trophy two years running

4

Why Swan Did Not Want That Call After All

Cheltenham has been good to Charlie Swan as Sandown was unkind to him first in 1991 when ill-fated Cahervillahow was disqualified after finishing first past the post in the Whitbread Gold Cup and then smiled on him when he took the same event in 1994 on the 25/1 outsider, Ushers Island.

After Cheltenham '93 the world was at Charlie's feet. He had returned to his native Cloughjordan in North Tipperary with the Ritz Club Trophy after emerging as top jockey at the Festival meeting with four winners for four different Irish trainers. Then followed victory in the Jameson Irish Grand National on Ebony Jane for the Francis Flood Grangecon stable and on Camden Buzz for Paddy Mullins in the Guinness Galway Hurdle. To crown it all, he had become the first Irish-based jockey to ride 100 winners over the jumps in a calendar year and in the process had broken the record of the incomparable Martin Molony that had stood the test for 42 years.

Cheltenham '94 would see Swan win the Ritz Club Trophy for the second year running as he recorded a treble on the Wednesday, winning on Time For A Run and Mucklemeg for the Edward O'Grady-J. P. McManus partnership and taking the Sun Alliance Novices' Hurdle on Danoli to an unforgettable "Irish roar".

It's Galway race week '93 and I am sitting in the lounge of the Corrib Great Southern Hotel chatting to Swan over coffee and bringing him back to the moment when Irish racing circles were aflame with reports that he had been sounded about taking the job as No. 1 jockey to the Martin Pipe stable following the retirement of Peter Scudamore in April of the same year. Credence had been lent to the reports when "The Duke" Nicholson issued what was to all intents and purposes an ultimatum to Richard Dunwoody demanding of him that he make up his mind one way or the other on whether he was going to stay with him or leave. It was not proving an easy decision for Dunwoody to make.

Yes, there had been feelers, Swan told me, and he had responded that he would be "interested" – but that, of course, was different from having to give a definite "yes" or "no". The final irrevocable question had not been put.

Martin Pipe did not come back with an offer – the kind of offer it would have been difficult to refuse. Obviously, he had put more than one top rider in the sights of his gun to begin with but when it came to "bagging" one, the ultimate choice was Richard Dunwoody.

"I do not know what I would have done if I had been asked to take over the mantle of Peter Scudamore", said Charlie Swan quite simply and very frankly.

You see the Irish National Hunt champion jockey had only recently completed building work on a lovely new bungalow-style home – "The Cobs" – about a mile from the training establishment of his father, Capt. Donald Swan at Modreeny, Cloughjordan.

❃ ❃ ❃ ❃

Tranqulity reigns in this corner of North Tipperary and when Charlie gets home, for example, from Cheltenham, the hurly-burly of the Festival meeting seems light years away.

Cloudghjordan is steeped in the lore of hurling, the game that is to Ireland what cricket on the village green is to England and baseball to America. Love of hurling and racing go hand in hand when you assess what are the passions of the people in the sporting sense in the Modreeny area. If you drop in to mingle with the pint drinkers in the Corner House, one of Cloughjordan's favourite hostelries, you will quickly discover that these are the topics you have got to be able to discuss – and with knowledge too, if you are to survive a long day.

Charlie is not a "hurling man" in the way that the aficionados of the game are classified in Tipperary. But he understands its place and its over-riding importance in the psyche of the people.

He is a "King" in this most picturesque of villages but "one of our own" at the same time to the residents of Cloughjordan and the surrounding area. They are proud of the way he has made its name known among lovers of the jumping game in Ireland and Britain and around the globe.

A man would not easily leave such an ideal setting. And for Swan and his wife, Tina, it's now HOME in capital letters.

Swan loves his life in Ireland too much to want to depart for pastures new. "Yes, I could earn a lot more money. But I don't think I'd be happy – and that's what counts."

When, for example, I interviewed him for a *Sunday Independent* feature prior to the Leopardstown '93 Christmas meeting, he told me that he would ride out at his father's place on Christmas morning – "and then I'll probably have two Christmas dinners, one in Cloughjordan and the other with Tina's family in Kildare. Or it may be half a Christmas dinner in each place", he laughed.

"This is my home and it's the place where I belong", he told Declan Kelly of the *Cork Examiner* when Declan travelled to Cloughjordan to cover the social function when the entire village came out to pay tribute to their favourite son.

"I have no desire to leave this place at all. In fact when I have finished riding, I want to train here at my father's stables", he added significantly.

While it does appear on the face of it that it is almost inevitable that he will assume Donald Swan's mantle, it must be stressed that Charlie is not one who wears rose-tinted glasses when he contemplates a future as a trainer.

Indeed, he is quite pragmatic and clear-headed when it comes to discussing the pitfalls of the training profession. "It's essential that you get the right owners from the outset and, every bit as important, that you are training good horses. I believe there is no point in becoming a trainer just for the sake of being a trainer, simply because people assumed that was the natural progression your career would take after you retired from the saddle.

"It can be a nightmare breaking your back with bad horses that are going nowhere. They will put the same demands on you – even more – than good horses and potential champions. I wouldn't like to end up enduring that kind of nightmare."

Like fellow-county man, Michael Kinane, Charlie Swan is a man for whom quality of life has a deep significance and he would not be willing to exchange it unless he got the kind of offer which he could not refuse.

Like Kinane he is able to enjoy the best of both worlds at the present time – retain the National Hunt Jockeys crown in Ireland while booting home 100 winners in the season and at the same time pick up plum rides for English trainers.

Nicky Henderson has come to deeply appreciate Charlie's talent and is quite willing to engage him whenever the occasion demands. He gave him the ride on Thumbs Up in the Arkle Chase at the '94 Cheltenham Festival meeting and Swan had this one close up and waiting to pounce at the third last when he was brought down in most unlucky circumstances.

Swan could have joined Henderson if he wished back in 1989 but turned down the offer as he would not have been No. 1 to the stable.

Around the same time "Mouse" Morris offered him a job as his No. 1. "Naturally I took that instead, even though I knew I would make more in England."

The arrangement worked out well for both jockey and trainer and it saw Swan become associated with that good staying hurdler, Trapper John. He rode this one to victory in the Bonusprint Stayers Hurdle at the Cheltenham Festival meeting in 1990. He also partnered the enigmatic Cahervillahow, who promised more than he achieved.

As Swan matured and his professionalism became more pronounced, offers of rides from outside stables increased.

"Mouse" Morris presented him with a decision that required a "yes" or "no" – nothing less – either he rode everything from the Fethard stables or else he would no longer be the No. 1 jockey.

"I told 'Mouse' I could not give him that commitment," said Swan. "Let me emphasise that there was no question whatsoever of a falling-out between us. It was a totally matter-of-fact discussion, like two businessmen talking over something, nothing personal about it whatsoever and he understood my point of view and I knew what he wanted."

So there came the parting of the ways – though not, as it turned out, permanently.

The bottom line was that Charlie Swan felt that he was losing winners by being tied to one stable as No. 1. If Pat Flynn came to him with the offer to ride Montelado, he wanted to be in a position to accept it. It was as simple as that.

When Charlie Swan vacated the position as No. 1 jockey to the "Mouse" Morris stable, he lost the ride on Cahervillahow but the greatest tribute of all to him was that "Mouse" eventually asked him to team up again with the Deep Run gelding, who wore blinkers when finishing third in the National Handicap Chase at Punchestown in February under 12st. Having made no impression in the Gold Cup, he gave Swan an exhilarating ride when he figured in "the race that never was" – the '93 Aintree Grand National, Wexford-born John White having the distinction, if one might call it thus, of being "first" past the post in that 154th renewal.

After a long delay to the preliminaries, caused by animal rights protestors on the course and two false starts – the second missed by all but nine of the 39 jockeys – the race was declared void.

If utter disappointment needed a visual definition, it was surely in the graphic photographs of John White's expression as the truth dawned on him after he and Esha Ness had "won" in a close four-horse finish with Cahervillahow, Romany King (Adrian Maguire) and The Committee (Norman Williamson).

At least Cahervillahow had shown that he had the ability to jump the Aintree fences and Swan likewise had proved that he had the horsemanship to win a National one day.

Many people would probably think in terms of Swan being "a lucky jockey" in the avoidance of serious injury. Yet it's an indication in itself of the fearlessness of our National Hunt jockeys that Charlie reels off to me the fact that he has broken his right arm twice and his left arm once, a leg, a hand and his nose – not to mention collar bone fractures – as if such injuries happened to be an everyday occurrence. He has also cracked his skull and he still has the scar on his forehead.

What the real professionals of this game fear is the kind of injury that terminates your career prematurely when you are right at the top – and it can all seem so cruel. What they fear is an injury that can leave you like a punch-drunk boxer – one resulting from a horrible fall from which you never really come back as you were in your prime.

Or it may be that you will have your career prematurely ended, as Martin Molony's career was ended by a cruel fall on Bursary at Thurles in 1951. Molony was only 26 when it happened. An English specialist advised him not to ride again.

Now that he is champion, Swan has the right to choose. "I will ride a bad lepper if I know he has a chance of winning. But I won't ride one who has no hope."

To put it bluntly, he is a "little bit more choosey" nowadays – and can afford to be.

When you ride horses that have no hope, all you are doing is giving yourself the chance of a fall. I know you are doing yourself out of IR£71, but a bad fall could cost you an awful lot more."

He sums up the philosophy of the risk-takers of the National Hunt game thus: "You learn to take it day by day."

Survival is more important in the final analysis than the breaking of records.

⌘ ⌘ ⌘ ⌘

Charlie Swan has come a long way from the time he started pony racing at the age of ten. While a boarder at school in Headford he played cricket and one might speculate now on Charlie progressing to the point where he was chosen to represent his country – even against the touring West Indies.

But, of course, he knew in his heart that the only profession he wanted to pursue in life was to be a full-time jockey. His father encouraged him in every way possible.

He was 15, going on 16, and still a schoolboy weighing six-and-a-half stone when he had his first ride in public at Naas in March, 1983 on Final Assault, a debutant in a two-year-old event. "I broke him at home, my father trained him and my grannie owned him", he recalled. "I was thrilled that my father had enough faith in me to let me ride him."

Drawn 16 in a field of 16, Charlie found himself heading for the winning post very much on his own and out wide from the rest of the field. Final Assault had been worked on his own at home. "The ground was very bad on the inside that day at Naas and father had advised me not to go over for the rails. He was certainly proved right in that as I came home the winner by six lengths."

He was hooked on riding from that moment. He had arrived – though with his cherubic countenance he looked almost too much the kid bringing Final Assault back into the winner's enclosure.

His father was mostly into jumpers, so it was inevitable that in order to further his racing education he should become attached to a regular Flat stable. He joined the Curragh establishment of Kevin Prendergast, son of "Darkie". He quickly won recognition as an apprentice of outstanding promise and was constantly in demand by "outside" stables. He would end up with the impressive record of riding 56 winners on the Flat. Not surprisingly, his experience as a Flat jockey would stand him in excellent stead when it came to riding a finish in the National Hunt sphere.

There came a stage when Swan realised that if he wanted to remain a Flat jockey he would have to resign himself to the rigid regime of wasting and he had a fierce aversion to this.

When he suffered a broken leg one day schooling, the result was that in the period of recuperation his weight shot up to 9 stone. "I was still growing at the time and it's work, believe me, to get weight off when you're in a situation like that. So I decided that the time had come to switch to the jumps."

"I informed Kevin Prendergast who immediately understood the problem", he added.

Prendergast rang Dessie Hughes and in a way it was the Hinge of Destiny that put Swan on the road to becoming Irish champion National Hunt rider and to lifting the Ritz Club Trophy at the 1993 and '94 Cheltenham Festival meetings.

Jumping was his first love really. He hunted with the Ormonds and Golden Vale and was quite accustomed to the point-to-point circuit.

In teaming up with Dessie Hughes, he was joining a man who had distinguished himself as one of the outstanding Cheltenham riders of the modern era – the man who had won the Gold Cup on Davy Lad in 1977 and the Champion Hurdle on Monksfield in 1979 after an epic battle with Sea Pigeon and Jonjo O'Neill from the last. Apart from these two successes, he won the Sun Alliance Novices Hurdle in successive years (on Davy Lad in 1975 and Parkhill in 1976, both trained by Mick O'Toole), the Supreme Novices Hurdle on Mac's Chariot in 1977 and the Bonusprint Stayers Hurdle on Bit of a Jig in 1976 and both these two were also trained by Mick O'Toole. He was first past the post on Mick O'Toole's Chinrullah (disqualified subsequently on technical grounds) in the 1980 Queen Mother Champion Chase, having won the Arkle Challenge Trophy Chase on this gelding in 1979. Overall an outstanding record.

Swan is the first to acknowledge the benefit he gained from the time he spent with Dessie Hughes and it is significant that Tom Moragn was also a pupil of the same Academy – Morgan who rode Miller Hill to victory for Hughes in the 1982 Supreme Novices Hurdle and who was only thwarted from winning the 1989 Gold Cup on Yahoo by the "people's champion", the great Desert Orchid.

✼ ✼ ✼ ✼

Charlie Swan rides easily at 9st 12lb and "with a sweat" can get down to 9st 7lb.

In common with most champions, he has a distinct preference for racing on the inside but not simply because it's the shortest way round.

He explained: "Horses tend to settle better when they have a rail alongside them, particularly in hurdle races. They will often run too freely when they are between other horses.

"Also if you are in the middle, you have to contend with the horses in front backing off at each hurdle, those on your left jumping across you and those on your inner jumping out.

"For the same reason I also like to be on the inside in steeplechases. But I find that on a good jumper you are better off out in front because it means you have a chance of making ground at the fences.

"If your horse is jumping well in behind, you have to keep pulling him back. This means that he loses what he has gained at his fences."

Swan's actual style is neat and effective. But coming into the last he will often ride like a demon and he is convinced that this do-or-die approach makes a big difference to the number of winners he rides.

"You can gain a length before you even get to the jump and probably another one as you take it. Whereas if you sit still, the horse will tend to back off and lose ground in the process."

❀ ❀ ❀ ❀

Charlie Swan will always remember 1993 as the year that lifted him on to an entirely new plane and brought his name to the notice of a vast public in Britain who up to the time of the Cheltenham Festival meeting may have thought of him as just another Irish rider of blossoming talent.

Swan's outstanding feat in recording a four-timer at the Festival meeting combined with his becoming Irish National Hunt champion jockey for the fourth successive year with 105 winners put him right in line to battle it out with Michael Kinane for the Personality of the Year Award in Irish Racing.

The Awards scheme was inaugurated that same year by the *Irish Racing Annual* in conjunction with Tipperary Crystal, who put up magnificent inscribed trophies for the winners.

Making the awards all the more prestigious and meaningful was the fact that the winners were chosen as a result of the

Irish Racing Correspondents and Writers expressing their opinions through a ballot.

In the final analysis the singular triumph of Vintage Crop in the Melbourne Cup made it inevitable that the main Award would be shared by Dermot Weld and Michael Kinane.

But Swan qualified for a Special Award as did also Waterford trainer, Pat Flynn, for whom Charlie rode Montelado to that memorable triumph in the Supreme Novices Hurdle.

Donald Swan and his wife were on hand at the Racing Board Headquarters at Leopardstown to see their son receive his trophy – and Donald, reflecting back a decade to that day in Naas when he legged Charlie up on Final Assault, had every reason to be a proud man.

The Tipperary Crystal trophy would take its place beside the other crystal trophies and inscribed silverware in "The Cobs" in Cloughjordan, all testifying to Swan's brilliance as a rider over the sticks and especially to the impact he had made at Cheltenham.

Ironically, on his first visit to Cheltenham in 1987 he broke his arm when Irish Dream came a cropper. It didn't end there. The ambulance taking him from the racecourse to the medical room was involved in an accident – "a car pulled right in front of us", Charlie recalled. "I was in enough pain at the time without wanting additional shocks", he added ruefully. So much for dreams of glory on a "dream" horse that wasn't up to delivering on the day. . . .

But four of Swan's rides at the '93 Festival meeting certainly delivered in style and the beauty of it was that all four were for stables – three of them based in County Waterford – that wouldn't rate in the big-guns category of Martin Pipe's or "The Duke" Nicholson's in Britain.

First there was Montelado storming up the hill to put twelve lengths between him and Lemon's Hill in the Supreme Novices' Hurdle, conjuring up memories of ill-fated Golden Cygnet pulverising his rivals in similar fashion in this race in 1978.

"This horse is something else again", was the tribute paid by Tony Mullins to Montelado.

❃ ❃ ❃ ❃

It was a great training feat by Pat Flynn of Rathgormack, County Waterford, to bring Montelado to winning peak on the day that mattered.

For, as the trainer himself told me, the horse had been very sick after Christmas. However, the patience shown by Flynn in avoiding giving Montelado any recent race was fully vindicated.

When he was nine years old Pat Flynn was one of the family sent by their mother to learn to ride at an equestrian centre in Clonmel. "The rest of them gradually drifted away from it but I stayed on a while longer than the others. I was playing hurling and football at the time, but after letting the riding go for a while I went back and then I got really interested in riding the ponies, hunting and at shows", he recalled.

A spell as a boarder at De La Salle Brothers College was a further interruption to his equestrian career. But he managed to keep in touch during the holidays and as well as riding he was lending a hand to his father with the yearlings at home. He had, after finishing school, started farming and enjoyed it, but deep down he knew that he was happiest around horses.

After breaking a filly bred by his father which went to be trained by Adrian Maxwell, he decided that horses must come first and farming second. In time the filly came home. She had been named Cheap Display. In 1981 he got a permit to train and she was his only racehorse to begin with. Fortunately, she won her last race of the year for him – and he knew then that he was on his way.

What followed is of the stuff of dreams. On an intuitive hunch he bought a colt from the Ballykisteen Stud at the Newmarket December Sales for 4,300 guineas. Now he had two horses, the newcomer being by Auction Ring out of Via Mala. The name he was given was Virginia Deer.

The Flynn gallop then was a modest one, comprising two fields sloping gently to the feet of the Comeragh Mountains under Drotty's Lake in one of the most scenic and idyllic parts of County Waterford. The horses walked to the bottom and work was done uphill through a stone-pillared gap in the second field, all the work being a stern test against the hill.

Virginia Deer in a way was the making of Pat Flynn initially in the sense that he brought his name to the notice of a wider public, leading on to his acquiring more owners. Third time out Virginia Deer won a Maiden at the Curragh and next time the Marwell Stakes at Naas. When Tony Power, then Racing Correspondent of the *Irish Press* asked Flynn in the winner's enclosure where he might go next with the colt, he replied: "The Windsor Castle Stakes at Royal Ascot."

When reminded by Power that it was Saturday afternoon and that the entries closed first post on Monday morning, Flynn airily replied: "That's O.K. I'll send a telex to Wetherby's."

"So you have a telex machine?", said Power rather tentatively. "Not at all, but there is one in the Creamery and I can send from there."

Christy Roche rode Virginia Deer at Ascot and the horse ran a blinder, finishing a close-up fifth. He came back to win the Curragh Stakes to break into the Group league. He ran second to Ancestral in the Railway Stakes before being fifth to Kafu at Doncaster in the Flying Childers and then winning the Listed Goff's Stakes at the Curragh.

He was sold that December and at the sales Pat Flynn met some of the Ballykisteen people, and through them Tom Cahill from Sydney, Australia. Cahill sent Flynn a filly called Madam Fair. Pat won three races with her and so a new partnership was established.

Subsequently Tom Cahill sent Maiden Fair to Pat Flynn and with this full sister to Madam Fair he won nine races. She was the third leg of a never-to-be-forgotten day at The Curragh when Pat saddled the last three winners on the card with Spottiswode, Quilty Rose and Maiden Fair.

"Maiden Fair really got me going. I never chased after owners, but she made them conscious of me. I have had some good horses such as Sweet Charmer which won eleven races for me and Lightning Bug which won the Naas November Handicap. Then there was Arcane which is now making a successful career as a stallion and Salmon Eile who was my 100th winner in September 1991."

Nowadays Pat Flynn has forty-five horses in training in the yard which he built, mostly himself, beside his bungalow, and he is twice blessed in that his wife, Catherine, does all the paper work.

It is a sign of Pat Flynn's character that friends from his school days at De La Salle have sent him horses, and kept in touch, while Dermot Cantillon from that era introduced him to Dr. Michael Smurfit for whom he trains a number of horses. Pat Sullivan from Kilsheelan is his right hand man and the yard is also blessed in having a loyal, efficient staff.

One of his proudest possessions is a huge wall plaque given him by his owners to mark his hundreth success. And he won the National Hunt Stallion Owners Award for the 1991/1992 season as top trainer of mares and fillies. In all he won fifteen races with eight mares during that season.

※ ※ ※ ※

As Charlie Swan brought Montelado back into the winner's enclosure to a mighty Irish roar, I heard one Irishman exclaim to the heavens: "The bumper in '92, the Supreme Novices in '93 and the Champion in '94."

The connections went wild with excitement – and who could blame them.

Montelado is owned by a County Roscommon quartet headed by Ollie Hannon, who owns a poultry factory, Brian Nolan, a State solicitor and brother-in-law of former EU Commissioner, Ray MacSharry (who was present for the occasion), Donal O'Rourke, a veterinary surgeon and his son, John, who is Products Manager of Sligo Dairies.

They brought off a nice "touch" and Donal O'Rourke told me that they took the best "morning board prices" available. But naturally he wouldn't reveal how much they took from the bookies. Montelado started at 5/1.

I liked the comment of Ollie Hannon, pinpointing the burning desire of the Irish for success at the Festival meeting: "We feel it and we accept it, and we're pleased to have this winner not for ourselves but for the people who wanted to see it."

As Paul Hayward noted in *The Independent*, the English daily: "It was delivered with an apple-sized lump in the throat and opened a new shaft in the mine of humility."

Montelado was bred by the O'Rourkes. Recalled Pat Flynn: "When he came to me as a four-year-old, he was still a big weak horse, so I gave him the summer at grass. When he came back in he thanked me by winning three bumpers. You know the rest of the story."

Tiananmen Square had gone to Cheltenham '92 being hailed as the Irish banker but he was beaten by Montelado in the Festival Bumper and this was the prelude to the gelding's sweeping triumph at the '93 Festival meeting, leading to the conclusion that he would complete a historic three-timer by winning the Champion Hurdle in '94. However, he had to be bar-fired on his off-fore and that killed the high ambitions entertained for him in the 1993-'94 season. Pat Flynn was confident that he would be back . . . but in the meantime a horse called Danoli had arrived on the scene.

❆ ❆ ❆ ❆

Charlie Swan's victory in the Gold Card Handicap Hurdle on the Wednesday of the '93 Festival meeting provided more grist for the mill of those who like a touch of the romantic to their Cheltenham yarns.

I was thinking that day that if you had an abscess in a tooth down Waterford way, you might have had to resign yourself to the fact that your favourite dentist was away "on business".

And the "business" in this instance meant one thing and one thing only – that he was over in Cheltenham having a flutter on Fissure Seal. At least that was the jocose way that friends of Waterford trainer, Harry de Bromhead were telling it as they arrived in Cheltenham.

In the Form Book the Syndicate that owned the horse was listed simply as the "Delton Syndicate".

It comprised four dentists, Richard O'Hara, Waterford, Sheila Keneally, Cork, Con O'Keeffe, Waterford, and Seán McCarthy, Enniscorthy, who went to college together and had kept in touch all through their careers.

All four had a deep interest in racing and decided to pool their resources to purchase a horse to carry their colours.

It was most appropriate that a horse owned by four dentists should have been named Fissure Seal. A seal in this instance is what a dentist performs when tackling a child's cracked tooth.

Fissure Seal did not come to Cheltenham simply to satisfy the ambition of owners wanting to have a Festival runner.

Far from it. He had a very good win at the Leopardstown Christmas meeting over three miles and won his previous outing over the same distance at Clonmel.

The connections had a nice "touch" at Cheltenham as Fissure Seal started at 14/1 – but they got better odds to their money. They had reason to keep the champagne flowing in the celebrations that followed.

I met the members of another syndicate of four from South Tipperary who cashed in on Fissure Seal's triumph and that of Montelado also. They combined to put £100 each way on the double (Montelado at 9/2 and Fissure Seal at 18/1) and this quartet were also making the champagne corks pop as they celebrated winning a cool £12,000 for a small outlay.

In case you think that this was one of those up-in-the-clouds coups, I was actually shown the docket by a member of the syndicate – *before* Fissure Seal went down to the start. I only regretted afterwards that I didn't take a piece of the action.

It was an unforgettable moment for laid-back Harry de Bromhead when Fissure Seal came back into the winner's enclosure – a man who has been all his life around horses. Both sides of his pedigree boast horsemanship of the top calibre and, indeed, his father, Johnny was one of the most respected amateur riders of his day, who between business, farming and racing managed to get the time to hunt the Gaultier Hounds for many years. Harry's sister, Iny was an international show jumper on the Irish team and her daughter, Jessica Willis was leading lady rider in Ireland on three occasions.

Harry de Bromhead started his racing career while working in the family business in Waterford, riding as an amateur and training one or two horses at home, his first winner being Meadowlark at Galway in 1958.

The training side developed slowly until 1979 when he decided to go into it seriously. With twenty-four boxes today at his Knockeen yard near Tramore he has just the right sized operation to maintain a mixed string for all year round racing, with the horses getting the vitally important personal supervision.

No one has known the ups and downs of the game more than Harry de Bromhead, for after enjoying a red letter day when Grand Henbit won the Thyestes Chase in Gowran Park and Bishop's Hall took the other featured chase on the card, he suffered a savage blow of misfortune when Grand Henbit was killed in 1993 at Killarney and at the same meeting Boro Buckle was lost after a crashing fall at the last hurdle.

It was in September '92 that de Bromhead was approached and asked if he would take a six-year-old chestnut by Tug of War to train. He took the horse and within a month knew that he had a smart one in this chestnut – none other than Fissure Seal. In the count-down to Cheltenham '93, Fissure Seal won the Gold Card Stayers Hurdle at Leopardstown, which qualified him for Cheltenham. The camp was actually divided on whether to send him to the Festival meeting or not but eventually they decided to take the plunge, after Harry had explained that the opposition could hardly be termed world-beaters.

For Paddy Kiely the 20/1 success of Shuil Ar Aghaidh in the Bonusprint Stayers' Hurdle represented the highlight of his career as a trainer. The euphoria it created in his stable and in the nearby town of Dungarvan was something, he admitted, that he had never encountered before. The mare's win spanned almost half a century of the Kiely family history. It was back in the forties that his father bought Chain Gang from local man Milo Walshe as a foundation mare from which to breed. She bred such as Shee Gaoithe and Sgeal Shee – and Shuil Ar Aghaidh became the fourth generation of the line.

Paddy Kiely had considerable success as an amateur rider and, after turning professional, he hit a peak in 1977 when his forty winners put him second to Frank Berry in the battle for the Irish Jockeys' Championship and with 34 wins he had been third to Tommy Carberry in the 1974 Championship.

He had a very good record over the Aintree fences, completing three of the Grand Nationals in which he rode, his best placing being on General Symonds, which dead-heated for third place with Black Secret in 1972.

"I had one of my biggest disappointments at Aintree in the Grand National when Roman Bar fell with me two before Becher's on the second circuit. He was flying at the time. Another moment at Aintree which I cannot forget about was in 1978 when I got pipped on Rathgorman by Another Dolly in an all-Irish finish to the Gillette Trophy Chase", he recalled.

Suil Ar Aghaidh was trained by Paddy Kiely for his wife, Marie, and was bred by the trainer's brother, Matthew.

The mare was completing a Thursday double for Charlie Swan, who had earlier used forcing tactics to telling advantage on Shawiya, the first filly to win the Daily Express Triumph Hurdle, and trained in County Kildare by Michael J. P. O'Brien, who did a really brilliant job in bringing her to her best on the day.

O'Brien had learned the ropes under the late Tom Taaffe at Rathcoole and had been a champion jockey in America until breaking his back in a horrible fall in 1974, which resulted in his being confined to a wheelchair. He never has what one might describe as a big string but still ranks among the best of his profession and he has achieved a remarkable strike rate in the bigger races. Bright Moments and King Spruce put him on the map in the eighties. And in 1982 he also won his first Irish Grand National with King Spruce, ridden by Gerry Newman.

His second success came in 1992 with another eight-year-old, Vanton, who was the mount of 21-years-old Jason Titley.

Bought out of John Oxx's yard for 12,000 guineas and racing in the colours of Gervaise Maher, Shawiya went on from Cheltenham to win again in the hands of Charlie Swan in the Murphy's Irish Stout Champion 4-y-o Hurdle at the Punchestown Festival meeting, beating Titled Dancer by no less than nine lengths and with the favourite, the English challenger, Lemon's Mill, unplaced. Shawiya was beaten only once in six races over hurdles that season.

With the Ritz Club trophy on his sideboard for his four-timer at the 1993 Cheltenham Festival meeting, Charlie Swan also had a four-timer over the three days of the Fairyhouse Irish Grand National meeting.

"Charlie was superb", was the spontaneous tribute of Grangecon, County Wicklow, trainer, Francis Flood to him after he had ridden Ebony Jane to victory in the Jameson Irish Grand National. Flood, who trained Ebony Jane for James Lynch, a businessman and jumping enthusiast from Coachford in County Cork, was winning this race for the second time after an interval of 23 years. In 1970 he sent out Garoupe, ridden by the late Cathal Finnegan, to beat a better-backed stable-companion, Glencarrig Lady, ridden by Tommy Carberry.

Francis Flood has been established as a top-class trainer for close on thirty years now.

A native of Wicklow with a National Hunt background he was associated previously with another famous Grangecon establishment, the racing stables of Paddy Sleator. During that period of his life Francis Flood was a leading amateur rider, with a formidable record on the point-to-point circuit, and was no less than seven times champion amateur jockey under rules.

❁ ❁ ❁ ❁

Before we parted that morning in the Corrib Great Southern Hotel, Swan told me that his great ambitions now centred around winning the Gold Cup and Champion Hurdle and he would also like to go into the records as the rider of an Aintree Grand National winner.

But that three-timer in 1994, following up his four-timer at the '93 Festival meeting and the winning again of the Ritz Club Trophy had already assured Swan of immortality as a National Hunt rider irrespective of whether he realised his ambition of winning the Champion Hurdle, the Gold Cup and the Aintree Grand National. The 1993-'94 season saw him become Irish champion jump jockey for the fifth successive time and he missed out by one riding a century of winners for the second year in a row (he had eventually ridden 104 winners in the 1992-'93 season and Kevin O'Brien was next in the table with 52).

One of the new features at Cheltenham '93 was a Hall of Fame. It includes a fitting tribute to the late Pat Taaffe, whose 25 winners, including four Gold Cups, over the famous course put him well ahead of all comers as the leading jockey at Prestbury Park.

Pat Taaffe's career was unusual in many respects, not least that he was in the top flight as a professional from 1950 to 1970, and for all of that period was first jockey to the late Tom Dreaper, a man unsurpassed as a trainer of chasers.

Clearly Pat's Cheltenham record will be very hard to beat. If it is to be beaten in our time – or even got close to – then Charlie Swan and Adrian Maguire are the two men with the ability to do so, if they can match Taaffe's durability in the saddle.

PART THREE

JIM BOLGER

A Rebel from the County of the Pikemen

5

The Winter of Virginia Kraft Payson's Discontent

As the field turned into the straight in the 1992 Budweiser Irish Derby, Jim Bolger experienced a moment which overshadowed everything else in his career up to that point.

It was the moment also that was to confirm his position unquestionably as one of the best trainers of the current era, for the planning that went into St. Jovite's preparation for that Classic and the ultimate execution of the plan itself, allied to the way the colt pulverised the opposition, was superb on one level and awesome on the other. And making the performance all the more breath-taking was the fact that Dr. Devious, who had trailed in twelve lengths behind St. Jovite, had beaten Jim Bolger's charge by two lengths in the Epsom Derby.

I could not have foreseen then – indeed no one could – that eleven months on from that red-letter Derby Day at the Curragh, Mrs Virginia Kraft Payson, who had been pictured all smiles beside Jim Bolger in the winner's enclosure, would almost break down as she talked to me on the trans-Atlantic phone from Lexington, Kentucky.

In that long interview, searing in the diamond-hard edge of bitterness that permeated her comments as she set down publicly for the first time her response to the headlines engendered by her decision to have Laffit Pincay Jnr. ride St.

Jovite in the Breeders' Cup Classic (over 1¼ miles on dirt) instead of Christy Roche, she admitted to being close to tears as she said: "I have been so brutalised, so crucified by sections of the Irish media over certain decisions that were made last year in relation to St. Jovite, especially the decision that Laffit Pincay Jnr. would ride him in the Breeders' Cup Classic, that I do not want to set foot inside an Irish race track for a long time."

That amazing outburst and all that surrounded it lay ahead as Jim Bolger listened to Des Scahill in the course of his racecourse commentary tell the teeming thousands thronging the stands and enclosures: "John Reid has gone for his whip on Dr. Devious."

"The roof nearly came off the stand in the roar that erupted around me. I knew then that bar a fall or that he would break a leg that St. Jovite would gallop all the way to the line," recalled Jim Bolger.

And then he added: "It was one of those days when everything went exactly according to plan. We had some very obliging owners who were prepared to supply pacemakers. We had a breakneck pace from the start and when the two pacemakers we ran had done their job, St. Jovite was brave enough to take it up and defy catching to the line."

There was not a cloud on the horizon on that beautiful summer's day – June 28th to be exact – as St. Jovite in trouncing Dr. Devious, Contested Bid (third in the Prix du Jockey-Club), Ezzoud (runner-up in the Irish Two Thousand Guineas that season and subsequently to win the 1994 Coral-Eclipse Stakes from Bob's Return and the '94 Epsom Derby winner, Erhaab) and Marignan (runner-up in the Prix du Jockey-Club) recorded the widest winning margin returned officially in the Irish Derby since it was first sponsored as a major international event by the Irish Hospitals Sweeps in 1962. Shahrastani and Assert had both won by eight lengths while Santa Claus, Troy and the ill-fated Shergar had won by four. The twelve-lengths margin actually equalled the record set by Portmarnock in 1895.

St. Jovite completed the twelve furlongs in 2 mins. 25.6 secs. – three seconds faster than the record set by Princess Pati in the Irish Oaks in 1984. It was all the more remarkable because the winner came back with cut heels after being struck into during the race. The time was unacceptable to a variety of experts in Britain, the Timeform writer in *Racehorses of 1992* claiming that "it looked too fast by around a second and a half", noting at the same time that it was three seconds inside Tambourine II's time for the race set in 1962.

However, Turf Club Chief Executive, Cahir O'Sullivan went on record to state categorically that as a result of eighteen months of research, a new system had been introduced for the Curragh and other major Irish meetings in April 1992.

"When the starter presses the switch to activate the starting stall, the same switch starts the timing apparatus and that is stopped as the first horse breaks an electric beam crossing the finishing line. No system is fool-proof but I'm sataisfied this one is working well and worked on the day," said O'Sullivan, who indicated that everything had been checked including the distance of the Derby, which, in fact, was found to be two yards over twelve furlongs.

The Taoiseach, Albert Reynolds, joined Michael J. Roarty of Anheuser-Busch Inc. in congratulating a delighted Mrs Kraft Payson as she received the magnificent Waterford Crystal trophy – a Derby Day graced by Dynasty star John Forsyth, Hart To Hart star Stephanie Powers and by film star Paul Newman among other famous personalities.

It would have been impossible to have imagained at that moment of singular triumph for the millionairess American owner that in the Spring of 1993 she would be severing her last remaining link with the Bolger stable when a "messenger" arrived at Coolcullen on the Carlow-Kilkenny border giving what was effectively one hour's notice that she was taking the remaining horses away from him.

The messenger was no mere nobody. He happened to be Dean Grim, son of Mrs Kraft Payson and President of the expanding Payson Stud in Lexington where St. Jovite was to be retired to stud.

While two of the horses being removed from Bolger's stable – Charette, a half sister of St. Jovite, and St. Elias – were in Mrs Payson's name, her son had an interest in both. He had come to Ireland from Britain where he was on business and, according to Mrs Kraft Payson, it was considered convenient that he should use the opportunity to oversee the bringing of the two horses back to the States.

This represented the last act in the breach of relations between Mrs Payson and the champion Irish Flat trainer.

❃ ❃ ❃ ❃

It would be easy to conclude that the defeat of St. Jovite by Dr. Devious in a photo finish to the Kerry Group Champion Stakes on Sunday, September 13th, saw the beginning of Mrs Kraft Payson's disenchantment with the man she had praised so highly in the aftermath of Budweiser Derby Day 1992. Then she told the world: "I was introduced to Jim at the Keeneland Sales. I was told that he was going to be the best trainer in the world, so I got in quick."

But Jim Bolger himself, amazingly enough, makes it clear that there was no "perceptible cooling" in relations in the immediate wake of that defeat. The real crisis would develop over the decision to have Laffit Pincay Jnr. ride St. Jovite in the Breeders' Cup Classic and the castigating of the owner over that same decision by sections of the Irish media, who saw it literally as the "jocking off" of the man who had ridden the colt to one of the most spectacular Derby triumphs of modern times.

Compounding the situation as far as Mrs Kraft Payson was concerned was the fact that the criticisms voiced of her in the Irish media found an echo in the most prestigious of American racing publications, the *Daily Racing Form*. Now she had reason to feel that she was not alone being painted a "baddy" before the Irish racing public but as a figure of real controversy also in the eyes of the American racing establishment. And no one was rushing to her defence.

Jim Bolger had walked the Leopardstown track with Christy Roche on the morning of the Kerry Group Champion Stakes and decided that the best going was towards the centre.

Ten furlongs, it was generally agreed, was short of St. Jovite's best and a strong pace would be required, therefore, if he was to stretch Dr. Devious to the limit.

Bolger put in Magic Carr to act as pacemaker and ensure an all-out gallop from the outset. To the argument voiced later that he should have utilised more than one pacemaker as he had done so successfully in the Irish Derby, he told me: "Magic Carr was the only suitable pacemaker I had on the day. Entries for the race closed some months beforehand and you could not take an overnight decision about putting in extra pacemakers, even if you decided to do so at the last minute. Anyway, St. Jovite had made all in winning the King George by six lengths without a pacemaker. Frankly, I don't think the lack of extra pacemakers was the cause of defeat. It was only in the last few strides that he lost it."

Magic Carr dwelt as the stalls opened. He recovered and raced through the field to lead after a furlong but compounded before half way and dropped right out of it. Great Palm took over the running but the sheer class of St. Jovite carried him to the front with three furlongs to go.

Christy Roche brought St. Jovite wide into the straight, sticking to the outside. Dr. Devious thus had a clear run up the inside.

St. Jovite, however, was in control right up to the time the winning post was in sight when Roche relaxed. He had told me in the course of an interview that his final ambition as a jockey was to win the Prix de l'Arc de Triomphe and he saw the Kerry Group Champion Stakes as a stepping-stone to the realisation of that dream. The man who had won the French Derby and the Irish Derby on Assert in 1982 and the Epsom Derby on Secreto in 1984 was convinced that he had confirmed the Curragh slaughtering of Dr. Devious as the winning post loomed. There was no way he was going to punish St. Jovite.

Jim Bolger makes it clear that he was not critical of Christy Roche's riding on that occasion – "and I will not criticise him now".

"I have every sympathy with Christy because on the occasion of that Leopardstown race he was not being cocky. He was really minding the horse with another day in mind. Two strides from the line he had the race won. When he relaxed, St. Jovite availed of the opportunity to take things easy and it made all the difference between victory and defeat."

83

The majority of racegoers at the track would certainly not have bet against St. Jovite getting the verdict in the photo finish. Christy Roche was almost one hundred per cent certain that the colt had won. And Peter Chapple-Hyam, trainer of Dr. Devious, came to the same conclusion, consoling himself with the words: "That should leave him (Dr. Devious) just right for the Arc."

Judge Percy Banahan called for a print before giving the verdict to Dr. Devious by the shortest of short heads.

"Most people, having seen the photograph, thought it was a dead-heat," said Jim Bolger. "I would still be interested to know from the judge how far St. Jovite was beaten."

While the primary target of St. Jovite after his brilliant win in the King VI and Queen Elizabeth Diamond Stakes (the winning distance over the high-class four-year-old Saddler's Hall, winner of the Coronation Cup and the Princess of Wales's Stakes, equalled the six-lengths margins achieved in the race by Dahlia and Mill Reef, surpassed only by Generous who won by seven) was always going to be the "Arc", Jim Bolger with that total frankness that has always been an integral part of his make-up, made no secret of the fact that he was very disappointed to lose the Leopardstown race.

"This was an important race and we wanted to win it," he emphasised. "There was no reason why St. Jovite could not pick it up on the way to the expected victory at Longchamp. This was the champion, rated 6 lb clear of anything else in Europe and 4 lb superior to A.P. Indy which Eddie Delahoussaye would ride to victory in the Breeders' Cup Classic at Gulfstream Park later that same season. And that, of course, was the very race that St. Jovite was earmarked to contest if all had gone right for him.

"I know that on the day of the Kerry Group Champion Stakes that St. Jovite was beaten by a colt that was inferior to him. It was just a case of the verdict going against him."

❋ ❋ ❋ ❋

Disillusionment did not set in either between Mrs Kraft Payson and Jim Bolger in the wake of defeat in the Prix de l'Arc de Triomphe, as some so readily assumed. Because it had to be accepted that St. Jovite's chance was gone when the rain came down in the proverbial bucket-fulls on the eve of the race itself.

I remember filing from Longchamp on that Saturday evening to the *Sunday Independent* in Dublin that St. Jovite had drifted significantly in the betting with the big English bookies and I entered a note of warning in my report that the going was now all against him, as his two finest performances of the season – in the Budweiser Irish Derby and the King George – had been recorded on a sound surface.

The general view of English and Irish experts in Paris for the weekend was that St. Jovite would be surmounting impossible odds to win the "Arc" in the circumstances.

Jim Bolger himself would reveal later to me: "I was not optimistic."

"However, it was his last race in Europe. We had nothing to lose. As it was, he ran fourth behind the French horse Subotica on ground that was totally unsuitable to him and again confirmed his superiority over Dr. Devious, who was sixth.

"I have no doubt that if he had got the ground conditions that suited him he would have won. I always believed that he was at least as good a horse, if not better, on 'Arc" day as he was on Irish Derby day."

It was generally assumed in Ireland that Christy Roche would ride St. Jovite at Gulfstream Park. Roche had proved his versatility and his adaptability as a big-race jockey in his Derby triumphs from Chantilly to the Curragh to Epsom. And on the score of experience he did not have to answer to anyone.

Mrs Kraft Payson was to claim in her interview with me, however, that she had discussed frankly with Jim Bolger the question of Laffit Pincay Jnr. riding St. Jovite in the Breeders' Cup Classic instead of Christy Roche – "because of Pincay's thorough knowledge of American tracks and his outstanding record in the Breeders' Cup series".

She asserted that Bolger had gone along with that decision.

She went further and said that she had confronted Bolger on the issue when they met in Lexington in January 1993 and expressed to him in no uncertain terms her disappointment at the fact that when she was castigated by sections of the media for replacing Roche with Pincay, he had *not* made a statement defending her.

Jim Bolger, when I talked to him in the Berkeley Court Hotel in February 1994, had this to say on the controversial decision to replace Christy Roche by Pincay: "The way she put it to me, I had no option but to go along with it. Frankly, I did not like it but, as I have said, I was left with no option."

Responding to Mrs Kraft Payson's charge that he had not defended her in face of the criticisms in the Irish media, he said: "She did not ask me to go to her defence. I always regarded her as a woman of the world – a woman who would not be easily phased by the media in any part of the globe.

"And because of this assumption on my part, I did not see any need to jump in on her behalf. I had full confidence in her to fight her own battles. A so-called roasting from the Press does not necessarily mean the same thing to me as to other people."

Laffit Pincay Jnr. never did get to ride St. Jovite in the Breeders' Cup Classic as the colt never got to the starting stalls.

Coming up to the race, St. Jovite suffered an upper respiratory track infection which manifested itself in a discharge from both nostrils.

"Mrs Kraft Payson had been understandably very keen to have St. Jovite run in the Breeders' Cup Classic," recalled Jim Bolger. "Some days before he was due to leave Ireland, he went down with the respiratory problem. It proved somewhat debilatating. It was not possible to train him further. Consequently, he missed the Breeders' Cup. This was a big disappointment to the colt's owner and shortly afterwards she decided to take St. Jovite to the States."

Jim Bolger stressed that there was no hint at that point that St. Jovite would not be returning to Ireland to be trained as a four-year-old in 1993. "Some time in November 1992, in fact, I presented Mrs. Kraft Payson with the programme I had already mapped out for St. Jovite for the 1994 season. It envisaged another tilt at the King George and the Arc and was to be climaxed with a bid for the Japan Cup.

"I sent two of my best staff to the States with St. Jovite to remain with him as he settled into his new surroundings. He was subsequently transferred to Roger Atfield's stable. It was announced he had suffered a recurrence of an old injury and was being retired to stud. So he never raced again after the Arc of 1992."

It remains a mystery to Jim Bolger to this day that the official cause of St. Jovite's premature retirement stemmed allegedly from an "old" injury. As far as he is concerned, the colt did *not* suffer an injury while he was in training with him that would have affected in any way his racing future.

Yes, there had been that respiratory problem in the countdown to the Breeders' Cup Classic, an infection, as seen already, that resulted in his being scratched from the race. But Bolger, as he supervised St. Jovite's departure from his stable to the States, knew in his heart that the colt was sound of limb and wind and was looking forward to welcoming him back in 1994 and training him, hopefully, for another glittering campaign that would take in not alone another crack at the Prix de l'Arc de Triomphe but be climaxed by a bid for the Japan Cup.

⌘ ⌘ ⌘ ⌘

Mrs Kraft Payson told me that her arrangement with Jim Bolger was that any of her horses in his charge that were not up to Group class would be sent back to the States. But it was generally assumed in racing circles in Ireland and Britain that Charette, as a half-sister of St. Jovite, would be trained by Bolger with top targets in mind.

Mrs Payson contended that Bolger told her Charette was not going to make top class and that was one of the reasons she decided to bring the filly back to America.

There is little doubt in my mind that, as relations between owner and trainer soured over the events leading up to the Breeders' Cup Classic, Mrs Kraft Payson sought to exercise greater control and an open conflict developed between her interpretation of what constituted a "trainer's agreement" and Bolger's.

Asked what the signing of a trainer's agreement would have meant for him, Bolger responded: "It would have tied me down and could have damaged my professional career. I refused to sign.

"You cannot have a situation where the owner wants to take decisions over and above the head of the trainer – to restrict his freedom of decision and action.

"In the States an owner-trainer relationship may be like that between a football or baseball club and the manager. A trainer may not enjoy, or expect to enjoy, the same loyalties that obtain in Europe."

Mrs Kraft Payson claimed Bolger made certain changes in the draft agreement she presented to him and claimed further that she did not get around to sending him the final draft for his signature as she was so caught up with other matters at the time. She said the signing of such agreements are normal between trainers and owners in the States.

"I did not seek to restrict Jim Bolger in the actual training of my horses but the horses were my property and I believed I had the right to bring my horses back to the States if and when I chose to do so. I would not see the autonomy a trainer might enjoy in the actual training of my horses extending to his having control over what should happen my property," she said with emphasis.

Mrs Kraft Payson contended that it was always understood that St. Jovite would return to the States when his racing programme in Europe had been completed. She said that Jim Bolger was aware of this from the outset.

❃ ❃ ❃ ❃

The epilogue came down to one word – loyalty. And the depth of significance it has on this side of the Atlantic as against the interpretation placed on it in the racing world in the States.

And here I am thinking of the kind of loyalty that saw Robert Sangster sticking with Vincent O'Brien through thick and thin, even when the number of horses trained at Ballydoyle had been reduced to a dozen or so – by Dr O'Brien's own choice – as he passed his 76th birthday in the Spring of 1993. Sangster would never forget what he owed to the Master of Ballydoyle – would always remember the golden triumphs they had shared together with such brilliant horses as The Minstrel, Alleged, Golden Fleece and El Gran Senor. In a word, you cannot quantify that kind of loyalty.

Jim Bolger was immensely proud of the level of consistency he had delivered with the horses he had trained in Mrs Payson's colours, apart altogether from the singular achievements of St. Jovite.

Carressed and Carrnassier both won on their debuts in 1992. In fact, four two-year-olds in the Payson colours went into the winner's enclosure first time of asking.

When Mrs Kraft Payson removed Charette and St. Elias from the stable and finally broke all ties with Jim Bolger, it was a far cry from the enduring bonds of loyalty between Robert Sangster and Vincent O'Brien.

Her argument to me was that she had so many commitments in the States that it would not be worth her while travelling over and back for "just two horses". She revealed that she had made no less than eleven two-day trips in 1992 alone.

As our long conversation on the trans-Atlantic phone came to a conclusion, I emphasised to her that no one could ever forget the job Jim Bolger had done in producing St. Jovite to overwhelm Dr. Devious in that memorable twelve-lengths victory on Derby Day 1992 at the Curragh, a performance described by *Racehorses of 1992* as "the most exhilarating exhibition of the European season".

I suggested that everyone in Ireland would have thought that she would have repaid it by continuing to provide Jim Bolger with the material to come up with a repeat. I suggested further that the Irish sense of loyalty demanded that the links between owner and trainer should not be irrevocably severed.

But I had to accept that we were on different planes entirely. This was certainly not a case of talking to the converted.

Never again would the twain meet. It was wishful thinking to believe that there could be a reconciliation, such was the sad souring of what at one stage had been a very happy relationship for the benefit of the Irish racing and breeding industry.

In the winter of Mrs Kraft Payson's discontent there would be no going back and I wondered if I would ever again see her setting foot inside an Irish race track.

6

Meeting the Rent Arrears Through a Horse named Kilmore

Jim Bolger was four weeks behind with the rent on his flat in Dublin. It was the longest period he had endured of "severe financial restraint", extending from March right through to April 1962.

He decided that Kilmore, the mount of Fred Winter, was going to win the Aintree Grand National. "I put £1 each way on him at 33/1 and he duly obliged in a field of 32."

Jim Bolger recalled meeting Fred Winter later when both of them had become racehorse trainers. "I was seeking to sell him an ex-Flat horse I favoured as a potential winner over the jumps. I told him the story of how I cleared off my rent arrears in one stroke by backing Kilmore to win the National. But he didn't buy the horse from me after all."

At the time of his coup on Kilmore he was working in an office during the day and studying at night.

"Let us say that I learned to shop in the bargain basement for flats and digs," he told me with a smile. "Accommodation that would be regarded as O.K. in the summer months was not so good in winter. But it was all part of my education.

"I met some wonderful people from all walks of life and all parts of the country both in digs and in flatland.

"I went to the races and to the dogs, to hurling and football matches and athletic meetings. But somehow I never got into following soccer and rugby. Hurling has always been the game that has meant most to me."

Mixing with ordinary people, people who were products of a rural background like himself, convinced him that one must never forget one's roots or assume a veil of pretence stemming from a basic inferiority complex. He expresses a certain pity for those, including members of the racing profession, who have felt the need to change their accents to an Oxonian or Old Etonian emphasis in order to progress in life or be at ease in the Royal enclosure in Ascot.

Jim Bolger today speaks with the same accent he had when he left his native County Wexford. And he makes no apology to anyone for being himself.

This is not to say that he eschews the best in favour of what sufficed when he was shopping in the bargain basement for accommodation in Dublin. It's par for the course for him to meet you for lunch or dinner in the main diningroom of Dublin's most prestigious hotel, the Berkeley Court, or in the George V off the Champs Elysees in Paris during Prix de l'Arc weekend. But he is totally at ease among rank-and-file Wexford supporters, proudly wearing the colours and favours of the Model County, on the day of a Leinster Hurling Championship, against Kilkenny, maybe, in Croke Park.

Jim Bolger is admired for his integrity, his straight-from-the-shoulder talking and for tilting at the windmills of authority when he believes that there is a case to answer. He is his own man – and will always be.

He came into the world on Christmas Day 1941. One of eight children – five boys and three girls – raised on a farm in Oylegate, County Wexford. It was a mixed farm, maintaining 25 cows and also cattle and horses. Jim's father, Walter, who died in 1987 aged 84, was a breeder of and dealer in half-bred horses. His mother, Katie (nee Doyle) came from the locality and at the time of typing this chapter in the Spring of '94 was still enjoying good health at the grand old age of 87.

Incidentally, Jim Bolger's uncle, also christened James, wrote on hurling and football under the nom-de-plume *Recorder* in the *Irish Independent* for a period of years. He had started in journalism on the *Enniscorthy Echo*. He was grandfather of Booker Prize winner and bestselling author, Roddy Doyle.

Ask Jim Bolger if life was hard for the family in those days of the Emergency when first Hitler's panzers were carrying all before them and then the tide turned and the Third Reich fell when he was still only four and he responds: "There was never any shortage as far as food was concerned. We were no different from any other farming family in the forties and fifties. My father as the principal bread-winner worked very hard and my mother, with eight children to look after, worked equally hard.

"They never complained. People didn't complain about their lot in that era. We had wonderful neighbours. You must remember that there was no thought then of a five-day week or a four-day week or holidays abroad in the sun. Daylight hours were for working. There was a wonderful happy family atmosphere in our home.

"I learned to milk the cows at 7 a.m. before I went to school. You took that for granted, as you took so many other tasks for granted. These were routine tasks, like helping to make the hay, like getting involved with the threshing.

"I can still recall the excitement when a pig was killed to provide bacon and all of us joining with mother in the making of the black puddings. It just seemed to be one long happy time.

"We were very fortunate that despite the fact that we were a large family, we had no bereavement while I was growing up. The first time that we experienced a death in the family was the passing of a near-relative of ours when I was 17. But I grew up to know the love of both my parents."

He cycled seven miles each morning to secondary school in the CBS in Enniscorthy and back the same distance in the evening. He got his Intermediate Certificate and his Leaving Certificate but didn't go to university. He admits that the only time in life that he ever entertained self-doubts was when sitting exams.

He had learned to ride at an early age, the nursery being to use his father's half-breds and workhorses.

When he left for Dublin at the age of 17, he carried with him an ingrained love of horses in his veins. From as early as he can remember he loved to have a bet but he didn't acquire this from his father. "As far as I can recall, my father never had a flutter, not even on the Grand National. But it gave me immense pleasure to stake a bob each-way on my fancies and to see my judgement proved right."

Bolger, amazingly enough, dabbled in the buying and selling of cattle before he got involved in horseflesh. He actually bought his first horse at the age of 16 with £50 he got together dealing in cattle. "You might say that I cashed the bovines and bought equine," he laughed, as if talking stocks and shares.

In his teens we find him buying and selling show-jumpers and hunters. And riding as an amateur. He did not exactly set the world alight with his riding exploits but still could boast three wins from twelve rides.

⌘ ⌘ ⌘ ⌘

On his arrival in Dublin Jim Bolger worked as a trainee accountant in an office by day and attended evening classes in the College of Commerce in Rathmines, progressing in time to a job as an accountant with a Dublin motor company. Deep down, however, he never intended to make accountancy his life. He saw it as a stop-gap career – a training ground on the way to what was going to be his chosen profession.

The area in which he had been born in Wexford is steeped in hurling tradition and he had played as a forward with the local Oylegate Club. In the metropolis he played a few times with Faughs, who invariably attracted quite a number of players from the rural heartlands including Billy Quinn, former Thurles C.B.S. Dr. Harty Cup player and Tipperary hurler and father of Republic of Ireland International and successful racehorse owner, Niall, for whom Jim Bolger trains.

His love of horses dominated much of his leisure time. He even arranged his annual holidays so that he could fit in the annual bloodstock sales. Again there was calculated method in this.

He was prepared to learn from the Masters – P. J. ("Darkie") Prendergast and the Master of Ballydoyle himself,

Vincent O'Brien. Indeed, Vincent O'Brien had been his idol from childhood and he was a keen follower of the stable when it came to betting, supporting Nijinsky to win the Triple Crown in 1970.

"I was particularly taken by the fact that Vincent O'Brien was a self-made man, that he had climbed up the ladder to the very top from what you might describe as humble beginnings as a trainer in Churchtown, County Cork," he said.

Bolger, able to move about unobtrusively because he was unknown then to the big players, noted carefully the yearlings that Vincent O'Brien and "Darkie" Prendergast bought, assessing the conformation that attracted them and the breeding lines.

"You might say that during all this time I was a trainee trainer, getting a grounding in the real essentials of what would dominate and dicate my life from 1976 onwards," he told me.

He would reach the point where he could go to the sales and with confidence pick out a yearling that he knew had the potential to be a Group or Classic winner and, more important still, he could evaluate an animal's worth, knowing how high to bid and when to fold.

The days, so to speak, at the feet of Vincent O'Brien and "Darkie" Prendergast had paid off handsomely.

Behind the scenes in his apprenticeship period, Jim Bolger was all the time buying and selling horses and he noted: "The secret, I knew, was that if you could buy intelligently, you could dispose of your purchases at a profit and in time build up the tank to move on to better things."

Although there were times during his days in digs and flatland that he would fall into arrears in paying the rent, he recalls with satisfaction that he was "never really skint".

He was too shrewd an operator both at buying and selling horses and in bringing off successful bets as a student of the Form Book to go broke entirely.

But one day when he went along to the Phoenix Park as an ordinary racegoer and punter he learned a salutary lesson that was to hasten his determination to control his own destiny when it came to horses – in a word, that he would be certain that an animal was running on its merits when he put his money on the nose.

That incident in the Park, in fact, was to imbue Jim Bolger with the try-for-your-life approach to training and to be able to look any man straight in the eye and say: "Mine always try."

"I recall putting my last tenner on a horse at the Park when a tenner was worth far, far more than it is today. I judged the horse in question a certainty on form. He never tried an inch and wasn't even put into the race. You can imagine my feelings when he bolted in next time."

In 1976 Jim Bolger took out a full training licence, having operated under permit from the previous year when he had purchased a filly called Lovely Rhapsody for 400 guineas. "I have never trained a more difficult filly than that one," he told me. "She finished fourth on her first outing as a two-year-old and then entered the winner's enclosure the following year and from that moment I became convinced that I could do it."

But Jim Bolger's first winner as a trainer with a full licence was Peaceful Pleasure who scored at Roscommon on 20 September 1976.

He was operating from a base at Clonsilla.

For a man who could not boast a blue-blooded racing pedigree, he certainly made a major impact very quickly on the racing scene. In his second season he sent out 22 winners and finished in the top six in the Trainers Championship Table.

In 1978 he trained Beparoejojo to win the Papermate Hurdle (4-y-o) in the hands of Dessie Hughes in record time. Beparajojo, incidentally, was dam of Project Manager, now a leading first season sire.

By 1981 he was challenging successfully in Britain. Form Book experts, looking up the record of Condessa, would have noted that she was the winner of a moderate handicap event at Clonmel in the Spring of '81. They would have scratched their heads and wondered what inspired Bolger to send her for the Lingfield Oaks Trial, in which she finished third.

But shortly afterwards they realised that Bolger was no fool but a man who had got to be reckoned with from that day onwards. Condessa appeared at York and landed the

Musidora Stakes. Three months later she won the Group 1 Yorkshire Oaks.

From the very outset he was prepared to adopt a bold attacking policy. If Vincent O'Brien was the idol of his childhood and youth, Bolger, the man, was afraid of no one when it came to throwing down the gauntlet for the prizes that mattered.

In cold retrospect now it can be argued that in the peak days of the Ballydoyle stable, Vincent O'Brien won races at the Curragh and at the Phoenix Park, Leopardstown and at other tracks because there were trainers who were just not prepared to take him on. Because he turned out the "goods" in horses of the quality of Sir Ivor, Roberto, Nijinsky, The Minstrel, Alleged, Saddler's Wells, El Gran Senor and Golden Fleece, it was presumed that almost everything from the yard was unbeatable. And, therefore, races were won in bloodless fashion that might not have been won so easily, if at all, if there were trainers with the courage of Bolger to step into the ring and challenge "The Master".

The old guard didn't like Bolger for his presumption – for his spurning of much that was seen as sacrosanct. They didn't take kindly to how quickly he made his mark in a profession that they regarded as the demesne of those born into it.

Bolger smiles now as he remarks to me with a touch of cynicism that "there are no doubt some octogenarian owners around who would not give me a horse to train under any circumstances because, in their minds, I have not got a true racing pedigree.

"Friends have told me that there is still a perception in some quarters that I can't train. That perception and the fact of being ignored by certain octogenarian gentlemen doesn't particularly concern me or cause me sleepless nights. What matters is the number of times the horses under my care occupy the No. 1 position in the winner's enclosure. I reckon I have been around that No. 1 spot pretty often."

I suggested to him that he had been admired for the way he had tilted at top Flat races in Britain when with a few notable exceptions other Irish trainers of his generation were loath to challenge outside of Ireland.

96

"I had the goods when I sent runners to England," he replied quite frankly.

"Look back through the records and you will find names like Park Appeal, Park Express, Happy Bride, Give Thanks Polonia – all Group 1 horses. And each one of them won a Group 1 race. I sent very few others, excepting Flame Of Tara, winner of the Coronoation Stakes and beaten a head in the Champion Stakes in 1983. She is, of course, the dam of Salsabil.

"I don't believe in wasting time or money in purely speculatory ventures," he said. "At best a trainer, even with 80 to 100 horses in his yard, would do well to have six horses in any given year capable of being sent to challenge for prizes abroad. And that would not mean, of course, that all six would get into the frame."

⌘ ⌘ ⌘ ⌘

In the summer of 1982 when he was just beginning to graduate to the top league, Jim Bolger returned from Gowran Park races to find that a fire had ravaged his Clonsilla stable.

The big career gamble was taken then to move to a new base at Coolcullen, a short distance inside the Carlow border with County Kilkenny. Bolger was reputed to have looked at seventy different possible locations before he settled on Coolcullen.

A throw-back to the exhaustive search undertaken by Vincent O'Brien before he finally settled in March 1951 – as he moved base from Churchtown in County Cork – on the virgin fields in the shadow of timeless Slievenamon that he turned into the world-famous Ballydoyle gallops.

Traditionalists naturally expressed surprise as to why Jim Bolger did not grasp the nettle and head straight for the Curragh. It would not be Bolger's style to share gallops on the Curragh with other trainers. He was intent when he left Clonsilla on creating his own pad to his own vision and Coolcullen answered his requirements to a tee. The loner in him made him act as Vincent O'Brien had acted thirty years earlier.

Glebe House, the new Bolger homestead, was aptly described by Ruth Buchanan in the *Irish Press* as "a house fit for a bishop". For it was, in fact, the Church of Ireland Bishop of Ossory who built it for himself in 1760.

Ruth Buchanan noted that he used it as a summer residence and spent many sunny days receiving the clerics from the diocese there. On other days he used to set out and tour his See – most likely in a carriage drawn by four horses.

As the years passed it became clear that the upkeep of Glebe House was too much for a Church that saw its numbers dwindling drastically with each passing decade. Parishes were amalgamated in pragmatic fashion to cater for a new era and smaller modern houses were erected to accommodate the men of the cloth.

Glebe House passed into lay ownership about twenty years ago. A lot of money was spent renovating it.

It was re-roofed and re-wired and new plumbing installed. Painted and re-decorated throughout. The heating was updated also.

When Jim Bolger arrived with Jackie and their two daughters, Una and Fiona, in the week before Christmas 1982 he knew that he was taking over a house that was in excellent repair, that required no expenditure on serious reconstruction and that could be lived in right away.

He realised that there would be substantial investment in modern boxes for 80 horses, a total that would rise in time to well over 100, requiring far more staff than he had at Clonsilla.

The old beech trees had immediately caught Jim Bolger's eye when he first saw Glebe House – a magnificent five bedroomed Georgian building – and the 240 acres going with it. Jim and Jackie are proud of the fact that they have added a further 20,000 trees since 1982 and now, in addition to beech, the visitor to the stable can pick out chestnut, birch and walnut as well as oak.

There is a rural splendour about the whole place now and when first I saw it, I was reminded to an extent of the impact Ballydoyle House makes on one.

The sun lounge is where Vincent O'Brien generally greets visitors, including media representatives.

The conservatory – all glass on three sides – is where you will find yourself chatting to Jim Bolger on a visit to Glebe House. In fact, it is here that you will discover him most likely at any hour of the day when he is not out on the gallops or engaged in other urgent tasks. He can see the sun rising at the front in the morning and setting at the back in the evening.

As in the O'Brien dwelling, where the prints on every wall tell better than any film, Vincent's amazing strike rate from Cheltenham to Aintree, the Curragh to Epsom and Longchamp and Laurel Park to Belmont Park, so under the wood-pannelled ceiling in the Bolger conservatory, your eye cannot fail but be taken by the photographs of the 149 winners the Master of Coolcullen turned out in that golden season of 1990 when he broke J. J. Parkinson's record of 134 winners for a full year that had held since 1923.

But, of course, there are other prints also that stand like milestones to his spectacular rise up the ladder to international stardom as a trainer.

In a way you could call Coolcullen a mountain-top base as it is roughly 1,000 feet above sea-level.

It was ideal for Bolger's training methods. Brought up in an atmosphere where there was no molly-coddling, he realised the benefit of this in his own life. And he certainly doesn't believe in molly-coddling his horses.

You cannot but note that the all-weather gallops rise steeply to an incline at the finish and it is Bolger's belief that this helps to develop the resilience and toughness of the charges he is training and ensures that they will not be found wanting when it comes down to an all-out battle for top honours.

Vincent O'Brien in the era when all-weather gallops were not yet in vogue exercised his horses in a field in Church-town that had an incline like the rising ground that horses have got to cope with if they are to win at Cheltenham. In that respect, the man who was "King" of Cheltenham in his day was leaving no stone unturned and, likewise, when he turned his attention solely to the Flat, he had a circuit laid out at Ballydoyle that reproduced the descent to and swing around Tattenham Corner.

"The key is fitness", said Jim Bolger to me when I discussed his training methods with him further on a day in July in '94. What he defines as "fitness" is the operative word here. He talks about his horses being "fitter and tighter" than many of the opposition they meet. He prides himself in the fact that when the rider of another leading contender for honours in a race throws down a challenge and maybe goes by his one a furlong out, he may find the Bolger runner fighting back and regaining the advantage near the line. He argues that it's "a precision game" acquiring this kind of fitness for one's charges.

"It's very hard to win any race", he goes on, rejecting out of hand the "myth", as he describes it, propagated by the critics of Irish racing that half the runners in any given race may be non-triers. "You don't get any non-triers at Galway, for example", he said. "Everyone wants to win there if they can."

So in that kind of atmosphere it's only logical that you have to be sure of your methods if you are to be successful. In a word, you have to be a precision merchant.

Bolger confesed to me that he prefers not to have to train horses that you have to be soft with – "that have to be molly-coddled".

He accepts that there are horses that have to be treated with great care early on in their careers, that there are others who may be too backward to run at two. "If I had not been very careful and as patient with Erin's Isle when he was with me, he would not have turned out to be the champion he was later in his career in the States", he said.

But he argued that the horses that had to be treated with exceptional care early on were not typical of the breed. "If they lack the requisite toughness, it can indicate a flaw in character and it can lead to a lot of frustration. Frankly, I do not get a lot of satisfaction out of training horses like that, though if you know you have a potential Classic or Group winner on your hands who requires immense patience, you will willingly devote the time to the task and not rush matters."

100

Jim Bolger sent out his first Classic winner from Cool-cullen in July 1983 when Give Thanks won the Irish Oaks in the hands of Declan Gillespie at 7/4. The filly enjoyed an outstanding season as she also won the Lingfield Oaks Trial, the Musidora Stakes and Lancashire Oaks.

Bolger was building a name for himself as a brilliant handler of fillies. Other leading ladies who helped establish his reputation even more firmly as the 1980s progressed were Park Appeal (1984 Moyglare Stud Stakes and Cheveley Park Stakes), Park Express (1986 Phoenix Champion Stakes) and Polonia (1987 Prix de l'Abbaye).

Likewise he was proving himself outstanding as a trainer of two-year-olds, especially in the way they were able to hold their form, despite the fact that they were not molly-coddled. The dawn of the 1990s, for example, saw him dominating the scene and he climaxed the 1990 season in fitting style when unbeaten Nazoo landed the Tattersalls Tiffany Yorkshire Stakes at Doncaster in September and in the process won a £500,000 bonus for owner Maktoum Al Maktoum.

He was working to the dictum that sport is about winning, whether it is in hurling or golf or racing – take your pick it's all the same.

He agreed that there are those who contend that involvement or playing the game for the game's sake is everything. He agreed that in some respects that was the way it should be.

But, as he put it to me, once the primary aim of involvement or participation has been fulfilled, then the overriding consideration has got to be winning. Yes, winning.

"It's unthinkable to me that a person can be involved in a particular sport over a long period of time and not be worried whether he won or lost," he said with emphasis.

Collating this with his first love – hurling – he added: "If I was the trainer of a hurling team going for a championship title and I had a man in the squad who gave me the impression that he wasn't all that worried about winning or losing, I would see only one place for him – the sideline."

He hastens to add, however, that once you become a participator in sport of any kind, you must learn to be a good loser. And you have always to keep before you the maxim – "you cannot win them all".

If one trainer were to clean up all the prizes, then there would be no competition. "Competition is the very life-blood of sport."

And he added significantly: "Racing would lose its appeal for me if the challenge went out of it."

It's the challenge that turns Bolger on. He loves nothing better than to confound those who have tended to cry "crazy" when he has aimed right at the top with a horse that they did not think was up to the particular challenge.

Take, for example, the sending of Jet Ski Lady to challenge for the English Oaks in 1991. The Form Book experts would not have given her the proverbial snowball's chance in hell against the 1,000 Guineas winner Shadayid. She started at 50/1. But she won in the hands of Christy Roche with Shadayid third.

Bolger's confidence is such at times that he can be exasperating for the racing writer. On occasions when I have asked him for a professional's analysis of a big race, a cold and unemotional assessment of the main opposition as he saw it to the colt or filly he was sending to carry the Irish flag, he would merely respond that his one was ready to run for its life and he did not care about the opposition.

Adopting an approach like that all the time would mean that the late "Darkie" Prendergast would have dismissed the claims of Sea Bird II when sending Meadow Court to challenge for the 1965 Epsom Derby. But Vincent O'Brien when I asked him one day in Ballydoyle House to name for me the greatest colt he had seen outside of his own super stars, like Sir Ivor, Nijinsky, Alleged and Golden Fleece, replied unhesitatingly: "Sea Bird II".

I believe that it is only by knowing the chinks in the armour of the opposition – as in the case of a colt not bred to get the twelve furlongs of the Epsom Derby or Budweiser Irish Derby – that a trainer can explain with authority why he believes he can lift a Classic with his challenger. If his one is facing an animal with superior class and finishing speed, then talking a winning race simply because your charge is 100% fit is talking to the moon. It does not take cognisance of the fact that a colt like Sea Bird II is not going to get beat simply because you have your one at the peak of his form.

Fulke Walwyn had to admit that great though Mill House was, his heart was broken in the end by arguably the greatest chaser of all time – the peerless Arkle.

Let it be remembered that Meadow Court came good at the Curragh on Irish Derby Day '65 when there was no Sea Bird II to face. As Mill House was most unfortunate to be born in the same era as Arkle, so Meadow Court had the misfortune to come up against Sea Bird II at Epsom. And it meant that "Darkie" Prendergast, despite his wonderful achievements as a trainer, never won the Epsom Derby. Jim Bolger in debate is likely to pose the rhetorical question: "How many Arkles and Sea Birds does one encounter in one's racing career?

❊　❊　❊　❊

It has got to be stitched into the record that Jim Bolger will almost certainly scale many more peaks before he retires but nothing will ever surpass his achievement in turning the tables so decisively with St. Jovite on Dr Devious, his Epsom Derby conqueror, in the 1992 Budweiser Irish Derby.

In cold retrospect now, it has to be acknowledged that Epsom came too soon for St. Jovite. Jim Bolger is the first to recognise that the Pleasant Colony colt was slow to come to himself as a three-year-old and Christy Roche said with emphasis: "He had plenty of problems going to Epsom. When you are competing in top company, you can't afford to have problems."

"He was very difficult to train in the early part of the '92 season," explained Jim Bolger. He was not eating well and on work days I would scratch my head wondering whether I should gallop him or leave him alone."

"No horse I ever trained has caused me to think so much," he added

Starting odds-on for the Gladness Stakes (7f) on his reappearance in April, St. Jovite lost a lot of admirers when beaten into fourth place. But those who wrote him off there and then as a Derby colt overlooked the fact that the heavy going was all against him. His subsequent victory in the Derrinstown Stud Derby Trial at Leopardstown was workmanlike without being unduly impressive. Again that was over a mile and a quarter and he had yet to race over his best distance – twelve furlongs.

St. Jovite made remarkable progress after that Leopardstown race – "and he improved still further after we galloped him again at the Foxrock track," said Bolger. "It was a well publicised gallop. Malvernico beat him a length."

Like a sleeping giant, St. Jovite was beginning to stir himself. But Bolger said significantly: "I knew in my heart that I needed more time and that Epsom after all might not be his day."

You could have backed St. Jovite each-way at what appear now amazingly generous odds of 25/1 on the Saturday before Derby Day, though he went off at 14/1 on the day of the race itself. From an inside draw Christy Roche was able to take up a good position from the outset but in the straight itself, St. Jovite did not reveal the sharp turn of speed and acceleration to go away from the field. Rallying though in fine style, he snatched second place from Silver Wrap – two lengths behind Dr. Devious.

Jim Bolger now concluded, after consultations with Christy Roche, that St. Jovite did not act left-handed. The Curragh would see him in a far different light.

Coldly and professionally the Master of Glebe House now prepared for the moment and the day when the new St. Jovite would be revealed to the racing world – when he would explode in the straight with awesome power and the crowd would rise to this colt in a fashion that I had not seen since Santa Claus left his field for dead in winning the 1964 Irish Sweeps Derby.

Bolger set out to convince St. Jovite that he had the ability to take on and beat any opposition. "We worked him with inferior horses and as he dismissed them contemptuously, you could see the change. He was a fit horse going to Epsom but he had not peaked. Ten days before the Irish Derby he did peak.

"We did not have a final gallop as such over the full Derby distance. I was concentraing on six-furlong spins. He was finishing ever piece of work very strongly. It was all coming so easily to him now – so easily, in fact, that he was a completely different colt from the one I had sent to Epsom.

"Seven or eight days after he came back from Epsom I rode him in a strong peice of work," recalled Christy Roche. "He was such a different animal that day, so impressive that I said to myself: 'I will win the Irish Derby'."

"All we wanted was pace and good ground," said Jim Bolger. "St. Jovite was very choosey. He had to have good or firm ground to show his real worth."

After Dr. Devious, who started 5/4 favourite as against the 7/2 on offer about St. Jovite, had been galloped into complete subjection at the Curragh – a race run on much firmer ground than at Epsom – and in the count-down to the King George VI and Queen Elizabeth Diamond Stakes Jim Bolger told the world: "The Jovite you saw at Epsom no longer exists. The colt is a totally different horse now and I am happy he's as good as he was at the Curragh."

St. Jovite was ridden this time by Stephen Craine in the absence through suspension of Christy Roche. Jim Bolger earned a lot of kudos for placing his trust in an Irish-based jockey rather than opting for an international "name" rider and his choice was to be handsomely rewarded.

It was not a lucky dip by Bolger into the pool of local talent. He knew exactly the worth of the man he was picking. It was not long after his arrival from the Isle of Man to serve an apprenticeship with Liam Browne that Craine began to impress the Irish public. Thirty-four at the time he got the ride on St. Jovite, he was holding down one of the top jobs in Ireland with Tommy Stack and Ascot was not the first venue where he had demonstrated that he had the temperament for the big occasion.

In 1988 he rode a brilliant race to win the inaugural running of the Cartier Million at the Phoenix Park on Corwyn Bay, beating a star-studded field of international jockeys, with Willie Carson and John Reid his immediate victims. Coincidentally, Carson was again on the runner-up, Saddler's Hall, in the 1992 "King George".

Christy Roche generously played his part in the singular Ascot triumph. As Craine himself subsequently related, his old friend had, on the eve of the race, gone over videos of the colt's earlier races and coached him exhaustively on how to deal with every situation that might arise. Craine went to post supremely confident and that showed from the moment the new partnership left the stalls. Craine's personal contribution, however, should not be diminished in the achievement of another brilliant victory.

St. Jovite fully vindicated the pre-race confident claims of his trainer in pulverising a high-class field that included Saddler's Hall, winner of the Coronation Cup and the Princess of Wales's Stakes; Opera House, the Coral-Eclipse runner-up; Sapience, the Eclipse third; and with Rock Hopper, the Coronation Cup runner-up, fifth. The winning margin of six lengths had only been surpassed by Generous who won this race by seven lengths.

After a relatively slow first furlong, Craine seized the initiative, set his own pace and made the rest of the running. He actually stopped riding short of the line and subsequently reported that his mount had plenty in reserve. "He is very, very good and when he spreads his wings he is a machine," said Craine who was 34 on the day of the "King George" triumph.

"I will not be surprised to hear St. Jovite described as awesome from another Continent when he moves to middle distances," was the confident prediction of Jim Bolger on his leading juvenile in a contribution to the 1991-'92 edition of the *Irish Racing Annual*. His confidence never wavered, despite the colt's slowness to come to hand and those early reverses when he made his reappearance as a three-year-old in 1992.

St. Jovite was a product of Mrs Kraft Payson's own stud in the States – but he had links with two Irish families made famous by the late Joe McGrath's Brownstown Stud. St. Jovite's dam, Northern Sunset (Northfields, by Northern Dancer), was out of Moss Greine by Ballymoss from Blath Na Greine, a daughter of Carpet Slipper.

St. Jovite turned out exactly what Mrs Kraft Payson was hoping to produce when she purchased Northern Sunset who had won two races on the Flat and had run over hurdles in Ireland for her owner-breeder Basil Brindley before being exported to the States. Mrs Payson, a sound judge of horses and their pedigrees and a shrewd breeder, bought Northern Sunset to inject some stamina and toughness into the breed, for she bleieved that the emphasis on speed had been over-done.

St. Jovite's sire, Pleasant Colony, a grandson of the mighty Ribot, had been America's champion three-year-old in 1981 when he won both the Kentucky Derby and the Preakness Stakes. Incidentally, St. Jovite's great-grandam, Blath Na Greine, not alone bred two good horses in Prince of Greine and Time Greine but was a half-sister to the English 1,000 Guineas and Oaks winner, Godiva, and the immortal Irish Triple Crown winner, Windsor Slipper. So there is class on every side of St. Jovite's pedigree.

❁ ❁ ❁ ❁

The Irish Derby and "King George" successes should unquestionably have gained for St. Jovite the accolade of "Racehorse of the Year", but it went to User Friendly, who received eight votes more than Rodrigo de Triano. "There's no doubt which of the three possessed the greatest racing merit," wrote the Timeform writer in *Racehorses of 1992*. "The marvellous achievements of User Friendly and Rodrigo de Triano rightly captured the racing public's imagination but St. Jovite's clear-cut victories in the Irish Derby and King George marked him unmistakably as a colt superior to the general run of Classic winners, something that couldn't be claimed by any other three-year-old in training in Europe in 1992 – not the way we read the Form Book anyway."

Jim Bolger had the right to frame that comment – even though he must have wondered how in their wisdom the panel of twenty-six racing writers could place User Friendly ahead of St. Jovite.

Bolger challenged with two runners for the 1993 Epsom Derby – Blue Judge and Desert Team.

Blue Judge, a Rainbow Quest colt out of Walter Splash, had been runner-up to Newton's Law, beaten a short-head, on his reappearance as a three-year-old at Newbury in April and later was third behind Commander In Chief and Oakmead in the Culford Stakes at Newmarket. He had run twice as a two-year-old, comfortably landing the odds in a Curragh maiden (1m yielding) in his final appearance of the

107

'92 season and Bolger had described him as "an exciting 1½ mile prospect".

Yet he was allowed off in the Epsom Derby at 150/1 and in a way it was not surprising that the punters should ignore him as stable jockey, Christy Roche, opted for Desert Team, a Blushing Groom colt out of Bemiss Heights, who had won over a mile at Gowran Park as a two-year-old and on his three-year-old debut was beaten a half a length by Placerville in the Feilden Stakes at Newmarket before finishing third, beaten a half a length and a half a length by Tenby and Planetary Aspect in the Newmarket Stakes (1¼m) over the same course at the end of April.

Desert Team, starting at 25/1, was no danger from Tattenham Corner in the Derby but Blue Judge, ridden by Bruce Raymond, finished very strongly, after being switched to the outside in the last furlong, and was three and a half lengths behind Commander In Chief at the finish.

Commander In Chief had not run as a two-year-old and at one stage it had appeared that Henry Cecil might put all his eggs in the one basket and leave it to Tenby, backed down to 4/5 on Derby Day itself, to be his sole runner in the Epsom Classic and hold Commander In Chief in reserve for the Curragh.

"If that had happened and the Epsom form had worked out as it did, I could have had my first English Derby winner in Blue Judge," said Jim Bolger. "That's racing. But I'm not complaining."

As it was, he had supplied the runner-up two years running (1992 and '93) and his Star of Gdansk was third in 1991.

✿ ✿ ✿ ✿

Normally Jim Bolger's day begins at 6.30 a.m. and he will be out on the gallops during the Flat season by 6.45 a.m. to supervise first lot. The other lots follow. There is a break for breakfast between 8.20 a.m. and 8.50 a.m. Breakfast consists of cereal and tea and toast. Always tea – not even coffee after lunch or dinner.

The gallops at Coolcullen have proved eminently suitable for Bolger's training methods. He has shown himself to be

adept at turning out two-year-olds fit to do themselves justice
– to the point of winning – at first time of asking and his
strike rate in this sphere has been particularly impressive.
Likewise he has shown that he can produce older horses to
run for their lives, maybe after a lengthy absence from the
track. In a word, if fitness is the name of the game he can
achieve it.

The beauty of Glebe House is that it puts him within a
drive of just an hour and a half from Dublin.

When he hits town at around 1.30 p.m. he will have a day's
work behind him. And then he can fit in a heavy schedule that
may take in a working lunch, followed by a series of meetings
and appointments, a working dinner perhaps and maybe
another appointment before heading home.

He doesn't smoke or drink. All he partook of during a long
lunch I had with him one day in the Berkeley Court Hotel
were two glasses of fresh orange juice.

He has an abhorrence of alcohol and what the evils of
drink have wrought makes him voice very strong opinions
publicly on this subject.

He is only too conscious of the battle one of Wexford's
greatest hurling sons, Nicky Rackard, fought with the demon
drink until he finally conquered, working unselfishly in the
years before his death to help others to conquer also (a
number of them formed a circle around Nicky's grave, paying their own special silent tribute the day in April 1976
when he was buried in his native soil in Bunclody).

Rackard was a trainer of horses in his own right, apart from
being a veterinary surgeon and landed a few famous gambles
in his time. A portrait of Nicky hangs in the front room of
Glebe House.

"I have heard more waffle talked in pubs than anywhere
else in Ireland or in any part of the world for that matter,"
said Jim Bolger very forcibly. "Over-indulgence in alcohol is
one of the greatest single problems in this country – a problem that many prefer to shove under the carpet rather than
face head-on."

I put it to him that after a day's writing, I liked nothing
better than to have a few drinks before dinner and then share
a bottle of wine over the meal itself. "You can count yourself

lucky if you can control matters in that way," he responded. "Not everyone is so lucky. So few can drink in moderation that I maintain that it's almost an impossible situation to achieve. People think they are letting their hair down and then go too far and the consequences can be terribly serious, especially if someone is involved in an accident after taking too much drink.

"The wisest course to pursue is to stay clear of it altogether," he added.

I put it to him that he had upset a lot of moderate drinkers – people who like a pint or a "small one" for relaxation – when he was quoted by Paul Kimmage in the *Sunday Tribune* as saying: "I can't see how shifting your butt from your fireside to the publican's fireside and getting a pint in your hand is a panacea for all ills." I put it to him that he was implying that to even mingle socially and enjoy the "crack" with friends over a few drinks was a total waste of time?

He responded that for his part a good long walk was more beneficial health-wise and provided as much relaxation as spending some hours in a pub. Some of his horses, he noted, were "head-bangers" but they seemed to want to cure the problem by walking the box. "Walk, walk, walk – they don't go to the drinking pot and drink, drink, drink."

I was left with a distinct feeling that Jim Bolger would benefit from taking a glass or two of a vintage claret, that it would make him relax more and reveal to far better advantage the acerbic sense of humour that breaks through when he is not caught up too much on one of his pet subjects, like the composition and sins of the Turf Club.

But then the very intensity of his make-up, that steely part of his nature that can be so unbending, would make him totally vulnerable, I feel, to becoming an alcoholic if he were to begin to indulge. You think of people who took just one sherry at a wedding reception and were doomed from that moment. Somewhere deep down in his being Jim Bolger, the third generation non-drinker, may suspect this – knowledge in the subconscious, as it were – and it may be at the heart of his total rejection of drink. I may be wrong, of course, in writing this, in even hinting at it but it is a conclusion I am forced to draw in all honesty.

Jim Bolger has the name of being one of the hardest task-masters in the business. He must live with the legends, some of them apocryphal I do not doubt, that have grown up around him – all indicating clearly that he is not one to suffer fools gladly. But more than that – he can push people to the point of demanding too much of them and the sensitive ones and those unable to take a lash of a figurative whip, pull up camp and leave. Those who have left abruptly keep their silence in public but the scars can run deep.

His relationships with jockeys would be seen by many regular racing followers not to have been the easiest. Yet, the stories that have circulated about these relationships have not always been true. For example, Declan Gillespie was with Bolger for eight years and had already made up his mind to become a trainer when he retired from the saddle when he became associated with Ballydoyle, knowing how valuable it would be to him to spend time with the Master of Bally-doyle. Kevin Manning left for a time, of his own volition. Manning, who was to become Jim Bolger's son-in-law when he married Una, was back riding for the stable and had a leading role as No. 1 jockey for the 1994 Flat season after Christy Roche went freelance.

Bolger has given every chance to rising young apprentices and has no qualms in putting them up on horses in with a very live chance in very competitive events, where other trainers would be loath to adopt this approach. It has often paid off.

Christy Roche, incidentally, joined the stable when David O'Brien decided to retire from training for personal reasons after winning the French Derby and the Irish Derby with Assert in 1982 and the Epsom Derby with Secreto in 1984 – Roche being in the saddle for these three memorable triumphs.

Roche, the old pro, was too long on the road to be upset by a touch of abrasiveness, too long around to take his cards and leave if it came to a clash over some point. Bolger respected his experience as Roche in turn respected the level of success that Bolger achieved but it was always going to be a purely business arrangement.

The public perception of Jim Bolger is of a man with a short fuse but he flatly rejects this perception and points to

111

the fact that in the years he was hurling he was never once booked by a referee.

"Darkie" Prendergast unquestionably had a very short fuse and yet Christy Roche understood "Darkie", admired him deeply for his talents and his eye for picking out a potential champion and before the Curragh trainer passed on had become his friend and confidant in racing matters. That same depth of understanding and friendship was never attained in the case of Jim Bolger.

Roche is quite frank about his relationship with the Master of Coolcullen. "It was always difficult and possibly unnecessarily so. Jim I found to be very, very critical of people. It appeared to me that he liked to come across as the perfect fellow, one almost incapable of making a mistake. Yet in the case of his own mistakes – and he made quite a share of them – he was never willing to accept criticism for these.

"I had an unbelievable amount of success while No. 1 jockey to the stable. He had the ability to get his horses fitter than anybody of his era. Yes, he was hard on his horses. That cannot be denied but his methods were his own and the strike-rate he achieved showed that he knew how to get one fit to run for its life – and win.

"I won the 1991 English Oaks for him on Jet Ski Lady by adopting the tactics which I knew in my heart was the only way this 50/1 shot could have any chance of beating the opposition. I knew that if the filly was held up she would have no chance. Stamina was her strong suit and she would have to be ridden to bring this into play – right from the start. As it turned out, my judgement was fully vindicated."

Jim Bolger, for his part, could hardly be expected to accept Christy Roche's criticism of him as one who liked to come across as almost incapable of making a mistake and unwilling to accept criticisms of his own mistakes. Bolger contends that he has never been afraid to admit his mistakes publicly and has done so in the racing press.

When the parting of the ways came between Bolger and Roche early in '94 it had nothing to do with a short fuse – nothing whatsoever.

The air was alive with rumour. Neither man went public immediately on the reasons why. But the racing world

CHAMPAGNE DAYS FOR CHARLIE

Champagne times for Charlie Swan at Cheltenham '93 as his victories on Shawiya (centre top) and Fissure Seal (top right) helped him win the Ritz Club Trophy and (below) he gets a congratulatory kiss from his wife, Tina. Swan won the Ritz Club Trophy again at the 1994 Cheltenham Festival meeting.

WALES . . . WALES . . . The sheer joy stemming from Norton's Coin's 1990 Gold Cup triumph for Wales is captured as the Griffiths boys lead the gelding into the winner's enclosure and (below left) Norton's Coin down on the farm with Sirrell Griffiths and his wife, Joyce, and son, Martin, and (below right) Peter Beaumont from Brandsby, Yorkshire, trainer of Jodami, winner of the 1992 Gold Cup at Cheltenham and the 1993 Hennessy Cognac Gold Cup at Leopardstown.

The O'Sullivans of Lombardstown, Mallow, and friends have their finest hour as Lovely Citizen (Willie O'Sullivan) is led in after winning the 1991 Christies Foxhunters Chase and (below) Eugene and Willie hold the trophy aloft as their father shares the moment of triumph.

THE PAIN AND THE GLORY . . . The fatal fall on his neck at the last by Golden Cygnet in the Scottish Champion Hurdle at Ayr on 15.April 1978 that was to result in the death of the brilliant hurdler seen (inset) winning the Supreme Novices' Hurdle at the Cheltenham Festival meeting that year by 15 lengths and (below) six years on Edward O'Grady was again a power at Cheltenham as he shared with Charlie Swan and J. P. McManus the joy of victory after Time For A Run had won the Coral Cup Handicap Hurdle. O'Grady also scored with Mucklemeg for McManus.

TOMMY'S TEARS OF JOY

THE EMOTION OF VICTORY . . . Tommy Stack (top left) coming in on Red Rum after winning the Aintree Grand National and (top right) shedding tears of joy at Newmarket after training his first Classic winner, Las Meninas, pictured here (below) winning the 1994 English 1,000 Guineas in a photo finish from Balanchine (Frankie Dettori), right, with Coup De Genie (Cash Asmussen) a further neck away third.

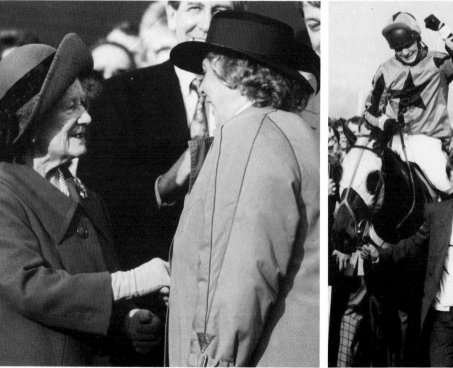

Jamie Osborne receives the Ritz Club Trophy as the top rider with five winners at Cheltenham '92 and (below) Mrs Jenny Pitman is congratulated by the Queen Mother after winning the 1991 Gold Cup with Garrison Savannah, ridden to victory by her son, Mark (inset).

A sextet of Irish trainers: (clockwise from top) — Arthur Moore, Jim Dreaper, ''Mouse'' Morris, Pat Flynn, Francis Flood and Paddy Mullins.

Martin Pipe and Peter Scudamore at Ascot (7 April 1993) after Scu's last ride before he retired from the saddle and (top right) Richard Dunwoody, who succeeded as No. 1 to the Pipe stable holds the British N.H. Jockeys' Championship trophy and (below) Pipe gives the thumbs-up victory sign after the enigmatic Carvill's Hill had won the 1992 Hennessy Cognac Gold Cup Chase at Leopardstown before being beaten in controversial circumstances at Cheltenham.

waited for a full explanation and it could only come from either one of them – or both at the same time. It never came.

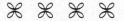

I put it to Jim Bolger that he could be brusque and short-mannered with people he felt had asked him silly questions – even media representatives – and that this was at variance in a publicity-minded age with the accepted norms where trainers could set out with the deliberate intention of courting popularity and cultivating an image that could assist them in acquiring new owners and also put them on very personable terms with the media.

"Very few owners these days are looking for entertainers when they decide on who will train their horses. They can readily arrange to employ comedians to entertain them if they so desire," he said.

"All right, I have never set out to be all things to all men. It's not my way, never has been and never will be. But it's not entirely true to say that I don't suffer fools gladly if by this you mean that I don't give people a chance to prove themselves. I have given every chance to a few lame ducks in my time.

"People, like horses, have degrees of ability. If you don't realise this fact, you will think that everyone is marked out to be a genius, as you will conclude that every Flat horse is a potential Classic winner. It doesn't happen that way in life and it certainly doesn't in racing.

"I can say quite truthfully that I have given people who have worked with me plenty of time. I have helped them along as much as I could. But there is one thing I can't abide and I don't mind admitting it – and that is that I find it very difficult to tolerate people who don't give of their best."

Bolger sums up by saying that while he has given every chance to a few lame ducks in his time when he gets on his staff a young lad of real potential and ability – "I will try to realise that potential to the full and that is where I will push because I know what can be achieved."

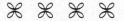

So in the final analysis it all comes down to discipline as far as Jim Bolger is concerned.

In fact, discipline is paramount in his relations with his staff and he accepts that it has played a major part in his success as a trainer.

The bottom line is that he expects no one to do more than he is prepared to do himself. He identifies discipline with presence in the stable on every day he can possibly be there – but more, with performance and the highest level of performance at that.

Again the motivation of his staff demanded that he didn't slip away and it was also demanded by the need to keep getting results. And bound up with that was to maintain the confidence of his clients in him.

Discipline, he argued, was something that permeated a stable when people realised its importance in the overall set-up. "As I see it, when you are training very valuable horses, a number of them worth big figures in dollars or guineas, there can be no fooling around or fool-acting. Again let me repeat – I expect the same from my staff as I do from my horses and myself."

The Bolger dictum can be interpreted as the Master of Glebe House wanting a 100 out of 100 every working day – *not* 75 out of a 100. "If somebody is giving me only 75 out of 100, he has a problem and he shouldn't be comfortable."

"He has got to put it right and he knows it," he added – and you realised that if he didn't do so, then there was only one place for him and that was the sideline in hurling terminology.

But herein, in a way, you put your finger exactly on the reason why, as Christy Roche so aptly put it, relations with Jim Bolger, even for experienced pros, will always be difficult. Even the best can make mistakes and even the best can have an off day.

In his unrelenting drive for success and to achieve that 100 out of 100 at all times, Jim Bolger can tend to forget that people are human, that they can get out on the wrong side of the bed, can even be suffering from a hang-over that he will never suffer from because of his total rejection of drink as a crutch. The hang-over might come from letting one's hair down to relieve the pressures. Not everyone will see the answer in his theory that a long walk is a better solution than sitting on a bar stool.

But one thing is certain – what Bolger believes he says straight out, dead on the button. None of your convoluted replies couched in careful diplomatic language in order not to offend.

He will continue to say what he thinks – and continue to offend. It's as simple as that.

7

Bolger's Bruising Battles with the Turf Club

In the spacious drawingroom of Glebe House are displayed many of the trophies Jim Bolger has won during his eighteen years as a public trainer, among them a bronze replica of The Pikeman which stands in the Bullring in Wexford.

Bolger received this nine-inch sculpture when he was nominated Wexford Sports Personality of the Year.

For me it has a special significance on two levels. Not alone does it ensure that Jim Bolger will never forget his roots but it gives clear and concrete expression to the rebel element in his character that compels him to wrestle with authority when he is convinced that there are still good causes worth fighting for in an age marked by a too-ready acceptance by the majority of the *status quo*.

One thing is certain – Bolger would never rest easy in any society in any age. In the Old West I reckon he might have been a loner wandering the hills, prospecting for gold or just like the Outlaw Josey Wales of the Clint Eastwood Western. The authorities would have felt the need to send a posse after him to take him out. Eventually he would have been gunned down. They would have seen it as the only way to silence him (though Bolger, who knew Dan Breen well and met him once in the company of Eamon de Valera, remarked laconically that the Tipperary freedom fighter survived, even if he had a lot of bullet wounds in him!).

Bolger will not be silenced in a more democratic age. Neither is he likely to mellow to the point where he will decide to take the easy route out when he thinks that his integrity has been impugned. The guarding of his integrity and the image the racing public have of him as a trainer whose horses are always allowed to run on their merits is all-important to him. Indeed, it has caused a fire to burn in his soul that is quite awesome. It has seen him go headlong into bruising battles with the Turf Club that men of less resolute character would spurn in the interests of peace of mind and what we term "the quiet life".

He subjected the Turf Club to scathing criticism in a much-publicised speech at the beginning of 1990, saying: "Racing in Ireland is governed by the Turf Club and Irish National Hunt Committee, a club where pedigree counts more than performance, where no politician is welcome, where 14% of its members are ex one army or the other, where 15% have a close relation to keep things cosy and where only 2% are female."

He again pulled no punches when I had a lengthy and wide-ranging interview with him in May 1990 on the democratisation of the Turf Club and other topics for a special feature in the 1990-'91 edition of the *Irish Racing Annual.*

"Democracy has got to enter the Turf Club," he said. "I look forward with great eagerness to an elected body replacing the Turf Club as we know it today.

"The new body would consist of people from within the industry as a whole – elected representatives including owners, trainers, jockeys, the racing public and media. The process is already under way in France with 20 members elected to their Societe in this fashion."

I put it to him that there were honourable men in the Turf Club, born and bred to the racing game, men of the highest integrity who might not be everyone's cup of tea because of their accents or because they were not viewed as "racy of the soil". Did he want to get rid of these in one fell swoop?

Jim Bolger replied that the last thing he wanted to do was to get rid of everyone in the Turf Club as it was formed at present. "But let's face it, let's be frank about it – no other concern, no other club in a democracy like ours is run as the Turf Club is run. It has no mandate from the people and yet it looks to the people to support Irish racing and provide the money to run it. It has no mandate from within the industry itself.

"It is a self-perpetuating body. Name me any other sphere where this is permitted? It does not even publish annual accounts. It is a relic of other times, of days before we got our freedom but I make absolutely no apology for asserting that the time has come to make it a more democratically-elected body."

Strong words, fighting words but said with all the conviction that Jim Bolger could muster and he was fearless in pronouncing them.

There was nothing personal whatsoever in his criticisms. Neither were they born out of pique. They were born out of his roots – and he had to be admired that the Irishness in him reacted, and reacted very strongly, to anything that he saw was a carry-over from colonial times. Ireland, as he saw it, had won its freedom at a very heavy cost. It was the last nation in the world that should preserve vestiges of an era when the bulk of the populace were expected to adopt a cap-in-hand attitude to a foreign ruler. As he saw it freedom should bring a rejection of everything that was associated with those same cap-in-hand attitudes. Logically, he argued, the Turf Club should be typical of the down-to-earth people who formed the very core of the racing industry in this country.

Bolger, as we have seen already, is a great follower of Ireland's national game of hurling. He moves easily in the company of hurling men, adopts no superior attitude – despite his outstanding achievements on the international plane – that would cause any of them to feel uncomfortable. Totally confident in his own ability, he can be himself always.

He argues that the Gaelic Athletic Association, the body that controls the games of hurling and gaelic football and the imposing of discipline on the playing fields, does not have in its ranks people at the top with a pedigree that might be described as alien to the very spirit that moves the Association. In fact, the GAA prides itself in being totally representative

118

of the grassroots followers who provide the powerful nation-wide support it enjoys.

Why then should the Turf Club, he asks, be different? Why this policy of perpetuating certain names, certain families, irrespective of the capabilities of those following on, almost automatically, in the footsteps of family-members who enjoyed membership of "The Club" in earlier decades?

Bolger has made the very relevant point that when Tom MacGinty, Racing Editor of the *Irish Racing Annual* since it was established in 1976, retired some years back as the distinguished Racing Correspondent of the *Irish Independent* and when Tony Power stepped down around the same time as long-serving and highly-respected Racing Correspondent of the *Irish Press* the Turf Club was presented with a golden chance of showing that it could go outside a privileged narrow circle by inviting one or both of these two to become members of the Club.

But the Turf Club for its own reasons could not bring itself to make such a step while it continued to have representatives of one army or another in the Club, continued a policy that indicated to the racing public at large that a pedigree counted more than pure knowledge and depth of experience – in a word, it would remain in many respects a self-perpetuating body.

The case rested there as far as Jim Bolger was concerned.

There were elements in racing who denounced him – privately if not publicly in all cases – for going a bridge too far in his criticisms. They even accused him of pursuing a vendetta because he had rocked the boat and made quite a few feel uncomfortable as his arguments struck home.

But it has to be said now – four years on from when he first went public on the issue – that he became a catalyst of change.

When the Government published – early in 1994 – the legislation to form a new Irish Racing Authority, which would effectively replace the Racing Board, we had arrived at the situation when the Senior Steward of the Turf Club was elected to the position, the accounts were published, there was a much bigger female representation in the Club and no longer at inquiries were jockeys addressed by their sirnames – as if they were foot soldiers being bawled out on parade by a burly sergeant-major – but in a fashion more in keeping with our times.

However, some of the stewards could still be seen wearing bowler hats on Budweiser Derby Day – even when it was 90° in the shade – and you asked yourself was there a need for such incongruity? Did Irishmen really have to wear such headgear in mid-summer to signify authority or maintain an outmoded practice from colonial days? The English might say it was essential for the Royal enclosure at Ascot to dress formally in mid-June as tradition dictated but the Irish should be able to do things their own way and sing: "Why can't the English be like us!"

The Government in announcing the new Racing Authority preserved the Turf Club as the body that would continue to police racing and see to it that discipline was maintained. But it was obvious that the very creation of the Authority would change and modify its overall area of control and, for example, the Authority would want to see that while black type was vital in the breeding area when it came to Group and Listed races, programmes would have to be so devised as to attract more customers through the turnstiles.

The Turf Club has over a period of two centuries (it celebrated its bicentenary in 1990) been charged with the task of ensuring that the rules and regulations governing racing in this country are observed.

To understand the weight of tradition behind it, one has only to point to the fact that the Racing Calendar was being published back in 1741 – the year of the first officially-recorded winner of a race in Ireland, namely the Earl of Bessborough's bay mare, Dairy Maid, who won at the Curragh on April 1st. By 1861 there were rules established for the King's (or Royal) Plates that prohibited riders from "crossing, jostling or striking" and those found guilty were not allowed to ride in any further King's Plates. And riders were to weigh out after a race to the satisfaction of the judge or judges appointed for the purpose.

The days of Turf Club inquiries were already being presaged.

Remember, when these rules were established in the middle of the nineteenth century, it was an era of outrageous gambling by the young bloods, some of whom would have thought nothing of fixing a race if they could – even a King's Plate or getting a rider to carry the wrong weight (the reason why weighing out became so important even then).

The efforts of the Turf Club to stamp its authority on the racing scene are well chronicled in Fergus A. D'Arcy's excellently researched *Horses, Lords and Racing Men* (The Turf Club 1790-1990). It was noted in a chapter, headed "Authority", that in the latter half of the nineteenth century the Turf Club and Irish National Hunt Committee enjoyed a power more arbitrary than the Czar of all the Russias and disqualification inflicted by them meant a sporting death. One "Pendarius", the sports commentator of the *Irish Sportsman*, noted that "jockeys are humble people and the fate of the best of them is a small matter to most of us, but they are entitled to common justice". His comments, according to Fergus D'Arcy, were prompted by concern at the fate of jockeys whose licences could now be withdrawn and whose families would suffer penury – all this as a result of Turf Club decisions taken, as "Pendarius" saw it, behind closed doors. "Pendarius" actually led a campaign against the Turf Club for acting like a secret tribunal, hearing evidence without the presence of the accused – something which would not have happened in a contemporary court.

But it has to be stressed that the Turf Club, battling to impose a strict code of conduct in an era when there was blatant pulling of horses, so much so that Fergus D'Arcy related in his book how one jockey received a warning-off sentence for an indefinite period (it was not lifted for six years) and a trainer who admitted to issuing an order to a jockey not to win a particular race was warned off and the owner involved in the same case was severely censured. The trainer in question had his warning-off sentence lifted in due course – but, despite five applications, his efforts to get back his trainer's licence were all turned down.

So if draconian penalties were imposed at times, they must be set against the attitude of some elements – trainers, owners, gamblers and certain jockeys sinking into the mire with them – who had no qualms whatsoever in flouting the rules to bring off their "killings", if permitted to do so. It was

121

no mean feat to bring order and respect for authority into a situation like that.

❀ ❀ ❀ ❀

Down the years the Turf Club did not always emerge with flying colours from situations where it was imposing its will in the upholding of the rules. In the course of my research for my book, *Vincent O'Brien – The Master of Ballydoyle*, I dealt at length with the dark episode that saw Vincent lose his licence to train for three months and unquestionably the penalty imposed on him five days before Royal Tan won the 1954 Aintree Grand National would have been heavier had not Pierce Molony, then Chief Steward of the Irish National Hunt Committee, threatened to resign if the drastic action being contemplated at one point was carried through.

The Turf Club Stewards, including Judge W. E. Wylie, "sat in" with the National Hunt Stewards during the inquiry (Judge Wylie had actually introduced the "sit in" to enable him to be present at all inquiries and as he was a retired judge, he had ample time on his hands and, with his experience on the bench, he tended to dominate the meetings). During the inquiry into the alleged discrepancy between the English and Irish form of four O'Brien-trained horses, Judge Wylie may as well have been in the chair as he just took over.

The suspension of his licence imposed on Vincent O'Brien did not become operative until April 2nd but on the night that Royal Tan came back to a tremendous home-coming victory reception in Cashel, with bonfires blazing on the hillsides on the way into town and the Rock floodlit, Mick Davern, local member of Dáil Éireann (Irish Parliament) stood on the platform and hit out at the fact that Vincent O'Brien was being subjected to a Turf Club inquiry. He talked of "green-eyed" individuals and his sentiments echoed the feelings of thousands who believed that Vincent was the victim of jealousy because of his outstanding run of success.

Vincent O'Brien himself was not prepared to go on the record about that episode but I know exactly how he felt it all evolved.

It is an extraordinary story in itself that will probably be revealed in full at some future date.

Vincent has never forgotten a remark passed to him one evening in the St. Stephen's Green Club by Judge W. E. Wylie (they were both members).

It was the day that the Stewards of the Irish Turf Club decided not to follow through on the decision of the English Jockey Club in the famous "Blue Sail Affair" (horses trained by "Darkie" Prendergast would not be allowed to run in England for a period). When Vincent asked the judge what was the finding of the Irish Turf Club Stewards, he replied: "we could find no discrepancy there" but then made the extraordinary remark that left the Master of Ballydoyle deeply shaken: "If it had been me, I'd have warned you off over Knock Hard last January at Leopardstown. He ran like a hairy dog."

Vincent's older brother, Dermot, has often pondered in the intervening years why Judge Wylie seemed so deeply concerned about the running of a chaser in an individual race at Leopardstown, why too a man whose principal concern and area of control as a Steward of the Turf Club was the Flat should be so inordinately interested in performances in the National Hunt sector that he should say what he did to Vincent.

Dermot, aware of the friendships the judge had in racing, has come to his own conclusions but he prefers to keep them to himself – and will carry them with him to the grave. Again I am aware of them and can only say that they leave a very nasty taste in the mouth.

On the broader plane Dermot O'Brien contended that it was only natural and human that there should have been jealousy of Vincent's success, extending right across the board, even to owners who did not have horses in the stable and to trainers who could not match his strike rate. And as Vincent, at that point, was still winning his biggest prizes in the National Hunt sphere, especially in Britain, one could expect that in a country where racing over the jumps meant so much, trainers of National Hunt horses had to be envious.

Vincent O'Brien's younger brother, Phonsie, argued that the sweeping indictment mentioning merely alleged discrepancy between the English and Irish form of four horses "without one single specific detail being elaborated" would never happen today. He pointed to the fact also that Royal Tan and Early Mist were essentially National types and could hardly be expected to sparkle at a place like Baldoyle – "a funny track" – or Tramore. In the case of Lucky Dome and Knock Hard there were explanations for poor performances they had given before they were successful at Cheltenham. "Yet, the Stewards in taking Vincent's licence off him for three months were not happy and seemed to have taken the view that these horses were deliberately stopped when that was not the case at all," added Phonsie.

⌘ ⌘ ⌘ ⌘

It would be an innocent man then who would think that *all* the Stewards who have served the Turf Club for over 200 years have been as white as the driven snow. Far from it. Some have been guilty of the frailties, weaknesses and prejudices that inflict humanity – a few should never have been in positions of command wielding the kind of power they did wield.

But if a poll were taken today among trainers and owners, among the followers of racing itself and the representatives of the media who write about the sport day-in-day-out, it is certain that they would not wish to see the independence of the Turf Club interfered with in the specific area of inquiries or the overall policing of racing itself in order that discipline be maintained.

Ask any of these people what could be put in the Turf Club's place and the response would probably be "leave well enough alone", even though they would obviously like to see a far more enlightened approach to its composition on the basis of the thinking of Jim Bolger and others. The consensus would appear to be that a body that has functioned for over 200 years has built up such a weight of tradition and authority that a new policing body would find it difficult to replace it.

Now that is not to say that the Turf Club does not have plenty of critics among the rank-and-file of racegoers. It has and will continue to have. Punters especially will assert that

Irish racing is a fertile breeding ground for non-triers, that the rules are observed by some trainers more in the breach than in the observance and that form at times can be made to look absolutely ludicrous in the manner in which it is upturned.

If there is a legitimate criticism, it is that not enough questions are asked often enough when a strongly-backed runner fails inexplicably to show the kind of form expected of it. As one experienced trainer put it to me: "No trainer ever objects to a question being asked by the Stewards. That is their right. If a trainer is running his horses on their merits, he has no need to fear being called in before the Stewards. And if he is a man of integrity he will be able to provide an acceptable explanation."

Jim Bolger has made it abundantly clear to me in more than one interview for this book that in his criticisms of the Turf Club, he has *never* set out to take from them the authority they have to pursue inquiries at the various tracks when the Stewards decide that a horse has not been allowed to run on its merits. He welcomes the harsh disciplinary code that endeavours to see to it that the rules are observed.

But he holds strongly to the view at the same time that an appeal against the decision of the local Stewards should be heard by an independent body – that is one independent of the Turf Club itself. "Under the existing arrangement when an appeal goes on from the local Stewards to Turf Club headquarters, it is akin to the employers sitting down to review and re-assess what was originally decided by its own employees," he said.

How that independent, impartial appeals mechanism would be constituted should be a matter for the new Racing Authority, he stressed. He pointed out that there was provision in the legislation for the appointment of such an impartial appeals body.

Again Jim Bolger repeated that he has no problem with inquiries being pursued at the racecourses themselves by the Stipendary and Acting Stewards of the Turf Club. "But from my own experience as a trainer, I feel very strongly that it has been shown that the appeals mechanism, as it has operated down the years, is not satisfactory. The urgent need for change is obvious," he added.

Consider now a minor race – the Rostrevor 2-y-o Fillies Maiden at the Dundalk evening meeting on 15 August 1990 – that was to become a *cause célèbre* in the list of battles Jim Bolger had with the Turf Club. The Bolger-trained runners, Nordic Tiara, ridden by Christy Roche, and Ashco by 18-years-old apprentice James A. (Seamus) Heffernan, finished first and second with the 4/6 favourite, Biki (M. Kinane) third. A Stewards' inquiry at the Dundalk meeting concluded that Ashco had been ridden otherwise than on her merits.

Jim Bolger was fined £500; the filly Ashco, who ran in the colours of his wife, Jackie, was suspended from racing for 28 days and Seamus Heffernan was stood down for five days.

Bolger, in cold retrospect, would recall for me later: "When I went racing that lovely day in August with Jackie, the last thing in the world I could have foreseen was that I would find myself in the middle of an inquiry over a race that had little or no significance in the racing calendar, that it would go on to lead to court proceedings and eventually to a marathon appeal at the Turf Club's headquarters on the Curragh. I just could not believe it was possible that so much could happen out of apparently nothing, especially when I didn't even have the favourite in the race."

And he would add significantly: "One horse in that same race made phenomenal improvement subsequently. Perhaps the attention of the stewards was diverted from him elsewhere!"

In November of the same year Jim Bolger went to the High Court seeking to win an order restraining the Turf Club from hearing his appeal against the penalties imposed by the Stewards at the Dundalk meeting. He failed in his bid.

Miss Justice Carroll said she was satisfied there was an adequate right of appeal available and it would be conducted by people not connected with the original inquiry at the racecourse. There was no reason, she said, to believe the appeal would not be conducted otherwise than in accordance with the principles of natural justice.

The appeal went ahead on 19 November 1990 at the Turf Club's headquarters right across the road from the Curragh racecourse.

In the chair was then Senior Steward, Dr Michael Dargan, assisted by C. S. Gainsford St. Lawrence, Seamus McGrath and Brig. H. J. de Waller.

Niall Fennelly, S.C., appeared for the Turf Club and Peter Maguire, S.C., for the Bolgers and Seamus Heffernan.

Rule 212, which requires that every horse which runs in a race "shall be run on its merits" was at the heart of the appeal which went on all day. In effect, the Turf Club hearing became a complete rehearing of the case, an assessment of the evidence by the Stewards of the Turf Club.

The head-on video of the race was shown twice to the Stewards and the side-on video twice also.

Seamus Heffernan's mount, Ashco, made the early running and, indeed, well into the straight. The boy looked around, first to his right and then he rode on a bit and looked to his left.

The Dundalk Stewards, having studied the videos, had decided that there must be an inquiry into the running and riding of Ashco. At the Dundalk inquiry Heffernan was asked why he had looked over his shoulders and he said he didn't know. He was unable to give an answer.

Jim Bolger intervened during that inquiry and asked the Stewards if it would be possible for him to direct a question to Heffernan. He was permitted to do this and asked the jockey: "Did you look over your shoulder in order to see how far you were ahead of the other horse?" and Heffernan replied "No."

Jim Bolger was then asked by the Stewards at the Dundalk inquiry if he would be concerned about the boy looking around in the race and he replied that he wouldn't necessarily be concerned with the boy looking around in the race but he would be concerned as to why he didn't know why he looked around.

Richard O'Brien, the owner of the winning horse, Nordic Tiara, was brought into the Dundalk inquiry at the request of Jim Bolger and he told the Stewards that he was in the parade ring while Jim Bolger was giving instructions to both Seamus Heffernan and Christy Roche. He heard the trainer say to Seamus Heffernan that if he could, he was to beat Christy Roche.

The Dundalk Stewards, stressing that they had failed to get a satisfactory explanation as to why Seamus Heffernan looked over his shoulder twice, decided that Ashco was not run on its merits and, therefore, they felt they had to impose the penalty they were imposing.

The issue of those two glances over the shoulder became, in fact, the kernel of the inquiry at Dundalk and would dominate the spell-binding question-and-answer session between Niall Fennelly and Jim Bolger at the appeal before the Turf Club, where Bolger would insist that the filly was a difficult ride and must not be ridden vigorously in a finish as it would not make her go any better.

Jim Bolger recalls that one of the Acting Stewards at The Dundalk inquiry (Robert Patton) made it quite clear at the appeal hearing at the Turf Club headquarters that it was obvious to him that the horse in front, namely Ashco, was not trying.

Indeed, Bolger remembers that the evidence of this Steward was quite extraordinarily in the totally-dogmatic conclusions drawn and it contrasted sharply with the eventual findings of the appeal itself in exonerating him completely.

Bolger recalls that as this particular Steward was being led by Niall Fennelly, he made the point that when Seamus Heffernan looked around, it seemed like he was looking for the stable jockey or the senior jockey (Christy Roche).

He was asked was that the conclusion he came to and he responded "yes".

Under cross-examination by Mr Maguire, he went on to say that the reason Heffernan was looking for the stable or senior jockey was that this jockey was likely to win the race – in a word, he was expecting Christy Roche to come past him and go on for victory.

In further evidence, Robert Patton described as "sinister" Heffernan looking back twice over his shoulder.

When it was put to him by Mr Maguire that there was nothing necessarily sinister in a jockey looking back, Patton replied that there was in this particular case, but not in the way other jockeys look back.

Pressed by Mr Maguire as to what he meant by "sinister", he explained that Heffernan looked back in a manner that no other jockey would look back in a race.

Asked then by Mr Maguire if he would accept that the instruction given by Jim Bolger to Seamus Heffernan was that he was to jump the filly out and make the running and beat Christy Roche if he could, Patton replied that he did not accept it.

Asked if he meant it was a lie then, he repeated that he didn't accept it.

Pressed further by Mr Maguire, he said twice in succession that he did not accept it.

Mr Maguire indicated that he wanted to be quite clear about one thing – was Mr Patton saying, in effect, that he totally rejected Mr Bolger's evidence that those were the instructions which he gave to the jockey?

"Yes", came the extraordinary response from Mr Patton.

Asked then if it was invention on Mr Bolger's part, he replied "maybe".

Mr Maguire then suggested that if it didn't happen, it could mean only one thing and that was that Mr Bolger had invented something and again Mr Patton responded that maybe that was the case.

Asked if that was what he was saying, he replied that he didn't know.

Mr Maguire told him bluntly that he had better know – either Mr Bolger had given specific instructions to his jockey or he had not given them. If he didn't say what he was purported to have said, then he was telling a deliberate lie to the Stewards.

To this Mr Patton replied "possibly".

Asked if "possibly" was the word he was actually using, he replied that he was merely saying that he wouldn't accept the evidence, otherwise he felt the jockey would have won.

The straight question – like a straight left – was then put to him by Mr Maguire that he didn't accept that Mr Bolger gave instructions to Seamus Heffernan that he was to beat Christy Roche if he could and Mr Patton replied with a direct "no".

Mr Patton went on to say that he looked upon the evidence of Richard O'Brien (owner of the winning horse, Nordic Tiara) with great suspicion. It was not very often that a trainer in front of other owners would say go out and beat the other horse. It would seem rather strange.

Mr Maguire put it to him that whether it was strange or not, was he (Mr Patton) now saying that Mr O'Brien was telling a lie about that when he gave his evidence and Mr Patton responded that he didn't believe it. Whether Mr O'Brien was telling a lie or not, he didn't believe it.

When Mr Maguire suggested that Mr Patton seemed to be hesitating in calling a spade a spade and asked again if Mr Patton was calling Mr O'Brien's evidence a lie, Mr Patton repeated that what he had said was that he didn't believe the evidence in question.

Another key factor in the appeal hearing was to be the veterinary evidence.

Terry Smyth, the Turf Club's veterinary officer in attendance at the Dundalk meeting on 15 August 1990, examined the filly Ashco on the instructions of the Stewards and found no evidence of lameness. He saw her leaving and entering the box but he did not have her trotted, as there was no satisfactory place at the Dundalk racecourse to have her trotted up. He had found no evidence of nasal discharge.

He stressed that if he had seen her to be sore or something questionable about her, it would have been a case of then trying to investigate lameness further – but he saw nothing. He asked the lad in charge of the filly had he seen anything wrong with her and he said no.

If the filly had sore shins, it might not be visible or palpable or obvious when he saw her but he would expect it to be visible within the hour or certainly before she went up. Yes, certainly the next morning. He would expect it to be visible by then.

He didn't see the horse later that evening or next morning or two days later but if the evidence was that sore shins had developed, it would be consistent with the filly having suffered jarring during the course of the race. Younger horses – two-year-olds – had a tendency to sore shins.

In cross-examination Mr Maguire put it to him specifically that he did not examine Ashco's forelegs and Mr Smyth replied that he ran his hand down the forelegs. It wasn't a very detailed examination but he did remember running his hand down her forelegs.

Mr Maguire then suggested that it was a cursory examination and Mr Smyth replied in the affirmative.

Kieran Bredin, a veterinary surgeon with a Certificate in Equine Orthopaedics from the Royal College, said in evidence that he had been the main vet to Jim Bolger stable since he started training.

The day he examined Ashco, some days after the Dundalk race, he found bilateral shin soreness affecting the left fore and the right fore but there was also a distinct new contour on the left shin which you would call a buck shin. There was a veritable degree of soreness.

The animal wouldn't trot for him. She trotted very reluctantly and in a stumbling sort of fashion, indicating that both legs were affected, but the pain elicited from the left one was greater than from the right. The conclusion he drew was that the filly had very obvious shin problems, very, very obvious.

⌘ ⌘ ⌘ ⌘

The exchanges between Jim Bolger and Niall Fennelly at the appeal hearing were fascinating as on the one hand you had a leading counsel, acting for the Turf Club in this instance, placing a particular significance on Bolger's intervening at the Dundalk inquiry to put a question to young Heffernan while the trainer himself made it perfectly clear more than once that there was "absolutely no innuendo" and the basis of his intervention was to set the boy at ease when he felt that Heffernan had become upset and it was important to make him feel that there was someone on his side.

Jim Bolger was at pains to lay it on the line at the outset of the appeal hearing that no one had ever disputed the right of the Stewards to ask for an explanation of an individual horse's running. In fact, it was something that he had not disputed from the word go.

Bolger insisted on the vital issue of Heffernan looking around that while it might not be as neat as people might like to see it in racing, there was nothing wrong with it as far as he was concerned.

When it was pointed out to him that the Stewards attached importance to the fact that Heffernan had glanced over his shoulder twice, Bolger responded that as far as he was concerned one of the Stewards at Dundalk had made up his mind that the horse was not trying.

He went on to emphasise that when the boy failed to give an explanation to the Dundalk Stewards as to why he glanced over his shoulder twice, he tried to get the boy to relax and tell the Stewards why he looked around.

Bolger claimed that at that point in the inquiry Heffernan was being barracked a little bit, was considerably upset and was shifting from one foot to the other and fidgeting with his hands. In a word, he was visibly upset. What he was trying to do was let him know that there was somebody on his side and to elicit an answer for the Stewards. He thought that the kind word in the boy's ear would help in that regard. But he failed to get an answer from him as he was considerably upset.

Now Niall Fennelly, in interpreting the reply Bolger sought to get from Heffernan at the Dundalk inquiry, suggested, in effect, that the trainer wanted the boy to tell the Stewards that the reason he looked over his shoulder twice was to find out how far in front he was.

Bolger told Niall Fennelly bluntly that he was wrong in this interpretation.

When asked why then did he put a question like that to the boy, Bolger insisted once again that he was trying to get Heffernan to relax.

Mr Fennelly then put it to Bolger that an outside observer might read something into what the trainer was trying to get the boy to say.

Bolger responded that there were no outside observers, only seven Stewards. And he contended that there was absolutely nothing ulterior in what he was trying to get the boy to say. He was trying to get the boy to know that there was somebody on his side. And he added that he understood why the boy was so upset.

Bolger claimed that as the trainer of Ashco he wasn't believed on the instructions he gave Seamus Heffernan. That was the situation in a nutshell. There was a problem with all of that.

He maintained that the Stewards didn't accept that he told Seamus Heffernan to jump the filly out, make the running and beat Christy Roche if he could. He maintained further that they didn't accept that these were the riding instructions. Secondly, he argued that when he said that he was convinced that if Heffernan had been more vigorous on the filly that she wouldn't have finished any closer, the Stewards did not accept this either.

These were the two basic areas where there was a problem, he stressed.

Jim Bolger came under strong pressure to explain why he did not tell the Stewards at the Dundalk inquiry that the filly had an extremely temperamental history and about the history of treating her for sore shins.

He didn't tell the Dundalk inquiry, he admitted, because the veterinary report came in that the filly was normal after the race, and anyway he was convinced that his explanation would have been accepted by the Stewards and that there would be no need for an appeal to the Turf Club Stewards themselves and all the hassle that it meant. He wasn't going to go out and tell the world that the filly wasn't genuine. He thought they could get her sweetened.

He was pressed strongly on the point that under the Turf Club's rules he should have told them at Dundalk about the filly's temperament and the sore shins problem and he replied that he had answered all the questions the Stewards had put to him truthfully and honestly.

He was pressed on why he had not explained to the Stewards that the filly must be ridden in a quiet manner and he replied that the question was never raised at the Dundalk hearing. The inquiry was conducted by the representatives of the Turf Club. They asked the questions and he answered them. When he told the Stewards that the filly would run better if she got a tender ride, he was not asked for any reasons. The Stewards had a right to ask for reasons. He repeated that he answered all the questions that were put to him. He thought it a pity he wasn't believed.

In his direct evidence to the Turf Club appeal hearing, Jim Bolger revealed how for a period of about six weeks before the Dundalk race the filly was treated for sore shins. The night beforehand she would have been on the anti-philagestine and hosed on the morning of the race and hosed in Dundalk. She was in superb condition on the way to the start.

It was put to him that under the rules he should have told the Stewards in Dundalk that the filly was being treated for sore shins, that he had a duty to do so and did not do so.

Again he repeated that he did not do so because the veterinary examination came back that she was post-race normal. He didn't feel the need to go through all that because it wasn't going to stand up.

It was midday the following day that he discovered – after talking to Seamus Heffernan when the riding out for the day was finished – that she was suffering from sore shins during the race and that in hindsight he should not have possibly run her on the ground at Dundalk on the day. She had fairly pronounced shoulder lameness.

When pressed as to why he had not mentioned it until that day – that is the day of the Turf Club appeal hearing – he pointed out that after the Dundalk inquiry he had gone to the High Court seeking a restraining order against the Turf Club hearing the appeal. The matter, as he saw it then, was under the courts and it was into a different ball game entirely. He felt it was something that should be sorted out in court and not by the Turf Club and that was where the matter of the sore shins and shoulder lameness should be kept for.

The filly next ran at Tipperary and it was suggested to Jim Bolger at the Curragh appeal hearing that this was a better race than Dundalk because the filly ran third to one of Vincent O'Brien's horses and Sheikh Mohammed had a runner in the race.

Bolger responded that it was not the owners who were important but the horses. The ground at Tipperary was different.

He explained that Christy Roche did not ride her to instructions. He hit the filly. He was instructed not to hit her.

When he gave instructions to a jockey in the parade ring they were not always adhered to. They didn't always do what he told them. Christy Roche was longer in the game than he himself and Christy thought he knew more than he did himself – and he probably did.

He repeated that the quieter you sat on this filly the better results you got. He agreed that in most cases by riding an animal out you got better results – that was because most of

134

the animals were genuine. But in the case of this one, you would get a better result by sitting quietly.

When it was suggested to him by Mr Fennelly that he would have to agree that with most animals you would get better results by riding them out, Jim Bolger replied that with genuine animals "yes" but they were dealing here with an animal that was not a genuine animal.

Mr Fennelly pointed out to him that at the end of the day he was saying that he gave (1) particular instructions to Seamus Heffernan; (2) that he was satisfied with the ride Heffernan gave the filly because he rode to instructions and (3) because of two special features of this filly.

Jim Bolger replied that he would like to take them one at a time. He asked Mr Fennelly to repeat the first part of the question.

Mr Fennelly asked him was he satisfied with Seamus Heffernan's riding of the filly because he rode in accordance with instructions?

Jim Bolger said that as he understood it, this was the second part of the question.

Mr Fennelly said that if Mr Bolger didn't know what he was asking, why did he ask for it to be repeated?

Jim Bolger responded that Mr Fennelly had asked three questions in one. He had got the second and third but he didn't get the first.

To this Mr Fennelly said, in exasperation, that Mr Bolger need not bother any further. That was it.

Later Jim Bolger would recall that Mr Fennelly seemed to have confused the situation by asking a three-part question at one and the same time and when he (Jim Bolger) tried to bring it down to specifics, it only led to more confusion and then counsel decided to give up and leave it at that.

❋ ❋ ❋ ❋

Christy Roche, who was Jim Bolger's No. 1 stable jockey at the time of the Dundalk race and had ridden Ashco on her debut at Leopardstown, told the Turf Club appeal hearing that he had actually suggested to the trainer after work on the gallops that this was one they shouldn't carry on with.

Anyone could see from the film of the Leopardstown race that her tail was going like a windmill.

In relation to the Dundalk race, Roche insisted that Heffernan rode to instructions in leading from the outset. He (Roche) knew that if it came to stamina his own filly would win and so he was quite happy to bide his time. Michael Kinane was challenging on the outside and would have shouted to Heffernan "get in, get in". At that point he himself would have shouted "get out" as he wanted a clear passage on the inside.

He argued that the look over the shoulder was obvious – and the reason it was obvious was from the jockeys shouting. The reason Heffernan was looking around was that he was being shouted at and this was not an unusual case for apprentices. The senior jockeys roar at them – "get in" and "get out".

Roche said that Heffernan on Ashco was never a concern to him, even though the filly was ahead of his one well into the straight. He knew that as soon as Heffernan gave Ashco a kick she would be gone. His own filly was a tough filly and every time he gave her a slap she put her head down. The only danger to him was Michael Kinane on the outside.

A key moment came in the appeal hearing when it was put to Christy Roche by Niall Fennelly that he had looked at the video of the race a number of times and Christy replied in the affirmative.

He was asked then what he thought, as a senior jockey, of the riding of Ashco? Was it ridden on its merits or not?

Roche replied that he saw the justification of the Stewards having an inquiry. Yes, he could see the justification of that. But he went on to emphasise that knowing what he knew about the filly – and he knew more about her than Jim Bolger – he had to say again that she was completely ungenuine and the more she would run, the more – he prophesised – that he would be proved right.

Seamus Heffernan, 18 at the time of the Dundalk race and with eight winners to his credit out of 100 rides, confirmed in his evidence that he was instructed by Jim Bolger to jump Ashco out and not to hit the filly under any circumstances . . . and to beat Christy Roche if he could.

There were a number of people present when he was given those instructions.

Asked what would have been his feeling about beating Christy Roche in that race, he replied that he would have loved to have beaten Christy as every rider wanted to beat the champion jockey.

Asked if he rode the filly on its merits, he replied "yes".

After the race the filly felt unsound under him and she wasn't moving perfectly. It looked as if she was jarred up front. Her action was not what it would normally be. That was probably due to the fact that the ground was good. She was very lame the next day. She was off for the best part of three weeks.

Asked why he had not given an answer during the Dundalk inquiry as to why he had looked over his shoulder twice, he said the reason he did not do so was that he did not want to bring any of the other jockeys into it, that is the jockeys who were shouting behind him. He looked around to try and ascertain what they were saying.

He said that he was upset during the Dundalk inquiry. He didn't understand what the Stewards were saying because they were saying it loudly and roughly.

In cross-examination, he was again asked why he did not tell the Dundalk Stewards that the filly had to be ridden a certain way because of her temperament, he responded that he didn't do so because he was frightened and afraid. The Stewards were asking him questions, using language he didn't fully understand. He didn't know what they were asking.

❊　❊　❊　❊

There had been a number of breaks during the long day – the Longest Day in Jim Bolger's career when it came to tilts with the Turf Club.

Peter Maguire in his summing up stressed that the onus of proof rested in this matter with the Turf Club, as it would rest in a criminal case and that was a very heavy onus indeed. The Turf Club Stewards must be satisfied, each one of them, beyond any reasonable doubt that the complaint against each of the three individually had been established. In other words, they would have to be satisfied beyond any reasonable doubt that the filly, Ashco, didn't run on its merits and then they would have to decide was it the responsibility and the fault of one, two or all three people?

They could not decide this by taking an *overall* view of it.

He argued that because of the very nature of things the examination of the filly immediately after the race was a cursory one but, bearing in mind the importance of what was involved – the inquiry itself and the subsequent appeal – he argued further that it was less than sataisfactory that the examination was not for a longer period.

One of the most significant pieces of evidence, he said, was Seamus Heffernan's statement that he would have loved to have beaten Christy Roche.

Mr Maguire contended that Heffernan would have beaten Roche – if the filly was capable of doing so.

He concluded by saying that there was no evidence whatsoever upon which the Turf Club Stewards could find that either Mr Bolger or Mrs Bolger did anything, said anything or caused anything to be done which would have resulted in Ashco being run on anything less than on its merits. Unless the Stewards could find that, then they had no other course but to uphold the appeal.

He emphasised that they could not put in evidence that was not there. They had to look at the evidence as given. They could not find evidence which would justify the results of the local Stewards as against the three people concerned.

Niall Fennelly said in his summing up that it was never part of the case that Mrs Bolger was in breach of any rule. She had a legitimate appeal, for she had done nothing that was responsible for the horse's running on the day of the race in Dundalk.

Mr Fennelly went on to say that it was accepted that the conducting of the inquiry at Dundalk was justified and legitimate. The Stewards were entitled to ask for an explanation as to why the filly was ridden in the manner in which it was.

The explanation which had been put forward during the appeal hearing that day was twofold, concerning the temperament of the filly and that she was a physical veterinary problem.

What was quite clear, however, was that this explanation was not given to the Dundalk Stewards. There was no question, he emphasised, of questioning the veterinary evidence. It was quite clear that the animal had a veterinary condition.

It was unfortunate, to say the least, that it was never disclosed at any stage.

They had heard no evidence which would suggest that Seamus Heffernan advanced the physical condition of the filly or any soreness as the reason he rode her in the way he did. The reason he put forward was that you had to ride her a certain way and that was the way he rode her on the day.

But Mr Fennelly said that Mr Maguire was correct that the Stewards of the Turf Club had to be satisfied beyond all reasonable doubt that an infringement of the rules had been committed. Applying that standard, they might believe the explanation that the temperament of the filly was the reason she was ridden the way she was in Dundalk. It was a matter for the Stewards to decide.

The Stewards might reach the conclusion that it was not possible to find an infringement of the rules against Mr Bolger. But they had to consider both separately. The evaluation of the fact was entirely a matter for the Stewards.

In the final analysis, the question was: did the animal run on her merits? It might well be possible for the Stewards to conclude that Mr Bolger's instructions were correct but that the riding was not.

That was entirely for the Turf Club Stewards to decide. They might conclude that an explanation was available but was not given to the Stewards in Dundalk, although it should have been given.

It was after 10 o'clock when it was all over. When the Stewards of the Turf Club finally gave their decision, it was shown that Jim Bolger was completely vindicated in bringing the appeal as far as his own reputation of integrity was concerned. Mrs Bolger was also completely vindicated.

The Turf Club Stewards, while finding that Ashco did not run on its merits, did not hold the trainer responsible and did not impose any penalty on the horse.

They did, however, find that the apprentice jockey, James Heffernan, made insufficient effort and confirmed the

139

suspension on him during a period when there was no racing.

They made the point that they had evidence before them that day which was not available to the Stewards in Dundalk.

On the insistence of Mr Maguire, it was included in the Calendar notice that the Turf Club Stewards allowed the appeal of Jim Bolger against the local Stewards.

Footnote: On Wednesday evening, 20 July 1994, Seamus Heffernan found himself in trouble with the Naas Stewards when he was banned for 28 days and his mount, Tirolean, was banned from racing for 30 days. The finish of the Jasmine EBF Maiden concerned the Bolger stable-mates, Pozzoli and Tirolean with the former prevailing by a head.

Following lengthy deliberations after the race, the Stewards found that Rule 212, which deals with "horses not being run on their merits" was infringed. The *Irish Field* in its report of the race stated that "Tirolean looked to be travelling easier than the 11/10 favourite, Pozzoli, but did not peg back the leader, who won by a head."

Jim Bolger, who was fined £1,000, announced the next day that he was appealing the fine imposed on him while Seamus Heffernan also appealed the ban on him and Mrs. Jackie Bolger, owner of Tirolean, the penalty the stewards had imposed on the horse.

The fine and suspension imposed on Jim Bolger, rider Seamus Heffernan and the horse Tirolean remained intact following the appeal hearing lasting six hours at the Turf Club on Wednesday, 3 August 1994.

After the failure of his appeal, Bolger issued a statement which declared: "I am at a loss for words to comment on the decision of the Stewards today as the Stewards declined to give any reason for same."

And he added: "I am appalled at the suspension imposed on Seamus Heffernan, a young married man with a family whose sole income is from riding and particularly without any specification as to what finding is being made against him."

There was a full line-up of leading lights in the legal profession including the barristers Niall Fennelly for the Turf Club and Kevin Haugh acting on behalf of the appellants.

Evidence was heard from the Stewards and Stewards' secretary Richard Teevan, the two Stipendaries Philip Lafarge and Peter Martin, plus Dr Marie O'Connor, the Turf Club veterinary officer, who had all acted at Naas.

The thrust and sentiment of Bolger's statement hinged on the lack of detailed findings by the Stewards – in effect, that a bare statement simply indicated which rule had been transgressed without issuing a full report on the matter.

However, as Valentine Lamb pointed out in the *Irish Field*, the appeal system had been proved legally acceptable and was not going to be easily altered.

In 1994 Jim Bolger was appointed a member of the Board of the new Irish Horseracing Authority and obviously he will be very keen to change the current system.

He holds very strong views on the appeals system and is convinced that it must change.

8

"The Man who Runs Irish Racing has Won" – said Sangster's Son-in-Law

The scene switches now two years on to the count-down to Budweiser Irish Derby Day '92 and Jim Bolger is making headlines both in Ireland and Britain as a question mark is put over St. Jovite competing in the Curragh Classic if Christy Roche is not available to ride the colt.

Roche had received a 15-days suspension from the Naas stewards for "improper riding" in the Clane Maiden Race on Saturday, June 13 (Roche was alleged to have struck another rider with his whip during the race but when I questioned him about this he vehemently denied that he was guilty of this offence).

The duration of the sentence meant that Roche would miss the Irish Derby, unless he appealed successfully to the Stewards of the Turf Club, or the hearing was held after the Derby. The Turf Club Stewards, in fact, named the Friday *before* the Curragh meeting as the crucial date.

Roche sought a postponement in the High Court on the grounds that he required more time to prepare his case. When that was thrown out, it seemed that his fate was sealed.

But at the eleventh hour there was a compromise. The Turf Club announced that "in the interest of the sport of racing" it had responded to a personal plea by Roche's solicitor and named July 6 as the new date for the appeal.

142

Bolger had previously intimated that he and owner, Mrs. Kraft Payson would be "reluctant" to run St. Jovite if Roche was unable to ride.

The *Sporting Life* reported the trainer was stating that "it is just possible St. Jovite might not run in the Irish Derby if Christy is suspended".

When I read this quote to Jim Bolger at a volatile press conference at the Curragh on the day of the Budweiser Irish Derby, he flatly denied that he made any threat to the Turf Club – direct or indirect. He repeated that what he had said in the count-down to the race was that "both the owner and I were reluctant to run St. Jovite without Christy Roche in the saddle".

He took a strong line with journalists who suggested that by implying that the colt would not run if Roche was not available because of suspension, he was in effect laying it on the line that there would be no renewal of the St. Jovite-Dr. Devious Epsom Derby battle if the Turf Club had pressed ahead on the Friday with the appeal and the 15-day suspension had been confirmed. He repeated more than once – in the strongest possible terms – that he had issued no threats.

However, in the days before the Derby a section of the racing public, rightly or wrongly, perceived that the authority of the Turf Club was being called into question. This perception was compounded by the fact that when it looked as if the Turf Club would insist on the appeal being heard on the eve of the race itself, Roche's legal representative went to the High Court seeking an order to have the appeal adjourned.

When the Turf Club did not go ahead with the appeal on the Friday, thus leaving Roche free to ride in the Derby, it was interpreted as a defeat for the Turf Club and the *Sporting Life* page 1 headline read: "Roche Wins Day as Club Climbs Down".

Cahir O'Sullivan, Chief Executive of the Turf Club was adamant when I talked to him subsequently that there was no question of the authority of the Turf Club or its integrity being damaged as a result of these events.

He explained that when the injunction was not granted, the Turf Club could have called the inquiry for the Friday

143

and Roche would have had to appear and also, assuming he was available, Jim Bolger as a key witness.

"What happened was that Niall O'Neill, Christy Roche's solicitor called to our office and requested that the appeal hearing be adjourned because there had not been sufficient time to prepare Mr. Roche's defence. The Turf Club acceded to Mr. O'Neill's request.

"We were not influenced in the least by who would or would not ride St. Jovite. If we had pressed ahead with the hearing on the Friday and Niall O'Neill had made the case that he had not time to prepare Mr. Roche's defence, it was certain it would have been adjourned anyway."

Mr. O'Sullivan added that nothing was presented to the Turf Club on the record that could in any way be represented as a "threat".

The fact remained, however, that if St. Jovite was not in the field the Budweiser Irish Derby would have been robbed of the clash that had caught the imagination of the racing public both in Ireland and Britain – the showdown between the Epsom Derby winner, Dr. Devious and the Irish-trained runner-up.

One who unfortunately chose to give voice to the opinion that the Turf Club had bowed the knee to Jim Bolger was Peter Chapple-Hyam, trainer of Dr. Devious and son-in-law of Robert Sangster. His post-race Curragh comment was: "The man who runs Irish racing has won".

It was not a very sporting jibe from a visiting loser, but it came at a moment of great disappointment from a relatively young and inexperienced trainer who in only his second season had completed a remarkable hat-trick when Rodrigo De Triano won the English 2,000 Guineas and Irish 2,000 Guineas – ridden to victory in both by the ageless Lester Piggott – before Dr. Devious took the Epsom Derby in the hands of John Reid.

Chapple-Hyam later recovered his composure and, while reporting the next day that Dr. Devious was not a well horse on his return to the Manton stables, conceded that he would not have beaten the winner. "You have got to say 'well done' to Jim Bolger who has got an improving high-class horse on his hands".

144

In the immediate aftermath of St. Jovite's demolition job on Dr. Devious, Jim Bolger at the subsequent crowded Curragh press conference said that if Christy Roche was not available to ride St. Jovite in the King George, the colt might not run – as he saw Roche as "part of the horse".

One could appreciate Bolger's gratitute to Roche at that moment. The Coolcullen trainer had interestingly given much of the credit for training St. Jovite to Roche. Bolger was able to forecast that whereas at Epsom, Roche was pushing and niggling his mount from the start, at the Curragh the jockey would have a double handful. And so it proved, St. Jovite producing for the first time in public what Roche and Bolger had always said he was capable of doing.

It was suggested to Jim Bolger that in even hinting that St. Jovite might not run at Ascot if Christy Roche was not available, he was putting the gun to the Jockey Club's head and at the same time to the Turf Club's head, for if the appeal before the latter was lost, then naturally Roche would not be able to ride the colt in the King George.

In what developed into a very tough public session between the winning trainer and the media representatives, Jim Bolger denied flatly that he was putting the gun to the heads of the racing authorities but at the same time, in face of repeated questions, he held firmly to the line that he saw Christy Roche as an integral part of the successful partnership with St. Jovite. He left it to the racing writers to put their own interpretation on his words.

I had no doubt in my mind – after putting some very direct questions to him at that news conference – how I should interpret what Jim Bolger had said and I concluded in an article in the *Sunday Independent* that clearly a question mark had been put over St. Jovite's participation in the King George if Christy Roche lost his appeal to the Turf Club and was not available to ride the colt. Some English journalists went further.

Christy Roche lost his appeal when it was heard by the Turf Club but then brought a case before the High Court in Dublin.

The High Court granted an interim injunction temporarily lifting the 15-day ban and enabling Roche to resume riding the day before the Irish Oaks, in which he partnered Ivyanna, trained by Jim Bolger.

But when the full case was heard by the High Court – taking three days and involving a heavy outlay in legal costs – the acting President, Mr. Declan Costello, refused Roche's application for an injunction against the suspension.

Accordingly, the suspension became operative immediately. And it took in the period that included the King George VI and Queen Elizabeth Stakes.

Christy Roche would say to me in his home in the Spring of 1994 that the one mistake he regretted in his life was to bring that case before the High Court.

"I was alleged to have hit the boy with my whip. I did not hit the boy. I think people who know me will accept my word for that. But in the end I got caught up in a clash between personalities and I could do nothing at all about it.

"I am a big boy now. I made a decision at the time and I know now I made a wrong one. It was a racing matter essentially and not a matter for the courts. It still bothers me that I could have been so wrong to take the decision I did."

But it could be argued perhaps that if Roche had not gone to the High Court in the first place the Turf Club might not have postponed the date of the hearing of the appeal on the Naas incident and he would have missed the ride on St. Jovite in the Irish Derby.

⌘ ⌘ ⌘ ⌘

His role in making St. Jovite the outstanding middle-distance colt in Europe in 1992 assured Jim Bolger of immortality but one day over lunch, he amazed me when he said that he was not driven by the need to achieve immortality. "I have no interest in being remembered or not being remembered, even inside the narrow confines of racing", he said quite frankly.

He then went on to make the point – and it struck home – that Noel Murless was probably one of the best trainers Britain produced in the last one hundred years and his record in winning nineteen English Classics, including the Derby three times, set him on a pedestal apart. "Yet, when he died, he hardly merited the column inches in the newspapers of the following day that one would have expected, given his truly amazing achievements", said Jim Bolger.

Likewise, when Tim Hamey died in 1990. How many of the younger generation were aware that he was one of the select band of jump jockeys to win both the Cheltenham Gold Cup (on Koko in 1926) and the Aintree Grand National (on Forbra in 1932)?

In his own case, he went on, he could set out to try and beat the overall record of Vincent O'Brien, "Of course, I know in my heart that it would be impossible, for even if I were to emulate the successes he achieved on the Flat, I could not hope to win three successive Gold Cups, three successive Champion Hurdles and three successive Grand Nationals. No, with the handful of horses I have at the jumping game in a stable that concentrates principally on the Flat, that would be impossible. Vincent's record will NEVER be beaten".

The "tunnel vision", as he described it, to try and achieve immortality had affected men in many sports – and not just in racing alone. Often they did not realise until too late, if not at all, how they had missed out on the other essential aspects of life.

"It seems futile to me if aiming at immortality is achieved at the sacrifice of the quality of life, especially family life."

It was at the coffee stage that he drew back the veil on his philosophy of life, rather eye-opening you will agree when most racegoers could be forgiven for concluding that such was the ambition driving one Jim Bolger that he would have absolutely no time to reflect on the quality of life.

There are those who would see the commanding of an obituary in *The Times* (that is the English *Times*, mark you!) as the ultimate when they passed on. The sure measure of immortality.

Jim Bolger is certainly one person who won't turn in his grave at such an appalling omission – if it were to happen.

But, of course, it will not happen. In my book it would be a brave man who would assert that he does not come into the reckoning for a place in the top six all-time great Irish trainers. He himself is the first to acknowledge that Vincent O'Brien is the undisputed No. 1 and because of his record no one will ever dislodge him from that pedestal apart.

Personally, if I were concentrating on a trainer with a brilliant record over the jumps, one who stood the test of time, then I would have to place Tom Dreaper second, bearing in mind those five Gold Cup triumphs achieved through Prince Regent (1946), the peerless Arkle (1964-'66) and Fort Leney (1968) and his tremendous strike rate in the Irish Grand National that included seven-in-a-row in the period 1960-'66 and a seven-timer also in the Harold Clarke Memorial Leopardstown Chase between 1962 and '68 (inclusive). He had 26 victories in all at Cheltenham to Vincent O'Brien's 22.

But if one were concentrating solely on the Flat, then P. J. "Darkie" Prendergast would be right up there after Vincent O'Brien vying for the No. 2 position, for he did it all and was desperately unlucky that Meadow Court arrived in the same year as Sea Bird II. Otherwise he would have achieved in 1965 the Epsom Derby victory that eluded him during an outstanding career.

By 1980 – the year he passed away – he had won 17 Irish Classics and four English Classics. Despite the shattering effect of the cough on some of his finest talent, he established a record in 1965 in that he topped the list of champion trainers in Britain for the third successive season.

It was quite unprecedented for a trainer based outside the country and Dermot Weld argues that for Prendergast to achieve it from his Curragh base represented the finest accomplishment of his entire career.

"There's no doubt he was a great trainer", said Lester Piggott to me one day in his Newmarket home.

With Vincent O'Brien, "Darkie" Prendergast was unmatched in the field of picking out a potential champion at the yearling sales. I have only to instance here the way he picked Windy City – a veritable flying machine – which others had let go by that day in the sales ring and the way he purchased

148

Ragusa for the Mullions after the American-bred colt had been cast aside from another quarter as being a "ragged or weedy" yearling.

Christy Roche summed up: "You have got to remember that 'Darkie' was operating on a shoe-string compared with the money that was spent at the yearling sales when the Sangster-O'Brien-Magnier syndicate hit Keeneland in the mid-seventies and then the Arabs moved in with a vengeance. Prendergast had unbelievable success with horses that were not fashionably bred. His eye was uncanny in spotting the conformation that told him that here was a champion in the making".

So in Vincent O'Brien, "Darkie" Prendergast and Tom Dreaper we have three who go in automatically into the top six all-time greats.

Dermot Weld because of his achievement in becoming the first European trainer to win an American Classic when Go and Go took the 1990 Belmont Stakes in authoritative style and then in 1993 became the first man outside Australia to land the Melbourne Cup – shattering all previous conceptions cherished by racing aficionados Down Under – has got to be considered for a high ranking in the Top Six honours list, and I, therefore, give him the No. 4 spot, just ahead of Jim Bolger at No. 5. I believe that Weld in breaching the American defences and winning one of their Triple Crown races and silencing the Aussies in taking their most prestigious race achieved a historic breakthrough on two levels that merits special reward.

Of course, Jim Bolger and himself at the time of writing had still ample time on their side to add to their record of achievements of recent times and even challenge for consideration for the No. 2 spot before retiring.

Christy Roche acknowledges that Jim Bolger has the ambition to be the greatest trainer in the world but, amazingly enough, he puts David O'Brien right up there in the Vincent O'Brien and "Darkie" Prendergast league as a trainer of genius, who had won three Derbys (French and Irish with Assert in 1982 and the English with Secreto in 1984) by the time he had reached his 30th birthday. Roche reckoned that if David hadn't decided to retire early from the game, he could have gone on to unparalleled heights of achievement, granted he got a few more horses in the class of Assert and Secreto.

"He spent so much time with the horses in his care", said Roche. "He came to know them so well. Few realise, as I do, the job he did in making Assert into a champion. He started out looking an ordinary horse. But such was David's patience, such his way with the colt that he trained him to the point that he improved 100 per cent and emerged as the leading three-year-old in Europe in the season he won at Chantily and the Curragh."

On Roche's reading of it, David O'Brien would be placed ahead of both Dermot Weld and Jim Bolger but that in itself must become an issue of fierce debate and controversy.

As fierce as whether David O'Brien should go in ahead of Mickey Rogers and Paddy Sleator.

Rogers, a man with a big vision, the mystique of greatness surrounding his name to this day, who turned out Hard Ridden to win the 1958 Epsom Derby and Santa Claus to make it a second English Derby in 1964 and supplementing that success by taking the Irish Derby in brilliant style.

Tom MacGinty, respected former Racing Correspondent of the *Irish Independent* and current Racing Editor of the *Irish Racing Annual* does not hide his deep admiration for Rogers' skill as a trainer and notes that what he achieved on the high plains with a comparatively small string was simply phenomenal. "He was very similar in character to David O'Brien, shy and retiring, and preferred to let his achievements speak for his ability," said Tom MacGinty.

But the admirers of Paddy Sleator rate him one of the finest trainers this country has produced – one, they argue, who must be included automatically along with Vincent O'Brien, Tom Dreaper and "Darkie" Prendergast in any top six. He didn't win the Gold Cup or the Aintree Grand National. He had one Champion Hurdle to his name with Another Flash (1960) but, as I wrote in my book, *The High Rollers of the Turf*, he was for "over a span of half a century always among the leaders of his profession, a breaker of moulds and a maker of them in that his very success saw rules introduced to clip his wings. And yet when he challenged those who set those same rules by reaching out to new horizons, it ultimately rebounded to the benefit of trainers who had been jealous of him and, indeed, to the benefit of Irish racing as a whole''.

There was no better illustration of this than the momentous decision he took to concentrate all his best jumpers in England and few episodes in the history of National Hunt racing match the strike rate he achieved when he teamed up with Warwick trainer, Arthur Thomas in the early sixties and the blitz campaign they waged over a four-year period saw the winners flow with a regularity that was unmatched in its consistency. Little Scottish Memories, who got nearly as fulsome a press in his day as Arkle did in later years, won in all 23 races while operating out of Warwick.

In his heyday the Master of Grangecon was the one the bookies, both in Ireland and England, feared most of all. He wasn't a gambling man himself as such but there were owners in his stable who loved to have a real cut at the ring and when the ring was hit, the bookies certainly felt it where it hurt most – in their satchels.

Michael O'Farrell, Racing Correspondent of the *Irish Times* contends that Paddy Sleator had no equal in the art of placing a horse to the best advantage and that is why the bookies came to dread him. But O'Farrell argued at the same time that Sleator was not very adventurous and was loath to send horses to Cheltenham or for other top National Hunt races in England unless he was certain they were in with a chance of winning. Sleator certainly was not one to make swans out of geese. But then if he was in Jim Bolger's shoes in 1993 he would never have sent Blue Judge for the Epsom Derby and would have missed runner-up position behind Commander in Chief – and possibly victory if Sheikh Mohammed's colt had not contested the Classic.

On the Flat four of the most prestigious races must be seen as the Epsom Derby, Irish Derby, King George VI and Queen Elizabeth Diamond Stakes and the Prix de l'Arc de Triomphe in the order in which they are run during the season.

If one argues that the winning of one or more of this quartet has to be the basis in the final analysis for deciding the

151

ultimate ratings on respective trainers in the Top Six rankings, then Jim Bolger automatically qualifies because of his phenomenal achievement with St. Jovite, who not alone pulverised the opposition in a twelve-lengths victory in the Budweiser Irish Derby but left no doubt whatsoever about his superiority over the older horses in the King George and, if he had got the ground he required in the Arc, I believe he would have climaxed the 1992 season by adding this race to his laurels.

In Bolger's case it must be noted that he had nothing going for him when he started out initially as a trainer – he wasn't following in the footsteps of an established father. He had no contacts whatsoever when he began from his Clonsilla base. As one friend of his put it to me: "He was like somebody left on the top of a bleak mountain in his underpants."

He made it entirely on his own.

If another of the criteria in deciding the placings in the Top Six is the ability to withstand the pressures of the game over a long period, then no one can compare in this respect with Vincent O'Brien, who started out in 1943 and was still training a half a century later in the latter half of his seventies. If Vincent's son, David, had not decided to leave the heat of the kitchen and had added more Classic successes to the French and Irish Derby wins of Assert and the Epsom Derby victory of Secreto, he would now be vying in my book for a place ahead of Jim Bolger or Dermot Weld – but we are left to ponder what his genius would have contributed under the line "trained by David O'Brien" in the record books if he had chosen to continue. His decision to opt out was taken on purely personal and family grounds.

My own view of the Top Six is: 1, Vincent O'Brien; 2, "Darkie" Prendergast; 3, Tom Dreaper; 4, Dermot Weld; 5, Jim Bolger; 6 (shared), David O'Brien and Mickey Rogers.

I realise I will come in for strong criticism for omitting Paddy Sleator from the top six – but Sleator's record at international level in the major events in the National Hunt field did not compare with Jim Bolger's, Dermot Weld's, Mickey Rogers' and David O'Brien's on the Flat and they have to go in before him.

✿ ✿ ✿ ✿

Jim Bolger has reason to be proud of the fact that he put two champion apprentices – Kevin Manning and Billy Supple – through his hands and another in Seamus Heffernan who had hit an impressive total of winners by the summer of '94. And Bolger had reason to be proud also that Aidan O'Brien, crowned Irish National Hunt champion trainer in the 1993-'94 season is a protege of his.

Peter Scudamore spent the summer of 1979 with him just before he turned professional and went on to be English champion National Hunt jockey eight times, amassing a total of 1,677 wins during a distinguished career in the saddle that also saw him create a record for most wins in a season – 221.

It was as a result of his father's friendship with Eddie Harty and his own with John, who died so tragically of motor neurons disease, that Peter Scudamore joined Jim Bolger when he was training at Clonsilla and noted in his best-selling autobiography, titled simply *Peter Scudamore*, that "despite his reputation as a hard man, I got on very well with Jim, and found working for him a totally enlightening experience.

Scu noted also that Bolger was "a self-taught and brilliant trainer and a very industrious man – on both counts like Martin Pipe, another trainer for whom I was to gain a huge admiration later in my career – he knew his horses inside out. He timed their preparation to perfection and when at peak fitness a Bolger horse would often win a sequence of races in quick succession".

Scu's outstanding memory of his time with Jim Bolger is of riding his first and only winner on the Flat – Pigeon's Nest in the John Player Amateur Handicap at the Galway Festival meeting on 31 July 1979.

The hinge of fate turned in his favour on that occasion as Scudamore only got the ride as Jim Bolger, who had planned to ride the filly himself, found that he had to go to Goodwood to saddle a runner there.

The victory of Pigeon's Nest resulted in Scu leaving Ireland a week earlier than he had intended. It happened this way. After the race it was discovered that he had claimed a seven-pound allowance when he should have claimed five, because of the number of winners he had ridden.

"It was thought better that I slipped away to England and got myself out of sight and out of mind until it was too late for the authorities to disqualify me", he recalled.

Incidentally, Jim Bolger, fifteen years on, still has happy memories of the remarkable weight-carrying performance of Pigeon's Nest in the Fortwilliam Handicap Hurdle at Tipperary on 11 October 1979. She was allocated 13 stone. It resulted from the fact that she was hit with two penalties at one and the same time. However, with Brian Nolan claiming seven pounds she actually carried 12 st 7 lbs to a three-lengths victory.

Like his great rival, Dermot Weld, Jim Bolger has always maintained horses in his string that can keep things ticking over during the winter months, among them also dual performers who can compete on the Festival round in summer.

He has had the distinction of winning the Irish Champion Hurdle two years running – with the four-year-old Nordic Surprise for Eddie Kearns in 1991 (with Charlie Swan in the saddle this one scored at 10/1) and the five-year-old Chirkpar for Dr. Michael Smurfit in 1992.

The race looked destined for export in '92, the English challenge being led by the reigning champion, Morley Street, predictably the odds-on favourite. Morley Street had no difficulty joining the front-running Minorettes Girl before the last flight and when the mare blundered he came away looking an assured winner.

Be that as it may, Liam Cusack produced the five-year-old, Chirkpar with a powerful late run to pip Morley Street on the post, much to the delight of Dr. Michael Smurfit and Jim Bolger. Chirkpar started at 20/1.

It is interesting to note that when Morley Street, Chirkpar and Minorettes Girl met in the Smurfit Champion Hurdle at Cheltenham that same season, they were sixth, seventh and ninth respectively and subsequently Minorettes Girl ran Morley Street to half a length in Aintree's Martell Hurdle.

As his 53rd birthday approaches on Christmas Day 1994, it had to be acknowledged that he had left significant footprints on racing's sands of time.

Even when he was not commanding the headlines, he was at the heart of speculation and rumour, something he knew he could not control but he wasn't deterred from his single-mindedness of purpose as a trainer who maintained an impressive strike rate.

I put it to him straight that he was reputed to have lost a cool £1 million when GPA ran into difficulties (the basis of this story, circulating in racing and business circles, being that he had made this investment because his wife, Jackie, is a sister of Maurice Foley of GPA) but he did not blink as he responded: "My financial position is the same now as it was before these rumours ever began to circulate".

I pointed out to him that it wouldn't have mattered one iota to me personally if he had lost £1 million – his reputation as the Man Who Trained St. Jovite would still remain intact. Just as Vincent O'Brien's reputation survived the collapse of Classic Thoroughbreds.

Then Jim Bolger remarked significantly: "There are those who like to argue that much of Vincent O'Brien's success as a Flat trainer was due to the money power of the millionaires he had behind him after he moved to Ballydoyle. But I maintain that he would have been a success even if he was training on the top of a mountain".

You get to thinking much the same about Jim Bolger himself.

PART FOUR

DERMOT WELD

*Epoch-making Return to
Banjo Paterson Land*

9

Stunning Triumph in the Melbourne Cup

The tumult and the cheering had subsided in the wake of Vintage Crop's stunning and epoch-making victory in the 1993 Melbourne Cup.

And now the hard-bitten representatives of the Australian media had crowded into the post-race press conference. Eyebrows were immediately raised when Dermot Weld told them that his love of Australia went back to childhood days when he received a copy of Banjo Paterson's book, *The Man From Snowy River*.

The Australians thought initially that Weld was giving them a bit of the Irish barney but then a respectful silence descended on the assembled gathering when Dermot quoted confidently and easily from *A Bush Christening*:

On the outer Barcoo where the churches are few,
And men of religion are scanty,
On a road never cross'd 'cept by folk that are lost,
One Michael Magee had a shanty.

Three months on from that historic day in Melbourne, I sat with Dermot Weld in Rosewell House on the Curragh and he recalled for me exactly how he came to acquire his prized copy of *The Man From Snowy River*, which occupies a central place on the bookshelf in his study and he recalled also how he first learned to recite *A Bush Christening* when he was ten years old.

"My father trained a number of good horses for E. P. Douglas, who resided at South Lodge in South Tipperary

159

where later Adrian Maxwell had his stable. One Christmas he gave me a copy of Banjo Paterson's book of verse as a present. I fell in love with his ballads right away and it wasn't long before I could recite most of them.

"You know Banjo Paterson was the best-loved Australian poet of all time, the man who also wrote "Waltzing Matilda". He came from the outback and captured the true spirit of the outback – the real Australia – in his verse."

Dermot Weld came to appreciate the real significance of the poems in *The Man From Snowy River* when he spent a period as assistant trainer to the legendary T. J. (Tommy) Smith back in 1971. Incidentally, Smith's biography, *The Midas Touch*, was launched in Australia at the time Weld was making his bid for the Melbourne Cup, a book telling of the most famous coups landed by the Sydney-based trainer who was thirty-one times leading trainer in New South Wales. He had won the Melbourne Cup, of course, and, as fate would have it, his daughter, Gai Waterhouse – the first woman trainer to have a runner in Australia's most prestigious race – turned out the New Zealand-bred Te Akau Nick to finish runner-up to Vintage Crop.

Weld had sent out Go And Go to become the first European-trained horse to win a United States Classic when the colt took the Belmont Stakes, beating both the winners of the Kentucky Derby and the Preakness Stakes and in the process also he recorded the seventh fastest time ever recorded in the last of the American Triple Crown races.

But Weld knew deep down that in bidding for the Melbourne Cup he was seeking to conquer the highest mountain of all in international racing. It was as if all the seemingly unconquerable peaks had been rolled into one. It was akin to testing one's climbing skill and experience against a sheer ice face with no oxygen to fall back on. It was taking on a challenge that all the experts said was impossible and which the Australians most of all deemed beyond the scope of a horse from another hemisphere.

There was the 12,000-mile trans-world journey, the quarantine periods at both ends of the trip, the loss of 7 kilos that Vintage Crop suffered during the long flight and overshadowing everything else, the fact that the gelding was jumping right into the unknown in racing in another hemisphere. It all added up to a body of evidence that seemed to support the theory that the Irish-trained challenger could not pull it off.

When Michael Kinane swept past Te Akau Nick in the final furlong to go on for a highly-impressive three-lengths win over 23 rivals, it represented what the *Racing Post* aptly described as "quite simply the greatest achievement ever in international racing".

For on this first Tuesday in November '93 – November 2nd to be exact – a race that up to then had been farmed exclusively by Australian and New Zealand horses was suddenly cracked open to the world.

And the man who had revolutionised the scene overnight by his courage and initiative was Dermot Weld.

❀ ❀ ❀ ❀

Now he is telling me: "It never entered my head that this victory would make such an impact globally. In the countdown to the race itself I was totally caught up with ensuring that the horse was right and I had put everything else out of my head. The closer we got to the Tuesday the more people were saying to me that it was not a practical proposition to bring a horse this far and hope to lift the prize.

"When Vintage Crop did succeed, it made the post-race euphoria all the greater, especially among the big Irish community in Melbourne and Australia generally. Naturally, they saw it as a histsoric victory for Ireland and their joy was unbounded. I was particularly happy for giving them that day."

Weld preferred to dwell on the consequences for international racing than on his own role in planning for this victory over an 18-months span.

As far as the Melbourne Cup is concerned, matters will never be the same again. The trail blazed by Dermot Weld will be followed by others. The Maktoums have already set their eyes on winning the principal race in the Australian calendar, leading French trainers also while, of course, the Americans will not want to be outdone by the Europeans.

"We are coming to the end of the twentieth century," said Dermot Weld. "Many people tend to forget that fact. Huge strides were made in racing during this century. The Breeders' Cup series, which brought European horses into contention with the best in America was inaugurated, and I see this as only a beginning.

"I believe that inside ten to twenty years remarkable new advances will have been made on the international plane. There will be huge developments in cargo transportaion by air and this will influence dramatically the transportation of horses on a global scale.

"We will go beyond the Concorde era to the ultra-sonic age and London to Sydney will take less than what it takes now between Dublin and New York. A two-hour journey by air will be a long one. And that will be between hemispheres."

He could visualise the Breeders' Cup series expanding to become a global contest involving European, American and Australian and New Zealand horses – a battle between the hemispheres, the new Star Wars, as it were, of the racing stratosphere. Horses would then be handicapped on a global scale and all the ratings would be computerised.

He was convinced that Ireland could hold its place in the new era of challenge and change. "Our horses are better than anything to be found in Europe or any part of the world for that matter. Down the years we have produced wonderful trainers like Vincent O'Brien and the late "Darkie" Prendergast, who, remember, from his Curragh base was three years champion trainer in Britain in the early 1960s and that was a fabulous feat in itself.

"Vincent O'Brien's achievements both over the jumps and on the Flat put him on a special pedestal. Of the National Hunt trainers, I have always felt that Tom Dreaper and Paddy Sleator were really outstanding. I don't have to refer to the immortality Dreaper gained with horses like Arkle and Flying Bolt while Sleator broke new ground when he teamed up with Arthur Thomas and completely dominated the English scene for a time.

"I would say also that for a country of our size we have a tradition of horsemanship second to none. We have

162

produced a stream of jockeys both in the National Hunt and Flat spheres who have shown that they are tops.

"I believe quite firmly that the Irish racing public show a knowledge of racing that excells. It cannot be found anywhere else in the world to the same extent, excepting maybe among the more knowledgeable of English racing followers.

"Where we do lag behind countries like France, America and Australia is in the level of prize-money. And that is something that has got to be rectified if we are to keep pace eventually with the dramatic developments I envisage on the world stage."

Dermot Weld through Vintage Crop's success in the Melbourne Cup garnered £628,000 for owner Dr Michael Smurfit and translated into Australian dollars, it was a handicap race worth in all 2½ million dollars.

Dermot Weld is adamant on one point and that is that the Australians have "the best system in the world" when it comes to betting on-track and off-track.

"We are talking about a continent which, despite its size, has a population of only 18 million," he said. "I believe that their system is the only system. Because they have bookies on track – and I mean bookies who will take a bet of any size – while there are no bookies off-track.

"The mony taken off-course in what is a complete Tote operation is channelled back into racing and into boosting prize-money. The Australians then have the best of both worlds. They have the excitement of the ring by allowing bookies on-course and their 'rails' bookies are the best to be found anywhere. But instead of bookies creaming all the profits to be garnered from off-course betting, it's racing itself that benefits in Australia.

"It benefits first of all in the level of prize-money, far outstripping anything owners and trainers could dream of in this country; secondly, you see the results in the outstanding facilities for the racing public and, thirdly, entrance charges to racecourses and the various enclosures can be kept at a realistic low level, again helping to boost attendances."

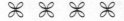

The weights for the 1993 Melbourne Cup were framed well before Vintage Crop won the Jefferson Smurfit Irish St. Leger. It meant that the gelding got in with a weight that ensured that he should beat a field of handicappers, granted he reproduced his Curragh form.

But if you were a betting man, you knew you could not "go to war" in the ring until you saw how Vintage Crop had recovered from the energy-sapping flight and how he adapted to his new surroundings.

The omens were not good as the Big Day approached. Drum Taps had settled in better and impressed the locals in a gallop at Flemington. The news filtered back to Ireland and Britain and, even though Vintage Crop had beaten him at the Curragh, the inspired money was now going on the English-trained challenger.

Vintage Crop – the loss of those 7 kilos the biggest worry – remained at the isolation centre at Sandown Park on the fringe of the city. As Tony O'Hehir reported: "The decision was to keep the powder dry and hope for better news."

On the Sunday morning – two days before the race itself – the tide began to turn. Vintage Crop goes a mile, ridden by his lad David Phillips. Dermot Weld is watching the training spin with his son Mark and Tony Smurfit, representing his father, who had business commitments in the States, and the owner's bloodstock manager, Dermot Cantillon. Weld can be seen smiling in the bright sunshine. The others are a lot happier also.

"He's coming right. He's beginning to roll. If I had another week with him I'd be confident," was Weld's reaction.

But there was another great imponderable – would Vintage Crop get the good ground on which he invariably acted best?

The rain came down over Melbourne on the eve of the race. Very heavy rain. Two of the Flemington car parks were flooded and couldn't be used. The going was declared "heavy". Would Vintage Crop's hopes be cruelly dashed even before Michael Kinane got him to the start?

However, "heavy" in Australian racing terminology is not "heavy" in the Irish sense. Tremendous relief in the Irish camp when it is learned that really it's more "yielding to soft", as we would know it. Weld believes his charge will handle it.

Vintage Crop has come right on the day history is there for the making. If J. P. McManus and Noel Furlong had been there they would have rocked the ring with this knowledge and so too would Terry Ramsden if he was around riding the range as he did in his betting heyday. I mean a Classic horse available at odds of 14/1 for a two-mile handicap and many of the Australian challengers very suspect on stamina for such a test.

As the field comes out for the Kentucky Derby at Churchill Downs, the vast crowd sings "My Old Kentucky Home" – a moment that makes the spine tingle.

Now at Flemington racecourse, Johnny Farnham, the popular Australian singer, launches into "Waltzing Matilda".

> *Once a jolly swagman camped by a billabong*
> *Under the shade of a coolabah tree*
> *And he sang as he watched and waited 'till his billy*
> > *boiled*
> *"Who'll come a waltzing Matilda with me?"*

Because of the weather and the gloomy forecast the attendance for the 1993 renewal was down to 75,000, where normally it would top the 100,000 mark. Many of Johnny Farnham's words are lost in the wind.

But always from this out when Dermot Weld hears the last verse of "Waltzing Matilda" he can be forgiven if he dances a jig in the privacy of his home or if his eyes mist over momentarily – just for the memories that can never fade from a day in a million.

> *"Waltzing Matilda, waltzing Matilda,*
> *Who'll come a waltzing Matilda with me?"*
> *And his ghost may be heard as you pass by that billabong*
> *"Who'll come a waltzing Matilda with me?"*

Yes, he had come and now he would conquer in Banjo Paterson land – conquer in a way that was as emotive for the thousands of Irish gathered at Flemington as it was as decisive in the thrilling late surge of Michael Kinane's victory sweep.

Dermot Weld replays the video of the race for me . . . noting that the only stage that he was really worried was when Vintage Crop, after a tardy start, had to make up ground in the first quarter of a mile, Kinane having to work to keep contact with the leaders.

But passing the post first time Kinane had him travelling smoothly, tracking Drum Taps. Vintage Crop was still ten lengths behind the leaders at the final bend but Kinane knew he had the goods under him.

Straightening for home, the Irish champion jockey, cool as a breeze when there is everything to play for and a world to lose, presses the button and Vintage Crop eats up the ground in a thrilling late run that sees the chestnut leave Te Akau Nick for dead in the last one hundred yards.

A great "Irish roar" erupted from the stands and enclosures. Now as a mud-bespattered but smiling Michael Kinane came back in on Vintage Crop, Dermot Weld slipped him a mini-Tricolour and he waved this to the Irish exiles who created victory scenes that outstripped anything in the history of Melbourne Cup Day. It was most moving of all for the long-term exiles who could never have contemplated that the Weld-Kinane partnership would give them such a happy link with the old land.

Among the first to congratulate Dermot Weld was Fr. Kevin Condon, who used to teach him in Newbridge College.

Tony O'Hehir noted in his report that David Phillips, Vintage Crop's closest friend – they call them "strappers" in Australia – had watched the race over a furlong from the finish. He wasn't sure the horse had won until he met a few photographers as he charged towards the action.

Phillips wasn't left out of the post-race presentations. He received the Tommy Woodcock Trophy, named after the "strapper" who looked after Australia's most famous racehorse, Phar Leap.

If Australian racing had been isolated – and insulated – from global challenges up to this day in November '93, this was no longer the case. A new era had dawned.

It had taken an Irish trainer of vision to internationalise the Melbourne Cup and open it up to the world. Yes, Weld acquainted with the significance of the outback in the Australian psyche through Banjo Paterson's verses, will always be remembered as the pioneer and those who were fortunate enough to be part of the day in Melbourne when he effected the great breakthrough will always cherish the memory.

Again he noted that he never thought it would create such headlines in the world's racing press. "The consequences of one race never entered my mind. I could never have foreseen all that would evolve from that one success."

He came home to a heart-warming reception . . . and to an accolade from the Taoiseach, Albert Reynolds, speaking for the Irish nation.

It didn't end there. He returned to Australia in the Spring of '94 to receive the Australian Sports Personality of the Year Award.

While he was away, Fortune And Fame, favourite for the Smurfit Champion Hurdle, was cast in his box. The gelding was withdrawn on the morning of the race and those who had backed him ante-post at all odds from 40/1 down could only smile ruefully and tear up their dockets.

At Cheltenham on the Tuesday, Dr Michael Smurfit was gracious and sporting as he said to me: "That's racing. We have enjoyed more good luck than bad. If it was a novice hurdle, perhaps we could have taken a chance and run him today but not in the Champion Hurdle. There will be another day."

The memory of the historic Melbourne Cup triumph helped in its own way to ease the pain of the withdrawal of Fortune And Fame.

Many an owner would give his right hand to have known the moment Dermot Weld had created for Michael Smurfit on a day in November '93 Down Under.

10

Go And Go's Historic Win
in the Belmont Stakes

They described Dermot Weld as being in the Columbus mould when he scored a unique and historic win on a dirt surface with Go And Go in the 1990 Belmont Stakes, the third of the American Triple Crown races.

But that pioneering success – making him the first European trainer to win an American Classic – had already been presaged when the same colt scored an equally-historic triumph by landing the £100,000 Grade Two Laurel Futurity at Laurel in October, 1989. The son of Coolmore's Be My Guest thus became the first Irish-trained or British-trained two-year-old to win in America. What is more, this tremendous breakthrough success was recorded on dirt and it had an extra significance in that Dermot Weld became the first Irish trainer to top £1 million in prize-money in a year.

If ever there was an instance of an ill wind blowing good for someone, then Dermot Weld had reason to remember always the old Irish saying when it rained cats and dogs at Laurel and it appeared initially that his hopes of landing this prestigious back-end mile race for two-year-olds had been sunk in the waterlogged turf track. For the Laurel executive decided that they had no other option but to switch the Futurity to dirt.

Weld had chosen the Laurel Futurity specifically as Go And Go's target on the basis that the colt would get the fast ground he needed to be seen at his best. He calculated at the same time that not many of the top American two-year-olds would, at that stage, be used to running on turf.

When the rains came down they made the surface on the dirt track sloppy. But "wet" or "sloppy" on American dirt does not mean the same as "soft" on an Irish racecourse.

Indeed, John Oaksey in his *Racing Post* column would describe it as akin to "galloping along a main road covered with a few inches of Brown Windsor soup".

A top-of-the-ground horse could handle the "soup", so to speak, as long as he did not mind it being flung in his face. Later when it came to the Belmont Stakes, Dermot Weld took the tactical advice of Bill Shoemaker, who told both Michael Kinane and himself to keep the horse's nose stuck right up the tail of the one in front, the legendary American jockey explaining that if Go And Go were to lie a length or even a half-a-length behind, he could expect to find himself galloping unprotected into a blizzard of filth.

With that advice and a visor to help, Go And Go was never troubled by the Brown Windsor soup!

But back to the Futurity. It was only part of the drama that the race had to be switched at the eleventh hour to dirt.

As Weld himself explained to me: "It was touch and go whether my colt ran at all. He bruised a foot when standing on something sharp two days before the race but, fortunately, he responded to treatment.

"His lad, Tony Flanagan, deserved the highest commendation for his efforts with Go And Go. He carried out my instructions to the letter up to the time I arrived myself in the States."

American jockey Craig Perrett stood in for Michael Kinane because Kinane was riding for Weld at the Curragh on the Saturday.

Go And Go handled the unfamiliar dirt surface with elan, beating a competitive field by a neck and ten lengths. He went on to finish eighth in the Breeders' Cup Juvenile.

From the time he worked as a track veterinarian at Belmont Park, Dermot Weld had always harboured a dream – to bring a colt over some day to bid for an American Classic and if it was not possible to attain the target of winning the

Kentucky Derby, then the Belmont Stakes, a really true twelve-furlong test, attracted him greatly.

Clive Brittain had blazed a trail by going for the Kentucky Derby with Bold Arrangement in 1986 and the English trainer deserved the greatest credit for that bold challenge, even though the colt had to settle for runner-up prize. A pathfinding bid to prove to the world that European horseflesh was superior to American had been made by the 1923 Epsom Derby winner, Papyrus when he took on Zev, the Kentucky Derby and Belmont Stakes winner in a match at Belmont Park but was slaughtered for his pains.

⌘ ⌘ ⌘ ⌘

Dermot Weld knew after the Laurel Futurity triumph that Go And Go could go on dirt and it was now decided to lay him out for an ambitious American programme. "It was very much on my mind to make a bid for the Kentucky Derby", recalled Dermot, "but our plans in that respect were knocked on the head for two reasons. First, wet weather made it extremely difficult to have horses forward in the early part of the Spring and, second, travelling and quarantine problems virtually ruled out any possibility of making it to Chuchill Downs. So we put all our concentration into the Belmont Stakes".

Go And Go wasn't rushed. He won a Listed Race over a mile at the Phoenix Park on his reappearance as a three-year-old and, while the winning margin was only half-a-length, Weld noted that it bore no relevance to his superiority over the rest of the field.

Next he finished fourth behind Anvari and Dovekie in the Derrinstown Derby Trial at Leopardstown. "I couldn't accept the outcome as his true form and that is why I decided to put a visor on him for his next race. Up to that point also, I had been very easy on him but I was convinced that he was a much better horse than he had shown and that now we had to start serious work with himn", Weld told me.

On the Saturday before the Belmont Stakes Go And Go worked with a visor on for the first time – a very strong piece of work on the grass up Walsh's Hill on the Curragh, a stiff ten furlongs.

"We had two seven-furlong horses to cut out the early pace and then a couple of other decent horses to take him on from there. He was impressive, working right away from them.

"I had no doubt then that he had improved considerably since the Derrinstown Derby Trial and also that the visor helped him to keep his mind on the job. That was the only long piece of work he did between the two races. All his other work was over five or six furlongs."

With the meticulous approach of a born professional, Weld was overlooking nothing. He even gave Go And Go a swim, then weighed him and took a detailed blood count.

Everything was spot on. And Go And Go before he left the Rosewell House stable on the first leg of his long journey was unquestionably the picture of an athlete in perfect trim for the task ahead.

But deep down Weld realised that the fitness attained on the Curragh gallops would not suffice if Go And Go came badly out of the trip to the States and failed to acclimatise when he got there. The very same worries would, of course, arise three years later when he sent Vintage Crop to make his historic bid for the Melbourne Cup.

No longer a worry, as we have seen, was Go And Go's ability to act on a dirt surface. Indeed, it was quite obvious that he preferred dirt to turf. He had only been given a rating of 110 in the 1989 International Classification – 15 lbs below Machiavellian. The enormous improvement he made from two to three was not achieved on grass but when he again hit a dirt surface in the Belmont.

John Oaksey asked the Jockey Club's Senior Handicapper, Geoffrey Gibbs if a colt could achieve such abnormal improvement when switching from one surface to the other and the answer was in the affirmative. As Oaksey noted: "The different surfaces have been known to make as much as 18 lbs difference between dirt and turf in the States and between turf and all-weather in Britain".

Weld knew that Go And Go answered in the strength of his legs what was essential to stand the strain of racing on dirt. "They must be very, very sound – good forelegs and most important of all, well-made feet".

171

He knew also that Go And Go had an outstanding temperament and his '89 trip to the States had revealed that he loved travelling and never turned a hair during a long flight.

But this was not going to be a direct flight from Shannon to New York. Go And Go travelled first by road from the Curragh to Shannon Airport, then by air to Paris where there was a change of planes. By the time he got to the quarantine area at Aqueduct racecourse in New York, twenty-four hours in all had elapsed.

During the flight he actually got through 20 lbs of nuts and drank all the water he was offered. "He never left a nut from the time he got his first meal", Raymond Carroll, then second jockey to the Weld stable would recall. "He'd eat what you gave him in ten minutes and then whinny for more. What he got through during that journey was enormous by any standards. And he drank half a bucket of water every time it was offered to him. He didn't dehydrate. In fact, he never batted an eyelid either on take-off or landing".

✾ ✾ ✾ ✾

Came the day of the Belmont Stakes. That morning, by special permission, Go And Go had a canter round the Aqueduct track with Michael Kinane in the saddle. He was so well in himself that he was bucking out of his skin.

He got to Belmont Park around mid-day. Now he faced a problem he had not faced when racing in Ireland, where the horses come into the parade ring beforehand and the media attention arises when one had come back into the No. 1 spot, especially on big race days.

The television cameras were on Go An Go from the moment he hit the barn area and, leaving aside the race writers, the most banal questions can be asked in the States by those doing "quickies" for the newscasts on the various T.V. networks or feature writers, who normally cover baseball, basketball or American football and switch to doing specials just for the Triple Crown events.

At one stage Dermot Weld had to tell the television film crews to back off – "to allow the horse and myself a bit of room".

"Normally the very essence of relaxation, Go And Go had a tendency to get tense as a race approached and became a bit of a handful with the crowds pressing in on him. But once Michael Kinane got on board and he was heading for the start, he was back to his old relaxed self", said Dermot Weld.

Dermot Weld's biggest worry was the going, which he saw as "muddy", though the *Daily Racing Form* rated it "good". He felt that Go And Go might find it more difficult to handle than the sloppy conditions he faced at Laurel the previous autumn.

But American breeding experts, seeking to set his mind at ease, told him that Go And Go's sire, Be My Guest, was by Northern Dancer and the latter was never unduly perturbed by a muddy track.

Go And Go, who came in from 12/1 to 7½/1 before the off, held a handy position in fifth place in the early stages of the race, Michael Kinane, riding superbly, saving ground from the inside draw. After a mile he had moved into third place behind Thirty Six Red and Baron de Vaux, the early leader, the Kentucky Derby favourite, Unbridled, having been ridden to conserve his stamina.

Entering the straight, it was clear that Kinane was in total command and once he pressed the button and asked Go And Go the question, the colt quickened away in magnificent style to win by eight-and-a-quarter lengths from Thirty Six Red with Baron de Vaux two lengths further away third and Unbridled in fourth place, two-and-a-half lengths adrift of the third horse home.

Unbridled had loomed up menacingly to the leaders turning into the stretch but his challenge faded as quickly as it had begun and the verdict was that he did not get the testing Belmont mile-and-a-half (the Belmont Stakes is a quarter-mile more than the Kenturky Derby). Then too it must be remembered that Unbridled was running that day without his customary dose of medication – Lasix in this instance. In New York medication is allowed only up to 48 hours before a race.

Did the fact that he was prevented from having that dose of Lasix make any real difference to Unbridled's performance? John Oaksey pointed out in the *Racing Post* that a series of tests had shown that Lasix not only "allows a horse to achieve his full potential" but may also improve him by several pounds.

There were those who claimed in the aftermath of Go And Go's spreadeagling Belmont Stakes triumph that it was not a vintage year on the American three-year-old scene, that there was nothing to be even mentioned in the same breath as Secretariat or Affirmed. In a word, it was a sub-standard season.

But that in no way can take from the authority with which Go And Go won this Classic or from Dermot Weld's courage in opting to take on the leading American colts rather than bid for the Irish Derby, for which he was also entered. As that most respected of American racing writers, Dan Farley, put it in his report for the *Racing Post*: "Dermot Weld was rightly elated that his daring decision to challenge for the prize had paid off so handsomely".

"Sensational" was how Farley – a man not given to easy praise – described Go And Go's runaway win and Michael Kinane summed up afterwards: "Once I saw Unbridled in trouble on my outside, I knew we could win".

Incidentally, Kinane was presented with a car and when asked how he would get it back to Ireland, he quipped: "I'm more concerned about how I'll get it converted to right-hand drive!"

In the euphoria of the Belmont Stakes success, it was hard to believe that Go And Go's first win as a two-year-old was achieved over seven furlongs at Galway on 31 July 1989. He started evens favourite in a field of sixteen. He followed that up by winning over the same distance at the Curragh the following month, starting joint favourite at 2/1, though he was beaten into seventh place in the Group One National Stakes on his final outing of the season in September.

❁ ❁ ❁ ❁

Dermot Weld was returning, as we have seen, to the land of Banjo Paterson, to the land where he had spent time as assistant trainer to Tommy Smith in the early seventies, when Vintage Crop brought off that epoch-making triumph in the 1993 Melbourne Cup.

174

And it was with a sense of nostalgia for times past that he had returned to New York three years earlier for the Belmont Stakes.

You might say that he knew every blade of grass at Belmont Park and at Acqueduct also.

Weld is proud of his New York connections. "My grand-uncle emigrated from Ireland and set up a bar in New York", he recalled. "His name was Sidney Weld and he was from County Kildare.

"He became President of the Kildaremen's Association in New York and was a personality in Irish-American circles."

The name of the bar? "Oh, I forget but I do know that his apartment was at 2160 Newbold Avenue in The Bronx".

It was back in the late sixties that he first got acquainted with Belmont Park, Acqueduct and the American racing scene generally. It evolved from a tacit understanding he reached with his father, the late Charlie Weld, a popular, respected and successful trainer in his own right, though he did not attain the international status of Paddy "Darkie" Prendergast and Vincent O'Brien.

Dermot Weld, who came into the world on 28 July 1948, was born into the racing game and bred to the training profession. But his father showed no great enthusiasm to see him following in his footsteps. Indeed, he made it abundantly clear to Dermot from the beginning that he would be happier to see him making his career in another field, as few knew better the constant pressures and pitfalls of the trainer's life.

So it was agreed that Dermot would study to be a veterinary surgeon and, on completion of his studies, they could then assess whether the amibition still burned in his soul to become a trainer. His father was happy with this compromise solution.

Before he actually graduated from University College, Dublin – becoming at 21 the youngest vet in the world – Dermot Weld spent a time working in New York with Dr. Bill Reed as an assistant at Belmont Park and Acqueduct. "I did all the menial jobs but I was learning all the time", he recalled with a laugh.

He went back to serve a second stint with Dr. Reed after he had received his degree. Few think of him today as one

175

who was ever interested in gaelic games – unlike Jim Bolger, who is recognised as a avid hurling man – but during his tenure in New York, he spent many happy Sunday afternoons in Gaelic Park with his uncle and a friend named Christy Burke.

He rode his first winner at the age of 15 and was already beginning to make his mark as an amateur rider at the age of 16 in bumpers (Flat races under National Hunt rules for potential hurdlers and chasers). In the very week back in 1964 that he celebrated his sixteenth birthday and received word from his school, Newbridge College, that he had passed his matriculation examination, he rode his father's charge, Ticonderoga to victory in the Player Wills Amateur Handicap (2 mile) at the opening stage of the Galway Festival meeting.

Ticonderoga went off at 100/7 but upset a gamble on the favourite, Running Rock, coming home a clear two-and-a-half lengths winner with Diritto, the second favourite, taking third place.

"Ticonderoga raced up to Running Rock in the dip and the pair were disputing the iussue on the sweeping turn into the straight. As they headed for home, Ticonderoga responded well to Mr. Weld's polished riding to run out a highly praise-worthy winner. Young Mr. Weld fully deserved the many congratulations showered upon him after the race", wrote the writer in the *Irish Field*.

Dermot Weld won this highly-competitive event and one that is invariably a tremendous betting race four times in all. He rode Mrs. M. T. Jackson's Spanner to victory as a five-year-old in 1972 and scored again on the same horse the following year. Then in 1975 Spanner, now an eight-year-old, justified 2/1 favouritism.

Weld also won the Player-Wills Amateur Hurdle at Leopardstown. He had the distinction of being champion Irish amateur rider three years running (1969, '71 and '72).

His successes in the saddle were not confined to Ireland alone. "While I was in New York as a vet, I went down to Camden in South Carolina where the Colonial Cup is run and rode the winner of a big amateur race on the programme", he recalled. He also rode winners in France and South Africa and took the Moet & Chandon Trophy at Epsom.

After his historic achievement in training Go An Go to win the 1990 Belmont Stakes, John Oaksey, himself an outstanding amateur rider, paid Dermot this tribute in the *Racing Post*: "He took a cosmopolitan view of racing long before he set up as a trainer. One of several occasions I wearily pursued him home was in Pietermaritzburg. The locals had unwisely put on a two-mile hurdle race in stifling tropical heat and I remember Dermot, who was already training as a vet, taking much more interest in the condition of four horses who collapsed after pulling up than in the winner he had ridden".

And adding this note to his pioneering spirit in bidding for the Belmont Stakes, he wrote, "He and Columbus would have had a lot in common".

⌘ ⌘ ⌘ ⌘

By the time he returned to Ireland after that stint with Tommy Smith in Australia, Dermot Weld was ready to get involved in the one and only career he wanted to pursue – training. By now his father had resigned himself to that fact and realised that it was useless trying to discourage his son any longer.

Dermot, in fact, spent a year as assistant trainer to his father. He was fortunate that it was a stable accustomed to success and so the winning philosophy was ingrained in him from the outset.

Charlie Ward turned out Farney Fox to win the Irish Lincolnshire Handicap in 1960 and the same horse had won the Naas November Handicap the previous year with Jimmy Mullane in the saddle. He trained Courtwell to win the Irish Cambridgeshire at 100/8 in 1965 and Arctic Kanda the Irish Cesarewitch in 1963 and Say The Word won this same race for him in 1965.

He again won the Naas November Handicap with Honest Injun in 1968 and with Boreen in 1971, the latter carrying 9-2 to victory as a three-year-old. And he won the Leopardstown November Handicap with Beaurette in 1963.

Say The Word and Honest Injun were both owned by E. P. Douglas, the man who gave Dermot Weld his copy of Banjo Peterson's *The Man From Snowy River*.

Other good winners trained by Charlie Weld were: Eucalyptus (1970 Ballymoss Stakes); Right Strath (1963 Phoenix two-year-old Stakes); Wily Trout (1963 Desmond Stakes); Cynthella (1954 Rockingham Stakes); Greenogan (1960 Rockingham Stakes); Pavella (1966 Madrid Free Handicap); Market Square (1969 Madrid Free Handicap) and Decies (1969 National Stakes). Incidentally, Decies won the 1970 Irish 2,000 Guineas in the hands of Lester Piggott when trained by Bernard van Cutsem.

Dermot Weld rejects any suggestion that he was born with a silver spoon in his mouth. "My mother and father both worked very hard and I was brought up to respect the work ethic. If I have been successful I put it down to constant effort".

That respect for the "work ethic" was evident even during his school days. Former school-mates of his in Newbridge College will tell you that he was a very bright pupil, one who was particularly good at English and at one point he entered – and won – an essay competition that drew entries from all parts of Ireland. He loved English literature and poetry.

The bookshelves in Rosewell House are the clearest pointer to his love of books and he has listed "reading" as one of his recreations in *The Turf Directory*.

While he likes music also, he admits with a laugh to being a "total crow" when it comes to singing, though at the same time he is naturally very proud of the fact that his eldest son, Mark, who has a very good baritone voice, has graduated to the Irish Youth Choir.

Weld acknowledges that his parents were very supportive of him when he started out on his own as a trainer – it was in 1972 that he got his licence – and did everything to advance his career.

Dermot has always given a special place to his mother whenever she has been present to share a major moment of triumph with him. And he owns the 300-acre Pipers Hill Stud in partnership with her.

In the same year that he began to train on his own on the Curragh he was married – on 25 November 1972 to be exact – and every racing correspondent and writer who has visited Rosewell House will vouch for Mary's very personable and pleasing manner and the relaxed atmosphere of hospitality she instantly creates. She has undoubtedly been a wonderful support to Dermot. And she has the very happy knack of doing it all in an unobtrusive way.

Dermot Weld has always operated in the top league and even before he had passed his first decade as a trainer, he was numbering among his patrons the leading American real estate figures, Bert and Diana Firestone, also newspaper magnate, Joe L. Albritton of the *Washington Post*, the Smurfit brothers, Michael and Jeff and Sir Cecil Boyd Rochfort.

He would also train for Allen Paulson and for Walter Haefner, owner of the Moyglare Stud; and the Moyglare Dinner in the Berkeley Court Hotel, hosted by the Haefners in December each year, is without question the most glittering social occasion of the racing calendar.

In recent years also Dermot Weld has been the principal trainer on the Flat in this country of the horses owned by Dr. Tony O'Reilly of the Heinz Corporation and Independent Newspapers while he also trains for Sheikh Mohammed and Sheikh al Maktoum. And he trains a filly for the President of Ireland, Mrs. Mary Robinson.

One of his most faithful patrons and closest friends has been Frank Conroy. Ray Rooney of Galway, the man who owned the ill-fated Golden Cygnet, is also a prominent patron of the stable. And one of the most popular successes on the opening day of the 1992 Galway Festival meeting was that of Ray Rooney's Arabian Treasure who won the two-year-old event. Ray Rooney, incidentally, is a long-standing member of the Galway Race Committee.

Three years after he got his licence, Dermot Weld took the Pretty Polly Stakes with Miss Toshiba, carrying Robert Sangster's colours and ridden by Johnny Roe. The previous year Klairvimy, carrying 9-13, had won the Royal Whip.

Weld won the Irish Lincolnshire Handicap with 25/1 shot, Shaw Park in 1978 and the Naas November Handicap (Division Two) with French Lane in 1977.

But it was in 1981 that he had his first big success outside of Ireland – Blue Wind triumphed in the English Oaks.

He was really on his way to the top of the ladder after that singular success. . . .

179

11

Blue Wind Gives Weld His
First Classic Success

"**A** true champion" was how Dermot Weld would describe Blue Wind, who gave the Curragh trainer his first Classic success when sweeping to a majestic seven-lengths victory in the 1981 English Oaks in a time that was almost four seconds faster than that credited to the ill-fated Shergar in the Derby on the Wednesday.

Controversy surrounded the victory in that Lester Piggott had been engaged over Walter Swinburn, who was on Blue Wind at the Curragh on Irish 1,000 Guineas Day when she earned her ticket to Epsom by running Arctique Royale to a short-head in a photo finish.

Asked about the jocking off of Swinburn, all Weld would say in the winner's enclosure at Epsom was: "I don't want to comment on the switch of jockeys. I booked Lester ten days ago."

He added: "Blue Wind is my first runner in the Oaks and she has given me my first Classic success. I've had some fast fillies but this one is very good."

Ice-cool Piggott, who was winning his fifth Oaks, said: "She did it very easily." Asked if Blue Wind was the best of his Oaks winners, he replied: "No, that was Petite Etoile."

In opting for Piggott, Weld was being coldly professional in his approach by ensuring that he had in the saddle on Blue Wind on the day that was going to mean a lot to him as a trainer a man who knew the Epsom gradients like the back of his hand, and who had no peer when it came to producing an inspired ride at the death – if it came to that – as he had shown for Vincent O'Brien on Roberto and The Minstrel.

Weld was not one to indulge in sentiment when he was tilting at the major prizes. Later we would see how he was prepared to engage Adrian Maguire to ride General Idea in the 1993 Digital Galway Plate, he had been so impressed by the manner in which Maguire rode Second Schedual to beat Dr. Michael Smurfit's gelding in a great battle from the last at Cheltenham in March of the same year – and Maguire duly delivered.

Walter Swinburn may have been disappointed at being denied the chance of making it a unique and memorable family double at Epsom in '81 as Walter, of course, was the hero of Shergar's scintillating Derby triumph.

But Swinburn Snr. was back on Blue Wind when on Saturday, 18 July 1981, she became the first Irish-trained filly to complete the English-Irish Oaks double. Starting at 4/6 she won in emphatic style from Condessa and Stracomer Queen with Arctique Royale, her conqueror in the Irish 1,000 Guineas, finishing sixth.

"She was always going well and, once I went clear, she had everything beaten," said Walter Swinburn.

It was the second year in succession that a filly had given Bert and Diana Firestone moments of singular triumph. For in 1980 their Genuine Risk had become the first filly to win the Kentucky Derby in sixty-five years.

A daughter of Irish National Stud stallion, Lord Gayle, Blue Wind was bred by Miss E. C. Laidlaw, County Dublin.

She was bought at Goffs Sales in the Autumn of 1980 for Mrs Diana Firestone and joined the Weld stable at a cost of 180,000 guineas.

She proved her worth in double quick time, being a winner first time out as a three-year-old over a mile at the Phoenix Park in the 1981 season. And then followed that highly-promising performance in the Irish 1,000 Guineas.

The sky seemed the limit for Blue Wind after her brilliant English Oaks triumph followed by her success in the Irish

Oaks, making her the only Irish-trained filly to complete the Classic double.

The ultimate target of that '81 season was going to be the Prix de l'Arc de Triomphe and it was thought that she might take in the Yorkshire Oaks and either the Irish or English St. Leger on the way.

As it happened, she started 2/1 favourite for the Joe McGrath Memorial Stakes (Group I) at Leopardstown on Saturday, September 19, but could only finish fourth behind the Vincent O'Brien-trained King's Lake, who had been awarded the Irish 2,000 Guineas in very controversial circumstances after initially being disqualified and placed second when beating English challenger, To Agori Mou by a neck (in the St. James's Palace Stakes, To Agori Mou had reversed the Curragh finish when winning by a neck).

Blue Wind went on to finish fifteenth in the Prix de l'Arc de Triomphe, seven lengths ahead of King's Lake. The race was won by the Alec Head-trained Gold River (G. W. Moore) from Bikala and April Run.

Dermot Weld said that Blue Wind had had a very busy summer campaign and the edge was gone when the ground came up very soft at Longchamp.

❅ ❅ ❅ ❅

Asked in the count-down to Go And Go's bid for the Belmont Stakes to name some of his favourite horses, Dermot Weld named three for John Manley of the *Irish Echo* – namely Blue Wind, "a true champion", Committed, who was a champion sprinter, winning the Prix de l'Abbaye at Longchamp two years running, and of the colts, Theatrical.

Dermot Weld won the Irish 1,000 Guineas with Prince's Polly (Walter Swinburn) in 1982 and when he won again in 1988 with Trusted Partner, Michael Kinane was now the No. 1 jockey to the stable.

The Weld-Kinane partnership was to evolve into one of the most successful in the history of racing. It is a tribute to Weld's understanding of how to deal with such a special talent – and not an easy one at that – and of Kinane's respect in turn for the Master of Rosewell House that when Sheikh

Mohammed made the kind of offer that many thought Kinane could not refuse, he chose instead to remain as No. 1 to the Curragh trainer while getting the best of two other worlds at the same time. He had a lucrative contract to ride in Hong Kong in the winter, returning to Ireland in April and he also got plum rides for the Sheikh and others during the Flat season in Britain, France and Italy. Weld was willing to release him to accept these rides when it did not interfere with the Rosewell House operation.

Kinane's big-race triumphs in 1993 included the Epsom Derby on Commander In Chief for Henry Cecil and the Coral Eclipse Stakes on Opera House for Michael Stoute, after Sheikh Mohammed's retained jockey, Michael Roberts, opted to ride Barathea.

Strangely enough, the Epsom Derby and Budweiser Irish Derby are two major Classics that have so far eluded Dermot Weld, which becomes rather ironic when you reflect on his pioneering successes in the Belmont Stakes and the Melbourne Cup.

The closest he came to winning the Irish Derby was when Theatrical was beaten by the Vincent O'Brien-trained Law Society in 1985. Michael Kinane was on Theatrical that day as he carried the famous green and white diamond livery of the Firestones. Pat Eddery was on Law Society.

"That was a first-rate Derby field and Theatrical was only caught close home by Law Society," recalled Weld. "They were very good horses, covering the last two furlongs in 22 seconds."

The half-length margin at the finish shows the thin dividing line between success and failure in a Derby.

When Theatrical moved to the States, where he was trained by Bill Mott, he won the Breeders' Cup Turf and, developing into one of the best turf horses in the States, amassing about 2.9 million dollars in total winnings.

Weld noted that he was a highly-strung horse who required a lot of understanding in his younger days – "but patience paid dividends".

"I believe that had Theatrical started his racing career in the States rather than in Ireland, he might never have seen a racecourse at all," he went on. "He suffered from claustrophobia in his early days when it came to starting stalls and it took an amount of work to try and get over that problem. It was a case of developing his confidence. If we had pushed him, he would probably have turned sour and that would have been that.

"I believe that we give horses a better chance mentally than is the case in the States. Most horses in the States, outside of the real turf specialists, train exclusively on dirt surfaces and leg ailments, especially shin problems, are very frequent."

He told one American journalist that he was proud to say that 99% of his horses were 100% sound. "If I have a two-year-old with a shin problem it is a rarity whereas in the States it rears its head all the time. It can be tragic to see potential champions ending up as crocks because patience was not the motto when handling them."

Weld has very clear and definite views when you turn the topic of conversation to the Breeders' Cup series. He is totally opposed to the idea of running these races at tracks in Florida and California as it does not give a fair chance to the European challengers. "I would only run them in Belmont Park or Woodbine in Canada," he said. "The heat and humidity, for example, in Florida can kill the prospects of the European horses even before they get to the starting stalls and then you can get a track with bends that mean that if a horse is not up with the pace from the outset, he will not figure in the finish.

"Belmont is an excellent track with a long straight that gives every possible chance to the best horse on the day to prove his or her merit. It was no mere coincidence that Royal Academy triumphed for Vincent O'Brien here where he might not have had a fair chance to succeed at a track in Florida or California. No, I maintain that if we are going to have fair contests between American and European horses in the Breeders' Cup races, the only course to adopt is to select the tracks on the basis that the European horses will not be facing obstacles that are well-nigh insurmountable."

As dawn breaks over the Curragh plain, they will already be moving to man battle-stations in the Weld stable. Indeed, one man will already have completed his stint and that will be the night watchman, whose job it is to carry out an hourly inspection of the boxes.

Long-serving Head Man, Joe Malone, an integral part of the success of the stable, will have arrived by 6 a.m., overseeing another morning of hectic activity from the feeding to the preparation of the various lots who will go out to the gallops between 7 a.m. and midday. Up to 45 work riders ride out with the Weld strings.

It's a massive operation between the main yard at Rosewell House (100 boxes) and the 100-acre Rathbride Stud (50 boxes) about a mile away where the fillies and backward colts are housed. Rathbride Stud was formerly owned by the late Mickey Rogers, who had the distinction of training Hard Ridden to win the 1958 Epsom Derby and Santa Claus to take both the Epsom Derby and Irish Derby in 1964. In a quiet corner in Rathbride Stud an inscribed granite headstone marks the spot where Rogers chose to bury Santa Claus.

I have been there in the early morning in the count-down to a Classic or other big race, as Dermot Weld casts his eye over the string exercising on the all-weather gallop. Everything in this stable is timed with an exactness that shows again his attention to detail.

Indeed, getting everything completed to a planned programme and precision timing is mandatory rather than optional in such a large stable.

Weld is fortunate that he has T. P. Burns as his assistant trainer. Burns, a pupil of the ultimate "Master", Vincent O'Brien himself, has a depth of knowledge and experience that is awesome. You reflect on the golden era when he was associated with some of Vincent O'Brien's finest triumphs in the Gloucestershire Hurdle at Cheltenham; you reflect also on his riding of Ballymoss to victory in the Irish Derby and St. Leger of 1957 and how he was for seven years assistant trainer at Ballydoyle before coming to Rosewell House.

I remember when I was doing my research for the biography of Vincent O'Brien, *The Master of Ballydoyle*, T. P. telling me that what impressed him always was Vincent's "wonderful grasp of the whole business of training. His insight was phenomenal, his patience quite extraordinary. It meant nothing to him to earmark a horse in his charge for a target a year ahead, maybe even longer. It was no trouble to him to put away a horse when he was going for bigger things.

"He was ahead of his time all the time, yes, a step ahead of the others. I rode for him a lot over a period of nearly twenty years, though not on a retainer for the stable. The stable had to gamble. The money in jumping in those days was peanuts compared with the prize-money today for the major events. I rode five to victory in the Gloucestershire Hurdle. They were all gambled on without exception. You knew the money was down. When there is gambling, there is always pressure. You felt the pressure. And, believe me, the pressure was far greater then, far more intense than when Vincent was turning out Derby winners for wealthy owners."

❊   ❊   ❊   ❊

With the kind of money garnered from Go And Go's triumph in the Belmont Stakes and Vintage Crop's success in the Melbourne Cup, Dermot Weld certainly doesn't have to gamble to survive.

But while we do not think of his stable as a gambling one, as we would think of some shrewd small trainer "down the country", Weld loves a tilt at the ring and gets immense pleasure out of delivering.

The big English bookies squirm still at the thought of how he hit them where it hurts most when Vintage Crop was the subject of a major gamble down to 5/1 from 25/1 when winning the 1992 English Tote Cesarewitch by eight lengths under 9-6 and you can easily realise how the gelding became one of the easiest winners in the history of this event when you measure the task he had that day with his winning of the Irish St. leger in '93. In effect, a future Classic winner taking on a field of handicappers!

The period taking in December '91 to November '94 became a high water-mark in the career of Dermot Weld – a

186

period that had some really memorable moments across the international spectrum.

At Sha Tin racecourse in Hong Kong on Sunday, 14 December 1991, before an attendance of 84,000 with another 40,000 looking at the race on the giant screen at the Happy Valley track, Irish champion jockey Michael Kinane left his rivals stunned as he came from the tail of the field with a sweeping run in the straight – a magnificent piece of timing – on Additional Risk to beat an international field at odds of 13/1.

The Thursday before that Sha Tin success Dermot Weld was at Clonmel to saddle a number of runners, Pippi's Pet winning the Ladbroke Handicap Hurdle for him. Then he took a plane home from Hong Kong on the Tuesday, arriving back on Wednesday and was at Fairyhouse the same afternoon – as if jet lag was something for the birds!

In May of '92 he won the Derby Italiano (Italian Derby) with It's A Tiff.

Then followed one of his finest achievements of the '92 Flat season in turning out Brief Truce to win the St. James's Palace Stakes at Royal Ascot at 25/1 in the hands of Mick Kinane with Rodrigo De Triano fourth and Arazi fifth.

In the Breeders' Cup Mile (Turf), Brief Truce, after being last away and losing a lot of ground, put in a fine finish – again ridden by Mick Kinane – to take third place, beaten three lengths and a neck, earning ST$63,830 in the process.

Dermot Weld, who is not easily given to fulsome praise, rates Kinane unhesitatingly as "the best Flat jockey in the world" while of Adrian Maguire he says: "He is unquestionably the best over the jumps at the present time."

General Idea, in the hands of Adrian Maguire, romped to a six-lengths win in the 1993 Digital Galway Plate. Maguire had ridden The Gooser to victory the previous year for Paddy Mullins. He became the first jockey to capture the Plate in successive years since Stan Mellor won on the Phonsie O'Brien-trained Ross Sea in 1964-65.

While basically his operation will always be geared principally to the Flat, Weld has shown that he can mix it in very versatile fashion. He keeps a sufficient number of dual performers in his yard to ensure that his name is always to the forefront in the jumping season.

187

Dr. Michael Smurfit loves the National Hunt scene and, despite his heavy business commitments on the global plane, tries to arrange his schedule to fit in meetings like Cheltenham, the Fairyhouse Irish Grand National meeting, Punchestown and Galway, of course.

Dermot Weld won the Digital Galway Plate for Dr. Smurfit in 1990 with the five-year-old Kiichi, ridden by Brendan Sheridan, and the Jameson Irish Grand National in 1988 with Perris Valley (also ridden by Brendan Sheridan) which he owned in partnership with Michael Smurfit.

Following the "Great Whitewash" at the 1989 Cheltenham Festival meeting – the first in 40 years – Dermot Weld through Michael Smurfit's Rare Holiday followed up the success of the "Mouse" Morris-trained Trapper John on the Tuesday of the 1990 meeting by taking the Triumph Hurdle on the Thursday and many Irish punters had a real "touch" at 25/1.

I recall Michael Smurfit, Frank Conroy, Paddy Fitzpatrick and Dermot Weld and his son Mark, who had taken the day off from school, enduring a nervous 20 minutes before a very long stewards' inquiry ended favourably. The British media believed that the Irish horse had to lose after he veered inside the final furlong, seeming to some race readers to squeeze compatariot Vestris Abu somewhat for room – but all was well in the end for the Weld camp.

On Champion Hurdle Day '94 the big English bookies were quoting Vintage Crop ante-post favourite to win the 1995 running of the race, though after his triumph at Aintree on Grand National Day Danoli became the new favourite at 5/1. It was a tribute in itself to the versatility of Vintage Crop that the bookies were taking no chances whatsoever with him twelve months ahead of the '95 Champion Hurdle. And then, of course, there was also Fortune And Fame to be reckoned with; Dr. Michael Smurfit certainly held a very good hand and it explained why he could take the rough with the smooth.

When Fortune And Fame won the Woodchester Credit Lyonnais Downshire Hurdle by seven lengths at the 1994 Punchestown Festival meeting with the Irish *Form Book* commenting "not extended", Dermot Weld had reason to be in a bullish mood in the unsaddling enclosure afterwards. "The best two mile hurdler in these islands," was his spontaneous comment to the assembled journalists and he indicated that the gelding obviously needed the race when finishing third behind Danoli and Mole Board in the Martell Aintree Hurdle (2m.4f.) some weeks earlier. Flakey Dove, winner of the Smurfit Champion Hurdle at the 1994 Cheltenham Festival meeting, could finish only fifth.

I put it to Dermot Weld that in describing Fortune And Fame as unequivocally "the best", he was putting him ahead of Montelado, Danoli, Flakey Dove and all the other leading contenders for the champion's crown in '95. Michael Smurfit smiled at that and more so when Dermot, with a fighting gleam in his eye, said: "That's what adds spice to the game."

Certainly all who were at Punchestown on that Wednesday in late April came away with little doubt in their minds that if Fortune And Fame had gone to the start at Cheltenham he would have beaten Flakey Dove and the rest of the field in the authoritative fashion that he dismissed the challenges of English challengers Dancing Paddy and Royal Derbi and Shawiya, the 1993 Triumph Hurdle winner.

Again the might-have-beens . . .

❦ ❦ ❦ ❦

Come to think of it, Dr. Smurfit could so easily by the end of the 1993-94 National Hunt season already be in the record books as the man who owned both an Aintree Grand National winner and a Champion Hurdle winner, apart from his victories in the Irish Grand National, the Triumph Hurdle and the Galway Plate and Galway Hurdle.

It was a case of so near and yet so far when Greasepaint (11-2) was beaten four lengths by Hello Dandy (10-2) in the 1984 Aintree Grand National.

No one had been more impressed by Greasepaint's bid as an eight-year-old to win the race in 1983 than Dermot Weld (that year Greasepaint was runner-up in a field of 41 to the Jenny Pitman-trained Corbiere).

Weld has always entertained an ambition to win the National and with patron Michael Smurfit he put together a syndicate to buy the horse from Michael Cunningham. The plan to train Greasepaint exclusively for Aintree received a minor setback when the weights were published. Greasepaint was given almost as big a hike as Corbiere and Weld took his time before confirming Greasepaint a runner.

By the time Greasepaint was despatched to Liverpool, Weld had already carried off the William Hill Lincoln Handicap with Saving Money, the first Irish-trained horse to win that event and hopes were high, as National Day dawned with Greasepaint in the pink of condition, that the trainer would pull off a historic double.

Greasepaint ran a marvellous race for Tommy Carmody. Apart from a mistake at the tenth fence, he hardly put a foot astray. While Burnt Oak was blazing the trail on the first circuit, Greasepaint was in the van of the main group and when the leader began to weaken, starting the second circuit, Carmody moved up to dispute the lead with Earthstopper, the pair being pressed by Two Swallows, Grittar, Broomy Bank and Corbiere.

At that stage Hello Dandy, which had been towards the rear from the start, was just beginning to make some ground, his jumping helping him to get nearer to the leaders until, taking Bechers for the second time, he was within striking distance.

By then Greasepaint was taking the measure of those nearest to him and he held a definite advantage at the Canal Turn. Hello Dandy moved into second place two fences later and before they crossed the Melling Road it looked a match – and a match which even Neil Doughty thought was going in Greasepaint's favour. "I think you have me beat," he called to Carmody.

As two brave horses faced up to the last two fences and the long run to the winning post, Hello Dandy started to come into his own. He produced a great jump at the second last to land in the lead; safely retained the advantage at the last and headed for home in a seemingly unassailable position.

But Greasepaint was equally courageous. In a similar position twelve months previously, he chased Corbiere all the way to the line, and here he was again running his heart out. A slim chance of recovery appeared at the elbow. Hello Dandy began to hang to the right.

190

Carmody spotted the opportunity, called for yet more effort and for several strides it was just possible that Greasepaint's tenacity would be rewarded. However, once Hello Dandy had drifted far enough off course to get the benefit of the running rail, he stretched himself in real earnest and at the post there was no doubt at all that the marginally-better horses had deservedly carried the day. Corbiere ran on with great heart under top weight (12st) to finish third.

"The weight just beat him," was Tommy Carmody's simple but accurate summing up of Greasepaint's defeat.

Dermot Weld concurred: "Giving a stone to Hello Dandy was his undoing."

Weld revealed that it was one of the most exciting moments of his entire career to see Greasepaint coming so close to winning the race that every trainer who ever handled a chaser wanted to win. "Tommy Carmody was in front earlier than I would have liked, for Greasepaint had a habit of idling a bit when he was ahead. But then the horse was jumping so well and going so easily that it was difficult not to go on when others began to weaken and drop away.

"In the final analysis, as I have said already, it was the weight that beat him and nothing else. Greasepaint looked like regaining the advantage and taking it when Hello Dandy began to drift to the right. Once he got the benefit of the stand rail, Neil Doughty was able to get him going again in a straight line and it was enough to win the day for him. Both Hello Dandy and Greasepaint were well clear of the rest of the field until Corbiere ran on again from the second last to take third place."

✴ ✴ ✴ ✴

Dermot Weld has been six times leading Irish trainer in terms of prizemoney won and sixteen times in respect of the number of winners trained.

The year 1994 saw him pass two very significant milestones in a distinguished career. When Michael Kinane passed the post first on Limanda in the Oatlands Handicap at Leopardstown on Saturday, 16 July '94, it saw Weld record his 2,000th training success in Ireland and it put him in sight of a historic achievement.

Only one other trainer, the legendary J. J. Parkinson has had more winners. He notched 2,577 between 1903 and 1947.

While Senator Parkinson operated for 44 years, Weld has been only half that time involved. Before he steps down, it's very likely that he will have set a new record but he conceded at the same time, "It's all in the lap of the Gods".

On the first evening of the 1994 Galway meeting – Monday, July 25 to be exact – Dermot Weld sent out his 100th Festival winner when Michael Kinane rode Union Decree to a 3/1 victory in the GPT Industrial Properties EBF Maiden. Incidentally, it was Weld's 15th time winning this two-year-old event and his ninth success in eleven years.

He has always enjoyed an outstanding strike rate on the summer Festival round from the big Galway six-day meeting to the three Kerry tracks, Killarney, Tralee and Listowel.

In 1993 he beat off the challenge of his great rival, Jim Bolger, to win the Dawn Light Butter dish award (a perpetual trophy plus £4,000) presented by the Kerry Group to the leading trainer at the three Kerry tracks and this was, in fact, his third consecutive Kerry award.

One of his most noteworthy achievements was to turn out ten winners at the 1993 Galway Festival meeting. Eight of these were ridden by Michael Kinane, including a four-timer on the Tuesday and on the Saturday prior to the Galway meeting the Weld-Kinane partnership recorded a five-timer at Leopardstown.

And he emulated his '93 Galway feat at the '94 Festival meeting when again turning out ten winners, eight on the Flat and two over jumps. As he celebrated his 46th birthday on the Friday, he was surely the "King" of the Galway Festival meeting.

If there is one basic tenant of the training game that Dermot Weld never overlooks, it is that you cannot afford to forget the bread-and-butter fixtures if you are to maintain an operation at the level of his establishment on the Curragh.

Weld is the total professional when it comes to dealing with the media. He realises that the racing correspondents and writers have a job to do and he knows too that they have got to be facilitated as they are the link between his stable and the racing public, who, for example, in the countdown to the '94 Champion Hurdle wanted to read everything they could read on the favourite, Fortune And Fame – and more so when he suffered the unfortunate setback that was ultimately to prevent him running in the race. It was the same in the case of Vintage Crop in the lead-up to the Melbourne Cup.

If Weld says he will be available on the phone to talk to a racing writer at one o'clock after coming in from the gallops, he will be available at that time. No messing.

Jim Bolger, similarly, is the essence of professionalism in this respect. But the very intensity of his make-up can make Bolger bring a journalist up short at times when maybe on the phone early in the morning he mistakes a filly for a colt by saying "he" instead of "she".

He did it one day in the case of a well-known commentator who was interviewing him on television.

Nothing much to a hard-bitten journalist who has been a long time on the road and prepared to let it pass – once Bolger meets the essential requirement of being there at the end of the phone when he says he will. And provides the information that is required without demur.

Weld is a born diplomat, easy of manner, seeming to take it all in his stride. But behind the friendly and relaxed exterior is a razor-sharp intellect and it would be a fool that would take liberties with him.

Weld has a suavity that if he got off a commuter train, wearing a pin-striped suit and was carrying a rolled umbrella in London during the rush hour in midweek you would be prepared to bet your last 50p coin that he was heading for the City.

You never find him locked in public battles with the Turf Club. It would never be his style to bring a High Court case against the body charged with policing Irish racing and guarding its image. You rarely if ever see him called before the Stewards. He is simply not a figure of controversy.

In this he differs to a marked degree from Jim Bolger, the man the racing public view as Weld's greatest rival. Rivalry there is and it will continue to be there while the two are training. They battle annually for the Trainers title in Ireland and they battle for the Leading Trainers Award offered by the Kerry Group each year (in conjunction with the Racing

193

Board and the three Kerry tracks) to the trainer who comes out "tops" at the Festival meetings in Killarney, Tralee and Listowel (Weld emerged winner in 1993 with Jim Bolger second and Aidan O'Brien third).

The rivalry is good for racing and both are mature enough to maintain it at a professional level without allowing it to affect their relations on a personal plane. They have both enjoyed sufficient success in recent times to be able to realise that one person cannot win them all.

To conclude that Dermot Weld is bland because of his general demeanour would be totally wide of the mark. Behind the smiling presence he presents in the winner's enclosure when greeting yet another winner and talking in easy and relaxed fashion to the circle of racing writers around him is an edge of steel – the steely edge that had made him what he is. And that is one of the most successful Irish trainers of the 80s and 90s.

Again nothing illustrates this better than the way he jocked off Walter Swinburn to utilise the services of Lester Piggott when he knew he had the "goods" in Blue Wind for the 1981 English Oaks. And likewise the way he passed over Brendan Sheridan in favour of Adrian Maguire when it came to deciding who would ride General Idea in the 1993 Digital Galway Plate. He didn't involve himself in tiresome public explanations. He confined himself to "no comment" to the media when they asked "why Piggott over Swinburn" and in the case of Maguire said simply that he was the best over the jumps at the present time – and he was booking him for that very reason. In each instance his judgement was fully vindicated. And no one thought less of him because of his steely approach – the approach of the true professional.

But Weld knows that racing is the great leveller. When I interviewed him in the lead-up to the 1994 Champion Hurdle for the *Sunday Independent*, he told me that after giving Fortune And Fame one spin over hurdles, he wasn't risking him again because of that doubtful leg. Anyway, he had no reservation whatsoever about his jumping ability.

And then Fortune And Fame gets cast in his box. A million to one chance – but it happened.

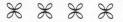

Dermot Weld stood on top of the world after that epoch-making triumph in the 1993 Melbourne Cup – a victory that was to see him travelling to Australia in the Spring of '94 to receive the Sports Personality of the Year Award Down Under, beating all the other top achievers in Australia in the process.

He was only too well aware of the fate of Classic Thoroughbreds, something few could have foreseen when it was launched in Dublin in 1987 as a £10 million bloodstock investment company – and with thousands of ordinary punters putting their faith in Vincent O'Brien's eye and judgement by buying shares in it. The victory of Royal Academy (bought by Vincent O'Brien for 3.5 million dollars at Keeneland in July 1988) in the 1990 Breeders' Cup Mile (Turf) at Belmont Park came too late to save the venture from eventual extinction.

The final rites performed by the liquidator – former Irish international rugby player, Tom Grace – took place in Dublin's Burlington Hotel on Monday, 23 May 1993, when two conservatively-attired shareholders were present to listen as the few loose financial ends were tied up and it was announced that the final pay-out would amount to 5.62p per share, slightly higher than the anticipated 5.25p per share. Of course, this was a long way off the original purchase price of 30p when the shares were launched in the heady days during the autumn of 1987 and some 4,000 shareholders believed that there were days of glory ahead as they invested in a string of blue-blooded horses trained by Vincent O'Brien.

Dr. Michael Smurfit had described it as "a noble experiment". All the shareholders took its failure on the chin for the Irish know better than any other people the risks involved in the bloodstock area.

The final irony was that as the curtain came down on Classic Thoroughbreds Tom Grace revealed that everything had to go – and this meant the trophies also and these fetched just £1,120 at Adams showrooms.

Weld was only too well aware also of how David O'Brien, who at 28 had become the youngest man ever to train an Epsom Derby winner when Secreto beat "wonder colt" El Gran Senor in 1984, suddenly decided to walk away from it

195

all for personal reasons. He had not alone just one Derby winner behind him but Assert had won both the French Derby and the Irish Derby in 1982.

Dermot Weld has gone on record to state that he is indeed aware that "there are other things in life besides training racehorses . . . something different perhaps to pursue in the future. At some stage I will just decide to quit and it will be final."

He is still only 46. And most people will maintain that, considering that Vincent O'Brien was still training as he celebrated his 77th birthday in April '94 that Weld need be in no hurry to quit the fast lane of the training profession. But, remember, he started early and, taking in the year he spent as assistant to his father, he is moving towards a quarter of a century of involvement at the highest level.

Sons Mark and Christopher are there – and Mark can be seen everywhere with his father outside of schoolgoing days.

In 1994 18-year-old Mark was in his final year at the Dominican College in Newbridge and confessed to John Kelly of the *Irish Times* that he would be sad to leave – "because I had a great life there. I'm involved with several of the school choirs and have been fortunate enough to get choirster of the year on a few occasions."

It was an eye-catching performance as Joseph in the school musical, *Joseph And His Amazing Technicolour Dreamcoat* that launched him on a course with Veronica Dunne's Musical Academy. "Ideally, I would like to join one of the good Dublin choirs or musical societies. At the moment, I'm a baritone, but my range is getting higher and I'm hopeful of getting up to tenor, as your options are that much better", he said.

Mark noted: "Both sides of the family have a great tradition in music, particularly on Mum's side. I have an uncle (Noel) who is a classical guitarist and all my aunts, as well as Mum (née Mary Nugent) are marvellous singers in their own right."

Then he laughed: "Dad, I'm afraid, sings like a jackdaw – he hasn't a note in his head. But my grandfather (Charlie Weld) was a great singer as well as being an accomplished organist."

196

It's difficult to imagine that the Weld operation will not continue at Rosewell House when Dermot eventually retires.

Mark gave a clear hint that he sees himself following in the footsteps of his grandfather and father when he said: "It's going to be very difficult maintaining the standards set by two highly-successful generations. I suppose if I can do half as well as Dad I'll be doing very well. At the moment, I have my sights set on going to UCD and studying law!"

It might appear an unusual road for a potential trainer to take but Mark Weld feels it will give him the experience he requires. "Nowadays, the legal element is creeping more and more into racing", he said.

Like his father he intends to travel and naturally Australia already has a special place in his affections for he was present on that memorable day in '93 when Vintage Crop won the Melbourne Cup. He had the honour of being part of the lead-in and will never forget the amazing scenes of excitement and emotion generated among the Irish exiles Down Under.

Mark's younger brother, Christopher – Chris to all the family – is a veritable mine of information about horses at the age of ten. "He's definitely the brainbox of the family", said Mark. "He even goes through *Turform* and *Timeform*."

⌘ ⌘ ⌘ ⌘

There was one Master of Ballydoyle in Vincent O'Brien, unparalleled in the level of his achievements.

And undoubtedly the two greatest milestones that the Master of Rosewell House has left in his careeer to date are the historic breakthrough victories in the Belmont Stakes and Melbourne Cup.

If Banjo Paterson were still alive he would be penning a ballad, entitled maybe *The Man From the Curragh Plains*, to follow *The Man From Snowy River* and it would evoke vividly a day in November '93, a day that bridged the hemispheres and one Michael Magee in his shanty in the outer Barcoo would have known that things could never be the same again.

Even in the Bush now there are men for whom the name Dermot Weld has meaning.

PART FIVE

MICHAEL KINANE

Scaling the Heights from Epsom to Longchamp and New York to Melbourne

12

"They could not call me Lucky after That!"

Michael Kinane believes that the race that made a major difference to the advancement of his career to a new pinnacle was the winning of the 1991 King George VI and Queen Elizabeth Stakes on Belmez for Sheikh Mohammed.

"I was involved in a great head-to-head battle with Steve Cauthen over the last two furlongs and I had to pull out all the stops to get home by a neck as Old Vic rallied again after I had headed him at the quarter-mile marker. They could not call me lucky after that!"

Kinane had won the 1989 Prix de l'Arc de Triomphe on Carroll House – the day after his success on The Caretaker in the Cartier Million at the Phoenix Park. Earlier he had won the Phoenix Champion Stakes on Carroll House, a victory that ensured that he would get the ride on the same horse in the "Arc", while in 1990 he landed the English Two Thousand Guineas on Tirol for the Horgans of Cork and Richard Hannon.

But Kinane knew deep down that there was still a sizeable and influential lobby that would not accept him in the premier league of jockeys.

Belmez with Steve Cauthen in the saddle had beaten subsequent Epsom Derby winner, Quest For Fame in the Chester Vase before finishing third – again ridden by

Cauthen – in the Budweiser Irish Derby behind Salsabil and Deploy. But with Cauthen siding with Old Vic, the dual Derby winner of 1989, Kinane was booked for Belmez, who had made a sensational come-back from injury when it appeared that he would have had to be retired to stud in May.

Kinane actually wore Sheikh Mohammed's third colours as the second went to Steve Cauthen on Old Vic and the first to the Coronation Cup winner, In The Wings.

He grabbed the opportunity presented to him with both hands. Holding a good position throughout on the El Gran Senor colt, he took the lead at the two-furlong marker and was seen at his brilliant best in withstanding Cauthen's fight-back in a driving finish. Thus Henry Cecil supplied both the winner and runner-up for Sheikh Mohammed. But whereas Old Vic and In The Wings had occupied the first two places in the betting, Belmez went off 12/1 sixth-favourite in a field of eleven.

Ironically, this win resulted in Michael Kinane emerging as the clear favourite to land the plum job of first jockey to Sheikh Mohammed in January 1993 after a statement from the Sheikh's Dalham Hall headquarters near Newmarket confirmed that the three-year association with Steve Cauthen was being ended.

The split came after the 32-year-old jockey from Kentucky had rejected what was a significantly-reduced retainer for the 1993 season.

Speculation on the size of the Cauthen retainer suggested that he had been receiving about £500,000 a year – before bonuses or prizemoney percentages – for committing himself to the Sheikh's horses.

Cauthen, who was dubbed "The Kentucky Kid" when he arrived in Britain in 1979, was back home in the States when the bombshell dropped about the link between himself and Sheikh Mohammed being severed. He had succeeded Lester Piggott in 1985 as No. 1 jockey to Henry Cecil, riding Slip Anchor to victory that same year in the Epsom Derby and he won this Classic again for Cecil in 1987 on Reference Point. Though he had a significant number of big race winners for Sheikh Mohammed, it had to be accepted that during the seasons he was under contract to Dubai's Defence

Minister, there had been overall disappointment at the lack of major success enjoyed by racing's biggest owner.

Cauthen, who had come to be accepted as one of racing's finest ambassadors, was gracious in the moment of disappointment, simply noting that he was sad that the connection with the Sheikh had been broken. "The reason is that we can't come to terms. They wanted me, but the terms offered were not acceptable to me and they weren't willing to up them. It was not as if I was asking for a rise.

"There is no animosity. Sheikh Mohammed has been very good to me and I can understand his position."

"If there is one regret, it is that I believe we were unfortunate not to have better horses during my time with Sheikh Mohammed", added Cathen, the only man ever to win the Kentucky Derby and the Epsom Derby.

⌘ ⌘ ⌘ ⌘

Anthony Stroud, who had pursued the negotiations with Cauthen on behalf of Sheikh Mohammed, now became the front-line personality in the contacts with Michael Kinane, who was in Hong Kong riding under contract for the winter months for British trainer, David Oughton – an ideal arrangement as it allowed him to be back in Ireland in April.

In a *Financial Times* survey in 1991, three of the top ten earners in British sport were jockeys. Steve Cauthen, Willie Carson and Pat Eddery between them earned £3.4 million that same year.

Pat Eddery was the second highest earning sportsman in Britain behind Grand Prix racing driver, Nigel Mansell. Eddery earned more from horse racing than Nick Faldo and Ian Woosnam earned from golf tournaments., Quite an achievement when you consider Faldo won the US Masters and the British Open in the same year.

In total Eddery earned just over £1.3 million in 1990. This stemmed principally from the lucrative contract he had forged with Khaled Abdullah when he was literally bought out of the Vincent O'Brien stable.

That highly-successful association stretched back eight years and when the racing world woke up to the stunning news in May '94 that Eddery's contract with the Saudi Prince was not being renewed for 1995, the 42-year-old Dublin-born jockey, who had been British Champion Flat racing jockey ten times – one less than Lester Piggott's record – up to the start of the 1994 season, singled out Dancing Brave, Warning, Quest For Fame and Zafonic as the high spots. He stressed that while it was a "knock" to learn that a long and happy association was being ended, "I'll not lose too much sleep."

You could understand why as in those eight years, following his seasons with the Ballydoyle stable, Eddery had become a very wealthy man and he was philosophical enough to add the rider: "I will go on riding. I like riding good horses. I have won Derbys and other Classics. A lot of things have gone on through my life and you have got to take the rough with the smooth."

It was generally accepted by the media that Michael Kinane would join the elite club of the super-earners if he became the first jockey to Sheikh Mohammed, wearing those famed maroon and white silks in the Classics and other major races.

But what many observers tended to forget – as they took it for granted that it was only a case of Kinane putting his signature on a contract drawn up by the Sheikh's advisers – was that the very fact that Steve Cauthen had been asked to accept a reduced retainer meant that there was not the same money being put on offer on the table now by the Arab princes as was the case when "The Kentucky Kid" was signed up by Sheikh Mohammed and Pat Eddery did his original deal with Khalad Abdullah.

It wasn't as if Kinane was a hungry young jockey ready to jump at the first offer that came his way. He was an established champion with an international reputation in his own right, a man who had proved beyond any shadow of doubt that he had the penchant to rise to the big occasion and could deliver at the very highest level.

The retainer he had with Dermot Weld and the contract he had to ride for six months each year in Hong Kong, on top of the "job" rides he landed in Classics and other big races, meant that he was secure financially.

More important still he had a quality of life centering around his Curragh base that he was not going to exchange unless, to put it bluntly, he got an offer that he couldn't refuse.

He would not vacate the 36-acre pad and the lovely bungalow-style home he had invested in for the honour that some would see attached to being head-hunted by Sheikh Mohammed's advisers to take over the job that had been Steve Cauthen's. He owns 50 boxes and is boss of Cloonmore Equine Services and the modern equine pool that is in non-stop demand from Curragh-based trainers, never more so than in 1989 because of the continued dry spell that same summer.

Quality of life and family mean a lot to Michael Kinane. He would weigh very carefully with Catherine, his attractive Kildare-born wife, the schooling of Sinéad and Aisling and how this and the friendships they had locally would be affected if signing a contract with the Sheikh meant moving to Newmarket and a far more punishing schedule than the one to which he had become accustomed. That in itself though had its own globe-trotting demands as when he flew from Hong Kong to ride Vintage Crop in the 1993 Melbourne Cup, or after riding in Ireland on a Saturday he took a plane out of Dublin Airport on a Sunday morning to ride in Italy and was back the same night, ready to ride out at Dermot Welds stable the next morning.

But Michael's quality of life meant that it wasn't all work and no play. As a native of County Tipperary, he loves Ireland's national game of hurling and whenever he gets a chance he will not miss a big game, especially a Munster championship tie involving Tipperary and Cork. His father, Tommy, and his uncle, Christy, are true aficionados and can talk about the game with knowledge and authority. Incidentally, I remember one day in Killarney greeting Michael Kinane as he walked into the Great Southern Hotel. It was the day in '87 when Tipperary met Cork in the marathon Munster final replay – an epic battle which Tipperary won in extra time and Richard Stakelum, the winning captain led the supporters of the Blue and Gold in the singing of "Slievenamon".

On afternoons when there is no racing, Michael Kinane may go golfing. He admits to the fact that he does not practice and plays essentially for relaxation but still he is no mean performer off a 17 handicap. In the summer of 1989 he teamed up with Christy Roche and Pat Shanahan to form part of the team that won the Vincent O'Brien Classic at the Thurles Golf Course.

He can also indulge in "a bit of shooting and hunting" and all told the Irish way of life offers the kind of outlets in the type of atmosphere that Kinane would be loath to leave.

However, in the final analysis, though the offer from Sheikh Mohammed was in the six-figure league, it was not of the scale that saw Kinane say "yes" to Anthony Stroud. At one point he actually flew in from Hong Kong to England as the negotiations reached a climactic point. Naturally he agonised for days and later he would confess: "It was a very difficult period and when it was finished I was so glad it was over."

It was as if a load had been lifted off his back, for reaching decisions like that can never be easy.

As he sat back talking to me in the sittingroom of his home on the edge of the Curragh in April '94 against the background of the paintings depicting peak moments in his career and trophies adorning the mantelpiece like the magnificent Ciga Arc jockey's trophy, I put the question to him that if he had been offered £500,000 a year or say a contract that would have netted £2 million or more over three years, would he have refused?

"No", came the quick and unequivocal reply. So in the final analysis it came down to a question of what was put on the table and when Kinane balanced the figure against what he was already earning, he was not prepared to accept it when it would have meant at the same time losing out on his quality of life.

"The offer was not good enough to give up what I have at present", was how he put it.

The Kinane quality of life was something Sheikh Mohammed and his advisers failed to quantify in naming their final figure. But then the Sheikh could never understand the "crack", the camaraderie and the bonhomie

206

stemming from a day out with "the boys" on the golf course or the way one brought up to see hurling as an integral part of life can be moved by the surging glory of a titanic battle between Cork and Tipperary, like the unforgettable contests in the 1987-'92 period in Thurles, Killarney and Cork. Or other epics involving Tipperary and Galway and Kilkenny.

But because I write this, it doesn't mean that Michael Kinane is a sentimentalist, swayed by nostalgia and remembrance of moments with his circle of friends that would cause him never to forsake the things with which he identified most. No, he is the essence of pragmatism.

There were professional and racing considerations that had to be carefully assessed as he came to the final decision. For example, it was obvious that the "numbers game" would not enter into it. By that I mean that his attachment to the Dermot Weld stable meant that he could be assured of riding over 100 winners in any given season in Ireland (he had 115 in actual fact in 1993 as he won his eighth Irish jockeys' title) and in addition there would be the winners he would ride in Britain, in Italy, Hong Kong and other countries.

He was very conscious of the Classic winners that a contract as No. 1 jockey to Sheikh Mohammed would bring as these would represent the real icing on the cake. "Frankly, I just couldn't see where the Classic winners would come from", he said on the phone from Hong Kong to Jim McGrath of the *Daily Telegraph* on the evening in January '93 – January 26 to be exact – when he announced that he was rejecting the Sheikh's offer.

Ironically, Kinane would end up later with a contract with Sheikh Mohammed anyway, so from purely diplomatic considerations he will never reveal what was the final figure offered to him at the outset of 1993.

When Kinane said "No", the South African Michael Roberts was signed up but after an unhappy year there came a split. No replacement was appointed as first-choice jockey for the Sheikh's entire international string. Kinane, however, became committed to the Sheikh for big races, though the other Maktoum brothers continued with the services of Willie Carson (Hamdan Al Maktoum) and Walter Swinburn (Maktoum Al Maktoum) respectively.

The new arrangement suited Kinane ideally. It meant that he could continue as No. 1 to Dermot Weld, ride for six months in Hong Kong and be in line to land Classics and other major races for Sheikh Mohammed. And he also appointed an agent in Britain, who ensured that he picked up other mounts apart from those he would ride for the Sheikh. Thus, for example, if he was riding at Epsom during Derby and Oaks week or at Royal Ascot, he would be assured of an enticing book of engagements, for trainers knew that in Kinane they were booking a jockey with an ice-cool temperament and at the same time one who could be expected to make no mistakes if he had the "goods" under him.

Dermot Weld was happy, of course, that Michael Kinane was staying with him and David Oughton was also happy that he would continue to have his services during the winter months in Hong Kong.

"It's a great day for our country", said Dermot Weld. "It was a very difficult decision for Michael to take. It was a great honour to be offered the job of No. 1 by the leading owner in Britain.

"But I am very pleased that he has chosen to continue his association with my stable and will be going into our tenth season together in 1993."

⌘ ⌘ ⌘ ⌘

The first time that speculation arose about the likelihood of Michael Kinane leaving Ireland was after he had won the Phoenix Champion Stakes, the Cartier Million and the Prix de l'Arc de Triomphe. It had been absolutely hectic for him from the moment he got back home on the Sunday evening on the last flight from Paris after riding Carroll House to a famous victory.

It was the day after the spontaneous victory party of the night before – something that happened out of nothing – when I arrived at the Kinane home to interview him for a special feature for the *Irish Racing Annual*.

Christy O'Connor Junr., the memory of his great singles triumph in the Ryder Cup at the Belfry and the emotional

Historic Triumph in Melbourne Cup

Dr. Michael Smurfit's Vintage Crop powering to victory in the 1993 Melbourne Cup (top) and (below) Tony Smurfit holds the cup aloft as Dermot Weld savours the moment with David Phillips (who travelled with the horse), Michael Kinane and Dermot Cantillon (right), manager of the Forenaghts Stud.

From Curragh Classic Success to Stunning Victory in Australia's Most Prestigious Race

A smiling Dr. Michael Smurfit leads in Vintage Crop (Michael Kinane) after he had won the 1993 Jefferson Smurfit Memorial Irish St. Leger at the Curragh.

Michael Kinane enjoys the glory of the most epoch-making victory of his career as he comes back to the acclaim of the crowds after riding Vintage Crop to an unforgettable success in the 1993 Melbourne Cup.

The Awesome Power of St. Jovite

Christy Roche (top) gives an arm-aloft victory salute to the heavens as he passes the post twelve lengths in front in the 1992 Budweiser Irish Derby and (centre) St. Jovite showing awesome power as he streaks away in the straight from Epsom Derby winner, Dr. Devious and (bottom left) coming home a convincing six-lengths winner of the 'King George' and (bottom right) Stephen Craine, who deputised for Christy Roche, enjoys his moment of triumph.

Jim Bolger (right) makes it a proud day for Irish racing fans as he holds the Budweiser Derby trophy aloft at the Curragh after St. Jovite's pulverising victory and (below) the Taoiseach, Albert Reynolds joins with Michael J. Roarty of Anheuser-Busch in congratulating Mrs. Virginia Kraft-Payson, owner of St. Jovite as she receives her Waterford Crystal trophy.

Caroline Norris's study of the proud head of Danoli, the people's champion (top left) and (top right) Dan O'Neill leads in Danoli (Charlie Swan) to a tumultuous and emotional welcome after victory in the 1994 Sun Alliance Novices' Hurdle and (below) Dan O'Neill and trainer, Tom Foley proudly display the trophy.

THE FIELD OF DREAMS: The victory of Flakey Dove in the 1994 Smurfit Champion Hurdle was right out of the Field of Dreams. Trainer Richard Price is a picture of delight as he holds aloft the winner's trophy and (below) Mark Dwyer gives a thumbs-up victory salute in the unsaddling enclosure.

VIVE LA FRANCE

Francois Doumen and his wife,
Elizabeth share with Adam
Kondrat the joy of victory after
The Fellow's triumph in the 1994
Gold Cup (above) and (left)
Kondrat comes back in to a
hero's welcome after the
frustrating defeats he had known
in previous runnings of the Gold
Cup.

scenes at the 18th green still vivid in the mind, had dropped in with an autographed photograph in colour for Michael Kinane – "To Mick, Best Wishes, 1989, Christy O'Connor".

"Friends came round. We sang and danced into the early hours. Christy, of course, was as always the life and soul of the occasion. Yes, it was great", said Michael with a smile.

Now it was around midday on Tuesday – still not much more than 48 hours on from what he described to me at that point as "the greatest moment in my career to date", though by the summer of '94 it would be dwarfed by his achievement in winning the Epsom Derby on Commander In Chief and in the autumn of the same year the Melbourne Cup on Vintage Crop.

He was finding the going hot in trying to meet all the demands of the media and with no racing that day, he had, in fact, decided to give over most of the afternoon to interviews. Colleague Vincent Hogan was due to arrive at 3 p.m. for an interview for the *Irish Independent Weekender*.

I could see that the mobile phone had become part and parcel of Kinane's life – of the new pinnacle he had attained as Ireland's undisputed champion jockey on the Flat but more than that – a jockey riding at such a peak of sustained consistency that the world had overnight become his oyster.

The phone rings. It's the Bibi Baskin RTÉ programme planners on the line. No, he's sorry he can't make it. It appears that they have been on the line now fairly constantly since early the previous day. Soon afterwards, just as we were getting well into our interview, the phone rings again. This time it's the RTÉ *Night Hawks* programme, Shay Healy's Jacobs award-winning programme. He is very polite, very courteous. But he's sorry, his schedule won't allow him to make it at the hour of the evening they suggest to the Montrose studios.

Three big wins coming right on the heels of each other had made him only too aware of the fact that he could be handing over to the Taxman half of the percentage "cuts" he would be earning from these triumphs. He remarked that he would have to think seriously "if I get the kind of offer that it is almost impossible to refuse".

In winning the Cartier Million and Ciga Prix de l'Arc de Triomphe, Kinane had won a total of around £950,000 in prizemoney for the lucky owners. A winning jockey's net "cut" out of that sum comes to 7½ per cent when one allows for what is taken from the normal 10 per cent (for example, what goes to the Jockeys' Fund).

If Ireland was a tax-free island, Michael Kinane would have banked a cool £71,250. But Ireland has one of the toughest tax regimes in the world. If the Taxman took say the top rate at the time of 56 per cent, Kinane would be handing over £39,000 leaving him with just over £31,000 from the original £71,250.

No wonder then that he was so coldly dispassionate as he outlined the options facing him.

"I don't believe in shooting at stars. I don't believe in talking about something up there in the clouds just for the sake of commanding easy headlines when there is no basis in fact for the stories. I believe in talking about realities", he said.

I pointed out to him that so much was happening on the jockey level in Britain, that it seemed inevitable that he could find himself facing the kind of decision Pat Eddery had to face when he left the Vincent O'Brien stable to become No. 1 for Khalid Abdulah and became overnight in the words of Brough Scott "the world's priciest rider".

He nodded.

"This is the way I see it. It am into my thirties now and all going well and assuming I avoid injury and retain my appetite for the game, I can keep riding until I am 45 at least. That gives me another ten years. The career at the very top for any sportsman is limited. He has to make his bread and butter, has to make enough over and above that to set himself and his family up in such a way that he won't have to worry about money when he retires.

"In a word, while things are on a roll for you, you've got to try and hit the jackpot. You don't always get a second or third chance."

He went on to admit that for the first time in his life – after the events of the Cartier Million and Arc weekend – he had to begin to think seriously about what it would mean remaining on in Ireland in a certain situation.

"What I mean is, if I were to win a number of races each season from this out bringing the kind of percentages that fall to a jockey from rich events like the Cartier Million and the Prix de l'Arc de Triomphe and not forgetting, of course, the Phoenix Champion Stakes, I could simply end up taking all the pressure and it would get more intense the more big races I won and have to hand over most of it to the Taxman. I don't mind the pressure at the top. I like the high of it. The greater the challenge, the greater I enjoy it.

"But you would look something of a fool if you were bringing in the big winners and having little to show for it in the end, especially if you had turned down offers from abroad that you could not – or should not – refuse, just to continue to enjoy aspects of Irish life that appealed a lot to you.

"At that point you would have to say to yourself – must I cash in my chips now, go with the tide while it is rolling for me, or just keep on handing over most of the really big percentages to the Taxman. I am afraid a point could be reached where I would have to think seriously about leaving – but, as I have emphasised more than once, I don't want to leave unless I am forced to do so."

Nowadays riders in the big international league are not just on retainers and percentages and presents but on stallion shares. The latter can represent the real "cream", like an Oscar-winning actor or actress getting a percentage of a film that hits the jackpot world-wide.

When Michael Kinane turned down the original offer from Sheikh Mohammed in January '93 new doors opened to him that ensured that, despite the tax commitments he had to meet, he was still assured of an income at a level that put him way beyond any other Irish-based jockey and up there with the biggest earners in Britain, though Eddery's income still outstripped everyone else's.

Apart from his standing arrangement with Dermot Weld, the contract to ride with David Oughton in Hong Kong and the agreement reached with Sheikh Mohammed following the split with Michael Roberts, Kinane was very much in demand – when available – in Italy while at home he was picking up extra rides outside of the Weld stable from the numerically-powerful John Oxx stable. And, as mentioned already, the appointment of an agent in Britain opened further vistas for him.

⌘ ⌘ ⌘ ⌘

He impressed the Italians so much during his Sunday riding engagements there – when his services were not demanded here at home – that the wealthy owners of Carroll House had no qualms about giving him the ride on the Michael Jarvis-trained four-year-old in the Phoenix Champion Stakes and then the "Arc". The Italians joined with the big British and Irish contingent at Longchamp in giving voice to *Danny Boy* as the victory anthem swelled over the winner's enclosure.

If anything, the fabulous week-end that saw him win the Cartier Million and the "Arc" made Michael Kinane realise that the media and its demands have become more than ever before part and parcel of his life. And it has intensified since he won the English Derby and the Melbourne Cup.

The new pedestal he stands on now, the international spotlight trained firmly on him sees him more relaxed in the presence of journalists. The media is the line of communication to the vast racing public out there. "There is no more critical public than the Irish racing public", he says.

We know from experience that when the media shower on you the kind of praise that he has received over the past twelve months and particularly since he won the Epsom Derby on Commander In Chief and the Melbourne Cup on Vintage Crop, it is inevitable that you will be criticised at the same level at which you have been placed if things go wrong – and that is a very exacting level indeed. And because you are paid to know what you are doing and to deliver the goods, the connections of the horses owned by your paymasters won't be that forgiving if you take the wrong option, get yourself in a pocket when the right decision taken a split-second earlier could have given you the gap you wanted – and victory.

"Kinane is The Man", wrote Graham Rock in *The Observer* in the count-down to the 1994 Epsom Derby. "You can admire Pat Eddery's raw strength, Frankie Dettori's deft touch, Michael Robert's judgement of pace, Kinane's style embodies elements from all of them and, ride for ride, he makes fewer mistakes than any of his contemporaries".

And Hugh McIlvanney in the *Sunday Times* in a special feature on the Irish champion Flat jockey that had the sub-heading "All Kinane Needs Is The Right Horse to Claim His Kingdom" wrote: "Some respected judges suggest that Kinane, who will be 35 next month (July '94) and is plainly at the height of his powers, is probably the most effective jockey currently active on any continent".

High praise indeed.

Pragmatically then he accepts that one cannot ignore the media, even though you may assert publicly that criticism doesn't bother you.

Why? "We all make mistakes. They are part and parcel of any game, any profession. You can't be afraid of criticism but, ultimately, you must have confidence in your own ability, you have got to trust yourself.

"It's funny in this game of racing. You begin to make mistakes and the media begin to ask questions. The shrewder race readers may spot that you are getting yourself into no-man's-land and the parting of the waters you seek, so to speak, won't come for you. The media look more and more into your mistakes, begin to assess where you are going wrong, what you are doing wrong, maybe even to the extent – if you have reached a certain age – that they begin asking if you are past it.

"They may at that point be reflecting the very questions that are being asked by the public. Only a fool can say it doesn't bother him, especially if he knows deep down that things aren't going right for him. If it's simply a case of the occasional mistake, you must learn from it, otherwise you are a fool".

Michael Kinane looks across at me and says in the tone of a professional who knows what he is about: "You try and make as few mistakes as possible. You plan things in advance so that the fault can't be laid at your doorstep if things don't work out as expected, particularly on the really big occasions".

213

Always the perfectionist, he has made it a practice to go through the videos of the most recent races he has ridden in. "I don't know whether other jockeys do this but I make a point of examining how I rode each race and seeing if I could have ridden it any better".

Perfectionism also in the way he approaches the Epsom Derby. On his very first ride in the race in 1983 he had been runner-up on Carlingford Castle to Teenoso and Lester Piggott. When he won on Commander In Chief in 1984 it was his fifth ride in the race. He had learned his own theories in the meantime and they didn't revolve totally around the accepted theories of the professionals, especially the theory that it was best to keep off the rails going down the hill into Tattenham Corner and endeavouring if possible to be in the first six when you came round it.

The bottom line as far as Michael Kinane was concerned was to avoid at all costs being caught up and having your chance ruined by "the dead wood coming back at you" as you make your descent into Tattenham Corner.

But there was much more to it than that. From the first time he walked the course – that was back in his days as an apprentice jockey when he went over to ride in a Listed event – he knew that riding Epsom was going to be different from riding any other track in the globe. Because it was all gradients and one moment you were going downhill and the next uphill and positioning was so important and judgement of pace even more important still.

So in the lead-up to any renewal of the race now he forms a mental picture of how he thinks it will go and that means studying every other horse, apart from his own, in the race and how he thinks he will go – be up with the pace or come with a rattle after Tattenham Corner and bound up with this naturally was how each would be ridden.

From experience he was convinced that it was best to be drawn in the middle as this allowed one to adopt one's own strategy rather than have one forced upon you. If drawn badly you will use up too much horse to get into a good position. However, if you get that middle draw you hope that you won't have to do too much in the early part of the race, coast down the hill and strike at the vital moment.

He believed in keeping a close eye on the major contenders, not allowing them to get away from you. This was where judgement of pace came into it.

In Commander In Chief Kinane knew he had a horse that would get every yard of the distance and he could take responsibility and kick on if the pace was such that he decided he had to go. But in 1994 he felt that there was a question mark on breeding over King's Theatre getting the twelve furlongs in a really true-run race, so there was the necessity to conserve stamina. In each case his judgement was spot on.

"Yes, being in the first six coming down into Tattenham Corner is obviously the ideal place to be", he said. "But I think it's wrong to say that you can't win if you are not in that position. I mean Pat Eddery came from what seemed an impossible position on Golden Fleece in 1982 but then he had a colt with a super engine, who could come from some way back and still win going away."

Applying his own theories Kinane was guilty of no pilot error in either winning the 1993 Epsom Derby and taking runner-up position in 1994. Perfection was his hallmark.

He brought the same touch of perfectionism – the approach of the true professional – in discovering the know-how of riding the Longchamp track in the Prix de l'Arc de Triomphe.

In 1984 when he rode 105 winners (a new all-time record) that included seven trebles and one four-timer, he had won the Prix l'Abbaye at Longchamp on Dermot Weld's dashing sprinter, Committed, but it was not until 1989 that he had his frist ride in the "Arc".

Kinane learned the "Master's Plan" from Christy Roche. The Master, of course, was Yves Saint-Martin, the now-retired French jockey, rider of four Arc winners like Pat Eddery.

"The Yves Saint-Martin rule was to get your position before you reached what they know as 'the little straight'. It was imperative, according to Yves, that you must not try and make ground in that straight, only coast along. Then once you got to the straight proper, you could go for your race.

"In a big field like that for the 1989 renewal, it can happen that things will get rough. And it was rough. But I avoided it because I had gained the right position as we turned for home. And, happily, everything went right for me from that point to the winning post."

But what about the objection by the rider of Behera and the angry claims in France that Carroll House should have been disqualified? What about the contention by French trainer, Francois Boutin that if Sagace was disqualified in 1985, then there was every reason to disqualify Carroll House in '89?

Michael Kinane contended that despite French claims that he had caused interference, the facts of the matter were that "I quickened past Behera and even though my one hung in a bit, there was absolutely no question of the French horse being stopped in her run and I noted that the rider, Alain Lequeux didn't say *definitely* that she would have won. She was beaten fair and square, beaten on merit".

The head-on camera left no doubt in his mind that the French Stewards had taken the right decision, he added.

The year 1989 had another peak for Kinane in that the first week of December saw him heading for Japan and the International Jockeys' Series. He rode for Europe with Pat Eddery, Willie Carson and Cash Asmussen against the cream of the world's jockeys, including two from the States and two from Australia plus one from New Zealand and four from Japan.

※ ※ ※ ※

I brought him back to the time when he was faced with the daunting prospects that he might have to drop any ambitions of climbing up the ladder as a Flat jockey and become resigned to becoming a jump jockey.

He had started at the age of 15 as a pupil of the famous Liam Browne apprentice academy, where apprentices were assured of not alone being given outstanding tuition in the art of riding but also worked in a no-nonsense, character-building atmosphere that stood them in good stead for the rest of their lives.

Michael was only in his second season as an apprentice, aged 17, when his weight jumped to 7st 13lbs. "You might as well have a few years on the Flat while you can but you will have to go jumping eventually", Liam Browne told him.

It was then that Michael Kinane turned to Dr. Austin Darragh, father of showjumper, Paul Darragh, and a man who had helped countless jockeys with their weight problems.

"He put me through a very tough regime for a time. It wasn't so much a case of cutting down on food but the monotony of missing certain foods you liked. I was quite plump when I went to him but had slimmed down by the time I finished. Most important, I learned how to control my eating and learned what to avoid."

Fortunately also, he stopped growing at the critical time – "and I was soon okay".

Standing 5ft 4ins, he rides easily today at 8st 5lbs and it doesn't entail sweating it out in the sauna, which he confesses he doesn't like.

Breakfast consists of a cup of tea on waking up and maybe a bowl of cereal later and at lunch he will have another cup of tea and a sandwich or two.

He's the envy of many another jockey in that he can tuck into a really good dinner prepared with loving hands by Catherine, maybe lamb with plenty of potatoes and vegetables.

There are rivals for whom it would be a mirage during the season and who, to break the fierce monotonous regime, will let fly on occasions and then go to the men's room and do what a man has got to do in order not to put on weight. Kinane is sorry for them, so is Christy Roche – but it is the nightmare that is hidden from the public who see only the flashing silks maybe on a sun-drenched day as they cheer home an idol on a horse that has carried their money.

After winning the Apprentices title in 1978, he became first jockey to Michael Kauntze. Then after he had ridden Dara Monarch to a 20/1 victory in the Irish 2,000 Guineas in 1982 for Liam Browne (winning the St. James's Palace Stakes also the same season), Browne had him back as his stable jockey.

In 1983 he finished runner-up to Christy Roche in the Irish Jockeys' title race and the season was highlighted by his finishing second on Carlingford Castle to Teenoso and Lester Piggott in the Epsom Derby.

At the end of that same '83 season, he was offered the job of No. 1 jockey to the Dermot Weld Rosewell House stable. He has never looked back since.

It is a partnership that has blossomed to the benefit of both. The Cartier Million triumph on The Caretaker was simply putting the icing on the cake.

As Michael was heading for the Phoenix Park on the Saturday of the Cartier Million with Catherine, he remarked: "I feel lucky".

Somehow, he had a premonition that he could strike gold not alone in the "Big One" at the Park but at Longchamp also.

"Why not the Lotto?", remarked Catherine laughingly – as there was over £600,000 in the kitty that same week-end to be won.

Michael didn't have time to think of filling in Lotto tickets.

He hit the jackpot, however, with his own cool riding and panache at two different venues – and didn't have to depend on luck as he went smiling all the way to meet his bank manager.

13

"Kinane the Best Jockey in the World Today"

"Michael Kinane is the best jockey in the world today." This was the tribute paid to him by Michael Kennedy during the summer of 1993 after he had ridden Commander In Chief to victory in the Epsom Derby.

Kennedy, a great stylist in his racing days when he rode for such leading trainers as Mickey Rogers, Seamus McGrath and Vincent O'Brien is currently the Chief Riding Instructor at the Japan Racing Association's Horseracing School. His opinion has got to be respected, though I know there are diehard racing enthusiasts both in Ireland and Britain who will never be swayed from the view that Lester Piggott was the "daddy of them all" in his prime when it came to the really big occasion, Epsom Derby day most of all. Who can forget, for example, those scintillating triumphs for Vincent O'Brien on Sir Ivor (1968), Nijinsky (1970), Roberto (1972) and The Minstrel (1977) as he won the Classic nine times in all?

Pat Eddery, Walter Swinburn, Ray Cochrane and John Reid have all gained the distinction of winning the Epsom Derby in the last decade or so. But following Christy Roche's unforgettable win on the David O'Brien-trained Secreto in 1984, Kinane stands as only the second Irish jockey, actually based in Ireland, to ride the winner of Britain's premier Flat race.

219

Commander In Chief was the less fancied of Khalid Abdullah and Henry Cecil's two runners, the mount becoming available to Kinane after Eddery had opted for the same combination's Tenby.

Eddery, with three Derby winners, Grundy (1975), Golden Fleece (1982) and Quest For Fame (1990) under his belt, could hardly be criticised for choosing Tenby. He had already won the English 2,000 Guineas on the brilliant Zafonic. Trained in France by Andre Fabre for Prince Khalid Abdullah, Zafonic had made a lasting imprint as a two-year-old and had topped the International Classification with a rating of 125. On that mark he was 3lb ahead of Tenby, who was likewise unbeaten during his first campaign which I saw being culminated with an impressive win in the Grand Criterium on Prix de l'Arc Sunday in Paris.

Tenby, furthermore, had won his two preparatory races, doing everything asked of him in the lead-up to Epsom and while the form hardly justified Tenby being an odds-on Derby favourite, it was difficult to oppose him with any degree of confidence.

Commander In Chief was yet another unbeaten colt. He had not, however, been raced as a two-year-old – it was 20 years since Morston had overcome that handicap in the Derby – and while he was looked upon in the yard as a very bright prospect, there was a general impression that Commander In Chief might lack the experience and maturity required for an Epsom Derby. Nonetheless, he started second favourite, marginally shorter at 15/2 than Fatherland, who represented the familiar old-time partnership of Vincent O'Brien and Lester Piggott.

Michael Kinane had gone over to Newmarket to ride Commander In Chief at work and was very impressed. "I knew he would get the trip and that he was really on the upgrade", he said.

Still the professionals rowed in behind Tenby because he had won that most revealing of Derby trials – the Dante Stakes – by three lengths and he had a pedigree that guaranteed him getting the twelve furlongs, being by Coolmore's Caerleon, who had won the French Derby and sired Generous, and he was out of the Park Hill runner-up,

Shining Water and the grand-dam Idle Waters went back to the great Mill Reef.

Pat Eddery had Tenby in close touch behind front-running Bob's Return but as Blues Traveller took it up three furlongs out, the favourite's backers knew their fate. Eddery had been niggling at him without much response and as Michael Kinane later explained: "Turning for home I looked across and spotted Pat Eddery hitting the panic button. I knew then we would win. Commander In Chief was travelling so well I decided to go on and he went away from the others."

Tenby faded to finish tenth and the *Timeform* writer in *Racehorses of 1993* described it as "a woeful display – beaten too far out to blame the trip and finishing almost at a walk having been well positioned at Tattenham Corner".

George Enor in the *Racing Post* pointed out that Tenby and Planetary Aspect (10th), who had met at Newmarket and York in the run-up to the Derby, had reproduced the form closely enough to suggest that Tenby may not have run below his true ability, a theory that was to gain weight as the summer progressed into autumn, and the colt named after a Welsh seaside resort failed to win in four more races. The best he could achieve, in fact, was a third in the Eclipse Stakes at Sandown and a fourth in the Champion Stakes at Newmarket. "A smart colt, no better", summed up the *Timeform* writer.

Pat Eddery, through his contract with Khalid Abdulla, had the mount on Commander In Chief in the Budweiser Irish Derby and the Henry Cecil-trained colt disposed of the Prix du Jockey-Club (French Derby) winner, Hernando, who was ridden by Cash Asmussen. There had been a tremendous built-up to this clash of Classic winners and the Curragh crowd got plenty to cheer about as Commander In Chief maintained his unbeaten record in holding off Hernando by three-quarters-of-a-length.

There were writers who went over the top in their acclaim of Commander In Chief because he had simply done what other colts had done before him and that was win two Derbys (English and Irish) back-to-back, overlooking the fact that the real test would come when he met older horses.

Cash Asmussen fell into the trap of promoting him to the rank of super star because he had repelled his challenge on Hernando and Pat Eddery said he would have to rank with the best of his three previous winners of the race, though, personally, I am convinced that he would not have lived with Golden Fleece (I remember Vincent O'Brien at Ballydoyle one day passing the box where Golden Fleece was housed and saying to himself aloud as he contemplated the awesome late surge that carried him to victory in the Epsom Derby – "what speed, what speed". And the Master of Ballydoyle confessed that it was acceleration that put Golden Fleece up there with Nijinsky).

The official assessment of Commander In Chief was more restrained than that of those who were acclaiming him a world-beater after his Budweiser Irish Derby success. There were a few eyebrows raised in reaction to the Senior Irish Handicapper, Ciaran Kennelly's rating of 127, compared with the 130 awarded to St. Jovite after the previous year's Irish Deby. St. Jovite attained the higher rating of 135 following his victory in the King George VI and Queen Elizabeth Diamond Stakes.

It is well to understand the function and thinking of the handicapper. Mr. Kennelly, who is deeply respected for his knowledge, explained: "When a horse is allotted a rating the handicapper is not saying this is a bad horse or a good horse. He rates the horse as he sees it, the form; it is up to others to make of it what they will. A bad horse never wins the Derby so obviously Commander In Chief is a good horse, but it is very hard to rate three-year-olds until they have met older opposition."

The handicapper had to be influenced by the fact that Foresee, who was 3 lengths off the winner in third place, and Massyar, were rated at that time on 109. I would suspect, furthermore, that having studied the video of the race Kennelly like myself would anticipate Cash Asmussen, with the benefit of hindsight, taking Commander In Chief on a shade earlier if the two colts met again. Hernando would appear to have failed on the score of pace rather than stamina for he was coming again, slowly, at the death.

It was not long before Kennelly's theory about the older horses was put to the test in the all-aged King George VI and

Queen Elizabeth Diamond Stakes run at Ascot on July 24. Henry Cecil decided to run Tenby in addition to Commander In Chief, and while Hernando declined the engagement in favour of an autumn campaign, the Italian Derby winner White Muzzle joined the party along with two cracking seniors, User Friendly and Opera House.

Where Nijinsky, Grundy, The Minstrel, Troy, Shergar and Generous went on from victory in the English Derby and Irish Derby to take the King George, Commander In Chief failed to win the accolade of greatness when finishing only third to Opera House and White Muzzle. He never ran again after that, being sold to the Yashun Company for a reported £4 million to stand at stud in Japan where his sire, Dancing Brave (sold for £3 million in 1991) also stands. And what a loss to the Irish and British breeding industries Dancing Brave was to prove to be when one considers that he sired not alone Commander In Chief but also White Muzzle, placed in the Prix de l'Arc de Triomphe and, as we have seen, the King George apart from his Italian Derby success, also Wemyss Bight, winner of the Irish Oaks.

❋ ❋ ❋ ❋

Michael Kinane returned from Epsom to the evening meeting at the Curragh to be the recipient of a special presentation from the Curragh Committee to mark his first triumph in the English Derby. "A fantastic gesture", was how he would describe it later.

What a hectic day it had been for him. Up as usual at 7.30 a.m., Catherine drives him, after breakfast (a cup of tea!), to Dublin Airport. He was carrying a new saddle and one of the new whips he got from Walter Swinburn when he went over to stay with him for the Guineas.

"Things are lucky for me when they are new", he confided to Michael Glower of the *Sporting Life* in a detailed diary that gives the perfect insight into how one of the greatest days of his life evolved.

"I am feeling lucky. I had much the same feeling going to the Phoenix Park in October '89 when I won the Cartier Million and the Arc little more than 24 hours later.

"I said so to Catherine that day. This time I keep my thoughts to myself. I kiss her goodbye. 'Don't forget to pick me up when the chopper lands at the Curragh'."

The plane leaves for Heathrow. Also on it are Charles O'Brien and his wife Anne. Kinane says no to breakfast even though he has at this point eaten nothing since lunch the previous day.

He is doing 8st 9lb in the first. He settles for a cup of coffee and goes through the *Sporting Life* and the *Racing Post*. He memorises the colours of the Derby horses and where they are drawn. He also tries to absorb as much about them as he can. On arrival, he picks up chauffeur-driven car. John Reid has given him instructions for the back route that avoids the worst of the traffic.

And now as he hits Epsom with midday already past, every incident-packed moment of that unforgettable day would be imprinted indelibly in his mind, as he logged those moments for Michael Clower:

12.40: Reach Epsom. There are a lot of people here already. I begin to feel a sense of occasion. I go straight to the weighing room. Tony O'Hehir nabs me for an interview for RTÉ and I then go to the trial scales.

I am light. Thank God. No sauna now. That's the first winner of the day. I sit down in the jockeys' room and watch the replays of past Derbys on the closed-circuit TV. It's a great way of filling in an hour, and it gives me some useful information on the opposition. It also helps the nerves.

I am beginning to feel edgy and I know the adrenalin is pumping. I am sure the other jockeys are much the same. Anyone who says they don't suffer from nerves on Derby day is just not human.

It's lucky I have that ride in the first. There is nothing worse than hanging about with nothinbg to do.

1.55: Henry Cecil comes in. I weigh out and he takes the saddle. We chat about the filly. We talk again in the paddock. She will go close, he says. She is the favourite, but I miss the kick. The draw does not help because I am out wide. We are beaten a length and a half.

Some people might regard this as a bad omen. I don't. In this game you get beaten a lot! I go back into the jockeys'

224

room and back to the TV. I watch the build-up, change into Prince Khalid Abdullah's second colours.

Immediately after watching the second race, I weigh out.

3.15: Some official shouts "Jockeys out". We all climb into the minibus that takes us to the paddock. I walk over to Henry. He introduces me to the Prince. Henry says: "We've had a chat already. You are probably sick of listening to me by this stage, anyway, I keep repeating myself. I think it must be the first sign of insanity."

I laugh, but the Prince says: "No. It is very important to have your plans worked out and everything in order."

When I stayed at Warren Place the previous week, we agreed tactics. I may well force the pace. My horse is guaranteed to get every yard and so I am going to make it a true test. No point in giving the speed horses a chance.

Pat Eddery is there too. He does not say much other than general chit-chat. He is on the favourite. Henry goes off with him to give him a leg up.

The travelling head lad swings me into the plate and Dave Goodwin, Commander In Chief's lad, starts talking. He says: "This horse is in great nick. I have never seen him as well as he is now. He is really ready for this."

Great. But the horse is getting edgy. Not so great. The one thing I expected was that he would stay calm. He gets worse when we go out for the parade. Dave takes off the chiffney but the horse has quite a sweat on him by the time we turn to canter down.

I don't know this until later, but Catherine is also getting nervous in front of the TV at home. She gets out a bottle of pink champagne to calm her nerves and to wish me luck.

By the time we get there he is dry. I check the girths. Fine. Keith Brown, the starter, calls the roll. Robinson two, Reid four, Kinane six. "Yes sir."

Brown calls: "Even numbers first, handlers." We are loaded. He then calls the odd numbers. I have Lester on one side and Alan Munro on the other.

I mutter something to Alan, I am not sure what. I change my grip on the reins to get hold of the mane so that I don't catch the horse's mouth as we leave the stalls. "Last horse loading," shouts the starter. I lean forward. "Come on, jockeys."

3.51: We're off, I break nicely and settle in just behind the leaders. We tack over to the right for the first bend. But, once we get round it, there is a real charge.

Tenby has gone right up with the leaders and everyone wants to get close behind him. John Reid on Planetary Aspect tries to move out a bit to get nearer. Christy Roche on Desert Team is trying to keep in. He gets squeezed.

There is a fair bit of jostling. Somebody shouts, somebody yells, somebody swears. This is getting tough. I ease back. I don't want to start fighting on an inexperienced horse. I am now a fair bit further back than I had planned. But at least it is a good pace.

The top of the hill. I have nine in front of me. Too many. But I am happy enough. The pace is still good. My horse is going easily on a lose rein and he is relaxed. As we go down the hill towards Tattenham Corner, I begin to poke him along. I look across at the others. Michael Roberts on Barathea seems to be going best of all.

We turn for home. Barathea is on my inner and Michael wants to get out. He is half a length up on me. I don't want to get jostled so I let him go. Barathea moves forward. Almost at the same moment, Pat goes for everything. He's gone. Hallelujah.

I change my grip on the reins. I want to get him balanced before I ask him. Come on, let's go. He really surges forward.

He is really motoring now. I pick up my stick and give him a couple as we pass Blues Traveller and take it up with over two furlongs still to run. Three times more I hit him. He is drifting in. But it doesn't matter. I know I'm well clear.

Suddenly it goes quiet. The Derby is different from other races where the roar of the crowd suddenly hits you somewhere in the straight. Here you hear the noise all the way. I am just about to give him another one when I decide to have a look and see why it is so quiet.

What a sight. They are all strung out with the washing. I switch the whip to the carry position and give him a tap backhanded. Then I put it down and ride him hands and heels. This winning post is taking a hell of a long time to come.

I look back again, a long one this time. It's fantastic. It's like looking at a long line of brown cows. The post flashes past. Brilliant. I give him a grateful slap down the neck.

"Well done." It's Bruce Raymond. "I finished second," he shouts incredulously. He seems as pleased with himself as if he had won.

As we pull up, Willie Carson congratulates me. There is a yell of "Gimme five." It's Frankie Dettori. I slam my hand down on his five. He laughs.

"Well done. Great stuff." It's Christy. I reach out to shake his hand. We canter back. Dave comes rushing up. He shakes my hand. So does Peter Chapple-Hyam. He's a lovely man.

Two mounted policemen come up on either side. One of the Prince's family takes hold of the horse's head and leads him in. I slip down and take off the saddle. The Prince says "Well done."

"It was a great performance by the horse, sir, and I would like to thank you for giving me the ride."

"Stewards' inquiry."

Hell. What's it about, the Prince wants to know. "I don't see how it can involve me. I was well clear by the time I started drifting across."

"That was great." It's Henry Cecil. "Wasn't it?"

"It worked out really well, Henry. This is a good horse and I want to thank you for giving me the shot at this race."

Two policemen escort me to the weighing room. I put my whip and helmet on the table and weigh in. I go into the jockeys' room. Everybody shakes me by the hand. I hear something over the public address.

"The inquiry does not involve the winner." Great.

I order two crates of champagne for the boys. Some press guy grabs me for Channel 4. Brief interview with Brough Scott. Then it's off to the presentation. I am not quite sure what I am being presented with. Somebody takes it back and says they will get it engraved.

Lord Carnarvon asks me to go to meet the Queen. I don't have a lot of time, I tell him, but, of course, I will. He says to go up after the next race. The press guy tells me he has told the chopper pilot to wait and he hurries me off to the press conference.

227

Tony O'Hehir comes rushing up with his microphone. RTÉ again. No, says the guy, come on, I ignore him. Tony must have his few words. We go into the conference room, on to a podium. A few questions. I go back to the weighing room, take off my boots and put my suit on over my riding clothes.

Put my shoes on and go up to the Royal Box. You are introduced as you go in. "It was a fantastic performance," says the Queen. "Thank you ma'am."

I have met her once before; at Ascot when I won the King George on Belmez. The Queen Mother, too. She is there again. What a lovely person. She is very chatty. You can tell she loves racing. They want me to have a drink. Sorry no, I can't. I have got to get moving.

I get my stuff out of the jockeys' room and dash off across the course in front of the stands. Hell. I am going the wrong way. The chopper is near the seven-furlong gate. I run for it. We quickly reach Heathrow but we land near Terminal four. Miles away.

I climb into a minibus. So does Charles O'Brien and his family. They have also come by helicopter. We reach Terminal One. We have to go through all the normal check-in procedures. It's a race against time. I had reservations on the 4.35, 4.45 and 5.45. This is the last of them.

6.00: I am now beginning to feel hungry. It's 29 hours since I have eaten anything. The stewardess brings me lamb and vegetables. Delicious. Plus two bottles of champagne. "To drink later," she says with a lovely smile.

As I get off the plane in Dublin there is another minibus. Another chopper. Twenty minutes later, we are at the Curragh. Catherine is there waiting for me. She gives me a kiss and a big hug.

She tells me she has fixed up a party at our house, family and friends. Just as well she doesn't tell me it's going to go on until four in the morning. Goodnight Kiss in the maiden. She was second in the Irish 1,000 last time and this is a formality. She is 4-1 on.

A mass of people congratulate me. One of the best sights of all is my father. He is so overcome with emotion, a mixture of pride and delight, that for once he is stuck for words.

The crowd gives me a tremendous welcome when I go out to ride the filly.

Just under two furlongs to run. Time to go. I switch into top gear and glance round. Bloody hell. Something that has never run before rockets past like Nijinsky. I am very disappointed.

There are a lot of people in the weighing room. "This is a great game," I tell them as I step on the the scales. "Just when you think you have got the game licked, it puts you straight back on your arse."

❀ ❀ ❀ ❀

It's coming up to a year on from that epoch-making day and I am back again in the Kinane bungalow, looking at photos of the Melbourne Cup triumph and of triumphant moments also in Hong Kong during the winter.

It's different now than when I did that extensive interview back in 1989. There was a time when with all the confidence he carred into the ring as a boxer, the confidence that made him a boyhood champion, he thought when he hit the trail as a young jockey he was ready to take on the big boys – to take on the world, in fact.

He was in for a rude awakening – like the small town champions from Texan towns who arrive in Las Vegas to take on the big boys, the guys who have ice water in their veins instead of blood. They've got to prove something to themselves, they've got to know and in the learning, they may wither in the fierce heat as one who is as tough as nails puts him all in at the Hold 'Em game and looking across the table he cannot read whether "The Man" facing him has the "nuts" or is merely bluffing. It can be so cruel.

Kinane found that it was only when he took on the big boys that he discovered how much he had to learn.

Now I was talking to a man who is right at the top himself – on top of Everest, the world's highest summit and his ascent could be described fittingly as a bravura one.

But like the celebrated figures of the mountaineering world – Edmund Hillery and Chris Bonnington among them – he knew you could not rest on your laurels. You had got to try and deliver all the time to the scale of achievement you had carved out for yourself. And that meant someone going along to Bellewstown of an evening in July would expect a repeat of his Derby ride on Commander In Chief when they put their money on the nose on a fancied one he was riding.

The comparisons can be hurling ones when the talk turns to how you can perform better when the adrenalin is flowing. I make the point to him that Eddie Keher, the great Kilkenny stylist of the 1969-'77 era, had said to me once that he had no butterflies at all before the 1966 All-Ireland final as the wearers of the Black and Amber were such raging hot favourites and somehow or other he never hit the peak that day that marked his displays on other epic championship-winning days for his county, as in the 1969 and '72 All-Irelands against Cork.

Kinane will be tense and edgy on the morning of a big race, especially a Classic like the Derby and that means that he is building up for the high that will result in one thing – when split decisions mean everything, his reflexes will be razor-sharp. "When the adrenalin is flowing, you ride better", is how he puts it.

So hyped up will he become as he rides the high waves like a surfer, that it will take him quite some time afterwards to come back to normal. Maybe as long as a few hours.

Toughness – mental toughness as well as physical toughness are essential ingredients if one aspires to reaching the top – and staying there. There will be an intense spotlight nowadays on Michael Kinane as he decides maybe on the gallops at Newmarket what he will ride in the Epsom Derby and it will become even greater as his chosen mount is closely analysed and the media move in to write about the man who simply cannot be left out of the reckoning.

But at a meeting like the Galway Festival meeting, for example, when the press of crowds is immense, especially on Galway Plate Day and Galway Hurdle Day, Kinane will almost certainly be on board a fancied runner in every one of the Flat races over the six days from Sunday to the following Saturday and on warm orders from the Weld stable.

"When you find yourself concerned in almost every finish, it calls for a lot of effort mentally and physically and it can leave you drained", he admitted.

But he is known as a man who recovers quickly and Hugh McIlvanney, when he met him off the plane from Dublin at Stanstead Airport to interview him for a *Sunday Times* Derby special recognised immediately that he was "in the company of somebody formidable".

"It is the impression of an inner, contained strength that comes across most forcefully", wrote McIlvanney. "Though he is naturally amicable and the firm planes of his face melt readily into smiles, the large, deep-blue eyes under the blond, luxurient eye-brows are alive with a challenging directness."

McIlvanney described the Weld-Kinane Antipodean coup in landing the 1993 Melbourne Cup as ranking as "the most spectacular, perfectly-executed act of international plunder racing has known" and it fully exemplified the potency of Kinane's approach to his career.

⌘ ⌘ ⌘ ⌘

When Michael Kinane flew into Melbourne to take the mount on Vintage Crop, he was followed by members of his "fan club" in Hong Kong – among them High Rollers who would make Irish punters, who think they bet big in the ring at Cheltenham, go pale if they realised the level of the wagers invested on apparent "good things" in the Colony. These High Rollers have come to have a blind faith in Kinane's ability. They weren't going to miss the opportunity to go for a "killing" on Vintage Crop, once they got the word that he had recovered from the dehydration and weight loss of the long and exhausting flight from Ireland. The price was right and in the ring at Flemington you had bookies who would put in the shade many of those who masquerade as fearless layers in both Ireland and Britain.

As with the Americans, the Aussie scribes place a lot of store on how it goes at work in the count-down to a big race, on sectional times and generally on what is sparking and what is not. Vintage Crop didn't appear to be sparking initially whereas the English challenger, Drum Taps, dual winner of the Ascot Gold Cup, was really catching the eyes of the gallop-watchers.

But Kinane knew – as Dermot Weld did – that his one had the measure of Drum Taps after beating him in the Irish St.

Leger at levels and, irrespective of what Drum Taps was showing at work, there was no way he could make up 5½ lengths giving half a stone to Vintage Crop – once Dr. Michael Smurfit's gelding came right on the day.

And what the Australian gallop-watchers did not know was that the lad who was riding Vintage Crop was using his own saddle and that meant that the Irish challenger was carrying what he would carry in a National Hunt race!

It worked out like a dream for Kinane, who recalled that he was only eighth or ninth as the taps were turned on and the front-runners sprinted for home more than four furlongs out. He knew what Vintage Crop was capable of when he pressed the "go" button. He knew that he had a Classic winner under him against handicappers who hadn't the acceleration of his one in a finish.

"When I asked my one to go, he jumped from under me and we strolled in by three lengths."

Looking at the video, you would have got the impression at one stage that Kinane was in trouble, that he couldn't make up all that ground, that he might even have left it too late.

But then you remember again what the man said – "You have to understand pace."

On a November day in Melbourne when he climbed one of the highest peaks of all in his career, he showed that he really understood pace and judgement of it at the finish.

⌘ ⌘ ⌘ ⌘

The clock moves forward six months – 25 May '94 to be exact – and on the Newmarket gallops Henry Cecil is seeking to persuade Michael Kinane that King's Theatre is the one he's got to be on in the Derby a week hence. You might almost think it was a scene out of a play being enacted on the Limekilns for the benefit of the assembled media representatives – but this is deadly serious stuff as Kinane, the big-race "King", knew when he flew over from Ireland that he had the choice of two colts, Foyer from Michael Stoute's yard and King's Theatre.

"Henry was very persuasive. He didn't miss his chance in front of the gallery", said Kinane. "There were a lot of press and television guys present after the gallop. You wouldn't see more people at some racecourses."

It didn't really take Cecil's selling pitch to convince Kinane that the Sadler's Wells colt out of Regal Beauty (by Princely Native) was the one he should partner. His mind had already been made up by the morning's work.

He worked King's Theatre over eleven furlongs, having already in a separate gallop found Foyer somewhat sluggish. "I was a little disappointed with Foyer. He did not pick up for me", said Kinane frankly.

"King's Theatre did work well", he went on. "He's a very handy horse, so I have no worries about the course. But I do have reservations about him getting the trip."

Kinane had King's Theatre placed perfectly to win the Derby and looked to have got the measure of Colonel Collins when Willie Carson, defying all the rules, managed to "get out of prison", to quote Tim Richards' very apt description in the *Racing Post*, and produced an electric burst of acceleration to win going away by one-and-a-quarter lengths. It was Carson's fourth Derby.

"He ran a great race but he just couldn't quicken in the final furlong", said Kinane of King's Theatre.

Still overall he had reason to be happy. One win and two seconds in six rides. Not a bad Derby record. Not at all.

Compared with Lester Piggott, who was riding in his 36th Derby – taking fifth place on Khamaseen – Kinane had a lot of ground to make up.

Even if he were to ride in ten more Derbys, he couldn't emulate Lester's amazing record and even in his wildest dreams, he could hardly hope to equal his "bag" of nine winners.

But in two years he had won international respect as a man who really knew how to ride the Epsom course in the most sought-after colts' Classic and it was a tribute in itself to him that immediately he opted to ride King's Theatre, Ladbrokes cut his price from 20/1 to 10/1, though on the Big Day itself he eased to 14/1.

14

Surviving a Horror Fall in Hong Kong

Afterwards Michael Kinane would say "I'm the luckiest man alive." For he had survived a horror fall in Hong Kong during his sojourn there riding for David Oughton in the winter of 1993-'94.

He was kicked by three horses after being thrown from his mount on the rails at the Colony's Happy Valley track.

"I honestly thought this was it. It was one of the worst falls of my career. I still don't know how I wasn't killed", he said. Then allowing his sense of humour to cloak how near he could have been to suffering fatal injuries, he added with a smile: "But I suppose it's very hard to kill a bad thing!"

"We were going flat out at the turn and I was trying to come in between two horses on the inside rail. But my fellow chickened out and clipped another horse. The next thing I knew he went down and I went flying over his head.

"The three other horses behind kicked me all over the place. It probably looked a spectacular fall but unfortunately I felt every bit of it."

Kinane was removed to hospital with two broken ribs and extensive bruising. "It's a miracle the injuries weren't worse. I'm in a hell of a lot of pain but I don't care, the main thing is I'm alive", he told a local newspaper at the time. "There is very little they can do to stop the pain. The only thing the doctors recommend is two weeks solid rest."

Later Kinane would realise just how lucky he was when 26-years-old Steve Wood was killed in a fall at Lingfield on Friday, 7 May 1994, and again it would be borne home to him very forcibly when he saw the brush with death that Declan Murphy had in the aftermath of a terrible fall at Haydock that same month.

Kinane himself had another amazing escape from serious injury – and possible death – when a young man from Berkshire climbed over the perimeter rail as the Ribblesdale Stakes was reaching its climax at the Royal Ascot meeting and ran right into the path of his mount, the Shiekh Mohammed-owned Papago.

The filly was disputing last place with Frankie Dettori's mount, Little Sister. Dettori, who was just behind Kinane, managed to take some kind of evasive action as Papago went down, noting: "The guy shot out from the rails and ran across the track. Mick saw him at the last minute and shouted at him but it was too late.

"Mick's horse hit him very hard and knocked him to the ground. I think I managed to avoid hitting him, although my horse collided with Mick's.

"We were so far behind the others that the guy must have thought the race was over. It's lucky we were only hacking at the time, otherwise the impact would have been much worse."

The young man was removed to Wexham Park Hospital in nearby Slough with multiple injuries.

Kinane, visibly shaken by the incident, said: "The fellow looked in a bad way. I didn't see him until the last second, as he ran out from underneath the rail. My horse went straight into him and hit him head on. He was looking the other way and didn't see me coming.

"For a while I was trapped with one leg in the iron under the filly. Luckily, she was winded and lay on the ground and did not attempt to run off."

Amazingly, Michael Kinane came out of it unhurt – the second time inside the one year that he had come out alive from two horrific falls.

And he was extremely lucky for a third time in '94 when winning the King George VI and Queen Elizabeth Stakes in

235

dramatic style on King's Theatre. Ezzoud, winner of the Eclipse Stakes, unseated Walter Swinburn at the start and then caused havoc as he proceeded to run loose, harassing the other runners all the way, Erhaab, the Epsom Derby winner, being one of those who suffered from his unwanted attentions.

Kinane first thought of coming outside the riderless Ezzoud, then went inside to tackle front-runner Bob's Return and drove King's Theatre clear to win by one-and-a-quarter lengths from White Muzzle, the mount of four-times Japanese champion jockey, Yukata Take. White Muzzle got boxed in on the rails as Ezzoud weaved in and out and trainer, Peter Chapple-Hyam said: "King's Theatre won fair and square but I would have liked to have seen what would have happened without the loose horse."

White Muzzle was flying at the finish after eventually getting a clear run.

"The loose horse was going everywhere", said Michael Kinane. "Some got caught up with him as he weaved about. I had to react quickly but I think a couple of horses were unlucky.

"When Ezzoud went right, I had to go left. And then he would go left, so I had to go right. Because he had a hood he couldn't see the other runners and my biggest fear was that he might go right across us and bring one of us down. That could have caused a real tragedy.

"But it was all right in the end, thank goodness", he added.

⌘ ⌘ ⌘ ⌘

Kinane said to me in his home on the Curragh in May '94: "Every time you go out to ride in a race, you know that a fall when horses are going at 40 miles an hour can mean serious injury, even death. It is something you have got to live with in our profession.

"It's worse, of course, for the jump jockeys and let me say that I would never begrudge them anything they get."

Michael Kinane rang his father, Tommy, in the immediate aftermath of that Hong Kong fall. He was seeking his advice on what way he should approach matters after his lucky escape, knowing that his father had seen it all during his career as a jump jockey.

Tommy Kinane told me that it was terrible to see jump jockeys who had lost their nerve completely after bad falls. "In some cases a situation could be reached where you could see terror in a man's eye as he left the weighroom to ride in a chase, more so if he knew he was on a dodgy jumper. His only purpose then would be to get round and try and avoid another crippling tumble.

"Those who lost their nerve like this could hide it for a while but shrewd trainers, knowing the game inside out, would spot that a man was stalling and pulling back instead of riding fearlessly into a fence and then the mounts would get fewer and fewer until eventually the one whose courage was gone had to accept the inevitable and call it a day."

Tommy Kinane said that he was lucky himself in that while he suffered the "normal injuries" – broken collar bones and cracked ribs and severe bruising – he was never out with a broken leg or arm. Therefore, he never had the kind of fall that would have really tested the undoubted courage he brought to the saddle.

"I didn't know fear", he admitted – and that was transmitted to his son Michael, who came out of the Hong Kong experience without any permanent mark as far as his own courage was concerned and he continued to ride at a level of excellence that won him the plaudits of racing enthusiasts far and wide.

✻   ✻   ✻   ✻

You come upon Tommy Kinane's training establishment – he has about a dozen horses in his charge – at Pollardstown on the Curragh. You reach Knockavilla Lodge, a comfortable bungalow-style house at the end of a drive-way and Tommy and his wife, Frances, make you feel immediately at home, Frances insisting on this lovely summer's morning that I have a "cuppa". In fact, if I hadn't already partaken of breakfast I could have enjoyed a full Irish breakfast.

Tommy reveals to me the hinge of fate that saw him returning from England to hit the top eventually as the man who

237

rode Monksfield to victory in the 1977 Champion Hurdle when he could so easily have continued to work on the building sites – and we might never have heard of Michael Kinane.

Frances revealed that Michael had a talent from childhood, expressed in different ways, that was special. And he was also a born character to boot who would have the rest of the family "in stitches" as he did his impression of Donald Duck.

His mother recalled that the very first prize he won was when he finished first in the under-12 sack race at the sports meeting in Glengoole. "He was so competitive that there was only one place for him always and that was in the No. 1 spot."

She recalled too how he entered an art competition that was linked with the Tidy Towns effort in Killenaule and the pupils of the school were asked to come up with the lettering for two posters – one for Ballingarry and one for Killenaule.

Michael's winning words were:

BIG, LITTLE AND SMALL SHOULD TIDY
      KILLENAULE

and

EVERY TOM, DICK AND HARRY SHOULD TIDY
      BALLINGARRY

His creative imagination also came into play when with his brother, Jayo he designed the crest for Killenaule Athletic Club.

And it didn't end there.

When he was ten, he walked in the fancy dress parade in Killenaule as Lester Piggott, complete with riding breeches and boots and carrying a little saddle.

No one could have foreseen that when Michael brought King's Theatre into the starting stall for the 1994 Epsom Derby he would be seeking his second successive victory in the Classic and Lester would be riding in his 37th Derby – and seeking a fabulous tenth victory on Fayor.

He was an outstanding boxer as a youth and champion of Tipperary, Waterford and Munster in his own class for three years. He was actually training for the Irish Championships

238

when he left home to join Liam Browne's stable as an apprentice jockey. But for a dispute arising in the Mullinahone Club that meant that he – and others – did not participate after all, it seems certain that he would have been crowned a national title-holder.

"He boxed southpaw", his father told me. "He was very skilful and at the same time very aggressive. One night he demolished the reigning Munster champion in two rounds. He had a vicious streak in him that made him deadly when he went after an opponent looking for a quick knock-out victory.

"When there wasn't a title or a trophy at stake, he would say jocosely 'Do you want this one short or long?' and then he might indulge in a bit of play-acting, a bit of codology and the like. Those of us who knew how funny he could be when he let the comedian in him loose would just laugh ourselves sick."

All the Kinane boys were champions. The love of boxing was instilled in them by their father who used box in the open air in London on Sunday afternoons. Tommy coached each of the boys individually as they were growing up and then in the Mullinahone Club they came under the wing of the official coach and trainer, Stephen Waters. The Club really had an outstanding record.

It was inevitable also that Michael should follow in his father's footsteps in another sphere – the hurling arena. When the family were based in Holycross – a great stronghold of the national game that gave John Doyle, winner of eight All-Ireland senior championship medals and Pat Stakelum, captain of his county in the All-Ireland winning year of 1949 and a brilliant centre-back, to the Blue and Gold colours – Tommy Kinane played junior for the club. He remembered, as he winced audibly but with a laughing gleam in his eye, one particular bruising game against Upperchurch-Drombane. "I won't say they were hatchet men", he laughed, "but, my God, it was tough!"

Tommy said that his son Thomas was "a skilled player" but "Michael would pull on anything".

"He'd take the ball and your ankles and all", he laughed again, adding – "put that in because it's the truth!"

239

Tommy Kinane bought a grey Arab-bred pony for the boys. A top-class show jumper, he carried Michael to a succession of successes and the rosettes that filled the Kinane home were evidence of his prowess.

But, whereas Adrian Maguire hit the pony circuit as the road to eventual stardom and overwhelming acclaim as a National Hunt rider, Michael Kinane only rode in one pony race that his parents can remember.

That was at a place known as Barrys of the Two Trees at Wilmount between Ballingarry and Mullinahone.

True to his determination to be in the No. 1 spot always, he came home the winner on the Arab-bred.

⌘ ⌘ ⌘ ⌘

The Kinane family hailed originally from the Glen of Aherlow, one of the most picturesque beauty spots in County Tipperary.

There were 14 children in the family into which Tommy Kinane was born. It was an era when it was not untypical to find families of that size in rural Ireland and, indeed, you might find 15 to 18 and as many as 20 children.

Nine brothers – Mick, Jack, Dan, Jim and Billy (the twins), Tommy, Christy, Ned and Ned the second time.

And five sisters – Alice, Breda, Mary, Nancy and Anne.

Tommy never met his brother Jack, who died in America three or four years ago – "he had emigrated to the States before I was born."

And when Ned died at the age of 21 when working in England, a child who came after his death was again called Ned, thus two Neds in the same family, which to the present generation accustomed to smaller families, maybe only two or three, would be something they could not possibly comprehend.

Dan, Christy, Billy and Jim were all associated with the Vincent O'Brien stable.

The Kinane family became synonymous with riding and horsemanship. Mick was associated with a famous show jumper called Aherlow which was bought by the British Army.

Danny rode a lot of winners in his prime and later turned his hand quite successfully to training. Jim and Billy entered the winner's enclosure also.

Christy was a good jump jockey in his prime, his happiest big-race memories being of dead-heating on the 33/1 chance Newgrove for first place in the 1961 Galway Hurdle with Cygne Noir, ridden by Pat Taaffe and coming fourth in the Irish Grand National and also winning the Munster National, two Ulster Nationals, the Independent Cup at Leopardstown and the Downshire Hurdle at Punchestown.

But these were dwarfed by his five training successes at Liverpool – especially the landing of a major gamble when Cooch Behar won the Weetabix Hurdle in 1976, with Liam O'Donnell in the saddle, from the 11/8 favourite Mwanadike and the same horse went across to Liverpool the following year and took the George Hurdle, again with Liam O'Donnell in the saddle. Cooch Behar was backed down from 33/1 to 4/1 when landing that "touch" in 1976 and there was an ante-post book then on the Weetabix Hurdle.

Christy Kinane, incidentally, has his training quarters at The Green, Cashel, the mid-Tipperary town that draws visitors from many parts to see the magnificent Rock, one of the most imposing historic landmarks in Ireland and compelling in the image it leaves on the mind when you swing around the bend on the road and see it for the first time in all its majestic splendour before you, rendered even more impressive when floodlit at night.

※ ※ ※ ※

Tommy Kinane started with the late Tim Hyde at Camas Park, where Tim's son, Timmy now has his stud.

Tim Hyde will always be remembered as the man who rode the great Prince Regent to victory in the 1946 Gold Cup – the first to be run after the Second World War. He was desperately unlucky not to justify 3/1 favouritism in the Aintree Grand National the same year, carrying the welter weight of 12st 5lb when finishing third behind 25/1 chance Lovely Cottage and 100/1 outsider Jack Finlay, beaten seven lengths.

Tim Hyde trained Dominick's Bar to win the 1950 Irish Grand National with Martin Molony in the saddle. This horse had an ill-fated time at Aintree where he ran in two Grand Nationals. He fell at the first in the 1952 won by Teal and two years later dropped dead at the second fence in the race won by Royal Tan.

"I was about to get my licence when Tim Hyde broke his back in a fall from a show jumper at Clonakilty on a July day in the early fifties", recalled Tommy Kinane. "I remember the day well. In fact, I can never forget it because of the consequences it had for me and others in the yard. Heartbreaker was a big black horse owned by Mrs. Peg Watt, who was a famous character in her day.

"I remember after Kinloch Brae, owned by Anne Duchess of Westminster, had run at Thurles one day, there was a party that evening at Willie O'Grady's. Mrs. Watt actually challenged me to a boxing match. I thought at first she was only joking but I realised she was serious when she took up a fighting pose and then caught me with one on the side of the face. I responded by giving her a tap of my finger under one of her tits. That was the end of it."

Legendary stories are told to this day of Mrs. Watt's exploits on the Festival round. If a piano went out a window in the early hours of the morning, there were characters in the inner circle who wouldn't have batted an eyelid if they hadn't been there but were told about it the next day.

Awesome card sessions. Awesome drinking sessions. Members of "The Set" on the road back from Kilbeggan or some other meeting and publicans locking up their doors and battening down the hatches because they knew that if they let them in, it was a case of getting to bed at some unearthly hour. "No" was never accepted as an answer if you were foolish enough to answer the door. The young jockey who got a lift with one of them resigned himself to being bleary-eyed and groggy on the gallops the next morning – even if his drink was only a mineral. It was that kind of era, that kind of time.

"Mrs. Hyde was left with a tremendous burden after what happened to Tim", Tommy Kinane went on to recall. "The whole thing fell asunder. Much as she would have liked to have maintained the staff at the same level as previously, we all knew that it was impossible for her to do so.

"I left. Others did also. I spent some time with Chally Chute and then with Lord Harrington. Soon, however, I was on my way to England with Jimmy Burke who had also been working in Hyde's. Two others who also left Ireland at the time were Johnny Kenneally and Tim Ryan – known as Tadghie – who enjoyed quite a deal of success and who died in 1993. Johnny Kenneally, who went to George Vergette, came very close to winning the 1964 Aintree Grand National on Purple Silk, who was much fancied for the race. He actually landed in front over the final fence from Peacetown but was caught in the last few strides by Willie Robinson on Team Spirit and beaten half-a-length.

"I was based first with a trainer called Thomas Robert Pettifer. I got my first English licence in 1953 when attached to the stable of Tom Yates at Russley Park, Bayden in Marlborough, Wiltshire.

"The first ride I had was on a two-year-old at Bath. Scobie Breasley rode a stable companion. Lester Piggott, Harry Carr, Bill Rickaby and Bill Marshall all had mounts in the race, so I was in exalted company.

"I got a few rides over hurdles and I remember riding one day in a race at Towcester that was won by Bob Turnell.

"Then in 1954 I gave up and went to London where I worked on the building sites with McAlpine. Yes, I was one of his 'fusiliers'. I was adept as a scaffolder and within two years was fully qualified.

"There was a big job in progress for the BBC and I was doing extremely well. But the call of the horses was in my blood. I used go down to Wantage to ride out and actually got the mount in the odd hurdle race. There was one very difficult horse and it was felt I was the only one who could manage him.

"My brother Danny, who is retired from training now, was doing very well at this time from his Mullinahone base. I decided to come home and team up with him. My employers offered to promote me to foreman. I was on the permanent staff at the time.

"While I saw it as a tribute to my work and a very genuine one at that, I had made up my mind to leave and nothing was

243

going to make me change. We parted on good terms and I was happy about that.

"I often reflect back, however, on the moment I made that fateful decision and I know that if I had decided to stay so much would have been different."

✼ ✼ ✼ ✼

Meanwhile Tommy had met in the Emerald Ballroom in Hammersmith the girl he would marry. She was from Knockavilla. "I saw her once in the distance before I went to England and I didn't bid her the time of day", he said with a mischievous gleam in his eye and Frances laughed heartily at that bit of Kinane provocation, as she poured Tommy another cup of tea and refilled my own cup.

The names of different ballrooms reeled off from Tommy's tongue – the Blarney, the Garryowen – as he recalled the Ballroom of Romance days with Frances. "We danced the night away from Hammersmith to Cricklewood, to Kilburn . . . you name them, we found the dance halls where they played the kind of music we wanted."

And when they married it was in the era when the Catholic Church threatened Hell's fire on any couple that practised contraception. The simplistic solution, if you went to confession and mentioned something to the effect that the wife's health might be endangered if she had another pregnancy or that it wasn't economically viable to have a dozen kids, was to sleep in separate rooms. The people accepted the ruling of Mother Church and her teaching – in Ireland anyway – that "God will provide" where there were big families.

Michael Kinane was one of seven, four boys – Thomas, Jayo and Paul were the other three – and three girls, Suzanne, Kathryn and Janette.

Frances Kinane can laugh now as she recalls the labour pangs as she arrived at Our Lady's Hospital, Cashel, to give birth to Michael and a good nun telling her – "offer up each contraction for your sins".

"I never got a whiff of anything and we hadn't the faintest notion what an epidural was."

✼ ✼ ✼ ✼

Tommy Kinane on his return to Ireland rode Kilmore, then a young and very promising horse, in five hurdle races for his brother, Danny, before he won at Mullingar with Danny himself taking the mount. "He landed a nice gamble for us that day", Tommy recalled and I preferred not to inquire why the horse that would win the Aintree Grand National of 1962 with Fred Winter in the saddle didn't figure in the five races in the lead-up to that Mullingar success.

Tommy's first big break came in 1958 – he doesn't forget the date, January 7 to be exact – when he rode Mrs. Michael Purcell's Trade Union to victory for trainer W. L. Cullen to a 10/1 victory by half-a-length in a handicap hurdle at Leopardstown.

When Michael Purcell was training on his own at Holycross, Tommy spent seven years riding for him and effectively acting as his Head Man. Before that he spent time with Andy Kennedy at Ballynonty and then moved to Arthur Morris at Powerstown Park, Clonmel. It would all stand him in good stead when he started training on his own.

He was with Arthur Morris when he went to the Easter Monday meeting at Mallow in 1961 and rode a double, winning the Stewards Handicap Chase (2m) on the 7/1 chance Fairice and the Mallow Novice Chase on Out And About. Incidentally, Out And About led all the way that day and similar tactics were tried in the 1963 Aintree Grand National but he fell at the 27th fence. Tommy Kinane did not ride him at Aintree when Josh Gifford had the mount and the owner, Bernard Sunley backed Out And About to win £250,000 with William Hill. The race, of course, that year went to the 66/1 shot Ayala, trained by Lester Piggott's father, Keith, and ridden by Pat Buckley.

In 1979, the year that Dessie Hughes had the mount on Galway-born Dr. Michael Mangan's Monksfield as he won the Champion Hurdle for the second successive year for trainer Des McDonogh, Tommy Kinane had the satisfaction of earlier winning the Supreme Novices Hurdle on the same trainer's Stranfield and the way he punched the heavens passing the post conveyed a world of meaning in itself.

Tommy, of course, had been on board when Monksfield

was victorious in the Champion Hurdle in 1978 – the peak moment of his career in the saddle.

Tommy Kinane spent twenty-two years in Killenaule and had his training establishment there before moving to his present quarters at the Curragh.

His ease in conversation and his ironic wit contrasts sharply with the way Michael presents himself today as a man who knows that there is a constant media and public spotlight on him and therefore, he has to choose his words very carefully and can often only be frank and forthcoming with very close friends – as things have a way of getting back.

But when you meet Tommy and Frances in their Curragh home and sit for a time chatting with them and they spin the stories, you can easily realise how it was that Michael was regarded as the comedian of the family in his younger days. And he was quite an independent spirit too from the outset.

Frances Kinane remembers the first day Michael went to school and learning later of how the future Irish champion Flat jockey asserted himself with a bully-boy.

"This cocky fellow said 'Hello'. Michael never acknowledged. The young fellow then gave him an elbow and a second elbow. Michael still didn't acknowledge. It was after the third elbow that Michael gave him one box and that was that.

"Another day Michael asked to go to the toilet. He was in infants class at the time. Mrs. Dwan allowed him out. It was almost an hour later when he returned. 'What kept you?', he was asked. 'I had a terrible long wee-wee', came the cool response."

⌘ ⌘ ⌘ ⌘

A lot had happened for Michael Kinane from those happy childhood and boyhood days in County Tipperary and later the apprentice days on the Curragh when he arrived at the Royal Ascot '94 meeting.

Already he had finished runner-up on Sheikh Mohammed's King's Theatre in the Epsom Derby and he was very much in demand – outside of the contract he had with the Sheikh – with trainers who readily acknowledged his prowess as a big-race rider.

The opening day saw him in absolutely brilliant form as he recorded a treble in winning the Queen Anne Stakes on the Luca Cumani-trained Barathea, the St. James' Palace Stakes on the William Jarvis-trained Grand Lodge and the King Edward VII Stakes on Foyer for the Michael Stoute stable. And he was third in a blanket finish on Chatoyant in the Prince of Wales's Stakes and third again in another blanket finish on Missel in the Coventry Stakes. So it might easily have been a fabulous five-timer or a six-timer if Vintage Crop had won the Ascot Gold Cup.

Then on the Wednesday he lifted – and lifted is the operative word – the Coronation Stakes on the Henry Cecil-trained Kissing Cousin. Geoff Lester in the *Sporting Life* reporting that "unstoppable Mick Kinane turned on another magic show as he landed his second Group One race in 24 hours."

Lester went on to say that in the process Kinane put the finishing touch to a monumental gamble. "Bookmakers almost ran out of chalk as Kissing Cousin's price plummeted from 20/1 to 13/2 and took well over £80,000 out of the ring."

Whereas Kinane came from well off the pace to snatch the St. James's Palace Stakes on Grand Lodge, this time he played catch-me-if-you-can and they simply couldn't. Cash Asmussen on Eternal Reve gradually reeled in Kissing Cousin but the French raider's final-furlong fling failed by inches.

Nothing, in the final analysis, matched the way he brought Barathea, in what *Raceform Note-Book* described as "an inspired ride", to lead in the closing stages and win by a neck from the 15/8 favourite, Emperor Jones with Gabr a short head away third.

Some would argue that he was seen to even better advantage on Grand Lodge and his power-packed finish saw him snatch the spoils in the very last couple of strides from Distant View. "This was Kinane at his best and the decision to hand him a two-day suspension for his use of the whip was nothing short of diabolical", said the race-reader of *Raceform Note-Book* in the frankest fashion possible.

Praise was heaped on Kinane by the most respected members of the race-writers profession for his riding on that June day at Royal Ascot.

"The race of the meeting got the ride of the meeting", was how Brough Scott in his *Racing Post* report summed up Kinane's performance in the St. James's Palace Stakes.

"Four hundred yards of as intense and committed a joint effort by man and horse as you will ever see. Hats off the Grand Lodge and Michael Kinane.

"On the television or from the stands, you forget the climb. From the turn into the straight right until a levelling-off in the final 100 yards, the race is against the collar.

"Up that climb Darnay and Royal Abjar now faced. Moving to the outside with a good five lengths to haul back, Kinane and Grand Lodge appeared to have the stiffest task of all.

"In 24 seconds, there will be the winning post and all the cheers and shouting which only Royal Ascot brings. At this moment, there was no breath for shouting. Just the whispering bite of hooves on deep green grass, the rush of air as the straining figures rocket past, and the memory of men's hard eyes and horses' dilated nostrils as they search for the ultimate.

"No eyes come harder than Michael Kinane's. You see them through the goggles locked on that upward climb. No amount of well-intentioned Jockey Club rules are going to change what he is there for. He is now going to force Grand Lodge to go where it hurts and more.

"All great jockeys have their time. Michael Kinane's is now. The style is different to Piggott's, Eddery's or Carson's. The best comparison is Laffit Pincay at his height in America. What you got, on Barathea, on Foyer, but most of all on Grand Lodge was the strongest motion of body and mind at present functioning.

"Running up to the furlong pole Michael had got Grand Lodge travelling, but there was a lot more work to do. The apricot silks are clamped low behind the mane, the polished boots drive hard in shared effort with the four-legged athlete beneath, and the arm which has already arched out four times to demand commitment will six more times insist that the chestnut colt puts every fibre into the closing battle.

"Ascot is the most glamorous front window in the racing game. It's great to welcome the world in. But let's not do so with pathetic concessions to pretend horses are not there to hurt. Overcoming the strain can be the greatness of it. Rewrite the rules. Rejoice in a jockey called Michael Kinane."

When an inspired few moments in the saddle bring out such an inspired piece of writing from one of the finest writers in the game – and such a spontaneous tribute from an Englishman to an Irishman – then you know that Michael Kinane had truly arrived in the summer of '94.

He had entered the pantheon of the immortals of his profession and globally at that. There was nothing else to be proved.

PART SIX

CHRISTY ROCHE

*Knowing the Glory with Assert,
Secreto and St. Jovite*

16

"It's All About Being Involved With Good Horses"

Somewhere in the South, on the morning of a big hurling match between Cork and Tipperary, I was chatting with Christy Roche over the bacon and eggs and tea and toast and he summed up his philosophy about the racing game in one sentence: "In the end life for a trainer, as for a jockey, is about being involved with really good horses."

Then he went on: "Look, the way I see it is this, you could break your back going everywhere to ride 100 winners and more in order to become champion jockey and then along comes a colt like Assert and it changes everything for you.

"The same too when I got up on Secreto to beat the seemingly unbeatable El Gran Senor at Epsom. And St. Jovite turning the tables on Dr. Devious at the Curragh. You wouldn't exchange moments like that for anything. If I had my choice between being champion and riding an Assert, a Secreto or a St. Jovite to victory in a Derby, I would jump for the latter any day."

Christy Roche has always been a man who savours the big occasion – a man too who has risen to the big occasions in spectacular style as a jockey. You might say that his love and understanding of the moments in sport that have a depth of significance equal to great occasions in life itself, where the life and death forces are mirrored truly with epic grandeur, stem from being such an avid follower of Ireland's national

253

game of hurling. The Man From Bansha loves nothing better than to be around the Tipperary hurling team.

I have sat with him on the sideline at Semple Stadium in Thurles on a sun-drenched July evening watching Tipperary preparing to throw down the gauntlet to Galway in the 1989 All-Ireland semi-final and I have talked about the merits of the team travelling back with him from Thurles in his friend "Babs" Keating's car.

Nothing moves him more than the intensity of a championship battle between Tipperary and Cork in Munster, like the dramatic matches in the 1987-'92 period. He was to be found then, when not caught up riding at a Sunday meeting, in the Tipperary dug-out and no one ever questioned why Christy was there. He became part and parcel of the scene. He lived and died a thousand deaths with "Babs" Keating and the rest of the management team.

On one particular Sunday afternoon when he was engaged to ride in the early races at the now-defunct Phoenix Park racecourse, he made arrangements in advance to be whisked from the course to Croke Park after changing from silks into his ordinary clothes. The man at the stile knew he would be coming through – and one moment Christy was seen on the television screens battling it out in a finish at "The Park" and the next, lo and behold, there, large as life in his customary berth on the sideline. If you weren't a hurling follower and didn't know about his involvement, you would have thought some kind of miracle had been worked!

As with fellow-Tipperarymen Michael Kinane and Charlie Swan, Roche has always put the quality of life above and beyond the mere banking of money for its own sake, though as I sat with him in the sun lounge of his comfortable home and spread on the Curragh one day late in May '94, he turned suddenly and said: "Racing has been good to me. I owe everything to the Sport."

Quality of life for Christy means that if he was offered a million pounds to ride in a country where he would have to reside permanently and there was never again an opportunity to watch a hurling match in the sun or hit a golf ball from a tee, he would see it, frankly, as exchanging heaven for hell – as hell must be a place devoid of the sound of the singing

254

ash and where no one ever had to sink a four-footer for the match and the money in a fourball where there was a lot of pride at stake!

They say of Christy that off his handicap he's one of the most deadly around. I have a dream of one day finding a place in the team with "Babs" Keating, Michael Kinane and himself in a big Golf Classic, a trio to compete with for the laurels, who know what pressure is all about and how to cope with it.

But back to the pressure that stems from riding Derby winners. When Christy Roche said to me with total frankness that he would prefer the glory any day of being associated with an Assert, a Secreto or a St. Jovite than being champion jockey, he wasn't talking as one who had never worn the champion's crown. No, he was Irish Champion Jockey six times.

However, he is the first to admit that when he really hit the high plains with David O'Brien and Assert, a new dimension came into his life as a jockey, for his French and Irish Derby triumphs in 1982 were achieved in the full spotlight of the television and satellite age – a long way on from the earlier Classic successes that he had for "Darkie" Prendergast.

Before St. Jovite arrived on the scene, Christy Roche had no hesitation in naming Assert as the best colt he had ridden – putting him ahead of Secreto. He contends that El Gran Senor didn't get the distance of the Epsom Derby in 1984 and winning the Irish Derby subsequently proved nothing, as the race was run at a dawdling pace early on and became a sprint finish in the end that suited El Gran Senor down to the ground. He would apportion no blame whatsoever to Pat Eddery for El Gran Senor's failure at Epsom.

He maintains that if Assert had met Golden Fleece in the Irish Derby in 1982 it would have been a fantastic race and Assert, he thinks, might have come out on top, though he acknowledges that Golden Fleece's performance in coming from literally nowhere to win at Epsom was breathtaking.

Where would he place St. Jovite in relation to Assert and Secreto? "I have to accept now that on the form that he produced in winning the 1992 Irish Derby, St. Jovite would have to be put ahead of both Assert and Secreto for he was absolutely unbeatable that day."

The wheel came full circle for Christy Roche in the sense that after riding for "Darkie" Prendergast, Vincent O'Brien and David O'Brien, he should have been honoured by Jim Bolger in being appointed his No. 1 jockey. And more than that – he dominated the race for the 1989 Irish Jockeys' Championship with Michael Kinane ("I rate Mick world-class as a jockey" was his spontaneous tribute to Kinane long before the world woke up to the latter's genius through his big-race triumphs from Belmont Park to Longchamp, Epsom and Melbourne).

In the end, Roche realised that it was impossible to over-take Kinane during the 1989 season. Kinane, powered by a spate of winners from his retaining Dermot Weld stable, was champion with 112 winners to Roche's 81, the next nearest to them being Stephen Craine on 53.

But the following year – 1990 – Christy Roche took the title from Kinane by riding a grand total of 113 winners. That season Kinane was on 80 and both of them again dominated the scene.

Ironically, when losing out in 1989, Roche had ridden his highest-ever number of winners and he had his previous best when runner-up for the title to Wally Swinburn.

The Bolger-Roche partnership was highlighted in 1989 by the winning of five races over the two days of the Budweiser Irish Derby week-end programme at the Curragh through Noora Abu (20/1), Eliakim (7/1), Elementary (7/1), Armanasco (4/1) and Upward Trend (9/1). That brilliant summer was made even more memorable also for Roche by the fact that Tipperary won the all-Ireland senior hurling crown for the first time in 18 years. And Christy was in the Tipperary dug-out when the final whistle sounded.

Roche is the first to acknowledge the "unbelievable amount of success" he enjoyed while attached to the Bolger stable as first jockey. And the first to acknowledge also Bolger's ability to turn out his charges fitter than anybody else could make them.

Overshadowing everything else during this period, of course, was St. Jovite's pulverising of Epsom Derby winner, Dr. Devious in the '92 Budweiser Irish Derby.

Was Roche confident that St. Jovite would turn the tables on Dr. Devious? "I was 100% confident going into the

Curragh Classic. I remember riding St. Jovite in a gallop seven or eight days after returning from Epsom and saying to myself: "I will win the Irish Derby."

"St. Jovite had plenty of problems going to Epsom. When you are tackling top company, you simply cannot afford to have any problems. But it all came right in the lead-up to the Curragh race. I knew in my heart that Dr. Devious would have to be something really out of the ordinary – a colt in the Nijinsky class – to stop St. Jovite and I knew he didn't rate in that category. So bar something going terribly wrong on the day, we were home and dried."

Roche derives immense satisfaction when he reflects on Jet Ski Lady's 50/1 triumph in the 1991 English Oaks. "I went against every opinion, all preconceived tactical assessments in deciding that I would have to make the running from flag-fall if Jet Ski Lady was to beat Shamshir, Shadayid and the rest. I knew she had more stamina in her make-up than Classic ability. My big chance then was to bring her stamina into play, to test the others to the very limit from the outset.

"This plan worked to perfection and when something like that comes off, you get a lot of pleasure out of it."

❈ ❈ ❈ ❈

Christy Roche was trained in the hard school of the late, great P. J. "Darkie" Prendergast, with whom he had instant success. Roche speaks with deep affection of "Darkie". He ended up riding first jockey to the stable, winning five Irish Classics – the 2,000 Guineas on Ballymore (1972) and Nikoli (1980), the 1,000 Guineas on Sarah Siddons (1976) and More So (1978) and the St. Leger on Mistigri (1974).

He was born in the little village of Bansha, famed because of its links with the late Canon M. J. Hayes, founder of the self-help Muintir Na Tíre movement that did so much to uplift life in the rural areas before the advent of television and the affluent society.

He was one of ten children, his late father, Billy, doing casual labouring to support his large family. Times were hard in that era when there were no proper social security services as we know them today and if you didn't get a job, you took the emigrant ship to Britain or the States or some other part of the globe.

Christy Roche left a desultory school career to work for local farmer and prominent GAA referee, John Moloney. He milked 25 cows a day and was paid 50p a week – the going rate at the time.

He had ridden a few ponies but was not enamoured of riding. It was only because his two older brothers, Pat and Tom had already found work with P. J. Prendergast that he too was despatched by his mother, Josie, to Mrs. Gallagher, his new landlady in Kildare.

He arrived as a homesick fledgling of 14 on the Curragh – a reluctant apprentice. He makes no secret of the fact that he tried to bunk home on several occasions. But somehow or other he survived while most of the others fell by the wayside.

On his third ride he won an apprentice race, on his sixth the Irish Cambridgeshire on 40/1 chance, Willya and on his ninth the Irish Cesarewitch on 100/6 chance, Say The Word. "I think I rode 15 horses the first year and was lucky enough to land the Autumn double. And I was champion apprentice for the next four years."

Then he graduated to riding as second jockey to the powerful Paddy Prendergast stable, understudying Australians like Des Lake, before in time becoming stable jockey.

Peter O'Sullivan in his autobiography, *Calling The Horses*, described Paddy Prendergast as "an Irish Volcano" and Christy Roche said frankly that "he was a hard man to ride for". Indeed, not many finished their contracts with him and when one of the Australians left, for example, before the end of a given season, Christy would invariably be called upon to fill in for the rest of that season. "Darkie" had a set way of doing things and no one – literally no one – was allowed to break the mould. You could take your papers and leave if you wanted it otherwise.

In an age when there were no big syndicates, no Arab money about, "Darkie" Prendergast could go to the yearling sales and buy small by the inflated standards of later years and pick out potential world beaters or he would purchase them away from the sales. "He enjoyed phenomenal success with

258

horses that he selected with a master's eye", said Christy Roche. "He was dealing on a shoestring compared with the prices paid at the Keeneland Sales when Vincent O'Brien, Robert Sangster and John Magnier hit the scene in the mid-seventies and then along came the power of Arab money. I often wonder what 'Darkie' would have achieved if he had had those kind of resources behind him."

One of Prendergast's most inspired purchases was that of Pelorus, which was to prove such an anchor to the stable over an eight-year period. Peter O'Sullivan relates in his book how the chestnut gelding by Sea Serpant out of Dinah's Daughter was knocked down to Kerr & Co. for 30 guineas in the sale ring at Ballsbridge on 30 September 1941 and "Darkie" Prendergast bought him from Bertie Kerr for £200 on behalf of one of his patrons.

"There's no doubt he was a great trainer," said Lester Piggott of Paddy Prendergast.

"He was a self-made man, who grafted for success and went right to the top of his profession from a difficult start," said Christy Roche. "But he was a fantastic judge of horseflesh."

Contrary to what many people thought, it was not on the "flying machines" – that is the brilliantly speedy two year olds – in his Curragh stable that "Darkie" brought off his cleverest coups. No, it was on maiden three year olds that he has assessed to a tee. Sometimes before they had even made their first appearance of the new season, he would have judged the ones that were just short of Classic standard. These were real betting propositions, literally "thrown in" against rival maidens he knew were totally outclassed on a line through other animals in his stable, formed the previous season.

"I was very, very close to P. J.," said Christy Roche. "He was like a father to me. I remember this day he was very ill and he called me to his room. He said: 'Christy, I have this horse lined up and I want you to ring up this friend of mine and tell him to do the needful for me'. I knew then that it wasn't medicine he was looking for but that he was going for a real old-style touch. I told him his instructions were already as good as carried out.

259

"As I walked towards the door, he called me and, as I turned back, he remarked: 'The only problem is that *two* of us know now.'

"In a situation like that P. J. seldom if ever failed – and the one he had lined up on that particular occasion romped home."

There was another occasion when "Darkie" brought off a famous "Sting", part of racing lore around the Curragh, and the story has it that in one stroke he cleared off a sum of £17,000 owed to one bookmaker, who promptly closed his account.

On the day Prendergast died, Christy Roche was riding Ardross at Ascot in the famous black and red halved colours. In a way he would have wanted it that way for Royal Ascot will always be linked in the minds of old-timers with the "flying machines" from Prendergast's stable like The Pie King, Martial, Typhoon, Young Emperor, Bold Lad, Prince Tenderfoot, Floribunda.

※ ※ ※ ※

After Prendergast's passing, Christy Roche linked up as second jockey to the Vincent O'Brien stable. In the early part of his career, there was no one better at laying out a horse for a gamble than Vincent O'Brien particularly when it came to races like the Irish Lincoln, the Irish Cambridgeshire and the Irish Cesarewitch (instance the successes of Hatton's Grace and Knock Hard, for example) and not forgetting either the way the bookies were hit with fearless gambles at Cheltenham.

But when Christy Roche became associated with Ballydoyle it was at the stage that "gambling was out", to quote his own words.

"It was an entirely different world to the world I had known in Paddy Prendergast's", he said. "It was all on the sale and value of class horses. And the winning of key races meant, of course, that their potential as stud properties was greatly enhanced. Everything was geared to this. Everything was pitched on a plane where a colt could be valued at millions and millions of pounds or dollars if he hit the target like Nijinsky or The Minstrel. You don't have to think of gambling in that world. The gambling was in the buying of the yearlings that would eventually be expected to become very valuable stud horses."

Vincent O'Brien's attention to detail was almost "unreal", according to Roche. His horses were never "overdone". When he set his mind on a major target, he would not rush an animal he knew had the class and requisite ability. He could wait and wait and wait.

But you could bet your last pound that on the day that mattered, he would produce the horse at its ultimate peak. There was no better illustration of this than the way he prepared colts like Sir Ivor, Nijinsky, Roberto, The Minstrel and Golden Fleece to win the Derby and Alleged to win the Arc two years running.

Vincent could be handling a one million dollar colt, even a three million dollar colt and ask him to train one costing £5,000 and he would show the same total attention to detail. His methods never changed.

The timing of his charges on the gallops – even down to sectional timing – was viewed as an integral part of his approach by Vincent O'Brien. "Darkie" Prendergast, on the other hand, had little interest in the clock. He was a great believer in trials, said Christy Roche.

His approach was to test his rising stars, his immature horses on the gallops with horses in the stable that he knew provided a reliable guideline.

P. J. could be as tough on the horses in his stable as the men who rode for him. His belief was that if they weren't good enough, they wouldn't survive. Good horses went by the wayside – that was the penalty. But, against that, "Darkie" enjoyed immense success with his methods and the only race of any consequence that eluded him was the Epsom Derby. And he would surely have won that with Meadow Court in 1965 but for the fact that this colt ran up against Sea Bird II, reckoned by many top judges to have been the finest Derby winner of the post World War Two period.

When David O'Brien started up in 1981 Christy Roche rode for him while still attached to Vincent's stable.

"The following year with David having such a good start, I went as stable jockey to him and things never looked back after that. David and I hit it off from the outset. I can never forget his loyalty. There was pressure on him, I know, to put up a different rider on the best horses in the stable, particularly Assert but he wouldn't hear of it. I cannot forget him for the fact that he gave me my chance of riding an Epsom Derby winner in Secreto and, in fact, I was to win three Derbys (a French, Irish and English) with David through Assert and Secreto."

Roche's admiration of David O'Brien as a trainer, as we have seen already, goes every bit as deep as his admiration of the qualities that made "Darkie" Prendergast and Vincent O'Brien outstanding world-renowned trainers. He believes that if David had not decided to opt out of the profession, he could in time have gone on to scale even greater heights than he did, granted, of course, that the right horses came along. And to any knockers of David, he points succinctly to the fact that he bought Assert for £16,000 and made him into a dual Derby winner.

From riding class horses for "Darkie" Prendergst, Vincent and David O'Brien and Jim Bolger, Christy Roche learned also that in the world of Hong Kong racing you discovered owners prepared to bet in awesome fashion on what they considered to be handicap "good things" and landing a gamble was more important than the glory of Classic success.

Christy came in this day after the horse under him had performed so promisingly that he enthused to the Chinese owner that it could even win a Classic. The response he got was: "What price will he be to win a handicap? – and that meant even if he was high up in the handicap.

"I suppose 6/1", replied Christy.

Then Christy was asked whether he felt he was certain the horse in question would win the Classic. Of course, he couldn't be certain as it would mean a rise in class. He was thinking of the honour and the greater reward in prizemoney that could accrue to the owner – if he pitched for a higher target.

But the Chinese owner was thinking only in terms of bringing off successful gambles. "Sure win, sure lose", was his motto. There was no in between.

In this atmosphere if you wanted to break with a stable you did not particularly relish riding for, you simply won on one that was in the "sure lose" category!

⌘ ⌘ ⌘ ⌘

When David O'Brien decided to walk away from it all – like a young composer of genius who has left a small body of compositions that leave us hankering for more of the same and weeping silently for all the might-have-beens – Christy was left, it seemed, high and dry.

An old pro, who had forgotten more about the game than many of the young ones would ever learn, finding himself with nowhere to go. Having always been around stables that accommodated "the goods", was it going to happen that he would suddenly, not by choice, be a journeyman freelance again, looking for the scraps from the table?

The prospect wasn't a nice one to contemplate after the highs of Assert and Secreto and Chantilly, the Curragh and Epsom.

He knew no other life, only a life around horses. He admitted to being hooked on the drug that riding horses meant for him. Hooked on the racing drug itself and, as you gave yourself another "fix" from a mythical syringe you knew only too well of its crass and ruthless side, of the sad rejects it left in all its facets, down to the guys who could not cope with the battle to keep the weight down, to others who fell victim to the bright lights or the inducements of those who had no pity for aspiring youth, to the sad flotsam and jetsam of the punting game.

He was like a journalist who after years pushing the pen knows there can be no other calling for him or those missionaries I met up with in Africa who could not call it a day, unwilling to return home after retirement, content to die under an African sky as the dawns and the sunsets had seeped into their bones.

"Looking back, I would be very happy with what I achieved", he told Pual Kimmage of the *Sunday Tribune* in the count-down to riding St. Jovite in the 1992 Prix de L'Arc de Triomphe. "I would never have any notions of people saying: 'Yeah he was a great rider'. I will never go down in the record books as one of the great riders.

"That would never worry me but at the same time I would like to think that I have mastered it more than anybody because I think I understand horses better than most. I have worked very hard on that end of it – really worked.

"From the time you are a stable lad you get to know horses, the feel of them, their trips, everything they can do. Racing is about beating the opposition."

When Declan Gillespie left him in 1987, Jim Bolger didn't have a No. 1 jockey. He needed a big race jockey. The destiny that shapes mens' ends was conspiring to bring Jim Bolger and Christy Roche together in a partnership that would be as rewarding for both as was Roche's brief but memorable partnership with David O'Brien.

Before he left for Hong Kong, Roche was in contact with Bolger and terms were agreed. The rest is history. . . .

When the break came in their relationship before the start of the 1994 Flat season close friends of Roche knew there was a problem. They knew also that it had nothing whatsoever to do with the short fuse, the volatility of either party. The two had shown in the High Noon of their golden days that they could live with one another. Like a volatile couple in a volatile marriage who have come to understand one another completely. No hang-ups about the petty squabbles.

When the "divorce" came, nothing was said publicly by Christy Roche to give any insight into why he had broken with Bolger. All that appeared in the media was that he would be riding freelance in 1994.

Bolger sat down beside him at a Naas meeting and asked him if he was prepared to ride for him again. Roche replied with a firm "No!", adding: "You know full well the reason why, Jim."

They left it at that. His son-in-law, Kevin Manning continued as No. 1 effectively to the Bolger stable during 1994.

It was obvious that nothing had changed Jim Bolger's admiration of the qualities of Christy Roche as a big race specialist. Back in 1992 he had made the point to Paul Kimmage that Christy might not be as polished as other top jockeys but then he was not a believer in "the sitting prettty technique".

Bolger went on to acknowledge that Roche was a tremendously keen competitor whose basic interest was "results". While he wasn't into style, he was certainly into "effectiveness".

And he summed up: "I think his big thing as a jockey in his finishing power. In those desperate head-to-head finishes over a furlong or two furlongs, he nearly always comes out on the right side. I'd say without doubt that he's the best finisher in the world today, due in no small measure to his physique. He's not very tall but he's very strong, built like a tank."

❊ ❊ ❊ ❊

I'm back in the sun lounge of "Curragh View" and Christy has come in from the yard and stables at the back of the house to chat to me about what the future will hold for him when he finally decides to call it a day as a rider. Now 44 and 30 years a jockey, it was something worthy of note in itself that among the stables he was riding for in 1994 was that of Vincent O'Brien's son, Charles, and also happy to use his services and derive all the benefits of his immense knowledge on the gallops – apart from booting home the winners for him – was Aidan O'Brien.

Roche doesn't see himself turning his hand to training. He will be content to continue to buy potential National Hunt horses – "get them ready and sell them on". At the moment he is buying between 20 and 25 store horses a year and it is the kind of no-risk business that he likes, bringing a steady income that keeps his bank manager happy. Somewhere up there in the Great Beyond "Darkie" must be smiling at Christy being into the buying and selling game and thinking that something must have rubbed off from him – "the father of my career" as Roche dubbed him – to the Man from Bansha.

Will one of his two sons, William, 12 now, or Pádraig, who is 8, follow in his footsteps? It's already out in William's case because of his size – "but Pádraig is showing great interest and who knows", says Christy.

Like most fathers in professions where arriving among the Top Ten or Top Twenty can stem from a talent ingrained from the cradle, Christy Roche would be loath to encourage a son of his to become a jockey if he thought he would end up being just a run-of-the-mill rider. Great at the top but rough if you fail to make it.

Noeleen emerges from the sitting-room to say a quick "Hello" in that so-relaxed friendly manner of hers.

Outside in the driveway the Mercedes with the car phone, one of the trappings of Roche's success – but now for a jockey not to have a car phone is like a journalist without a tandy in this computer age.

Paul Kimmage had asked him for that *Sunday Tribune* interview if he had seen the Eiffel Tower or been to the Moulin Rouge and enjoyed the Can Can?

No, he had not seen the Eiffel Tower – "and I've no wish to". It meant nothing to him really and neither did the Moulin Rouge or any other "in" touristic place in Paris that you wished to name.

Like the foreign correspondent who is doing the "beat", concerned principally with getting out his copy from the theatres of war and strife and meeting deadlines, Roche had come to see different cities in different countries as places that had race tracks where you rode in a particular race, maybe in more than one.

All the better if the hotel you stayed in – if it meant an overnight stay – had a sauna, for it could help in the continual battle with the scales.

But for him the tourist sights held no attraction.

Paris during Prix de l'Arc de Triomphe week-end became like Galway during Festival week or Tralee or Listowel. It was the racing that concerned you – the drive to ride winners.

Yes, Noeleen might go shopping in Paris while he was in the sauna and all he would say to that, with that spontaneous laugh of his, was "I hope she doesn't spend too much." But even if she did, it would be no big deal, the two are so close that theirs has been one of the happiest marriages among the racing fraternity.

You get back to where you started, talking about hurling and golf when you are not talking about racing and horses. Back to subjects that have real significance for him.

Basically, all the fame that Assert and Secreto and St. Jovite brought him . . . the money he banked as a result of those big-race successes never affected the essential Christy Roche.

He has his feet as firmly on the ground now as he always had . . . when he started out as a reluctant apprentice in those far distant days on the Curragh.

PART SEVEN

TOM FOLEY

And the Horse that Money Could Not Buy

"I Thought Every Horse in Ireland was For Sale"

The Englishman had spent over half an hour on the phone trying to cajole Tom Foley into a sale – the sale of Danoli. Tom wasn't budging, irrespective of how much the offer was being upped. Finally, in exasperation the Englishman could only exclaim: "I just can't believe it. I thought every horse in Ireland was for sale."

At one point there was a firm offer of £250,000 on the table.

But Tom Foley knows that more would have been paid if the gelding by The Parson had actually been put on the market.

In his home in Aughabeg in June of '94 he told me that he had a call one day from a prominent Irish National Hunt trainer, trusted by potential English buyers as one of the top judges of horseflesh in this country (I am keeping my promise to Tom not to go public with the name), and the money he was talking far outstripped the original top offer of £250,000.

"These boys won't take 'No' for an answer", is what Tom Foley heard down the line.

Would they have gone to £300,000?, I asked. "I believe they would and more if I had demanded it and we had been willing to part with the horse."

Ted Walsh said to me once that "every horse has his price". That may be true – but it doesn't take account of the fact that the owner in question may not be willing to sell.

Dan O'Neill, the bonsetter, who lives in Myshall, which is within a stone's throw of Aughabeg, had paid just £7,000 for Danoli. He doesn't have to worry about money. He knew, as Tom Foley did, that you could be going to the sales all your life and only once might you strike gold. He could lay out a fortune and yet fail to find another Danoli. And if he were to sell the horse that had opened up for him the world of ownership and given him such pleasure, he would probably end up regretting it for the rest of his life.

Danoli was the first horse that Dan O'Neill ever owned. Just imagine that. Men spend their lives trying to acquire an animal good enough to carry their colours at the Cheltenham Festival meeting, apart altogether from having the ability to win one of the prestigious prizes. They may never succeed in that ambition.

Along comes Dan O'Neill and not alone does he see his colours carried to a famous victory at the first time of asking – one that engendered the greatest "Irish roar" and most enthusiastic scenes in the winner's enclosure since Dawn Run and Jonjo O'Neill triumphed in the Gold Cup in 1986 – but Danoli went on to Liverpool and won the Martell Aintree Hurdle by eight lengths, beating into third place Fortune and Fame and into fifth the Smurfit Champion Hurdle winner, Flakey Dove.

Dan O'Neill's wife, Olive, anxious that her card-playing husband should get out and about more often, suggested racing as a suitable outlet. In Ireland the bonesetter holds a proud position and if he is good, his position is more privileged in its own peculiarly "specialist" field than that of any Harley Street specialist. As the man said "if you put it out, he will click it back in again".

But it's not as simple as that. The recognised bonesetter, who knows his job and does it not so much for the money but for the easing of pain he brings to those who arrive at his door crippled and leave thanking him to the high heavens for what he has achieved by the manipulation of his hands, won't enter the arena where he thinks medical treatment, maybe surgery is required. If there should be tuberculosis or cancer he won't profess to usurp what medical authorities alone can

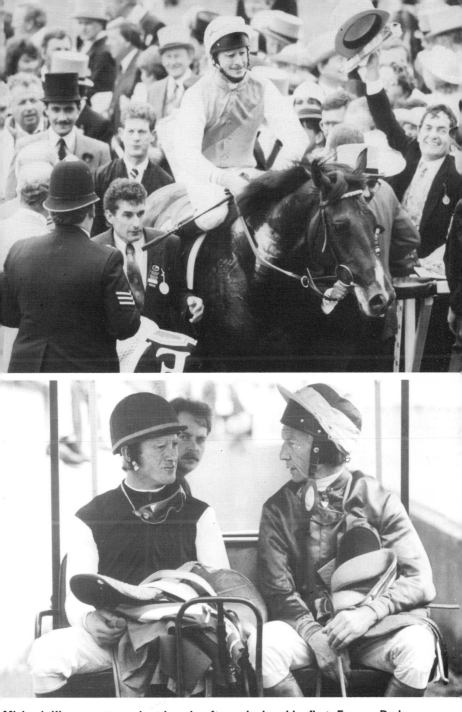

Michael Kinane returns in triumph after winning his first Epsom Derby on Commander-in-Chief in 1993 and (bottom) a rare picture by ace racing photographer, Ed Byrne, of Michael Kinane and the ageless Lester Piggott together at the Curragh. When Michael Kinane was ten, he walked in a fancy dress parade in Killenaule, County Tipperary, as Lester Piggott, complete with riding breeches and boots and carrying a little saddle.

Michael Kinane winning the 1990 English 2,000 Guineas on Tirol for the Horgans of Cork and landing a massive ante-post gamble in the process and (bottom) Kinane and Dermot Weld share with Maura and Stan Cosgrove and Brig Sam Waller, then Senior Steward of the Turf Club, at right, the pleasure of Additional Risk's sweeping victory in the 1991 Hong Kong Invitation Bowl race.

The mobile phone like the car phone is now part and parcel of Michael Kinane's daily round; (top right) Michael's father, Tommy and (bottom) under the Arch of Triumph with the Italian connections of Carroll House after winning the 1989 Prix de l'Arc de Triomphe.

Dermot Weld receives the congratulations of Ireland's Taoiseach (Premier), Albert Reynolds on Vintage Crop's historic triumph in the 1993 Melbourne Cup and (below) his wife, Mary is congratulated by Raymond Smith (left) and Tom McGinty (right), Editors of the *Irish Racing Annual*.

David O'Brien (top left) and Christy Roche (top right), who combined in the dramatic short head victory of Secreto (left below) over El Gran Senor in the 1984 Epsom Derby. El Gran Senor was trained by David O'Brien's father, Vincent, pictured bottom right with his son-in-law, John Magnier, boss of the Coolmore Stud.

Peter Chapple Hyam cannot
refrain from giving a victory
salute to the heavens after it
announced that Dr Devious h
got the verdict over St Jovit
the photo finish to the 1992
Kerry Group Champion Stake
Bottom picture shows just h
close it was between the tw
colts, as John Reid came on
inside to snatch victory at th
post from Christy Roche.

UNDER THE ARCH OF HIGH PROMISE . . . Aidan O'Brien, the most talked-of young trainer in Ireland today with his wife, Anne-Marie, and son, Joseph, at their imposing new stables in Piltown, County Kilkenny, and (top right) Aidan on the new all-weather gallop and (bottom right) Anne Marie with her imposing crystal award when she won the Irish N.H. Trainers' Championship crown in 1992-'93.

A sextet of leading British trainers: (clockwise from top) — Richard Hannon, Henry Cecil, Michael Stoute, Luca Cumani, John Dunlop and Mark Johnston.

deal with and, therefore, there is no conflict between a man like Dan O'Neill and doctors and specialists who realise the unique function he can fulfil.

In Ireland too the most famous of the bonesetters never have to advertise. It's all by word of mouth. One who has been successfully treated will tell another and it becomes like a chain letter, passing from village to village and town to town, beyond the boundaries of counties and even outside the shores of this country to reach people in Britain, who come by boat or by plane to get "the treatment".

For the successful bonesetter, one whose services are constantly in demand, the pressure on his time is such that he will have no life of his own if sympathy for those in pain and wanting immediate treatment dominates his outlook. And it can go beyond the human field. The queues become endless in the long days because there are sportsmen who will bring their horses and their greyhounds. For example, a month before Cheltenham '94 Paddy Kiely arrived from Dungarvan with Shuil Ar Aghaidh wanting Dan O'Neill to have her injured back probed. Does that name – that causes such problems to non Irish-speaking commentators in Britain to pronounce – ring a bell? Yes, the same horse that won the Stayers' Hurdle at the 1993 Festival meeting.

So it's not surprising that Olive O'Neill should want her husband to seek another form of relaxation in addition to the camaraderie of the cards in a rural setting.

Dan responded to her suggestion that he get involved in owning a horse. He turned to Tom Foley. At first Tom was rather sceptical because he had known people to say to him that they would like to see him training a horse for them – but when it came to going to the sales to buy one, nothing happened.

But Dan O'Neill pressed Tom Foley again some twelve months after the initial sounding on the subject. "Now I realised he was serious", said Tom.

No figure was mentioned. Tom Foley would just have to decide how far he was going to go.

"We went to Goffs the week of the Derby Sales in 1991 to buy a well-bred filly. The reason I had a filly in mind was that if she broke down, then at least we would have a brood

273

mare. I marked out eight or nine in the catalogue that I felt might fill the bill – if the price was right. There was nothing that attracted me, so Dan and myself wandered round the boxes.

"Danoli stuck his head out of this box and there was something about that intelligent head of his that immediately caught my eye. I kept going back for another look. And each time I kept saying to myself: 'I like that horse'. When I returned, as often as not I found him asleep. That indicated to me that he was a very relaxed type and there would be no bother in getting him to settle."

The irony of it was that Danoli was one of the horses that failed to qualify for the Derby Sale itself. He went through the ring in the pre-Derby Sale and failed to reach his reserve of IR10,000 gns. In fact, he was only making IR5,800 gns.

Outside the ring Tom Foley offered IR£7,000. Willie Austin, the gelding's disappointed breeder, held out for his price.

Foley pressed him hard. "Listen, Willie, the Derby Sale starts in two days time. I can go there and buy what I want and get it for seven. You have 48 hours to think about it."

Two days later the phone rang in Tom Foley's. It was Willie Austin on the line. He would take the seven grand.

"I often look back on that summer's day in Goffs and leaving for home with Dan O'Neill and wondering if we had lost a good one in Danoli. And to think that three years on the horse I managed to get for Dan for £7,000 would have won a total of £114,000 in prizemoney and in the process changed things completely for me", recalled Tom Foley.

Yes, a sea change if ever there was one.

❊ ❊ ❊ ❊

Tom Foley had known days when he almost despaired of making a living out of the 62 acres he farmed in County Carlow. To find his farm you head first for Bagenalstown and if you experience difficulty, you will easily get directions at the Lord Bagenal Inn, a great haunt of racing folk before and after Gowran Park races.

He was into cattle mainly but it was difficult to run more

than 35 cattle on 62 acres. "You get fed up doing the same thing year in, year out and all you're doing is scratching around and making no money."

You wondered if the life that could have prompted another epic in *The Great Hunger* category from Paddy Kavanagh (Kavanagh who loved a flutter in Dublin betting shops in his days of struggle) had added to the grey hairs on Tom Foley's head, making him look older than his 47 years.

Indeed, as we headed through this area of Carlow, through tillage country and sheep country also, lines from what was unquestionably one of Kavanagh's greatest poems readily sprang to mind:

> *Watch him, watch him, that man on a hill whose spirit*
> *Is a wet sack flapping about the knees of time.*
> *He lives that his little fields may stay fertile when his own body*
> *Is spread in the bottom of a ditch under two coulters crossed in*
> *Christ's name.*

It struck me that if there had been no Danoli, Tom Foley's continuing back-breaking struggle with the soil might have evoked the same summing up as Maguire's uneventful struggle evoked for Kavanagh:

> *He will hardly remember that life happened to him –*
> *Something was brighter a moment. Somebody sang in the*
> *distance.*

But life DID happen for Tom Foley from the day he acquired Danoli for Dan O'Neill.

The lead-up to that began when in 1986 he decided to diversify into training horses.

A January day at Tramore, the seaside town in County Waterford that we associate more in our minds with the August Festival meeting and the laughter of children on the sands. Thursday, January 28 to be exact. A very significant day for Tom Foley in that it saw him turning out his first winner.

Foley has Rua Batric in the opening race on the card, the Lismore Ltd. USD Handicap Hurdle. The mare by Energist goes off at 6/1 second favourite in a field of 14. She takes the lead between the last two flights and, coming under pressure at the last, holds on to beat the 20/1 shot Queen of The Glebe by a neck with the favourite, Cormac's Lass unplaced.

"Trainer Thomas Foley" in the results sheets made no headlines, for in British terms it would be akin to some "unknown" of the training profession coming up with a winner at Cartmel of Fakenham. The Jenny Pitmans or "The Duke" Nicholsons weren't suddenly beating a path to Tom Foley's door with cheque-books waving!

Foley and Dan O'Neill had been friends long before Dan asked Tom to buy a horse for him. Foley found that he had to utilise O'Neill's magic as a bonesetter not on his own limbs but on a mare of his called Motility. "She had a shoulder and disc problems and he put her right. She won for us at Gowran Park but eventually had to be retired due to arthritis."

⌘ ⌘ ⌘ ⌘

Danoli got his name from a combination of the Christian names of husband and wife – Dan and Olive – hence Dan-Oli.

Deep down Tom Foley had a secret fear – that Danoli might go the way of other promising horses that had passed through his hands. "Every decent horse I had in the past had been sold at the owner's insistence, the first time it showed anything on the racecourse", he said. "It was frustrating. You picked one out, you broke it. You did everything to put it on the road to achieve something that would help put you on the map and then it was gone from your yard. You were back where you started, beginning everything all over again."

Danoli was making his debut in a bumper at Naas on Saturday, 31 October 1992. On the way to that meeting Tom Foley felt he had to know – it was imperative that he get some inkling from Dan O'Neill as to his intentions if Danoli won first time out. Foley already believed he had a potential champion on his hands, was so convinced, in fact, that he was prepared to have the biggest bet of his life on the gelding that particular day. As it happened, he heard at the last minute that Arthur Moore was confident that he would win the race with Atours, the Chief's Crown colt that had been fourth on his debut. "I chickened out", said Tom.

"If Danoli wins today and you feel you should let him go, you should name your price now, so that I will be able to strike the best bargain possible for you", said Foley to his friend and new-found owner.

O'Neill didn't commit himself at that point one way or the other. In reality he had no knowledge as yet of the thrill to be derived when you saw a horse carrying your colours go past the post – a winner.

Atours was backed down to 11/10 favourite in a field of seventeen. When he came to challenge Danoli in the straight those who had backed him as if he was a cold-stone certainty thought that he would go on and win easily. But Danoli, then a four-year-old, withstood the challenge to win by a length and the form was franked when Atours justified 4/5 favouritism on his next outing at Punchestown.

Now Dan O'Neill realised that his life had changed in a twinkling. "Before I bought Danoli I had virtually no interest in horse racing. When people brought horses to me with bad backs and bad shoulders I used to think to myself that they were crazy in a way to keep them, especially when they had all these problems to cope with. But that win at Naas gave me the biggest thrill of my life and it also changed my entire outlook."

No money was going to induce him to sell the horse that had become his pride and joy. "Money doesn't come into it. The value is the thrill of watching him run and win", he said.

Tom Foley returned to Aughabeg a happy man on two counts. He knew now that he had a horse that was going places and he would be able to concentrate on training him to bid for prestigious events he would never have given a second thought to challenging for before – as he just didn't have the material in his yard.

And he had money in his pocket out of the bet he had on Danoli – not, mark you, anyway near what he would have had if he had not "chickened out" in face of the word around the course for Atours. A fraction was all he laid of his original intended bet but at odds of 16/1 the return to a self-confessed "small man" (in the betting sense as in every other sense!) was still quite rewarding.

Danoli came home with sore shins after that first win. It was to teach Tom Foley the lesson that he must NEVER run the gelding on going other than soft.

From his Naas success, Danoli went on to win a winners' bumper at Naas on 30 January 1993, starting at 10/1 and completed a hat-trick of bumper wins when he disposed of previous winner, Diplomatic by no less than nine lengths at Punchestown on Sunday, 21 February 1993, with Hotel Minella, a winner at Limerick on his debut, third. Danoli was returned at 5/2 that day.

Tom Foley now came under intense pressure to challenge for the Guinness Festival Bumper at the Cheltenham Festival meeting. Mick O'Toole was sending Diplomatic despite that defeat by Danoli at Punchestown.

But in the final analysis Foley, once he heard that the going at Prestbury Park was likely to ride fast, took a cold, calculated decision not to risk Danoli. And no one was going to sway him from that decision. "I was afraid of jarring him up", he said.

If Danoli had gone to Cheltenham and suffered sore shins on the firm going, the very people who had been encouraging Foley to send the horse across would have turned on him and accused him of rank bad judgement. By listening to no one in the first place but knowing what was best for the gelding and his future, Tom Foley proved that he was his own man – a man who was already reaching for the stars with the first true star he had in his stable.

⌘ ⌘ ⌘ ⌘

The 1993-'94 National Hunt season garnered pace and Danoli reappeared at Fairyhouse on Tuesday, November 16, carrying 12st on his hurdling debut. With Charlie Swan in the saddle he led from start to finish and, jumping well, was not extended to land the odds of 4/6 as he passed the post 4½ lengths in front of Fambo Lad.

He again started at odds-on (8/11) when scoring by four lengths from previous winner, What A Question at Punchestown on December 5 with another previous winner, If You

Say Yes in fifth place. On that occasion he was ridden by T. P. Tracey as Charlie Swan had the mount on Legal Profession, the second favourite, who finished fourth. Swan left Punchestown deeply impressed.

There seemed no reason why Danoli should not make it six victories on the trot when he left Aughabeg to contest the 1st Choice Novice Hurdle (2m 2f) at Leopardstown on Monday, December 27, the second day of the four-day Christmas meeting. The Paddy Prendergast-trained Winter Belle, third in the bumper at the Cheltenham Festival meeting behind Rhythm Section and the 9/4 favourite, Heist had won his previous race over hurdles at Naas in November and Minella Lad and Cockney Lad had also both scored on their previous outings. Still Danoli was installed 4/5 favourite.

Those who supported him purely on the Form Book could never have known what happened on the road.

Tom Foley revealed to me that, as was customary, Danoli was being taken in his normal horse-box to Leopardstown – the one that allows him to look out the window – when it broke down on the way. Along came Jessica Harrington, who trains in County Kildare. She offered to take the horse in her waggon which could accommodate four horses. Danoli resisted strongly being put into this, as he had never been in one before.

"We tried and tried again", Tom Foley recalled. "It was no use. He was getting into a lather of sweat and I said 'we'll give it one more try'. This time we succeeded. I believe he left the Leopardstown race behind him because of the way he got so upset."

The race itself was not run the way Danoli likes it. "Danoli is a horse that likes to come off a strong pace", the trainer noted. "If he's ahead too early, he gets the feeling that he has it over the opposition and he will be inclined to idle. But if they go with him from the outset, then he will conclude that he has to battle for victory and that brings the very best out of him."

At Leopardstown on that afternoon in December, Danoli had to make the running from flag-fall and, as Tom Foley noted, this played right into the hands of Winter Belle, who was held up and did not make his challenge until approaching the last. Danoli, after making a number of mistakes, actually surrendered the lead in the straight and the race was fought out in the end between Minella Lad and Winter Belle who won convincingly by two lengths, with Danoli a half-a-length away third.

Tom Foley was philosophical in defeat making the point that "you have got to take races as they come and sometimes there's nothing you can do". But deep down he knew that Danoli had not given his true running. In light of subsequent happenings, it is clear now that what happened on the road when his own horse-box broke down, contributed in the main to the only defeat that the gelding was to suffer in the 1993-'94 season.

Foley's faith in Danoli remained undimmed. But he felt he had to know how good the horse was. He had to know was he really up to the challenge of Cheltenham and performing at the festival meeting at the level demanded there – for victory.

The only way, he decided to himself, that he could ascertain this was to throw Danoli in at the deep end by taking on some of the current crop of top hurdlers. And he would learn if Danoli could go "at Cheltenham pace and take hurdles at the speed they go at Cheltenham".

That meant going for the AIG Champion Hurdle (2m) at Leopardstown on Sunday, 23 January 1994. In the field was the 1993 champion hurdler, the Martin Pipe-trained Granville Again. The other contenders included Fortune And Fame, ante-post favourite to win the '94 renewal and also Shawiya and Destriero.

"I had had a call from Charlie Swan, who said to me 'I'll ride Danoli at Leopardstown if you give me the ride'. I thought to myself that if Ireland's champion jockey over the jumps thinks that Danoli is the one for him in a race of this class, then it means that he believes he's a really top-class hurdler.

"I told Charlie Swan that we would talk it over and come back to him with our decision. I knew what we were taking on. I knew also that we would know exactly afterwards what the horse was able to do."

There were those who argued that Tom Foley was going a bridge too far in pitting Danoli, a novice, against the champion hurdler of '93 and the potential champion of '94. "One neighbour actually said to me that I was flying too high altogether and that Danoli would finish in the next parish."

Foley was undeterred. He rang Charlie Swan and told him he had the ride.

Fortune And Fame went off at 4/5 favourite with Granville Again next best at 7/2, Noel Furlong's Destriero at 11/2 along with Shawiya, Danoli was on offer at 12/1, having touched 14/1 at one stage in the betting.

Danoli was actually in the lead before the second last and going extremely well. Even when Fortune And Fame took over, he could not shake off the novice with the ease and authority that the professionals had anticipated. In fact, Danoli rallied so well that momentarily it seemed he might even cause a sensational upset. However, a mistake at the last did not help his cause but, nevertheless, he stayed on strongly to finish only one-and-a-half lengths behind Adrian Maguire's mount.

"That race made a man of Danoli", said Tom Foley. "It confirmed for me what I had always believed – that I had on my hands a horse that was something special and now I knew that I didn't have to fear any opposition in Ireland or England in the novice class."

⌘ ⌘ ⌘ ⌘

When Danoli went on to pulverise a field that included some of the most highly-thought novices in the country in the Deloitte And Touche Hurdle (2m 2f) at Leopardstown on Sunday, February 13, I wrote the next day that it was the finest performance by a novice hurdler that I had seen since Golden Cygnet had won the Supreme Novices Hurdle in 1979. I couldn't see him beaten at Cheltenham.

It was not just the fact that Danoli put ten lengths between him and Coq Hardi Affair but the manner in which he won the race that was awesome. For he was in command from the outset and when he was driven clear after the second last, it was merely a question of how much Charlie Swan would win by as the admiring cheers rose from the stands and enclosures.

To put the outstanding merit of that performance into true perspective it has to be noted that Coq Hardi Affair had won his two prevous races; What A Question, who was third, had finished '93 by beating Dee Ell by nine lengths at the Leopardstown Christmas meeting, having earlier won at Punchestown; Idiot's Venture had won four of his previous five races; Court Melody had completed his '93 programme with two successive victories while Padashpan had finished '93 by winning three on the trot. And the Charles O'Brien-trained Yukon Gold had won his previous race at Fairyhouse by 5½ lengths and before that he had won from a field of 24 at Naas.

Charles O'Brien had hoped that exactly forty years after his father had recorded a treble at the festival meeting with Stroller (Gloucestershire Hurdle), Lucky Dome (Spa Hurdle) and Quare Times (National Hunt Chase) he would have his first runner at Cheltenham in Yukon Gold. Coming down off the stand, he remarked to me that it was no good now sending Yukon Gold across – "after the way Danoli had destroyed his field in the Deloitte And Touche Hurdle".

You might have thought that the agonising was over for Tom Foley, that it was merely a question of travelling to Cheltenham and knowing the glory that many trainers had hankered for and some with far greater ambitions had failed to experience.

Foley had to decide between the Supreme Novices Hurdle (2m) and the Sun Alliance Hurdle (2m 5f).

Some had even suggested that he should go for the Champion Hurdle. "I want to win at Cheltenham. I am not going to take on the best for the sake of possible glory when I know that, on the form of two races at Leopardstown, Danoli looks a certainty to win one of the novice hurdle events at the festival meeting", was his frank summing-up.

He had one fear in relation to the Supreme Novices Hurdle. "I was a small bit afraid that they would go a fierce fast pace in the two-mile event. I feared that Danoli might not lie up with the pace and if he made a mistake, he might not have the time to get going again to produce the kind of finish I knew he was capable of.

"All right, he had run powerful races over two miles but Cheltenham, I knew, was different. English runners were quite accustomed to the pace at which they would be going in any two-mile event but an Irish challenger might need to adjust."

Before he made the fateful decision, Foley put Danoli into a schooling hurdle at Punchestown. "I told Tom Taaffe to go like hell on his mount to really test Danoli at Cheltenham pace and to find out finally that he could take hurdles at Cheltenham racing pace. Taaffe told me afterwards that when Danoli came up beside him, he went by with ease and was still running away as strongly as if he hadn't to call upon all that was in the tank.

"Danoli had never been asked a question like that before in a gallop. I was more convinced than ever that, bar a fall, he would win at Cheltenham."

The fateful decision was taken to challenge for the Sun Alliance and in hindsight Tom Foley was correct in all his planning and in the final execution of that plan on the racecourse itself.

However, he died a thousand deaths before Charlie Swan gave that arm-aloft victory wave to the heavens as he passed the winning post – and the Irish contingent let rip with an explosion of cheering that made the spine tingle and the emotional scenes that followed in the winner's enclosure were the most inspiring I have experienced since Dawn Run and Jonjo O'Neill won the Gold Cup for Ireland in 1986.

A small man became a "King" overnight in the eyes of every Irish aficionado of National Hunt racing. He needed no crown to know what it was for royalty to be acclaimed and acknowledged in a manner that seemed only for the dreamers and star-gazers.

In his quiet dignity, in the way he remained himself amidst all the back-slapping, he won for himself a special niche in the hearts of all the English enthusiasts too who crowded Cheltenham on that Wednesday afternoon in March and millions more looking in on television.

Afterwards he would say simply: "I'm still a small man and always will be."

Tom Foley had never been abroad before in his life. Cheltenham '94 marked his first trip to England and the first time he travelled by plane.

He was a notorious bad traveller – even in a car. "I must always take a seat in front, otherwise it's a certainty I will get sick."

His introduction to air travel could not have been worse as he accompanied Danoli on the flight to Bristol. Gale-force winds had compelled ferry companies operating across the Irish Sea to suspend the transportation of livestock for the time being.

Tom was very worried that Danoli might get upset on his inaugural trip in a plane. As it was, the gelding took it all in his stride while Foley, true to form, never let the sick bag out of his hands from the moment of a rough take-off from Dublin in very strong winds to the stomach-churning descent itself.

He arrived green-faced from the buffeting and was sick three times on the motorway between Bristol and Cheltenham.

But there was no time to bemoan his lot as he was photographed on the tarmac at Bristol, open-necked, as he watched Danoli treading British soil for the first time – a picture that made the front page of the *Sporting Life* next day.

The hint of a smile conveyed that he was happy despite that upset stomach. "Now that we had got here, I knew the horse was going to be alright for the challenge that lay ahead. And I had a feeling too that he was not going to be affected by the atmosphere of the big occasion."

No four-star or three-star hotel beckoned Tom Foley. He was not one of those world-weary travellers who thought in terms of a jacuzzi in a spacious suite, or a bottle of claret over dinner and a VSOP cognac to go with the coffee.

So intent was he on keeping a watchful eye on Danoli for every minute of every hour in the count-down to the Sun Alliance Hurdle that he sought – and got – permission from Edward Gillespie, the personable Manager of Cheltenham, to stay with "the lads" in their quarters at the edge of the racecourse itself.

And who could blame him.

284

When he dreamed his dreams he could have been forgiven for hoping that some day he might win the Lotto.

"But a Cheltenham victory wasn't even in my wildest dreams. I used to watch Cheltenham on television every year and it never entered my head that I would ever even have a runner. How could I when I only had fifteen horses in my stable and not one real star among them. I always thought the festival meeting was reserved for the big boys."

Now he had arrived at the Mecca of the National Hunt game. As he caught his first glimpse of the course, as he looked over towards Cleeve Hill as dawn came over the countryside on Monday morning, the nightmare journey from Ireland behind him, burdened with the knowledge that all of Ireland was willing him and Danoli on, he said to himself: "This horse is my only chance. I will probably never have another good enough to run at the festival."

His wife Goretti (a local girl from Aughabeg despite the Italian-sounding Christian name) stayed at home with the children, three girls, Sharon (18), Adrienne (16) and Goretti ("we call her 'little Goretti' ") who is eleven and one boy, Pat who is nine.

They would watch the race on the television set in the sittingroom. They would all get very excited, yes, and Goretti Foley confessed to me: "Before the start the tension was unbearable because I knew how much was at stake for Tom and I thought too what it was going to mean for him and the rest of us if the horse won."

Fr. Dowling would speak off the pulpit at Mass on the morning of the race itself, leading the congregation in prayer. His words were simple and heartfelt, echoing the inner emotions of the people of the villages and the townlands all around. After Danoli had triumphed in the manner in which everyone had hoped – and prayed – Fr. Dowling would drop around to the Foley homestead to offer his congratulations. He had no bet because his modest investment at odds of 7/4 wouldn't have represented "value", as he put it later. A pastor in a rural townland would be looking for odds of 10/1, maybe more to his money.

285

"I am what I am. I tell the truth and I know I cannot go wrong that way", Tom Foley said to me in his home three months on as he looked back on all the build-up of media pressure before the race that was completely new to him and to the demands of the television, radio and newspaper representatives on the day itself and in its aftermath. He confessed to losing almost a stone. There were days when he had hardly time to eat. There were times too when he felt he was caught in a maze from which he could not extricate himself.

After his run in the A.I.G. Europe Champion Hurdle the papers, as Tom Foley recalled, began talking about Danoli being the Irish banker for Cheltenham. It reached a peak following his brilliant win in the Deloitte And Touche Hurdle.

Then there were the phone calls from well-wishers, the letters, the cards. Some of the people were friends and neighbours – "but many of them I'd never heard of before".

Advisors came too to his house or button-holed him in the most unlikely of places. Well-meaning advisors who wanted to whisper in his ear the "do's" and "don't's" of Cheltenham because they feared that, having never been there before, he might walk unthinkingly into quicksands of his own making.

"A few who came to me wouldn't know one end of a horse from the other and knew even less about Cheltenham than I did."

There seemed to be no escape when you were in charge of the one horse that was carrying the flag of Ireland in a manner that bore comparison only with the way Dawn Run, who had been trained not all that far away in Gowran, had carried it on Gold Cup Day in '86.

Enterprising news editors in Britain, especially those on the tabloids looking for a new angle in the lead-up to Cheltenham, had caught on to the idea that Tom Foley, the man who NEVER wore a tie, was going to shatter the sartorial traditions of the parade ring and, more so, the traditions surrounding the presentation should Danoli win. And, of course, inherent in all this was the unthinkable – a winning owner stepping up to be greeted by the Queen Mother without a tie!

"I don't even wear a tie when I go to Mass", said Tom Foley with total honesty to the newshounds who rang him looking for "colour".

"If I fasten the button of my collar I start to get dizzy. If I was to put a tie on, I would have to pull it down and leave my shirt open at the neck. There is not a lot of point in that."

In the area around Aughabeg and Myshall you don't judge a man by sartorial splendour and whether he wore a collar and tie or not. And what Old Etonians felt was essential on certain august occasions, as when one was in the royal enclosure at Ascot or mounting the presentation stand at Cheltenham in the presence of the Queen Mother and other dignitaries, didn't wash in personal judgements. They identified fully with Tom Foley when he said: "I am what I am."

And they understood perfectly what his wife meant when she said: "Tom Foley isn't a man of airs and graces."

He would remain himself always, come what may. And his directness, the very simplicity and total truthfulness of his manner shone out like a beacon and, frankly, the spin doctors trying to shape him to their ends would simply have had to walk away and surrender their fat fees.

Edward Gillespie, a frequent visitor to Ireland, who has gone on record to state categorically that Cheltenham without the Irish would be nothing, took the trouble to ring Tom Foley at home and assure him that there was no compulsion whatsoever on him to wear a tie. "I appreciated that gesture very much. Indeed, he could not have been kinder and more co-operative in every way possible and I will always remember him for it."

As he left the house on the Sunday on the way to Dublin and the flight to Bristol, Goretti Foley slipped a tie into Tom's pocket. He put it on at the moment he felt himself he should put it on. No big deal. He was wearing it when he was presented to the Queen Mother.

Newsmen would crowd around him afterwards asking hm what he had said to her and what she had said to him. "I don't know what I said to her. I was just myself. She's a lovely woman, a very gracious lady."

All that was afterwards. After Danoli had done the business as the Irish nation expected it of him.

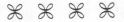

Wednesday morning, 16 March 1994, dawned and if Tom Foley had known Kavanagh he would have recited quietly now to himself lines echoing the days when he was only a farmer, the days of real struggle before Danoli arrived to so-dramatically change his fortunes:

He saw the sunlight and begrudged no man
His share of what the miserly soil and soul
Gives in a season to the ploughman.

The pressure on him that morning was intense, intense beyond anything you can imagine. A tightening in the stomach that he thought would never leave him.

He had to carry it himself. And no one could help him. He thought of Winter Belle failing in the first on the Tuesday, backed down to 4/1 in a field of 18 and finishing only eighth. Winter Belle who had inflicted on Danoli his only defeat at the Leopardstown Christmas meeting.

A whitewash for the Irish. Atone finishing only fourth in the Arkle, Gimme Five backed off the boards in an awesome gamble spearheaded by "The Sun Dance Kid" himself, to start 4/1 favourite in the Stayers' Hurdle and coming home in 20th place.

Fortune And Fame, considered by many an Irish banker for the opening day, had been pulled out of the Smurfit Champion Hurdle because of injury and ante-post punters had suffered accordingly.

"The Irish punters had been cleared out on the Tuesday and I knew they were looking to Danoli to rescue them", said Tom Foley.

More than that – they were looking to Danoli to rehabilitate wounded Irish pride. It was unthinkable that he should fail now.

The day became one long mad whirl for Tom Foley. Meeting Peter O'Sullevan on the course at the crack of dawn. The early-birds love it when the horses come out to exercise and you rub shoulders with trainers, owners, jockeys and race writers and there seem to be no barriers, for every horse is trying at Cheltenham (or should be!) and "whispers" mean nothing, only if it is the kind of solid information that

288

conveys that a horse is suddenly running a temperature or is not right for some other reason and then you can hedge if you have had a substantial wager ante-post or avoid going in with "the head down" on the course itself.

Tony O'Hehir wants to interview Tom for RTÉ. "I had to oblige Tony."

Then it's Colm Murray for RTÉ News. Again he obliges.

There's a call from the Pat Kenny Radio Show. They want him live on air. They mention a time, 12.30 p.m. to 1 o'clock. "Impossible", Tom tells them politely. At that time he'll be completely caught up with the preparations for the race itself, the first on the card. But he will be only too willing to do it earlier, if that suits. They fix a time that is convenient to him.

Other television cameras. The radio microphones seem to be constantly in front of his face. The questions from the reporters seem to go on endlessly. Later he would get letters from Carlow exiles telling him they saw him on television in different countries.

He was suddenly a celebrity but celebrity status didn't stir any special emotions in Tom Foley.

He came across to millions of viewers on television in Britain as someone totally different – a refreshing difference from what they had become accustomed to on the "talk shows" and the "phone-in" programmes.

A non-drinking Irishman, a non-smoker, a non-gambler, who had never been out of his country before. A man who wasn't burdened by tradition or what the status quo demanded. Who said things simply and directly and with feeling.

They loved him for it. Later he would show me in his home the hundreds of letters he received from people in all corners of Britain, people telling him how he came across to them, that they were thrilled when Danoli won because they wanted to see the horse triumph – because of the man who trained him.

A small man, so different from the big men. The champion of all the underdogs in the mean back streets and out-of-the-way corners in Old England, aspiring to nothing more than a big win on the pools maybe and retirement to the sunshine of the Costa del Sol – all dreaming dreams that might never be realised.

289

"One of our own", they could say over their pints of bitter when they read in some tabloid of the Irish trainer who didn't wear a tie and thought nothing of it.

No need to dwell on the race itself. The Irish Formbook would catch it for posterity in one line "held up, headway sixth, led four out, stayed on well flat".

Yes, a slight mistake at the last but that probably stemmed from the fact that he knew he had the race won or was distracted momentarily by the deep, sustained victory roar that now swamped the Cheltenham racecourse as Irishmen below me in the standing area near the rails' bookmakers gave vent to their feelings by tossing their hats and caps in the air. The place had suddenly gone mad, it seemed.

Back then into the winner's enclosure. There were those who claimed that the modern amphitheatre lacked the intimacy of the old one, that the tiered rows for the spectators, when not entirely filled, couldn't generate the atmosphere of other times. Now half of Ireland appeared to have gathered, crowding every conceivable vantage point to welcome back Danoli.

Someone in an official capacity had said to Tom Foley beforehand that he would have six extra badges for close connections so that he could bring them in with him to the unsaddling area, past the security men at the gate. "I was being tossed up in the air and swept along in a sea of people. I felt as if I was in the middle of a tide of humanity and I hadn't time to think whether I had a badge on or not and I couldn't think either whether any of my party had a badge. The next minute I was standing beside the horse and the cheers were erupting all around me.

"My legs were gone with the excitement from the moment Danoli passed the line in front. The sensation was something I never experienced before in my life, something I could never have imagined experiencing. The scenes in the unsaddling enclosure were indescribable. I had read about the victory scenes after Dawn Run. But it is only when you go through it yourself, when you train a Cheltenham winner like Danoli that the whole Irish nation is behind, that you know what it is like really."

"A great wall of noise to welcome home their own", was how Alastair Down graphically described it in the *Sporting*.

Life. "The Irish opened their throats in a roar the like of which has not split the Cheltenham air since Dawn Run sent English and Irish delirious alike eight years ago."

And he added: "It had nothing to do with the price – 7/4 would not have made the majority of Danoli's supporters rich – but it had everything to do with pride. Their best had taken on our best and carried the day. The cheers came from heads held high. The rivalry between the home team and the visitors is the gin in the tonic of this meeting. And the fierce but respectful competition is contained within the boundaries of the British and Irish relish of this great occasion. Greater divisions and older animosities have no place here."

No champagne flowed for Tom Foley in the immediate aftermath of the race. Or to put it another way, he did not think personally of vintage champagne, he wouldn't have been able to have it if he was a drinking man. He wouldn't even have been able to drink a froth-topped pint of Guinness or Murphy's.

He slipped away from the racecourse, from the tumult and the shouting . . . back to the lads' quarters and lay on the bed in his room.

He lay there for what seemed an eternity and on his own admission, "I wasn't able to move a limb, wasn't able to think straight, I just waited to put everything out of my mind for a while, let go and relax completely."

He could have slept then, all through the evening and through the night and well into the next day and beyond. The weariness of weeks of pressure would have been swept away.

But it wasn't possible with the celebrations in Cheltenham itself before the renewed excitement of the homecoming celebrations in Myshall . . . mounting a trailer as the cheers of the people of the locality echoed in the night air out over the rural heartlands for him and Dan O'Neill. And, as Goretti would tell me, "the bands playing and the dancing into the early hours and all the local talent contributing to make it a night we will remember always."

"I am what I am" . . . and Tom Foley was still himself in the homecoming, wearing no tie now.

And no one cared an iota.

Danoli had delivered for Aughabeg and Myshall and for Ireland.

And if Paddy Kavanagh were alive and if he had been present, he would, with the poet's eye have applauded the falling of the curtain on the first act of Danoli's Cheltenham odyssy and he would have known that "the hysterical laughter of the defeated" would no longer be heard over there.

PART EIGHT

SIRRELL GRIFFITHS

*When the Bonfires Blazed not for
Rugby Heroes but for
a Steeplechaser*

293

17

When Norton's Coin Won For Wales

Sirrell Griffiths milked 70 Friesian cows at 5.30 a.m. on that never-to-be-forgotten Thursday morning in March 1990 before driving his cattle-truck (he did not have a horse-box) to Cheltenham to take on Desert Orchid, the pride of England, in the Gold Cup.

It's history now how 100/1 outsider, Norton's Coin scored a famous victory for Wales. And that same evening in the village of Nangaredig, not far from the town of Carmarthen, which had given the legendary stand-off half Barry John and flying winger Gerald Davis to Welsh rugby, they put up a banner which read: "WELCOME HOME NORTON'S COIN".

The bonfires were blazing not for rugby heroes in an area where hero worship is legendary but for a steeplechaser who had upheld the honour of Wales against the most popular chaser since the incomparable Arkle.

It was a fairytale story in itself – one that disproved for all time, in the National Hunt sphere of racing at any rate, that you need to have the millions of the Arab Sheikhs at your back to win one of the major prizes at the Festival meeting.

The prophets of doom had been lifting their hands to the heavens in despair on the Tuesday when Kibensis, in the colours of Sheikh Mohammed, won the Champion Hurdle. They argued that it would be only a matter of time before the oil-rich Arab princes dominated the jumping scene and there would be no place anymore for the Willie Lomans – the small men with a dream.

After the success of Norton's Coin on Gold Cup Day '90 they knew with new certainty that such dreams could be fulfilled.

Sirrell Griffiths had blazed a trail out of the Welsh valleys. A year later the O'Sullivans of Lombardstown, Mallow, County Cork, enjoyed their finest hour as Lovely Citizen was led in after winning the Christies Foxhunters Chase. We heard the Cork anthem, *The Banks of My Own Lovely Lee* echo out from the unsaddling enclosure to Cleeve Hill and the Cotswolds.

The bonfires blazed in Lombardstown that night – and, yes, they had a party, quite a party, in the Becher's Brook pub in Mallow the night of the homecoming celebration with the Cup.

Then in '93 came Tom Foley with Danoli and with a twinkle in his eye he would say that compared to Sirrell Griffiths with his herd of 70 Friesians he was "the smallest of the small men". And who was to argue with genial Tom when he said that.

And Flakey Dove's victory in the 1993 Smurfit Champion Hurdle had about it all the elements of the romantic also . . . a victory right out of the Field of Dreams.

Dylan Thomas could have written a poem about 50-year-old Sirrell Griffith's return to Wales with the Gold Cup trophy – transporting back in the same vehicle in which he had headed for Cheltenham that same morning. And Norton's Coin ran with the cows in summer months.

Griffiths hailed originally from Herefordshire but he had lived locally in the village of Nantgaredig for seventeen years and Welsh folk had adopted him as "one of our own". A three-horse permit holder, he admitted that farming was his No. 1 source of income. He could have gone into training on a much bigger scale after the success of Norton's Coin ("I had offers to train 22 more horses") but he declined all such offers. "We are to far out of the way to start training on a big scale. You need to be in a major centre. Anyway getting a full licence would mean employing extra labour – we're just a small family concern. It's Joyce, me and the boys."

On the evening of the homecoming, Sirrell's wife, Joyce and his sons, Martin and Linley hardly knew what hit them, such was the excitement in the village.

"Unbelievable", said Sirrell, recalling it all some months later when Geoff Lester of *The Sporting Life* called to talk to him for a feature for the *Irish Racing Annual*.

"We never dreamed anybody would be waiting for us at home. Remember it was 10 o'clock at night by the time I got Norton's Coin back in the lorry from Cheltenham. Then, passing the Railway, I saw this banner across the road: 'Welcome Home Norton's Coin' and our lane was completely blocked with cars.

"There were TV crews and hundreds of well-wishers from the village and afar, and I had to send the boys out for ten bottles of Scotch. There wasn't much left by the time they all went – I can promise you."

Astonishingly, however, not one of the Griffiths family had a solitary shilling on Norton's Coin. "I've never backed him", said Sirrell. "I like a bet now and then, but I've just never brought myself to have a few quid on Norton's Coin.

"We told the whole village he'd run well, though. They took a coach-load to Cheltenham and with their £2 bets and fivers they came home with £17,000. My, it was one hell of a day."

❉ ❉ ❉ ❉

It was a miracle in a way that Norton's Coin ever got to run in the 1990 Gold Cup – and having got to the start, he might not have been allowed to run if the tapes had not already gone up just as he was being kicked.

"I thought our Gold Cup hopes had gone up in smoke when Norton's Coin coughed three times in the paddock before his pre-prep race at Newbury", recalled Sirrell Griffiths. "The vet had him scooped the next day and his lungs were full of muck. He was amazed how the horse had finished the race. Time was against us for Cheltenham now and we had to restrict his preparation to walking."

Norton's Coin was put on a course of antibiotics. Six days before the Gold Cup he was boxed up and despatched east along the M4 to Peter Cundell's Compton stables. Graham McCourt rode Norton's Coin in the crucial gallop, accompanied by Cundell's smart horse, Ryde Again.

The speed that "Norton's" displayed over a mile and six furlongs surprised even Griffiths, who had always maintained that the gelding had the pace to win over two miles on the flat.

McCourt, who had persuaded Griffiths to enter Norton's Coin for the Gold Cup in the first place, told the trainer after that full-scale workout that, provided his jumping did not let him down, the horse had a first-rate opportunity of finishing in the first three.

Fast ground diminished Griffiths' confidence somewhat – "He loves the muck and the softer the better" – and then disaster seemed to strike at the start when Toby Tobias lashed out and caught Norton's Coin on his front leg. "Graham (McCourt) called out to the starter that he had been kicked", Griffiths recalled, "but the tapes were up and they were on their way."

Desert Orchid was never allowed dominate matters as he had done in his races at Kempton, Sandown and Ascot. Norton's Coin was always going well within himself just in behind the leaders. Under a brilliant ride from McCourt he won the battle up the hill with Toby Tobias and Desert Orchid, outstaying "Toby" to win by three-quarters-of-a-length with Desert Orchid third.

Norton's Coin was lame on pulling up, the legacy of that kick at the start. And then when Sirrell Griffiths got to the stable area, after the customary interviews, he found the nine-year-old had drunk half a bucket of water – "but at the bottom were two handfulls of green slime. If he had coughed that up before the race, no way could I have allowed him to run."

❀　❀　❀　❀

When Fiona O'Sullivan set off with the horsebox carrying Lovely Citizen to England for his bid for the 1991 Christies Foxhunters Chase, she was entertaining the hope that the Golden Love gelding which the O'Sullivan's had bred themselves from the mare Kelenham, who they still had at home, would uphold the standard of County Cork.

But in a way she felt it was too much to contemplate that the point-to-pointer trained by her husband Eugene, and which would be ridden by his brother, Willie, would beat what many judges were predicting was an "unbeatable" favourite in Teaplanter. The latter had a string of victories to his credit.

Fiona's destination was the stable of Richard Hannon where her brother, Brian Meehan, was assistant trainer at the time. Each morning in the countdown to the Festival meeting she rode Lovely Citizen at work.

Lovely Citizen had won two hunter chases and three point-to-points but when the experts were analysing how many victories Irish-trained horses might win at the 1991 Festival meeting, the Cork-trained challenger wasn't even mentioned in the reckoning with such as Nordic Surprise, Minorettes Girl, Chirkpar and Kitchi.

Eugene confessed later that he would gladly have sold Lovely Citizen in August, 1990, if anyone had offered him £4,000 for the horse. There wasn't one offer.

When Lovely Citizen was a three-year-old he suffered a broken hock and Eugene was advised to put him down. He decided to take a second opinion. This resulted in the gentle and patient nursing of Lovely Citizen back to the point where he could race. However, the swollen remains of that hock injury meant that the leg was so big and awkward that no one would buy the horse.

He was a horse too with a mind of his own. He got to know how to open the latch to the horsebox in the O'Sullivan stable. Once he went missing for two days. Eugene was beginning to fear the worst when Lovely Citizen found his own way back. Now they have a special lock on his box.

He proved his ability on the point-to-point and hunter chase circuit and the O'Sullivans decided to go for the BIG ONE – the Christies Foxhunter Challenge Cup. Their friends and relations booked for the Festival meeting knowing in their hearts that they would never forgive themselves if the gelding won the massive trophy. No use looking at the race on television when you could be there in the shadow of the Cotswolds cheering your head off as the racecourse commentator announced that Lovely Citizen had got into the firing line coming down the hill. And you would want also to be part of the celebrations if he did pull it off.

No, you might never get a chance again in a lifetime to cheer home a winner from the little village and townland of Lombardstown.

They put on their tenners and fivers at odds of 16/1 and 14/1 and they didn't even ruffle the waters of the Cheltenham betting market – the strongest in the world beside that of Royal Ascot. The professional money was on Teaplanter, quoted at 2/1 in offices in the morning but going off at 6/4.

I will never forget the moment when Lovely Citizen came back into the unsaddling enclosure to a special "Cork roar" inherent in the Irish cheers.

The connections, forming a half circle as they linked arms, broke spontaneously into "Olé, Olé, Olé". Then they began singing *The Banks Of My Own Lovely Lee.*

Joy was written on their countenances. Fiona O'Sullivan was being hugged and kissed by friends as she exclaimed: "I just can't believe it." It was one of the happiest scenes I have ever seen at Cheltenham.

Mary O'Sullivan, mother of trainer Eugene and jockey Willie, combed her hair and smoothed her dress before she went up for the presentation. There was a world in that gesture speaking of the rural heartlands. Her husband, a man of no airs or pretensions, was smiling a broad and happy smile as he gave a victory wave to the circle of connections.

The cameras clicked. I know that there would be colour and black and white prints catching a moment that would never fade for the O'Sullivan family, "Hold up the Cup, Owen", one photographer shouted. He lifted the big, heavy trophy and held it aloft in triumph – and in a way it was as if Cork had completed the treble in the space of six months, the Liam McCarthy Cup and the Sam Maguire Cup having been brought back to the banks of the Lee already.

"The bonfires will be blazing in Lombardstown tonight," said Eugene. "And they will be blazing still stronger again when we arrive home with the Cup."

The finish of the race itself was a heart-stopper. Half-way up the run-in Dun Gay Lass was still holding on, looking to have the race won. Then suddenly her rider Martin Claxton lurched sideways and nearly fell out of the saddle. Claxton, half-way up the horse's neck, and doing the best he could, almost recovered the advantage but Willie O'Sullivan, riding like a man inspired, got Lovely Citizen up on the post to win by a head. It transpired that Claxton had performed miracles to stay on board as his off-side iron had broken clean through.

But the ill wind that cost Martin Claxton the race was blowing on this day in favour of the O'Sullivans. It was their hour and no one was going to take it from them.

There are few stories to match that of Lovely Citizen's triumph at the 1991 Festival meeting. It will go into the annals of Cheltenham legends – and they are many.

⌘ ⌘ ⌘ ⌘

From sheep country in Herefordshire emerged a success story in 1994 fit to stand beside the most romantic associated with the Cheltenham Festival meeting.

Where Sirrell Griffiths had milked his cows before setting off for Cheltenham on Gold Cup Day 1990, now on Smurfit Champion Hurdle Day 1994 36-years-old Richard Price delivered 20 lambs on his 400-acre farm before travelling to the Festival meeting with Flakey Dove and saw her succeed where her grand-dam Red Dove had failed in the race 31 years previously.

And adding to the romance was the fact that Flakey Dove, the first mare to win this race since Dawn Run in 1984, shared a Herefordshire field with a flock of sheep when not being asked to do the business on a racecourse.

Richard Price on the day of his greatest triumph told the media representatives in the winner's enclosure that he had a public licence for only three years but had a permit for six years before that. And he revealed also that Flakey Dove was one of only half a dozen horses he trained.

Where was his father, Tom, we asked? A lover of the hunt, he had been out that very morning with the North Herefordshires but at 70 he didn't like crowds and, frankly, couldn't be bothered trying to elbow his way through the crush of humanity at Cheltenham. So he stayed at home and would have watched the race on television.

Tom Price saddled Red Dove to finish unplaced in the 1963 Champion Hurdle. Now thirty-one years on from that day compensation was being made by Fate to the Price family, for another member of the family, Gordon, had finished third in the Champion Hurdle on 100/1 outsider, Stano Pride in 1985.

Flakey Dove's victory struck a blow for the unfashionably bred and proved once again that you don't have to spend six-figure sums to guarantee success at the Festival meeting.

Her dam's pedigree was listed in the racecard as "untraced" and it was left to her trainer to provide her family history.

The eight-year-old mare traces back to Cottage Lass and was bought in the mid-1950s by Richard Price's grandfather, Tom.

She produced Red Dove from whom at least 100 winners have flowed including Shady Dove, dam of Flakey Dove.

Shady Dove, now 22, was in foal to Epsom Derby winner, Henbit, on the day of Flakey Dove's triumph at Cheltenham and is turned out in the orchard of the Price farm, worked together by the three brothers, Richard, Ivor and Ernie.

They had quite a celebration in the village of Stoke Prior, near Leominster when Flakey Dove returned to a hero's welcome . . . and the pride of the villagers and the community in all the surrounding countryside was all the greater when they reflected on the slur they felt was offered by one scribe that same morning when he implied that really a mare from the sheep country of Herefordshire had no place taking on the more fancied runners like Large Action and Oh So Risky. "Disgraceful", said one of the connections.

But all was forgotten when Mark Dwyer, deputising for the suspended Norman Williamson, brought all his experience and talent into play in riding a perfectly-judged race to beat the 9/4 favourite, Oh So Risky by one-and-a-half lengths with Large Action a further three-quarters-of-a-length away third.

The two inns in the village, The Lamb and The Wheel-barrow had a whale of a night and the extended nature of the Price family ensured that there was a lot of back-slapping.

They would remember always the moment when Mark Dwyer thrust his fist into the Glouchestershire skies in a fitting victory salute as he returned in triumph to receive the acclaim that echoed out to the Cotswolds.

Sirrell Griffiths . . . the O'Sullivans . . . and now the Prices. From Wales to Lombardstown, near Mallow, to a sleepy village in Herefordshire. And the day after Flakey Dove had won, Tom Foley, the smallest of the small men, from out of County Carlow wrote his own special chapter in the annals of the Festival meeting with Danoli.

With romance like this you understand more fully why men dream dreams at which the Festival meeting is at the centre. And those for whom the dreams are fulfilled are privileged, as nothing in racing can quite compare with experiencing the roar that swells around the amphitheatre of the unsaddling enclosure at Cheltenham.

That roar represents the challenge and the spur.

PART NINE

AIDAN O'BRIEN

The Piltown Man is a Real Champion

18

A Pupil of
The Bolger Academy

You drive into the heartlands of Kilkenny hurling and up in the hills beyond Thomastown in the area around Piltown you come upon the stable of Aidan O'Brien, who according to Christy Roche is booked for greatness.

"This lad is something different", said Christy. And Christy's opinion is one you've simply got to respect for he has ridden in his time for P. J. "Darkie" Prendergast, Vincent O'Brien and his son David, and for Jim Bolger.

The view looking out over the sweep of the valley below, stretching away to the Comeraghs and majestic Slievenamon is breath-taking on a summer's day. "Over there is Pat Flynn's", says Aidan and you realise how distance shortens from this vantage point. You find yourself endeavouring to pinpoint Ballydoyle on an imaginery wall map and it strikes you at that moment that you are talking to an O'Brien with the kind of ambition and attention to detail that Vincent O'Brien displayed when he first started out on his own in Churchtown, County Cork, after the death of his father, Dan in 1943 and then moved in 1951 to the green sward in Tipperary that he was to fashion into the most famous gallops in the world. Aidan O'Brien, of course, is no relation to Vincent.

You realise too, as you watch the activity in the magnificent new yard and take in the new all-weather gallop which

307

winds its way for almost a mile up the hillside to your right – a 300 ft climb from bottom to top – that you have arrived at the establishment of a man in a hurry – one who at the end of the 1993-'94 National Hunt season in Ireland had not alone been crowned champion trainer but also champion amateur jockey. And still only 24.

He hails from County Wexford – the same kind of country that gave Jim Bolger to the training profession. Aidan O'Brien actually spent three-and-a-half years working with Jim Bolger and was assistant trainer to the Master of Glebe House before he left. Where others terminated their tenure at Coolcullen abruptly and departed with no love lost, O'Brien will tell you frankly: "Jim Bolger is a very good and a very fair man. He expects the best from you but if you respond as he wants you to respond, then he is good to you. I learnt pretty well all I know from him."

And Bolger, for his part, has nothing but the highest praise for Aidan O'Brien, naming him unhesitatingly as "one of the top three people to have worked for me since I became a trainer."

"He is a wonderful human being and one of the nicest young men I have ever come across", said Bolger. "If anyone was to epitomise the attributes of a gentleman and a scholar it is he. Aidan is intelligent and clever and picks things up quickly.

"Any operation with which he is associated can only prosper. His industry and dedication are tremendous. I'd have done anything to keep him working for me."

Aidan O'Brien was born in Killegney, Clonroche, near Enniscorthy and it was inevitable that like Jim Bolger he should have been involved as a youngster playing Ireland's national game of hurling and he also played Gaelic football. He played at midfield in under-16 competitions with his club Cloughbawn. He still follows the game but now such is his all-consuming passion for the horses and such are the time-consuming demands of his chosen profession that he cannot any longer be put into the category of a diehard enthusiast.

But like Jim Bolger he has no pretensions. There is not an ounce of affectation in his make-up. He presents a boyish and unassuming manner that surprises when you contemplate his achievements to date and the impact he has made in such a short space of time on the Irish racing scene.

That impact becomes all the more significant and praiseworthy when you reflect on the fact that unlike Dermot Weld, John Oxx, Jim Dreaper and Edward O'Grady, he did not spring from an established training family. However, his father Denis was a very keen point-to-pointer. "He rode many winners and there were always horses around the yard", Aidan told me.

O'Brien left secondary school midway through fifth year. "First of all I got a job weeding strawberries and later did shift-work as a forklift driver in Waterford Co-op.", he recalled.

The call of the horses was in his blood. Long-term he saw no other life. And already deep down the ambition to become a trainer was stirring in his veins.

�֍   ✖   ✖   ✖

He got the break that was to set him on the ladder that would lead eventually to making him the most exciting talent to burst on the Irish racing scene in the Nineties when a family friend, Pat Kelly, put him in contact with Curragh trainer, P. J. Finn, a son of the legendary Tipperary hurler, Jimmy Finn, who was selected at right wing back on the Hurling Team of the Century in 1984.

He was with P. J. Finn for two months before the latter opted out of the game and, fortunately for Aidan O'Brien, Pat Kelly then arranged a job for him with Jim Bolger. He was on his way.

You don't come away with a full note-book after interviewing him. He's at one with Vincent O'Brien in the sense that he's much more at home and far more relaxed when you put aside pen and paper and switch to a conversation taking in a broad range of subjects. In a word, you must come unaware to touch on the points that matter and you gain a hint as to why he has become the talk of the racing fraternity as they ponder the heights he will eventually scale. As one insider put it to me: "The Sheikhs have already taken note of his talent."

There are 70 horses in this yard, overlooked by the hill known as Carriganog, or Rock of Youth and to reach the stables you come through the little village of Owning. Twenty-five of them are Flat horses. But in truth the operation he is now involved in with his wife Anne Marie and her father Joe Crowley, who lives four miles away, embraces three yards all within the proverbial stone's throw of each other. Aidan O'Brien likes it that way, for as he put it to me very shrewdly: "If you have only the one yard you are left wide open if a virus strikes. By having three we are far better placed to isolate the horses that avoid becoming affected."

Anne Marie feels that in time Aidan would like to be basically a Flat trainer, though like Dermot Weld and Jim Bolger he would always train a few good jumpers and this would be facilitated by having dual performers in the yard. Reflecting on such a move, Jim Bolger says: "I'm sure he will become a force on the Flat . . . but I hope it's later rather than sooner."

It was on the racing circuit that Aidan and Anne Marie met and fell in love.

It happened at Galway in 1989. Aidan was riding Midsummer Fun in an amateur race for the Jim Bolger stable – it came home a winner, incidentally – and down at the start his eye was caught by the dark-haired Anne Marie, who also had a mount in the race. Shy and all though he was, he was so smitten by love at first sight that it was inevitable that he should take it from there and the rest is history.

Fate stepped in to cause his departure from Jim Bolger's stable in a rather unusual way. Six weeks before his wedding he broke his shoulder in a fall – "and I just never went back".

At that stage Anne Marie had just started training on her own and Aidan found himself completely involved in assisting her in the operation. He was the first to acknowledge that the three-and-a-half years he had spent with Jim Bolger represented "an invaluable experience" and that, having started off as a stable lad doing the most menial jobs around the yard and then being given more and more responsibility as time went on, he acquired a tremendous amount of knowledge of every facet of the training profession. "I would start work in the dark and finish in the dark.

I would ride out in the morning and do just about everything", he recalled.

Life has changed for Anne Marie since the arrival of Joseph, who celebrated his first birthday in June '94. A most lovable child, he is "King" of all he surveys in the kitchen of the home when his mother is doing the domestic chores.

She confesses to me that Aidan and herself decided to make the building of the new yard the priority before erecting a new house. All that can come later. Now there are many potential owners out there who are only too eager to send him horses as week-in-week-out he commands the headlines with his strike rate ("we've never had a problem getting horses. We're full all the time, thank God", he tells me, adding: "We have good owners, great owners, in fact, both Irish and English").

And on this evening in June '94, as Anne Marie serves the tea with that natural hospitable touch for which the O'Briens have become renowned, Aidan apologises for the fact that if he couldn't give me all the time I might have liked, it was because he had to be in Waterford in less than half an hour. He was going to pick up a brand new £20,000 Subaru Legacy car from the sponsor, T. Farrell & Sons of Grannagh and it would carry the legend: "Aidan O'Brien Drives a Subaru".

He doesn't drink or smoke – something that would have endeared him to Jim Bolger when he was riding as an amateur for him. Neither does Anne Marie drink or smoke.

⌘ ⌘ ⌘ ⌘

Aidan, one might say, was carrying on where Anne Marie left off when he took over the licence from her. In the two years she was a public trainer she carved a unique niche for herself in Irish jumping history. She was Ireland's champion National Hunt trainer in the 1992-'93 season with 26 winners of 53 races earning a total of IR£206,458 in prizemoney, putting her ahead of Noel Meade, Arthur Moore and Paddy Mullins. Her father was top owner the same season.

It captured the imagination of the race writers in Britain that this girl, described by one as "the 23-year-old with the stunning looks and killer instinct" should emerge overnight as the leading trainer in that area of the racing game that has generally been viewed as the natural terrain of hard-bitten men heading for Cheltenham with their charges come March each year. It was in 1993 that she sent her first challengers to the Festival meeting. Much play was made in the British media of the fact that at 29 per cent, her strike rate in Ireland was better than Martin Pipe's in Britain.

The tabloids made hay of the fact that she had forsaken the catwalks for the life of a trainer. But in reality she only took modelling assignments in Kilkenny as a teenager "as a hobby" and from the outset she knew deep down that her life would be spent in racing. "I was brought up to believe that horses were part of life itself", was how she put it to me.

One of six sisters, it was from her father that Anne Marie took over the licence. Joe Crowley didn't just fade away into the background. No, he remained very much involved as did Anne Marie's mother, Sarah. The Crowley operation could best be described as a classic regime – added to when Aidan married Anne Marie – and bearing comparison with other notable examples like the Dickinsons, the Rimmells and Reveleys.

Anne Marie's sisters could be found riding out for her and helping out in different ways when they were at home. Anne Marie herself was very successful in the saddle, riding 23 winners as an amateur, one of her happiest memories being the double she recorded at the 1991 Galway Festival meeting. Of course, when she held the licence, she partnered the stable's bumper horses.

Before assuming her father's mantle she furthered her racing education by spending some time at Jim Bolger's stable, so both Adrian and herself can be described as pupils of the "Bolger Academy".

Anne Marie readily acknowledges the debt she owes her father, recognised as one of the shrewdest characters in the game.

Now 64, he has a leading role in assisting Aidan in buying the horses for the stable. He can claim the distinction of having bought and developed and eventually sold on a young horse named after the hill under which he worked his own string, namely the 1983 Cheltenham Gold Cup winner, Bregawn.

Back in 1985 – the year he landed the Irish Cesarewitch with 20/1 shot, Ravaro – Joe Crowley was entitled to chuckle heartily at the suggestion that he was an overnight success in the racing game. He had been involved for quite a few years in the business as a hobby before circumstances conspired to propel him into the limelight.

Rejection of some of his produce at the sales and the realisation that a few of the other home-bred fillies wouldn't make their value in the ring saw this most unassuming character start 1985 with a promising though largely unproven string consisting of seven fillies, the 800 guinea purchase Camtown being his solitary "import".

But with only the help of his family and local amateur Frank Dalton, a young man who had spent two seasons with Michael Dickinson's all-conquering jumpers, Joe Crowley managed to win as many races as some more established stables.

By the start of November '85 six of those seven fillies had captured a total of 19 races between the flat and hurdling.

But he had no cause to complain as Rivero won four Listed Races, two under each Rules including the Cesarewitch, of course.

Ravaro's Curragh triumph in the hands of Gabriel Curran was indeed a remarkable training feat by any standards. Lacking inches if not gameness or courage, the daughter of Raga Navarro was scoring for the fifth time in '85 when defying top weight of 9 st 12 lb – her first outing for almost four months.

❊ ❊ ❊ ❊

When Aidan took over the licence from Anne Marie, he combined training with riding and finished the 1993-'94 season as the top amateur in Ireland with a total of 26 winners.

"But I won't ride that much from this out", he told me in June '94. That was only to be expected as the demands on his time increase all the time.

Anne Marie and himself find themselves supervising three yards – Joe Crowley's original yard, then the one that was added when Anne Marie was training and now the span new one, a model of everything that one expects in a modern stable and with a capacity to accommodate 100 horses.

The day I talked to him he told me he was planning to build a lab to facilitate the taking of regular blood tests. A canteen was also being planned for the staff (33 strong at the moment and including Head Men, Brendan Doyle and J. J. O'Gorman, both of whom followed him from Bolger's).

As Vincent O'Brien eschewed the Curragh plains when he moved from Churchtown to Ballydoyle and Jim Bolger did likewise when he chose to move from Clonsilla to Coolcullen, it was not surprising that Aidan O'Brien was happy to be training in hilly countryside. Bolger had proved that this hardened his string to be winners and the hillsides around Pilltown are doing the same for O'Brien's string.

Aidan O'Brien doesn't see horses as just inanimate machines. "You have got to approach it as if you are looking into their minds. You have got to make sure that they come out of their races as if they hadn't had them."

He is a great believer in feeding his horses well and this is something he gets involved in himself. He has a lot of faith in electrolytes and gives all his horses these before and after they race. "I find that it enables them to recover very quickly and run frequently."

Aidan confessed to me that he thrives on hard work. It's the same in the case of Anne Marie. "We enjoy every minute of what we are doing and the days seem to just fly by."

There are days when they will work right through until 9.30 in the evening, leaving no time for socialising. But with Joseph a bundle of boundless energy, Anne Marie finds that she has plenty on her hands outside of assisting Aidan by looking after the secretarial work (of course, a full-time secretary will be taken on in due course).

It's easy to understand why Aidan is satisfied to have Anne Marie's parents combining in the overall operation. "We all work together – we have got to with all the horses we have", he said.

The immediate aim is to keep the winners flowing with the consistency that has been his hallmark since he took over the licence from Anne Marie.

Over the jumps he utilises the services of Charlie Swan and Trevor Horgan while on the Flat his associationship with Christy Roche has already blossomed into a very fruitful one.

The respect between Christy Roche and Aidan O'Brien is a deep and mutual one. O'Brien fully appreciates the depth of experience Roche brings to the task when he arrives at least once a week to ride work.

"When he's down here, he often rides between 30 and 40 horses in a morning, flat horses, bumper horses, jumpers, the lot", said O'Brien and, of course, Roche's run-down over what he has discovered in the potential say of a two-year-old will be invaluable. Has got to be from the man who rode Assert, Secreto and St. Jovite to Classic victories.

The two became acquainted when Roche was No. 1 jockey to the Bolger stable and O'Brien was moving up the ranks to become assistant trainer before he left. And now Roche gets immense satisfaction from every success achieved by O'Brien. He noted that this young man has a special way with horses – an understanding of them and "an uncanny ability to keep them at peak form."

"What I like about him also is that in the ring before you go out to ride one of his horses, he doesn't beat about the bush, doesn't get involved in almost lecturing you on how to ride the race. A man of few words, he says exactly what has to be said and what you want to know. He leaves the rest to your judgement and experience."

Looking further ahead, Aidan O'Brien is setting his sights very high and admits that he would like to win a Classic, though he admitted to me that he would also like to train a Gold Cup winner. It's obvious that for the immediate future anyway he will aim at big targets in both fields but acknowledges that eventually he may be forced to take the ultimate decision that Vincent O'Brien before him had to face – a complete concentration on the Flat.

He knows that good horses winning good races help make a trainer ultimately.

Yet as I took the road back down from the hillside above Piltown, I knew that his head was not going to be turned by all the success that had already come his way, that the qualities that made Jim Bolger so effusive in his praise of him would not be easily destroyed.

⌘ ⌘ ⌘ ⌘

The O'Brien bandwaggon rolled on all that summer and into autumn days like Rommel's panzers sweeping through France. He had become overnight the headline maker and when he was announced in the *Irish Independent* of Friday, 9 September 1994, as the winner of the *Irish Independent*-Bisquit Cognac Racing Personality award for August, John Comyn wrote that he "had hit the Irish training scene like a blast from a thunderbolt."

On August 15 he had joined the elite band of Irish trainers who had 100 winners to their credit in a calendar year, reaching his century at Tramore through Moorefield Girl. The only other four to do so have been J. J. Parkinson, Paddy Mullins, Dermot Weld and Jim Bolger. But what made Aidan O'Brien's achievement unique was the fact that he produced "the ton" in his first FULL season as a trainer.

At the time of writing in September '94 his grand total for the year had jumped to 132 (88 N.H. winners and 44 on the Flat) and he was obviously in line to make a major bid to break Dermot Weld's record of 150 winners in a calendar year.

O'Brien had his first Group winner when Dancing Sunset was awarded the Royal Whip at the Curragh on August 13 on the disqualification of Blue Judge. He took his first Listed two-year-old prize with Glouthane Garden at Leopardstown on August 20 and started the Tralee Festival meeting the next day with a treble.

Dermot Weld had shown that he had the ability to turn out ten winners at a Festival meeting like Galway or Tralee (he achieved the distinction at both in '94). But Aidan O'Brien proved at Tralee that he was not going to allow anyone to dominate the Festival scene by producing eight winners and again was making it a battle right down to the wire for the Dawn Light Butter Dish Leading Trainer's Award, put up by the Kerry Group (in association with the Racing Board and the three Kerry tracks) for the leading trainers at the Festival meetings in the Kingdom. In 1993 O'Brien had finished third to Dermot Weld with Jim Bolger in runner-up position. And in 1994 he brought the battle for the "Dish" right down to the wire, to the Listowel meeting, eventually finishing second to Dermot Weld with Michael Hourigan third.

⌘ ⌘ ⌘ ⌘

One cannot journey through County Kilkenny and Goresbridge without reflecting on the unforgettable moment that Paddy Mullins, in partnership with Jonjo O'Neill, gave National Hunt enthusiasts through the victory of the gallant mare, Dawn Run in the 1986 Gold Cup and the unforgettable and emotive scenes engendered by Jonjo's triumphant arm-aloft gesture to the heavens as he passed the winning post, I chronicled in my book, *The High Rollers Of The Turf.*

Today Paddy Mullins's two sons, Tony and Willie, are both training successfully in their native county while Paddy himself continues to turn out the winners. The Mullins name is part and parcel of the Irish jumping scene.

So too are the names of Jim Dreaper and Arthur Moore, carrying on the proud traditions set by their fathers. As is John Oxx on the Flat.

Jim Dreaper will always be remembered as "The man who trained Carvill's Hill". In a way, the period when this chaser was with Martin Pipe was something of an anti-climax for, as we have seen earlier, he failed in the ultimate challenge – in his bid to win the Gold Cup.

He really caught the imagination of the public while he was with Jim Dreaper, for then the horizons were tinged with the glow of high hopes. We all entertained the dream that, as Jim Dreaper's father, Tom, produced Arkle to lower the colours of Mill House on a red-letter day at Cheltenham in 1964 and went on to become the greatest chaser in National Hunt history, so Carvill's Hill might produce an "Irish roar" on Gold Cup day that would bring pride to every Irish heart. And sent over, remember, from Ireland to challenge for chasing's most prestigious prize.

Jim Dreaper had turned out Ten Up to win the 1975 Gold

Cup and there is no doubt in my mind that he would have won a second in 1978 had the race not been postponed because of snow to April 12 (the Cheltenham Stewards erred badly by not putting back for just twenty-four hours the third day of the '78 Festival meeting and Peter O'Sullivan went so far as to describe it as "a massive blunder").

If the race had been run in the soft going that Brown Lad needed to show his real talent, then he would have fully justified the Irish singing "Brown Lad in the rain . . .". But on April 12 it was "good" and, not surprisingly, in the circumstances Brown Lad drifted to 8/1. The Fred Winter-trained seven-year-old Midnight Court, still a novice, won deservedly in the hands of John Francome from Brown Lad, who stayed on up the hill to gain runner-up position – but the Irish were left to ponder the might-have-beens.

Brown Lad went on to make racing history at Fairyhouse on Easter Monday, 27 March 1978, when he became the first horse in the 108 years of the Irish Distillers (now Jameson) Grand National to win the event three times (he had won it previously in 1975 and '76). The 12-year-old gelding, bred by Joe Osborne and owned by Mrs. Peter Burrell, carried 12-2 to a three-quarters-of-a-length victory over Sand Pit. The rains came to provide the soft going that Brown Lad needed.

It was a tremendous training feat by Jim Dreaper to produce this veteran chaser to contest the event, after the setbacks in training the horse had experienced. Dreaper was enjoying his fourth Irish Grand National triumph, as aside from the three successes of Brown Lad, Colebridge, also owned by Mrs. Burrell, had won the race in 1974.

The greatest moment that Carvill's Hill gave Jim Dreaper was when he won the 1989 renewal of the Hennessy Cognac Gold Cup (first run as the Vincent O'Brien Gold Cup in 1987) at Leopardstown in breath-taking style. Dreaper had adopted the patient approach of his father, preferring not to send Carvill's Hill to contest a hurdle race at the '88 Cheltenham Festival meeting following his wins in the Paddy Power Hurdle at Leopardstown and the Seán Graham Hurdle at Punchestown.

Carvill's Hill had become a "talking horse" and every aficionado of the National Hunt game in Ireland felt he had a right to voice his opinion but Jim Dreaper wasn't resentful. "The man on the spot has to do what he thinks is right", he said simply.

Carvill's Hill had a terrible fall when schooling later in '88 and then back problems set in.

Really the rest is history.

After the controversial Gold Cup showing in 1992, he never recovered properly. Martin Pipe announced that Paul Green's chaser would not appear during the 1992-'93 season. He never did appear again on a racecourse and was retired.

We were left to remember what Peter Scudamore, who had ridden him in the '92 Gold Cup, told the Stewards inquiry: "He did not like being taken on in the early stages and, as a result, jumped poorly. After he had jumped the last, the heart had gone out of him and he was unable to persevere to the line."

Martin Pipe couldn't achieve what Jim Dreaper tried his best to achieve. Carvill's Hill goes into history as the Great Enigma – the big chaser who pulverised the opposition when he had matters his own way but did not have the athleticism to conquer the Cheltenham fences when he had to go at Gold Cup pace and was taken on from the outset.

But still we were all sad when the music died on that March day at Cheltenham in '92.

�֍ ✤ ✤ ✤

Arthur Moore admitted to being a proud man at the Punchestown Festival meeting on Wednesday, 26 April 1994, when his five-year-old hurdler, Klairon made it seven wins on the trot in landing the Country Pride Champion Novice Hurdle in the hands of Trevor Horgan, who was highly praised by the County Kildare trainer.

At the 1994 Galway Festival meeting Moore won the Digital Galway Plate for the first time with Feathered Gale. Frank Woods, the successful jockey, had earlier in the season taken the Jameson Irish Grand National on Son Of War, trained by Peter McCreery, a son of the late Peter McCreery.

Moore is a man who has always aimed for big targets. In keeping with the standards set by his father, who won the

Gold Cup two years running with L'Escargot (1970 and '71) and again with Tied Cottage in 1980 (though he was later disqualified on purely technical grounds) and an Aintree Grand National with L'Escargot in 1975, he is to be found tilting for top prizes both at Cheltenham and Aintree and on the domestic front he has an unique record in the Ladbroke Handicap Hurdle having won it five times through Irian (1979), Fredcoteri (1983 and '84), Bonalma (1986) and Roark (1988).

At Cheltenham he has won the Queen Mother Champion Chase with Drumgora (1981), the Arkle Chase with The Brockshee (1982) and the Cathcart Challenge Cup Chase with Second Schedual (1993).

Trainer Tommy Carberry, one of the finest National Hunt riders of modern times in his prime, who is married to Arthur Moore's sister, Pamela, was associated with Dan Moore's greatest triumphs. He won the Arkle for Arthur on The Brockshee the year after winning this race for the Durkans on the outstanding mare, Anaglog's Daughter. Paul Carberry is following in his father's footsteps, showing rare talent both on the Flat and over the jumps. It was his proudest day to date when he rode Rhythm Section to victory for Homer Scott in the Guiness Festival Bumper at the 1993 Cheltenham Festival meeting.

❃ ❃ ❃ ❃

John Oxx is the perfect diplomat and, while coping with the responsibilities of being the Aga Khan's only trainer and Sheikh Mohammed's main trainer in Ireland, he can still make the time to act as Chairman of the Irish Racehorse Trainers' Association. Remember, he has 100 horses in his Currabeg stables on the Curragh and admits that he doesn't have room for any more.

On the retirement of his father, John Senr., at the end of the 1978 season, he took over the licence. By 1991 when he achieved a career best of 91 winners, he was unquestionably one of the most respected members of his profession – a man admired for his integrity and the high standards he set.

Nothing has given him greater pleasure in his career to

date than the winning of the Irish St. Leger – his first Classic triumph – with Eurobird in 1987 because it came in the same year that his father died.

It meant even more to him when he recalled the controversy surrounding the disqualification of Sorbus after she had won the Irish Oaks for his father in 1977. Sorbus was owned by Gerald Jennings, whose colours Eurobird carried.

John Oxx is not one to involve himself in opening old sores but he said to Tony O'Hehir in the course of a *Racing Post* interview: "Many people believed that the disqualification of Sorbus was a very harsh decision."

He acknowledges that "training better horses is what everyone in my job wants more than anything else". And he adds: "Having a really decent horse, who can win one or more of the top prizes, means most to me."

Oxx is never one to make facile predictions in order to command a headline. Behind that cool and calm exterior is a very sharp racing brain – and he certainly knows his horses and how to place them.

⌘ ⌘ ⌘ ⌘

A visit to the Royal County of Meath – now linked in every jumping enthusiast's mind with Adrian Maguire and the village of Kilmessan – is never complete without reflecting on the contributions that Des McDonogh, Michael Cunningham, Noel Meade and Michael Kauntze have made to the lore of racing annals, Kauntze who makes no secret of the fact that when he retires he would like to be remembered simply as the man who trained Kooyonga, brilliant victor over Opera House and Sapience in the 1992 Coral-Eclipse Stakes in the hands of Warren O'Connor and earlier Kauntze had been deeply admired for the manner in which he sportingly accepted the disqualification of the filly from first place in the Prince of Wales Stakes at Royal Ascot.

In *The High Rollers Of The Turf* I related how the Heaslips of Galway threw the biggest champagne celebration that Cheltenham has known after For Auction, trained by Michael Cunningham, had won the Champion Hurdle in 1982 at 40/1 and how memorable victory parties were thrown in the Queen's Hotel by County Galway-born Dr. Michael Mangan following the Champion Hurdle victories of Monksfield, trained by Limerick-born Des McDonogh.

Noel Meade in the count-down to the 1992 Cheltenham Festival meeting had in his Tu Va stables near Navan the biggest "talking horse" outside of Carvill's Hill. None other than Tiananmen Square who was looked upon by many as the Irish banker of the meeting in the Tote Festival Bumper. But he got "done" by Montelado and it was the following year, of course, when Pat Flynn's gelding won the Supreme Novices' Hurdle by twelve lengths that we realised what Tiananmen Square had come up against. And to think that Montelado went off at 8/1 in that bumper race!

Tiananmen Square reversed the Cheltenham result when beating Montelado by 2½ lengths in a bumper at the '92 Punchestown Festival meeting. He was again being talked about as a Cheltenham banker for '93 when he won two hurdle races on his reappearance for the 1993-'94 N.H. season and then went on to take the Orchard Inns Rathfarnham and Stillorgan Hurdle at the Leopardstown Christmas meeting.

But he was plagued by setbacks and didn't make it to the Festival meeting after all in 1993. And again he failed to make it to the 1994 Festival meeting.

Meade is a man who has always to be reckoned with at the Galway Festival meeting and, indeed, on the Festival round generally. A man who has mixed it successfully and who, while having the ability to enjoy life and the "craic", harbours a keen racing brain and true professionalism behind the easy affable manner.

Yes, a man for all seasons.

Footnote: Just as this book was going to press, the news broke on Thursday, 6 October 1994, that Aidan O'Brien was going to become linked with famed Ballydoyle in a new exciting venture. On the retirement of Vincent O'Brien, it became clear that his son, Charles, was not going to move from his Curragh establishment. So Aidan O'Brien would use the Ballydoyle gallops for the training of an expanded team of Flat horses while continuing to maintain his Piltown base for the training of jumpers. The full details had not been released officially at the time of writing.

PART TEN

TOMMY STACK

*The Kingdom's Aintree Hero
Knows Guineas Glory*

19

Tears of Emotion as Stack Wins His First Classic

The tears of emotion welled up in Tommy Stack's eyes before trickling down both cheeks in the moment of euphoria after the long wait at Newmarket on Thursday, 28 April 1994, when the announcement came over the public address system that Las Meninas had won the English 1,000 Guineas.

It had taken the judge seventeen minutes to decide that Las Meninas had edged out Balanchine by the shortest of short heads in the photo-finish, thus giving the 48-year-old Kerry-born trainer his first Classic triumph.

"Waiting for the photo was all a bit trying and I must confess I would have settled for a dead-heat", said Stack. "I shouldn't be crying but it was the same when I won the Grand National on Red Rum. It is that sort of day."

Yes, that sort of day . . .

His mind went back seventeen years to Aintree and etched still vividly in his memory was the roar – the great roar that he heard rising from the 40,000 crowd as he hit the elbow on Red Rum and all the way up the run-in it was deep and sustained, a mighty wave of sound breaking over him and it was like nothing he had ever heard before – "something out of this world".

"I know now I may never have an experience like it again in my lifetime", he had said to me back in 1977 in the immediate aftermath of Red Rum's third Grand National success (he had won in 1973 and '74 in the hands of Brian Fletcher and was runner-up in '75 to L'Escargot and in '76 to Rag Trade).

In the sun lounge of Thomastown Castle Stud, leading out to the patio and the Galtees beyond, Tommy Stack is talking to me now on a day in June '94 of how a man's ambitions can change when he becomes a trainer. "The ultimate ambition for every jump jockey is to win the Aintree Grand National. If you are training horses for the Flat the big target is to capture a Classic because you know that even if you turn out 100 winners it's not the same really as breaking into the big league through success in the Classics", he said.

Now Tommy Stack had carved out a new identity for himself as the man who had not alone triumphed over the Aintree fences on National Day but who had shown in '94 that he had the ability to produce a filly to win an English Classic. In cold retrospect the form of the race took on a new meaning and significance when set against the later achievements of Balanchine. For Balanchine, after winning the English Oaks impressively, trounced her field in the Budweiser Irish Derby, scoring by no less than 3½ lengths from King's Theatre, runner-up in the Epsom Derby and who would go on to win the King George and Queen Elizabeth Diamond Stakes.

❀ ❀ ❀ ❀

The emotion Stack showed at Newmarket revealed more about his character in one flashing instant than any in-depth interview. He has never forgotten his Kerry roots. "We are close to animals in Kerry", he said. And that same closeness has resulted in the involvement of the Stack family with greyhound racing and coursing. Not surprisingly, amid all the trophies and all the honours from his days in the saddle and more recently those stemming from his successes as a trainer, you find on the mantel-piece a depiction in bronze of a slipper letting two dogs away from slips in a moment of perfect symmetry and poetry, conjuring up days at Clonmel and Clounanna or at some meeting when there is frost in the air in the shadow of the reeks and glens of Stack's native Kingdom.

Tommy's sister, Helen Roche of Rathkeale, County Limerick, was associated with Ballinderry Ash, winner of the Blue Riband of English greyhound racing, the Derby at Wimbledon in 1991 in a time of 28.78 secs and Ayr Flyer, with which she was also associated, was runner-up to Moral Standards in this year's English Derby, also won the valuable International 525 at Dundalk and reached the final of the Respond Irish Derby, finishing unplaced. Tommy's brother, Stevie of Moyvane ran up for the Waterloo Cup in 1985 with Waterloo Lass and he trained the bitch himself.

Stack himself and his wife Liz hit the jackpot at the National Meeting in Clonmel through Wing Bell Wendy, the Oaks winner in 1980 and Little Scotch, winner of the same event in 1983 when she was Coursing Greyhound of the Year. And Stack, of course, was associated through "The Syndicate" with Believe Him dividing the Derby with Knockash Rover in 1981 and the same dog won the Champion Stakes the following year.

It was fitting then that Jeremiah Carroll – just "Jer" to his friends – the man from Sixmilecross, near Listowel, whose name will always be linked with the incomparable Master Myles should join in the celebrations at Newmarket on Guineas Day. Big Jer, at Tommy's invitation, joined Robert Sangster and John and Sue Magnier and others of the inner circle as the champagne flowed.

Stack would have been remembering Master Myles going up the stretch at Clonmel on a February day in 1978 as he produced what Eugene Murphy described in the *Cork Examiner* as one of the greatest triumphs ever recorded in this event.

Stack would have been remembering to himself also how, in the wave of celebrations that followed that epoch-making Clonmel triumph, Jer Carroll sold Master Myles for £30,000 to Captain Tim Rogers of Airlie Stud and then tried to buy him back and the tragic manner in which the wonder dog died in March of the same year – tumbling over very heavily while exercising at legendary trainer Dick Ryan's kennels at Gooldscross, County Tipperary, and fatally injured his back.

327

A whimsical gleam came into Stack's eyes as he recalled for me how Jer Carroll entered fully into the spirit of the Newmarket celebrations – "and then he went back to London and rang me from Soho in the early hours of the morning and said what a day it had been for Kerry, one of the best since Master Myles's Derby triumph."

And before I parted with Tommy Stack that day, the phone rang. It was Jimmy Deenihan, member of Dáil Éireann (Irish Parliament) on the line. The man who captained Kerry when they won their fourth successive All-Ireland senior football final in 1982, was inviting Stack down to a party in Listowel on the Saturday night in the establishment of Tim Kennelly, who was centre-back on the same team.

Tommy promised he would do his best but Royal Ascot beckoned the following week and there was much to do and, frankly, he would have to be Myles Roche's bird to meet all the invitations.

Stack is that kind of person – a man who can walk with kings and keep the common touch, who has never lost the essential qualities that can permit him to rub shoulders with his own and enjoy the "craic".

❀ ❀ ❀ ❀

Tommy Stack came into training almost by accident. He started off as a permit holder with just one horse, Northern Express, but quickly made his mark when winning the inaugural running of the Cartier Million with Corwyn Bay at the Phoenix Park on Saturday, 1 October 1988.

The colt by the Coolmore stallion, Caerleon, which he bred himself resisted a strong English challenge for the rich prize when coming home a 7/1 winner. Stack knew he would be smiling all the way to the bank as he lodged his percentage of the £500,000 which the four-man American partnership, owners of Corwyn Bay, earned in the space of the 1 min. 22.9 secs. it took the colt to complete the 7 furlongs.

The scenes in the enclosure were reminiscent of Cheltenham

in their overflowing enthusiasm as Tommy and Liz were mobbed by delighted well-wishers.

Stack had been manager of Longfield Stud, just outside Cashel, part of the Coolmore empire of which John Magnier is the Supremo and Vincent O'Brien and Robert Sangster are also very much involved.

Appropriately enough, Stack, Sangster and Magnier are credited with being the joint-breeders of Las Meninas, a daughter of Glenstal, who stands at Coolmore.

Las Meninas is out of Spanish Habit (by Habitat), the dam of Head Of The Abbey, a winner first time out for Stack in the colours of Robert Sangster at the Park in 1987 and beaten later that same season a head and a short head in the Tyros Stakes by Project Manger (received 7 lbs). Spanish Habit was sold to Denmark at Goffs. Stack, knowing she could produce winners, tried to buy her back when the Danish interests offered her for sale publicly a few years later but failed to do so. However, she was then bought privately.

Spanish Habit died after delivering a foal by Danehill – but she ensured that her name would live in the breeding records through the Classic triumph of Las Meninas.

"We reared her and she's always been around the place", said Stack with unmistakeable affection in his voice to the assembled racing press at Newmarket after the photo finish verdict had gone in his favour.

Generously, he acknowledged that a victory like this must invariably be "a team effort and not just a one-man show."

"It's great for the lads in the yard who are responsible for the filly", he said. "Because they know at first hand what is involved in the preparation."

Stack brought all his professionalismn to timing Las Meninas's preparation for the day that mattered.

He knew she had plenty of speed as the previous year she had been runner-up to Turtle Island in the Heinz 57 Phoenix Stakes. "I knew she would run a big race, but I wasn't sure if she had done enough. We'd been held up with the ground and the weather and I knew the fitness that was required to win a race at that level. It's not easy", he said.

Stack utilised the gallops at Ballydoyle and also all the experience of renowned work riders, Tommy Murphy and

Vincent Rossiter and rehearsed the waiting tactics employed under Vincent O'Brien's instructions for the 2,000 Guineas bid by El Gran Senor in 1984.

John Reid, the Down-born jockey, carried out Stack's plan to the letter but it became touch and go in the end as he ran into a number of problems. The filly had been drawn low and it was inevitable that she would be blocked behind a wall of horses. It was only inside the last furlong that Reid could produce his challenge and utilise Las Meninas's pace. "Eventually we found a way out, but I had to switch in order to get there", said the jubilant jockey.

"If the filly had been able to get clear earlier, I think she would have won by three lengths", said Robert Sangster, who, incidentally, after breeding Balanchine sold her as part of a four-horse package to Sheikh Mohammed's Dubai-based Godolphin Racing at the end of the '93 season. Ever the businessman, he added candidly: "I want all the horses I sell to Sheikh Mohammed to do well. He is my best customer."

Stack added his own special word of praise to John Reid for his role in giving him his first Classic triumph.

He did not forget either the support he had been accorded since he set up as a trainer by the Magniers and Robert Sangster. "John and Sue have been very close friends for years. We go back a long time. And Robert (Sangster) is, of course, a marvellous owner to train for and I am delighted to have come up with a Classic winner in his colours as he has had horses with me from the outset."

"Days like this are magic", summed up John Reid.

Yes, sheer magic for Tommy Stack and Robert Sangster and the Magniers and all connected with a singular triumph.

✼ ✼ ✼ ✼

Tommy Stack has come a long way from the time he left Moyvane, which is about seven miles from Listowel, for Dublin where he worked for a short time in the sixties as an insurance clerk. At the weekends, however, he was already acquiring that knowledge of horses and ease in the saddle that would blossom in later years as he reached the top as a professional jockey.

His closest friend in those days was Barry Brogan. The late Jimmy Brogan, Barry's father, was a trainer at the time. When Jimmy Brogan died suddenly, his son endeavoured to keep the establishment going – and Tommy Stack lent a willing hand. Those were rewarding years, maybe not financially, but in building up a store of valuable experience. Tommy doesn't forget how Barry Brogan set him on the road to the career that was far more fulfilling than selling insurance. "I am only sorry that life hasn't been as kind to Barry", he said with deep sincerity.

Moving to England, Stack joined the stable of Bobby Renton, a master of the training art, whose name will always be linked with that great Aintree favourite, Freebooter. Tommy rode for two years as an amateur before turning professional in 1967.

He went on to become British champion jump jockey for the first time in the 1974-'75 season and he took the title again in 1976-'77.

Red Rum stands out like a beacon when one charts the course of his career right to the top of the ladder.

Videos were not an integral part of the scene then as they are now – but Stack needs no video to recall for him the drama and the trauma of Grand National Day '77 and ultimately the moment when he raised his arm aloft to the heavens in a victory salute as he passed the winning post twenty-five lengths clear of Churchtown Boy. It was the era when the Aintree fences were far stiffer than they are today and 42 went to the start that year and twelve horses had fallen at Becher's Brook first time round. "Where are all the horses gone?", Stack would ask himself as the race reached its climax.

⌘ ⌘ ⌘ ⌘

Tommy Stack going down the middle when other jockeys were choosing to go inside or ourside. "The main thing is to keep out of trouble."

Andy Pandy sailed over Becher's Brook ten lengths in front second time round but had taken it almost too well. The "drop" got him and he crumpled on landing.

Now Red Rum was ahead – with rather more than a mile still to go and eight fences to jump. Anxious moments for Tommy Stack at the Canal Turn as two loose horses came perilously close to him. Then the climax.

"Crossing the Melling Road I knew that Martin Blackshaw was going well on Churchtown Boy – and this one was now the only real danger to me", Tommy recalled.

Martin Blackshaw would say later: "Three fences out I thought, 'I'll eat Red Rum'. But Churchtown Boy made a mistake there and again at the second last and that finished him."

Now seventeen years on, Tommy Stack is saying to me: "A National is like a Grand Prix race. It's about total concentration all the way. One mistake and you are gone."

From the height of Grand National victory Tommy Stack found himself later that year in traction in hospital for three-and-a-half months – the result of a terrible moment at Hexham when a horse fell back on top of him in the parade ring.

Listening to him describing the internal injuries he suffered would, I'm afraid, make you sick over breakfast if you had a delicate stomach. He underwent twelve operations while in traction. You have only to look at the photo of Tommy lying in his hospital bed to realise what superhuman courage and will power he displayed in fighting his way back to fitness. Imagine this – he was ready to ride Red Rum again in the 1978 Grand National but the gallant veteran went lame in the count-down to the race and had to be withdrawn.

There was consolation for Stack that same season when he won the Whitbread Gold Cup Chase. After that he wisely called it a day.

⌘ ⌘ ⌘ ⌘

Today he trains some 60 horses at his spacious 200-acre spread amid the rolling green fields of County Tipperary and, fittingly, there are five jumpers among them, including Gale Again, who was sent over by Stack to win a 2½-mile chase at Sandown in very impressive style under 11-11 on 29 March '94.

Owners who were loyal to the late Arthur Stephenson

(who helped him become champion jockey for the first time by producing a string of winners) have now sent horses to Stack to train. The friendships he has made right across the board from the time he was riding in Britain, to his days at Longfield and hitting the yearling sales from Goffs to Newmarket, to Deauville and Keeneland in Kentucky are reflected in the broad cross-section of people who have placed their faith in his training ability. The triumph of Las Meninas has shown that their faith will not be misplaced. The promise is a rich one.

There is laughter in the Stack home as owners drop in and friends come by – if only for a chat. Liz fits perfectly into this setting. And 14-year-old James – "we call him Fozzie", laughs Tommy – seems equally at home as the conversation about horses and sport in general flows easily over the impromptu coffee session in the kitchen on this lovely summer's morning – a break for Tommy Stack himself between lots.

And Serena, now eighteen months old, makes her presence felt as she looks for her bottle – and Liz soothingly takes it all in her stride.

The Stack household is a happy one. Somehow as I said goodbye to Tommy and Liz I could not but think back again to a man in an Aran sweater saying to me in Clonmel on the eve of the Coursing Derby '78 that saw Master Myles acquire a mystique that can never fade: "There are things in life that money cannot buy."

✽ ✽ ✽ ✽

From his Killeens stable at Ballynonty, seven miles from Thurles, Edward O'Grady sent Golden Cygnet in Raymond Rooney's colours to win the Supreme Novices Hurdle in breath-taking style at the 1978 Cheltenham Festival meeting and the late Fred Rimell described it as the greatest display by a juvenile hurdler that he had seen over the course. Unfortunately, Golden Cygnet was to suffer a neck injury that proved fatal in a cruel fall at Ayr before the season's end and so we were left to wonder how great a champion hurdler he would have been.

For a time in the Eighties O'Grady concentrated solely on the Flat but by 1990 he was back challenging at Cheltemham and Liverpool again. Although Blitzkreig failed to win the 1990 Arkle Chase – finishing fifth after being hampered by a faller – we knew that it would be only a matter of time before O'Grady was hitting the winner's enclosure again.

The patronage of the intrepid J. P. "The Sundance Kid" McManus, for whom he had won an Irish Grand National with Bit Of A Skite in 1983, meant that he got some very good horses and at the 1994 Festival meeting he brought off a notable double on the Wednesday with Time For A Run, who won the Coral Cup Handicap Hurdle, and Mucklemeg, the easy winner of the Bromagrove Industries Festival Bumper. Both carried J. P.'s colours. It might well have been a treble but Gimme Five, medium of an awesome gamble by McManus in the last race on the Tuesday as he came down to 4/1 favourite, could only finish 20th.

A decade had elapsed since O'Grady's Northern Game beat the favourite, See You Then when taking the Triumph Hurdle in 1984.

Now in his forties, O'Grady is a man who knows the game inside out. We can expect that he will be challenging strongly at the Cheltenham Festival meeting from this out. No one knows better how to prepared a horse for the ultimate test that Prestbury Park can present, for the emphasis there is on quality and you won't win if you are not good enough – or prepared to a tee to deliver on the day.

❧ ❧ ❧ ❧

Just a mile-and-a-half beyond Fethard town with its famed haunt of racing and sporting men – McCarthy's pub – you come upon the establishment of Michael "Mouse" Morris, son of Lord Killanin, former President of the Olympic Council. The magnificent vista of the gallops at the Everardsgrange stable would tempt you to sit down and do a colour painting taking in the Commeraghs, the Galtee and Slievenamon, so majestic and timeless. A stone's throw away is the Coolmore Stud, currently housing Europe's most renowned stallion in

Saddler's Wells and that in turn leads to Ballydoyle and The Master himself.

When I visited the stable in the count-down to the 1991 Leopardstown Christmas meeting the only sound to shatter the early-morning silence was that of the pounding hooves over the rich setting of a land that breathes in all the greenness of its Golden Vale pastures. With a sweep of his hand, as he took in the glory of the land around us, "Mouse" said: "I wouldn't exchange this for anything in the world."

Morris stood in windcheater and blue jeans, his shock of hair tousled in familiar manner, his shoulders hunched in that distinctive stance which immediately called to mind Steve McQueen walking out into the night after losing the last big hand to Edward G. Robinson, The Man in *The Cicinnati Kid*. A cigarette is never far from his mouth.

The eyes sharpen. He is oblivious, momentarily, to my presence at his shoulder as he casts a cold glance at a quartet of horses galloping past that would spearhead the assault on Leopardstown.

Would he ever think of training Flat horses? "Maybe – if some oil-rich Arab came along. But it's all sewn up. For me, it's the jumping game."

His patrons include the Magniers and Dr. A. J. F. (Tony) O'Reilly and appropriately one of the horses he trained for Dr. O'Reilly was named Beanz Means.

The ill-fated Buck House, who will always be remembered for that great match with Dawn Run at Punchestown following the gallant mare's triumph in the 1986 Gold Cup, provided Morris with success first in the 1983 Supreme Novice Hurdle and then in the 1986 Queen Mother Champion Chase with outstanding rider Tommy Carmody in the saddle, while Trapper John was victorious for him in the Stayers' Hurdle in 1990.

Another ill-fated horse, the enigmatic Cahervillahow could have been anything. He looked at one time a potential Gold Cup winner but, while he won some fine prizes for the Morris stable, he didn't deliver at the highest level, though it was a terribly galling experience for "Mouse" and a day when he had the sympathy of all aficionados of the jumping game in Ireland and Britain, when the gelding beat Docklands

Express by three quarters of a length in the 1991 Whitbread Gold Cup Chase at Sandown only to be deprived of the race in the Stewards' room.

Ironically, having failed in the 1993 Gold Cup, Cahervillahow gave Charlie Swan an exhilarating ride over the Aintree fences when figuring in the four-horse finish to "the race that never was" – the '93 Grand National – Wexford-born John White having the distinction, if one might call it thus, of being "first" past the post on Esha Ness.

Now in his early forties, "Mouse" Morris will always view Cheltenham as "tops" – the place where the best horses from Ireland and Britain take each other on for the best prizes but he thinks that the Leopardstown Christmas meeting is an outstanding meeting now in its own right with outstanding prizemoney. He got his share of it at the 1990 meeting when he won the Findus Chase with Rawhide while Cahervillahow took the Black and White Champion Chase.

⌘ ⌘ ⌘ ⌘

Back in Thurles in June '94 for a special birthday party for Imelda Harney, wife of Billy Harney, the man who trained Monanore, I heard Noel O'Meara, the Nenagh solicitor, singing *The Road To Nenagh* in that distinctive and rousing fashion of his. Memories came flooding back of the road to Aintree in 1988 – Saturday, April 9th, to be exact – when the rain came just in time for the eleven-year-old Monanore and he finished third behind Rhyme 'N' Reason and Durham Edition.

The Monday before Aintree Monanore was sold to Colin Tinkler of Woodland Stables, Malton, Yorkshire, director of Full Circle Thoroughbreds plc. Monanore up to that point had been owned jointly by Noel O'Meara and Dr Richard Fogarty of Nenagh and John Meagher from Toomevara but Billy Harney still trained him for the 1988 race.

The horse had been good to his joint owners and had done his trainer proud. He had never fallen at Aintree. Ridden by Tom Morgan on both occasions, he had finished eighth in 1986 and tenth in 1987. When Tom was claimed by his retaining John Edwards stable to ride Little Polveir in the

1988 renewal, Tom Taaffe, son, of course, of the legendary Pat, sought the ride on Monanore and Billy Harney was happy to give it him.

Monanore had won the Harold Clarke Leopardstown Chase and he had also won the prestigious Thyestes Chase at Gowran Park.

John Meagher, a sportsman through and through, had seen to it that written into the contract of sale was a proviso that when Monanore's racing days were over, he would return to Toomevara to enjoy his retirement on the Meagher farm. That proviso was duly observed.

John Meagher, Noel O'Meara, Dr Richard Fogarty and a legion of lovers of the jumping game had their hour as Tom Taaffe brought Monanore back into the spot reserved for the horse placed third. Great scenes of emotion were witnessed. Some did not hide their tears of joy. John Meagher gave Monanore an affectionate kiss on the head and said simply: "A great old horse."

He was remembering then, as the others were, all the memorable moments they had enjoyed over three seasons – remembering how five fences out in the 1988 race Monanore was going so well that it looked as if he would win the race and Billy and Imelda and Noel, in his fedora hat, and John and Richard and all the others lived and died a thousand deaths. Back at the Phoenix Park, where there was racing that same afternoon, a great roar went up as the commentator announced that Monanore was moving well, for he was carrying the hopes – and the money – of literally thousands of Irish people.

The hope did not die until the second last – but the unforgettable thrill of it all could never fade. On the tube back into Liverpool Noel O'Meara led the singing of the Tipperary anthem, *Slievenamon*, and John Meagher sang a song redolent of times when "The Greyhounds", that brilliant band of hurlers under "Wedger" Meagher, were famous throughout the land:

> Then here's to Toomevara
> May your banner never fall,
> You conquered Clare and Galway
> And then shattered Cork's stonewall;

But I never can forget the day
Kilkenny's pride went down
Before the skill of Wedger's men
In old Dungarvan town.

It was good to be alive and singing with them on this day
– the day of the 150th renewal of the Aintree Grand
National.

Yes, Monanore had certainly upheld the honour of
Kickham's Tipperary and the little village of Toomevara and
you can understand now why I was back on that tube again
as I listened to Noel O'Meara leading us in the chorus of
"We're on the road to Nenagh . . ." on a June night in
Thurles in '94.

That's what makes the camaraderie of the National Hunt
game so special.

PART ELEVEN

Pitman To Pipe And
Doumen Of Lamorlaye

20

How Martin Pipe Finally Silenced The Knockers

I t took a long time. But Martin Pipe finally silenced the knockers when he won the Aintree Grand National for the first time with Miinnehoma in 1994, supplementing his Champion Hurdle triumph with Granville Again in '93. These two big-race successes were thoroughly deserved and proved beyond any shadow of doubt that Pipe could no longer be viewed simply as the director of a conveyor belt-type operation that put seasonal winning totals before class.

No one has suffered more at the hands of the rumour factory than Martin Pipe. And no one has been so much a victim of the green-eyed monster – jealousy.

Pipe had, with his amazing strike rate, shifted all the markers and made feasible the attainment of every horizon, no matter how distant.

But the stark truth of it was that he was seen as a blow-in with his clipped and unaffected West Country accent. The bookmaker's son had had the temerity to tell the world that when he started out training point-to-pointers in the 70s he was totally ignorant of the business. "We started as idiots and learned", he said.

It was too much for a number of "The Club" to stomach, I mean those who would put themselves into the category of "gentlemen trainer", advocates of methods, they believed, had stood the test of time. And now they were being made a laughing-stock by this dapper little chap out of Pond Farm House, Nicholashayne, near Wellington in Somerset who, while he might drive a blue Rolls – the one with the number MCPI on it – still didn't cut the kind of figure that "The Duke" Nicholson or Dermot Weld would cut in the winner's enclosure in Cheltenham. And who, frankly, would not find himself surrounded by the gossip columnists looking for "name" personalities in the Royal Enclosure at Ascot.

He wouldn't have been human if he wasn't hurt by the jealously and suspicion that cast a long shadow over him, reaching a peak when in April '91 the news broke that a new investigation into his training methods was being prepared in the form of a Cook Report on Central Television.

You could understand him voicing to John Karter of *The Sunday Times* the rhetorical question: "Why are they investigating me? What have I done except train more winners than anybody else?."

And then he said aloud to himself: "It's depressing when you've worked so hard at something. Sometimes I feel like giving it all up."

Because he put such an emphasis on blood-testing, it was hinted that he must somehow be guilty of blood-doping, a device that apparently emanated from Finland where it was claimed that athletes had their winning capabilities greatly enhanced by substituting oxygen-rich blood into the system.

Not one iota of evidence was produced to substantiate this innuendo, even though one tabloid paper went so far as to send a reporter to pose as a stable girl and who actually managed to get work for a period in the yard. Not alone did she admit failure but came up with the immortal conclusion that the only charge that could be levelled at Pipe was that he was too obsessed with winning!

The Cook Report delved into the allegation that there was an unacceptable high wastage among Pipe's horses and, as he interpreted it himself, that "the percentage of horses that stay in my yard from one season to the next is far lower than in the case of other trainers."

Again the Cook Report failed to make anything concrete "stick". Pipe met the insinuations straight on by explaining to John Karter that "I train mostly ex-Flat racers who already have plenty of mileage on the clock, not the more expensive, slow-maturing types that Jenny Pitman favours. When a horse has fulfilled its potential, I advise the owner to sell it. I am looking for a quick return to provide an owner with enjoyment and value for money, and that means winning as many races as possible. I cannot see the point in running a horse out of its grade when it could win a little race somewhere else."

❋ ❋ ❋ ❋

When you consider all the headlines Martin Pipe has commanded in recent times, the column inches in features analysing his skills and unique achievements, it might seem difficult to believe that he took quite some time to break through and, having started off in 1974, he didn't enjoy his first winner until 9 May 1975; it took him four more years to achieve double figures and we had to wait until 1983 to see him break the twenties barrier.

He was a classic example then of the struggling small-time trainer, buying cheaply and quite content if he entered the winner's enclosure with a selling hurdler. But there came a day when he tired of the normal trainers' excuses and began to bluntly ask himself the question: "If a horse ran badly, I wanted to know why. I tried to cope with every possible problem that could arise."

So, with the financial support of his father, a millionaire in his own right, he converted his Somerset stable into the most modern, high-tech yard in Britain and where there had been pig-sties when Martin first took over the 300-acre farm, the visitor in time was introduced to a world where the laboratory to monitor every horse's blood and well-being was the centrepiece; but more, the other innovations included the horsewalker aimed at eradicating half the time his horses spent on tarmacadam; the gate-measurer, the swimming pool, the all-weather gallop with its woodchip surface that made it like a carpet (3,500 tons of stone were put down before being topped with the special woodchip). Once when heavy snow in the area looked like causing a complete shut-down of operations, Pipe just didn't sit around but went out and purchased a snow-blowing machine to clear his gallops.

By the latter half of the eighties he had become a mould-breaker and record-breaker, so much so that in the 1987-'88 season, he smashed Michael Dickinson's old record of 120 winners by reaching 129. On 26 October 1989 he reached the fastest 50 winners and on December 14 of the same year the quickest 100.

On 19 May 1989 he became the first trainer (NH or Flat) to reach 200 winners in a season (his final tally was 208) and in the 1989-'90 season he broke his own record by turning out 224 winners. And in 1991 he attained a prize-money total of £1 million.

❊ ❊ ❊ ❊

He reached a point where he made it seem that records were there to be broken.

He put a special spotlight on his system of interval training but, basically, it came down in the end to the fact that his horses were fitter and harder and were aimed at attainable targets. Others followed where he gave the lead. And some of the copycats, who were so dismissive of his methods and innovations early on, had to swallow their pride and his stream of winners was the best tribute of all to the standards of perfection that he set in everything he did.

Peter Scudamore, who was so much part of the Martin Pipe success story, summed up that the simple secret lay in the fact that Pipe did not allow himself to be governed and dominated by the old-fashioned approach to training. He set the pace. And the more he went ahead, the more ground others had to make up.

Now coming up to 50, Pipe is really an introvert, a shy man at heart who as a trainer may have the sure touch with the horses in his charge but in life presents the image of one who has yet to arrive. He will continue to be cold-shouldered by many of the Establishment in Britain who don't see him as "one of us". They don't have to say it in so many words but it's conveyed in cruel unspoken ways.

Pipe will go his merry way regardless – his eyes darting everywhere, the portable phone now a part of his person as he comes in beside another winner. Interview him at length on the phone, as I did one evening in the count-down to a big winter meeting at Leopardstown where he had a runner, and you are as likely as not to have your questions answered by other darting questions but still he is helpful and courteous, though never totally at ease with the media. "He is still a fox: quick, inquisitive and uncatchable despite a limp which ended a short and singularly unsuccessful riding career in 1973", wrote Brough Scott in *The Sunday Times*.

He lost his British Trainers' crown to "The Duke" Nicholson in the 1993-'94 season and word had it that Pipe was seeking to concentrate now more on quality than on the conveyor-belt approach. But still, where "The Duke" and others all but closed up shop when the Aintree Grand National meeting was over, Pipe was to be found sending out the runners to unfashionable racetracks at the climax of the 1993-'94 season, as Spring merged into early Summer, that ensured that his No. 1 jockey, Richard Dunwoody, the successor to Scu, just held off the powerful challenge of Adrian Maguire and Dunwoody was the first to thank Pipe for his role in helping him to retain his crown.

At least Pipe was no longer the victim of the rumour-factory. He was now taken solely on his merits and when the virus hit his yard he had to battle with it like any other trianer. All the high-tech innovations in the world don't make the virus depart any quicker.

⌘ ⌘ ⌘ ⌘

The contrast between Jenny Pitman and the Martin Pipe of the years when the numbers game – that is winner totals – seemed to be Pipe's all-pervading purpose in life was never better illustrated than by what Mrs. Pitman said to Geoff Lester of the *Sporting Life* when he interviewed her in the summer of 1991 for the 1991-'92 edition of the *Irish Racing Annual*: "I buy my horses to be champions. I'm not interested in winning any old race – I won't run them if they are not right on the day, because I am always gearing them to reach their pinnacle."

She went on: "When I go 'shopping' I am looking for a

horse who catches my eye. If he's got a good pedigree that is a bonus, but basically I've got to like him."

Asked why she did most of her buying in Ireland, she responded: "Why do people fish in streams?".

Stressing that some people were under the misapprehension that her success had been derived from going out with an open cheque book to buy "made" horses, she explained: "Most of our horses are bought as unbroken youngsters. There are few exceptions. When certain owners request an early return we will oblige. But, frankly, I get more satisfaction from seeing a young horse come through the nursery school."

A lot of water has passed under the bridge since the summer of '91. Fierce controversy stemmed from the allegation that her Golden Freeze was run in the 1992 Gold Cup to act as a "stalking horse" or an *agent provocateur* to upset the favourite, Carvill's Hill (it must be noted that a Jockey Club inquiry cleared Mrs. Pitman of the charge); the number of horses in her stable had dropped from 90 to 50 by December of that year as a result of the recession and Bill Robbins and his wife, Shirley, taking away their 16 horses and sending them to Andy Turnell and "The Duke" Nicholson; where once she was seen by the media as a journalist's dream, a natural and the most quotable of trainers, her relationship with the press deteriorated sharply for a time over the Golden Freeze v. Carvill's Hill affair and then when the ice was broken and she started talking again, she insisted that those who were accorded the privilege of an interview should make a donation to a specific charity.

Under the heading "Why Winners And The Fun Stopped For Mrs. Pitman", John Garnsey wrote in the *Daily Express* as if the heady days were over for good for this outspoken trainer, noting that "she finds herself playing a minor role to the new talent among women trainers, Mary Reveley."

But, of course, Mrs. Pitman could not be dismissed as easily as all that. Nobody could take from her the proud record of being the first lady to train either an Aintree Grand National winner (Corbiere, 1983) or a Gold Cup winner (Burrough Hill Lad, 1984, and Garrison Savannah, 1991) and her son Mark could well have had the distinction of bringing off the Gold Cup-Grand National double in '91 had not Garrison Savannah been caught and beaten in the run-in at Aintree by Seagram.

She had the galling experience of seeing Eshna Ness and John White pass the post first in the Grand National that never was on 3 April 1993 and one could understand her distress, for after the second false start she knew that her charge was on a futile exercise and foresaw the dreadful disappointment that awaited owner and jockey. She pleaded in vain for some form of intervention that would prevent the "race" continuing.

In the autumn of 1991 she spent a week in the Brompton Hospital being treated for chronic bronchitis and asthma and found herself in a public ward alongside cystic fibrosis sufferers and the experience was a humbling one.

When she returned to Weathercock House, her pin-neat yard in the pretty village of Upper Lambourn, she told Colin Mackenzie of the *Daily Mail* that "every time I lose sleep over a horse running badly, I now stop and think of those poor kids and I realise it isn't the end of the world."

"There is more to life than our glorious triviality. I'm devoting my next Open Day to their needs. The first thing I'm going to do is buy the hospital a new whirlpool bath because it does the patients so much good."

Behind the formidable front she could present when hitting out at the powers-that-be and when embroiled with the media, there was a heart after all and no doubt her feeling for the kids who were victims of cystic fibrosis was a throw-back to the dazzling summers she enjoyed as a child on the 100-acre family farm at Hoby in Leicestershire. She was very close to her father and her earliest memory was of "being sat on a pony at two and a half . . . my father would bring me on the pony across the fields, teaching me to ride as we went . . . he taught me most of the things I know about horses."

She married Richard Pitman of the BBC and they had two sons, Paul and Mark. Now they are divorced, of course. You recall Jenny Pitman telling Joe Steeples of *The Times* in 1992: "I was 19 when I got married and it was only then it dawned on me that I was no longer a child."

Kim Bailey, like Jenny Pitman, is a trainer who aims for big targets always and, coincidentally, his yard is also to be found in Upper Lambourn. Still only in his early forties, he is the first to admit that winning the Grand National is every jump trainer's dream – "and winning it with Mr. Frisk in 1990 was the most exciting day of my life."

"It did me a tremendous amount of good, keeping the name forward and generally creating a lot of interest. The National has always been part of English heritage."

As Richard Edmondson pointed out in *The Independent*, statistics showed that Kim Bailey was training as many winners five years prior to his Grand National success, though the standard of winner had improved. "It takes a long time in this business to get recognised", he said.

"We haven't been doing anything different now since we started, but we have probably collected some better horses along the way. You've got to keep churning out the winners. And good winners. It's a long old hard business and there are plenty of people who have been at it for years who train bloody well but who just don't get the breaks. We've been lucky enough to have them."

All he always wanted to be was a trainer but then it was in his blood as his father, Ken Bailey used to train in Northamptonshire. However, he didn't rush into the business, preferring to first spend a season in a ski resort and then he headed for Australia where he ran a restaurant in Sydney and started a landscape gardening business in Darwin.

He summed up his philosophy thus: "You get only one chance to break away for a while and try other things and I wanted to see what other sorts of life might suit."

At his Old Manor Stables, he can very easily give the impression of taking it all very easily, even in lazily-relaxed fashion but the man, who spent time in the academies of such celebrated jumping masters as Tim Forster and Fred Rimell, learned from the best and it has shown in the way he can bring a horse to its peak on the day that matters.

And it is revealed also in the manner in which he has chosen a really first-class Irish-born jockey in Norman Williamson to be his No. 1.

Mr. Frisk . . . Docklands Express . . . Kings Fountain . . .

and Master Oats, who started at 9/1 for the 1994 Aintree Grand National and was chasing the leaders when he fell at the fifteenth. In his previous race he had beaten Moorcroft Boy, the runner-up in the Grand National, by fifteen lengths and the then eight-year-old was receiving just one lb.

On his own admission, he adores it all really, "the whole Aintree thing".

Yes, Kim Bailey can never be left out of the reckoning when it comes to the Grand National.

❃   ❃   ❃   ❃

Francois Doumen, the Man from Lamorlaye, saw Lady Fortune smiling on him at last at Chaltenham when The Fellow beat the reigning champion, Jodami in authoritative style to land the 1994 Gold Cup. And no one deserved more to share in this singular triumph than Adam Kondrat who had come in for a lot of criticism when The Fellow was beaten by Garrison Savannah in 1991 and by Cool Ground in 1992.

Doumen, to his eternal credit, kept faith with Kondrat and the two were accorded the kind of spontaneous cheer that echoed the sporting feelings of all present when they came smiling back in to the winner's enclosure.

"We go back a while", said Francois Doumen to me as I offered my congratulations to his wife, Elizabeth and himself.

He was remembering the time in the Spring of 1988 in the count-down to the Cheltenham Fetival meeting when I talked to him on the gallops at Lamorlaye, beside Chantilly outside Paris as he was preparing to launch a bid for the Gold Cup with Nupsala and his compatriot, Yann Porzier was bidding for the Champion Hurdle with Marly River.

Doumen had the consolation then of seeing Nupsala jump the Cheltenham fences and finish a very creditable fourth. He was on offer at no more than 8/1 which was understandable as the bookies had allowed him off at 25/1 when he won the King George VI Chase at Kempton the previous December by fifteen lengths (Doumen himself had backed Nupsala ante-post at 50/1 to win that event).

"So we come to the Mecca of English National Hunt racing in search of the Holy Grail and, as tradition will have it, the pilgrimage was fraught with hazards", wrote Elizabeth Doumen, a well-known freelance journalist in her own right, at the outset of the article I commissioned from her at the time for the *Irish Racing Annual*.

And she concluded: "No, we did not bring home the Holy Grail in the shape of the Gold Cup but we returned to Chantilly with a host of memories – memories that will last us a lifetime and we realise now why those who have once experienced the atmosphere of this unique Festival meeting want so much to return. We shall return. . . ."

And return they did . . . not just once but every year from the time The Fellow launched his first bid for the Gold Cup in 1991. And Francois Doumen fittingly wore shamrock on Gold Cup Day '94 – St. Patrick's Day – and remarked to me, as I shook his hand: "It must have been the lucky shamrock that did it this time!"

The search for the Holy Grail was over and The Fellow had proved himself a most worthy champion.

❈   ❈   ❈   ❈

We end this chapter where we came in . . . with that man again, Martin Pipe.

He had just the one winner, Balasane in the Stayers' Hurdle at the 1994 Cheltenham Festival meeting and Richard Dunwoody, his No. 1 jockey was in the Alps skiing, as he was under suspension.

Meanwhile, "The Duke" Nicholson landed a double with Viking Flagship taking the Queen Mother Champion Chase and Mysilv the Triumph Hurdle and it would have been a three-timer for him and Adrian Maguire had Baydon Star, the 5/2 favourite, not been beaten into second place by Nakir in the "Arkle".

You were left to wonder if Dunwoody was right after all to leave the Nicholson stable for the "Pipe line" with his 30th birthday behind him that January? Was he, on his own admission, putting the cementing of the title and the attainment of 200 winners in a season before the constant pursuit of quality?

If Richard had doubts, they must have been eased when he won the Aintree Grand National on the Pipe-trained Miinnehoma.

He has now won two Grand Nationals (West Tip being his first in 1986), a Gold Cup (Charter Party, 1988) and a Champion Hurdle (Kribensis, 1990) and, in addition, he won the King George VI Chase two years running on Desert Orchid (1989 and '90) and the Irish Grand National on the popular grey in 1990. He has come a long way from his childhood days in County Down, so well chronicled by Jimmy Walker in his book, *Richard Dunwoody: Bred to be Champion*.

But still at Cheltenham he has been overshadowed in recent seasons by the sheer brilliance of Adrian Maguire. Nothing finer, to my mind, than the ride Maguire gave Viking Flagship in winning the 1994 Queen Mother Champion Chase by a neck from Travado and Jamie Osborne with Declan Murphy, third, a further length behind, on Deep Sensation.

If Cheltenham, in the words of J. P. McManus, is about quality and class, then this trio of riders and Charlie Swan too, of course, have set the scene alight with their exploits. Jamie Osborne recorded a fabulous five-timer in winning the Ritz Club trophy at the 1992 Festival meeting (Flown, Young Pokey, Nomadic Way, Remittance Man, Dusty Miller) and it included a treble on the opening day. And Limerick-born Declan Murphy, aptly described as the rider with the best pair of hands, displayed all his outstanding qualities as one of the finest horsemen of our time by winning the Queen Mother Champion Chase from Cyphrate and Katabatic on the Josh Gifford-trained, Deep Sensation in 1993. How happy everyone was when Declan survived that horrific fall in 1994 when he lay at death's door for days.

The traditions of great horsemanship and brilliant riding at Cheltenham go back to what Martin Molony and Audrey Brabazon produced in their epic battles in the late forties and the dawn of the fifties, to Pat Taaffe on Arkle and G. W. Robinson on Mill House, Tommy Carberry on L'Escargot, Frank Berry on Glencarrig Lady and Bobby Beasley on Captain Christy, to John Francome and Dessie Hughes and, of course, to that unforgettable moment when Jonjo O'Neill on Dawn Run won the Gold Cup in 1986 and the balladeers sang of it and intrepid characters did their Peter O'Sullivan-style commentaries all over Ireland.

PART TWELVE

RICHARD HANNON

*More Than One "Sting" From
The Cork Connection*

21

Singing *"The Banks"* at Newmarket and The Curragh

Newmarket had never seen anything like it on English 2,000 Guineas Day. And likewise the victory scenes at the Curragh dwarfed anything ever witnessed at the headquarters of Irish racing on the occasion of the running of a classic race.

The Horgans and their friends were celebrating first in impromptu fashion the victory of Tirol in the English 2,000 Guineas and then the completion of the double as the Richard Hannon-trained colt won the Irish equivalent at the Curragh on 19 May 1990.

The bowler-hatted members of the Turf Club could only raise their eyebrows and sigh, maintaining a dignified silence all the time, as those who had been part of the great "Leeside sting" broke into the Cork anthem, *The Banks Of My Own Lovely Lee* in the winner's enclosure. Making it all the more memorable for them was the fact that Tirol, purchased for 52,000 guineas at the High Flyer Sales in Newmarket and considered cheap at the price by Hannon, easily repulsed the challenge of the Gallic invader, Machiavellian. I still smile to myself as I recall one intrepid Corkonian exclaiming to the heavens: "Who put the ball in the back of Freddie Head's net?". And then with cool aplomb, he turned to me and shouted: "Put that in your next book, Raymond."

Richard Hannon and the "Cork Connection" had been an

integral part of the racing scene ever since the burly Wiltshire trainer won the English 2,000 Guineas and the Irish 2,000 Guineas with 19,000 guineas purchase, Don't Forget Me for Jim Horgan in 1987. This was the first time that a major coup, masterminded by Hannon, stung the ante-post layers badly – so badly, in fact, that it was estimated that they were hit for a £250,000 pay-out.

The Horgan brothers had started backing the colt for the Newmarket classic at 66/1 in September of '86 and continued consistently to take all the odds from 33/1 to 30/1. And then to cap it all, they waded in on the course itself until Don't Forget Me eventually went off at 9/1.

But that gamble was to be overshadowed by the "killing" the Horgans and their friends made on Tirol. The overall winnings were reputed to have topped the £500,000 mark.

Tirol carried the colours of John Horgan as Michael Kinane brought him home a two lengths winner. "We all started backing him back in January 1990 when he was at odds of between 40/1 and 50/1", John told me in Cork when I was researching my book, *The High Rollers Of The Turf.* "As the price came down, we continued to put money on him. There was a lot of money bet in Cork on the day of the race itself, as we didn't mind telling people that we expected him to win.

"Everyone was backing him. It didn't change the odds as the prices were being set in England. The bookies didn't give him the chance that we did. In the end he started at 9/1."

It is understandable in a way why the English bookies didn't see Tirol as posing a real threat. For months before Machiavellian had been the "talking horse" for the race. Indeed, Francois Boutin confidently asserted that the colt was "one of the best horses I ever trained."

Little wonder that the "inspired" money had gone on him in the ante-post betting and when they went to the start at Newmarket his price was down to 6/4.

They flew across in their own plane, the members of the Horgan family and close friends. Already the champagne was on ice in The Briar Rose, the Horgans' "local" in the Douglas area of Cork (adorning the walls of the bar are two fine prints of Don't Forget Me and Tirol in victory).

The fact that Tirol had two lengths to spare over Machiavellian at the finish was academic to the victory scenes in the winner's enclosure. The Horgans and their connections took over the place. It was more reminiscent of Cheltenham during the Festival meeting in March after a major Irish success than the normally staid reaction you get nowadays when a horse belonging to one of the Sheikhs wins a Classic.

"All it needed to complete the impromptu party was a céilí band", wrote John Karter in the *Sunday Times*, as he described how the connections of the winner "jigged ecstatically around the horse and trainer, Richard Hannon."

"It was like a breath of fresh air in racing's stuff citadel", added Karter.

Meanwhile back in Cork that Saturday – 5 May 1990 to be exact – was already going into gambling lore as "Black Saturday" for the bookmakers by the Lee. They took such a hammering that some had to close as they didn't have the cash to pay out what they owed. "But everyone got paid on Monday", said John Horgan.

Tirol confirmed with greater authority still the superiority he had shown at Newmarket when he beat Machiavellian into fourth place at the Curragh. This time Pat Eddery had the mount. John Horgan on the day feared Royal Academy more than Machiavellian. And he was proved right in that. Reports during the week that Royal Academy had done an outstanding gallop were reflected in the sustained support the 3.5 million Nijinsky colt received in the betting and he started at 4/1 with Tirol 5/4 favourite and Machiavellian at 9/4, having opened at 7/4.

Vincent O'Brien, aware of Royal Academy's stamina limitations, was reported to have told John Reid that he did not mind how long he held up the colt, he would not blame him if he got beat. The Ballydoyle representative had the rest of the field beaten when he led briefly inside the last furlong – but he could not repel the late surge of Tirol and Pat Eddery. It was either going to be a case of Royal Academy winning right on the line or not at all. He got beat a neck.

❀ ❀ ❀ ❀

It was only natural – fitting you might say – that the Horgans should turn to Richard Hannon when they were seeking a man to go into the market-place for them and purchase a potential Classic winner that could in time be described as a very shrewd one.

Hannon, who is himself of Irish extraction, eschews pretension just as the Horgans do. Secondly, he has the reputation of being as staight as a die in an industry noted for hustlers and trick-of-the-loop merchants who have no qualms whatsoever in taking a greenhorn to the cleaners. And, thirdly, he has a remarkable eye for a yearling as evidenced by the inexpensive horses he bought that turned out to be big winners (apart from Don't Forget Me and Tirol, one had only to pinpoint brilliant sprinter, Lyric Fantasy, which was purchased for 12,500 guineas for the Earl of Carnarvon, the Queen's racing manager and she won nearly £200,000 in prizemoney, including victories at Royal Ascot and York, before being sold for 340,000 guineas. Enstone Spark, winner of five races including the Lowther Stakes, cost only £3,000 as a yearling while Fly Baby, who won the Queen Park Stakes at Royal Ascot, was picked up for £1,700. And one must never forget Tokyo Tommy ("the cheapest horse I ever trained", says Hannon) who was purchased at the Doncaster Sales for £200 and won three races as a two-year-old, including a victory at Epsom on Derby Day with Lester Piggott in the saddle – "and that was a day when you had horses running at Epsom that cost hundreds of thousands", added the trainer.

The reason he has bought so cheaply and so successfully can be put down to the fact that where others get totally caught up in breeding lines, Hannon buys what catches his experienced eye and conformation is of immense importance to him. He is willing to put his money on the line in backing his own judgement and he has been known to go to sales and buy up to 20 yearlings maybe and then places them with owners who have faith in him – and he can take a leg himself in some of them.

Hannon was born and bred then to be a down-to-earth, fun-loving individual – yet at the same time he is a thorough professional and a credit to his chosen profession.

His first love in life was the pop music business and he delighted in his time the teeny-boppers when he was drummer with groups like the Trogs and Dave Dee, Dozy, Reaky, Mich and Tich.

Now for the generation that missed out on the impact they made, it has got to be noted that the Trogs were semi-legenday rockers from Andover who enjoyed a string of hits during the Sixties. Richard Hannon seeks to play down his association with the group, preferring to say simply: "I just left school and played once or twice for the Trogs – just as a fill-in."

Hannon's Irish-born father, Harry, was a trainer and something of a legend in the eyes of those who worked in his Lewis yard.

In the period when Richard was still a schoolboy, Mick Masson, son of a neighbouring trainer, was a playmate of his and would be invited to tea from time to time.

"I shall never forget those tea parties", Masson told Christopher Poole, Racing Correspondent of the *Evening Standard*. "We always had beans on toast and for years afterwards I used to refer to Richard as 'Baked Beans Hannon'."

Harry Hannon's time was a hilarious time. He was wont to enjoy a lunchtime drink at a local hostelry. It became a habit of his when he returned from these "liquid soirees" to sack half the staff.

"Many's the time I had to tour round and re-engage the lads", said Richard Hannon, recalling the era when he had just taken over the family stable while being "helped" by the advice of his father. "After a while the lads got used to it and turned up for evening stables irrespective of what my father had said to them at lunch hour."

When Richard Hannon, just three years after he had taken out a licence, won the 1973 English 2,000 Guineas with 50/1 longshot Mon Fils, he thought he was set up financially for life.

"I'm on the gravy train for life", he boasted that rainy day on Newmarket Heath and he could have been forgiven for going over the top somewhat in the exuberance and excitement of victory, as he had "a nice few quid" on at 200/1. However, he hadn't reckoned with rapidly escalating costs.

359

And there was a large family to care for; his wife Jo, to whom he had become married in 1966, had presented him with three daughters. They decided in 1975 to have a last try for a son.

Hannon telephoned the maternity hospital from the racecourse and was told by someone with a sense of humour matching his own at the other end of the line: "You have a fourth daughter – but you also have two sons."

"They were like peas in a pod. When they were small I would place them on the carpet in their nappies and get my friends to bet on which was the odd one out", he recalled with a hearty laugh.

Hannon, who is now a grandfather, found that "triplets were expensive" – and in the days before he built up his stable to the powerhouse it is today, he became adept at placing horses to win at remunerative odds and he was willing then to go to the small tracks where he knew the opportunities were better rather than tilting at windmills just to satisfy his ego. That skill in placing is still every bit as evident today.

⌘ ⌘ ⌘ ⌘

Today he trains 200 horses, divided between his two yards four miles apart at the East Everleigh stables on the rolling Wiltshire plains where Queen Boadicea routed the Roman adversary. And, amazing as it may seem, he feels underworked at that, making the point that in France you find trainers with maybe 300 horses in their care.

His link-up with Tony Budge, a millionaire tycoon in the civil engineering sector, enabled Hannon to use more financial muscle at the sales, saw him win the Gimcrack Stakes three times in recent years and, more important still, take on the power of the biggest Newmarket stables.

He emerged as top trainer in 1992 with 154 winners and £1.7 million in prizemoney and the impressive strike-rate continued when he set a new record in 1993 in saddling the winners of 182 races (the previous record of 180 was set in 1987 by Henry Cecil) – and those 182 victories meant prizemoney of £1,229,061.

For a long time he had reason to wonder to himself why the oil-rich Arabs hadn't come "knocking at my door".

"I expect I'd be quick enough to open if they did", he said on one occasion.

Now Saudi Prince Fahd Salman, Deputy Governor of Dharan, is numbered among the Arab owners he trains for – but you can rest assured that Hannon will remain true to the dictum he expounded three years ago: "I'm happy to cater for the small man who has one horse. They are the backbone of the sport."

Richard Hannon knew days of struggle starting out. Today, however, as he stands at the very pinnacle of his profession and looks at the pictures in his home of Don't Forget Me and Tirol in their Classic triumphs, he can reflect calmly that his father was a trainer of handicappers – but never lost his zest for life. And the fun-loving, comedian, wise-cracking part of Hannon's character allows him to note philosophically that "the one thing about this training business is that you can be flying one minute and the next it all comes crashing down about you" and yet he doesn't get all serious and strung-up about it.

When Dessie Hughes saw his 21-year-old son, Richard, join the Hannon stable in '94 he was very happy about it and Richard quickly hit the winning trail in Britain. The "Curragh Connection" following on the "Cork Connection". . . .

The Irish identify with the Irishness in Richard Hannon and his ability to enjoy the "crack". As he reaches his half-century in life, the horizons carry the promise of more rich harvests – and you can bet with confidence that the winners will continue to flow from East Everleigh.

PART THIRTEEN

HENRY CECIL

The Champion Who Rides
The High Sierras

22

Back On Top Again After Days Of Trauma

Henry Cecil is a real Tiger of the Turf on the Flat – a man who has ridden the High Sierras for twenty years in that his strike rate in the Classics and major races has been awesome. He has won every English Classic at least twice.

The Master of Warren Place invariably comes into the reckoning as winter closes in and men look ahead to the following year's Classics. It's impossible to imagine the antepost layers devising their lists and not giving the closest possible attention to the exposed material in Cecil's yard while at the same time looking for "inspired" information for the "dark ones", especially any likely Derby candidates, that may not have made a racecourse appearance as yet. The way Commander In Chief came out and won the 1993 Epsom Derby represented a tribute in itself to his mastery and skill.

Where Richard Hannon came to the profession with no silver spoon and, on his own admission, knew days of struggle at the outset, Henry Richard Amherst Cecil whose CV lists him as being the son of the Hon. Henry Cecil (brother of 3rd Baron Amherst of Hackney) and Rohays, daughter of Sir James Burnett, 13th Bt., certainly had everything going for him when he became assistant trainer to his stepfather, Sir Cecil Boyd-Rochfort back in the sixties. When he married Julie Murless, he had as his mentor, Sir Noel Murless, one of

England's greatest post-World War Two trainers and whose name will always be linked with Derby winners like Crepelo (1957), St. Paddy (1960) and Royal Palace (1967) and that smashing filly, Petite Etoile, who in 1959 became the greatest of his five Oaks winners and she also, of course, won the 1,000 Guineas, Champion Stakes and the Coronation Cup.

It seemed unthinkable that Cecil should fail to reach the top of the ladder – and very quickly. Yet his first 30 or so runners were losers and, as Rodney Masters revealed in a profile in the *Racing Post*, Noel Murless was so concerned for his son-in-law that he brought himself to say quite bluntly: "Your horses are galloping like a lot of old gentlemen. Make them *work*."

Indeed, Cecil was so depressed during this difficult period that he gave up going racing for a time in case he overheard would-be backers of his runners saying openly: "That's one of Cecil's. Don't back it, he couldn't train ivy up a wall."

All that changed from the moment his first winner, Celestial Cloud, went in at Ripon on 17 May 1969. And when Bolkonski won the English 2,000 Guineas in '75 and Wollow made it two back-to-back in the Newmarket Classic in 1976, Cecil had entered the Premier League.

He won the Epsom Derby for the first time in 1985 with Slip Anchor; Reference Point followed in 1987 and then Commander In Chief made it three Blue Ribands in '93. Old Vic, already winner that season of the French Derby, became his first Budweiser Irish Derby winner in 1989 and Commander In Chief completed a Derby double when holding off French Derby winner, Hernando in the Curragh Classic in 1993. He has won the King George VI and Queen Elizabeth Stakes three times with Reference Point (1987), Belmez (1990) and King's Theatre (1994).

Amazingly, the Prix de l'Arc de Triomphe, Europe's most prestigious all-aged race, has so far eluded him but he has reason to argue convincingly that he might have won with Old Vic if he was not retired prematurely after injuring a tendon in a racecourse gallop at Nottingham when being prepared specially for the Longchamp race. And then to compound Cecil's ill-luck in this event, Belmez, who became the substitute for Old Vic, tread on a stone two days before the race and though it killed his prospects of winning, he still managed to finish a brave fifth.

The final irony for Cecil was that he housed Saumarez in his stable until May, 1990, and then Charles St. George sold the colt to America. It was accepted – even by Cecil himself – as the wisest decision at the time but he couldn't have visualised the extraordinary progress that Saumarez would make, so much so that he won the Prix de l'Arc de Triomphe that same year. "It was just one of those things", said Cecil ruefully.

✿ ✿ ✿ ✿

Cecil experienced traumatic days and went through a time of "enormous pressure", to quote his own words, after the break-up of his 24-year-old marriage to Julie and it was even tougher on Natalie, the girl he was later to wed, as the news hounds and gossip columnists of the tabloid press went to town literally on the story. "Natalie is young and it was very difficult for her to take. Personally, I could take it, but when one half suffers so does the other one", he confessed frankly to Richard Edmondson of *The Independent* and a bitter taste remains from those days of media hounding.

He maintained that the upheavals at Warren Place (with Julie moving to the other side of Newmarket to set up new stables and Willie Jardine, Cecil's long-serving assistant joining her) hadn't really disturbed his training operation. But one was left to wonder all the same, despite the fact that he didn't have any outstanding ammunition in '91. He consoled himself by saying: "I can't be champion trainer every year, can I?".

At the time I was finishing this book in the sumer of '94 Cecil had already been champion trainer in Britain ten times (1976, '78, '79, '82, '84, '85, '87, '88, '90 and '93). Those ten titles meant that he had won one more than Sir Noel Murless, who was leading trainer nine times between 1948 and 1973.

Fellow Newmarket trainer, Italian-born Luca Cumani, who was assistant for two years to Henry Cecil before setting up on his own, is a man who has always thought big and

367

aimed big and you feel that if he had the fire-power at his disposal that the Master of Warren Place has, his record in the major races would be even more impressive. He was one of the main sufferers when the Aga Khan moved all his horses out of Britain, distributing them between Ireland and France, over the "Aliysa Affair". Cumani had won the Epsom Derby and Budweiser Irish Derby for the Aga Khan with Kahyasi in 1988 and the following year he won the Irish 1,000 Guineas for Sheikh Mohammed with Ensconse. One of the other outstanding horses he trained was Commanche Run, winner of the English St. Leger in 1984 while Old Country won the Italian and French St. Legers and Jockey Club Cup and Tolomeo took the rich Arlington Million in Chicago in 1983.

Cumani paid the generous tribute to Henry Cecil that he has been "Britain's best trainer over the last 20 years and he's still terribly ambitious and competitive."

"He's one of the most generous people anyone could hope to meet, totally open-hearted", added Cumani, who made the significant point that Cecil had taught him the very valuable lesson that "it's just as important to have a horse mentally happy as physically fit, unless there is a combination of both values, you are not going to get results."

Cecil is renowned for his range of designer suits and Gucci shoes but then when you have trained over 2,400 winners and your Classic total in Britain alone has reached 14, then you can indulge in sartorial splendour to your heart's content because you don't have to prove anything to anyone anymore. In Cecil's case, as he put it so aptly to John Karter of the *Sunday Times*, the excitement still comes from watching new stars appear. "I love the training more than the racing. I find the actual process of bringing a horse to its peak for a race particularly satisfying, although, being extremely competitive, I naturally enjoy winning as well.

✼ ✼ ✼ ✼

I could never imagine *Hello* putting the shaved domed head of Barney Curley on its front cover – Barney who talked to me during my research for *The High Rollers Of*

The Turf in his seven-bedroom mansion with its indoor swimming pool and snooker table at Stetchworth on the outskirts of Newmarket. Terry Ramsden was down in his luck, broken by the financial markets and the bookmakers, when Curley bought his mansion from him for "a reasonable price" ("I wouldn't have had the money to buy it if I had to bid the price it would have gone at auction"). Barney's horses are in a different league entirely – the bottom league – compared with those trained by Henry Cecil. But Curley is a survivor. And from the time his father was "skint" at the dogs he vowed that he would NEVER allow himself to be broken by the bookmakers. Nothing gives him greater pleasure in life than to make them squirm and they have had good cause to remember a Curley "sting" or two.

I could not imagine either the editorial executives of *Hello* waxing enthusiastic about doing a "special" on Neville Callaghan, a man who is no stranger to controversy.

But I recall a very pleasant poached salmon lunch given by Neville and his wife, Jenny, in the sun-drenched garden of their Hamilton Road home (just across the road from Lester Piggott) during the Newmarket '91 July meeting and there was a millionaire Irish owner, based in the South of England, present as the chilled wine went down easily over the racing conversation and the banter. His staunch patrons have never wavered in their loyalty to Neville Callaghan and he has rewarded them by landing a few nice "touches", as when Corrupt won the Bonusprint Easter Stakes at Kempton in March '91 at 20/1 and followed up by taking the Maxime Club Derby Trial Stakes at Lingfield in May of the same year, the connections getting in at 8/1 before the Lear Fan colt eventualy went off at 9/2.

After racing on that July day in '91 I had a relaxed game of snooker with Neville Callaghan and a few friends in the Newmarket club frequented by the racing fraternity.

❊ ❊ ❊ ❊

Michael Stoute has been one of Henry Cecil's great Newmarket rivals. The Barbados-born trainer has an outstanding record in the Classics and unquestionably he had a fabulous 1986 season when he recorded a notable Classic treble at the Curragh, his Epsom Derby hero, Shahrastani winning the first running of the Irish Derby with the Budweiser brand name attached to it, Colorspin taking the Gilltown Irish Oaks and Sonic Lady the Irish 1,000 Guineas.

Stoute won the English 2,000 Guineas twice with Shadeed (1985) and Doyoun (1987), the 1,000 Guineas with Musical Bliss (1989) and he had his first Epsom Derby triumph in 1981 with the ill-fated Shergar, who like Shahrastani was owned by the Aga Khan and who also went on to win the Irish Derby. Stoute had a third victory in the Curragh Classic through Shareef Dancer in 1983.

He won the English Oaks with Fair Salinia in 1978, the year he landed the Ascot Gold Cup with Shangamuzo. His other Irish Classic triumphs saw Shaadi win the 2,000 Guineas in 1989, Fair Salinia the Oaks in 1978 and Colorspin's success in this race in 1986 was followed up by Unite making it two back-to-back in 1987 while his Melodiet dead-heated with Henry Cecil's Diminuendo for the 1986 Irish Oaks.

Of course, Shergar followed up his English Derby and Irish Derby successes by also winning the King George VI and Queen Elizabeth Stakes in 1983.

As in the case of Cecil, the ante-post layers will always keep a close eye on the material in his yard, for he is a trainer who has operated on the High Plains for sixteen years now.

Stoute has always been a great favourite with the Irish racing fraternity and they obviously identify with the sport-loving side of his character – in this instance with the game cricket that is part and parcel of life in his native Barbados.

When Geoff Lester called to his Beech Hurst stable back in 1986 to discuss the high spots of that memorable season for an article for the *Irish Racing Annual*, he found him practising at the net in his own back garden and revealing his one remaining sporting ambition as wanting "to improve my batting average".

And he was bemoaning the fact that Willie Haggas, skipper of the Sunday side, "had the audacity to tell me that I was in the squad for the final match of the season. Me? I used to be an automatic choice but it seems I'm slipping", said Stoute, then turned 40, with a roar of laughter.

In that '86 season the swashbuckling Stoute left Henry Cecil in his wake as he smashed his way to a record-breaking prizemoney haul of well over £2 million and in the process mopped up 10 Group One races in Europe. What rankled with him was that Shahrastani was viewed as the horse who won Dancing Brave's Derby – as if it was a fluke.

After the controversy that surrounded Greville Starkey's riding of the Guy Harwood-trained Dancing Brave at Epsom, Stoute was naturally very anxious to put the record straight at the Curragh. He noted that "it would have taken something very special to have beaten Shahrastani on Irish Derby day. He was at his peak and clocked a good time."

Reverting back to Epsom, Stoute praised Walter Swinburn for a superb ride on the Aga Khan's colt. "We won the Epsom Derby and nobody can take that away from us. I felt the media were a bit hard on Greville Starkey because I have seen the video many times and it is patently obvious that Dancing Brave did not act on the course. Greville had given him a slap down the neck six furlongs out and the horse made no ground whatsoever coming down the hill."

Stoute so badly wanted to prove a point at Ascot in the King George VI and Queen Elizabeth Stakes but, sadly, Shahrastani ran a stone below his Curragh form and trailed in a well-beaten fourth to Dancing Brave, who went on to prove what an outstanding colt he was by winning the Prix de l'Arc de Triomphe that same season in the hands of Pat Eddery.

"I am not saying we would have beaten Dancing Brave at Ascot but something was definitely wrong with Shahrastani", said Stoute. "We still reckon he got a clod of dirt stuck in his throat but, even allowing for that, he probably had an off-day. In Britain we seem to get totally uptight about losses of form, whereas in the United States it happens all the time and is an accepted thing. It's a bit like the reigning champion being beaten in the first round at Wimbledon. Even champions have to lose some time!"

⌘ ⌘ ⌘ ⌘

Tall John Gosden, who holds a degree in land economics from Cambridge University, had been training with marked success for a decade on the west coast of America, when Sheikh Mohammed's advisers made him an offer that he simply couldn't refuse and came back to Britain to establish himself at his Stanley House Stables on Newmarket's Bury Road (he trains around 150 horses for the Sheikh).

No one could question his credentials or his experience of every facet of the training profession. He is a son of "Towser" Gosden, who had the misfortune to be struck by a fatal illness when he had Charlottown in his yard and he was forced to allow the colt to pass to Gordon Smyth, who trained him to win the 1966 Epsom Derby in the hands of Scobie Breasley.

John Gosden's 'education' consisted of two years (1975-'76) as assistant to Noel Murless and he also spent an invaluable year (1977) with Vincent O'Brien – and it was the year of The Minstrel, Alleged, Be My Guest and Artaius. With Murless and O'Brien, Gosden learned the value of patience when it came to handling horses of Classic and Group potential and he put the lessons to good use when he set up on his own in California, having first spent a period assisting the late Tommy Doyle.

Out in the early mornings at Hollywood Park and Santa Anita, Gosden became closely acquainted with Charlie (The Bald Eagle) Whittingham, a legend in his own lifetime and, as he told Hugh McIlvanney of the *Sunday Times*: "Charlie is a man who learned everything for himself and he is not reluctant to share the knowledge he has accumulated. He was a very good adviser to me, and a good friend."

Bates Motel and Royal Heroine were two of the top horses that made Gosden's name known right across America. Now he is seen as a leading light among the current crop of English trainers with the fire-power at his disposal to make a telling impact.

When Paul Kelleway, who has only 12 horses in his Newmarket yard, pulled off a sensational victory with 20/1 chance Belle Genius in the Moyglare Stud Fillies Stakes at the Curragh on Sunday, 11 September 1994 (relegating the hitherto unbeaten Jim Bolger-trained filly, Eva Luna to third place), he said in the winner's enclosure: "I now go out with only four horses in the first lot and there to the right of me

372

are 100 Cecil horses and to the left 90 of Gosden's, not to mention 80 of Cumani's – no wonder I know how General Custer felt!"

Incidentally, Kelleway, a former jump jockey, who won a Champion Hurdle on Bula and a Champion Chase on Crisp, has now trained six Group winners and some years ago saddled Gulf Key to win the Beresford Stakes at the Curragh.

❋ ❋ ❋ ❋

I was at Newmarket on the day in 1989 when Major Dick Hern in his wheelchair was acclaimed in the unsaddling enclosure after the 2,000 Guineas triumph of the brillliant Nashwan – and it was repeated at Epsom when he completed a Classic double. The Hamdam Al Maktoum's Blushing Groom colt went on to win the King George VI and Queen Elizabeth Stakes, the race Hern had previously won with Brigadier Gerard (1972), Troy (1979), Ela-Mana-Mou (1980) and Petoski (1985).

The 73-year-old trainer, who won the St. Leger as far back as 1962 with Hethersett when private trainer to Major L. B. Holliday and then set up on his own at West Isley in Berkshire the following year, put some of the greatest horses of modern times through his hands, none more so than Brigadier Gerard, winner of seventeen out of eighteen races. He also handled St. Leger and Coronation Cup winner, Bustino, who was narrowly beaten by Grundy in an epic battle for the 1975 "King George"; Derby winners, Troy (1979) and Henbit (1980) and Oaks winners, Bireme (1980) and Sun Princess (1983) and 1981 St. Leger winner, Cut Above. Dunfermline won the Oaks for the Queen in her Silver Jubilee Year in 1977 and the same filly was successful in the St. Leger that season.

Joe Mercer was associated with some of Hern's greatest triumphs and he was succeeded by Willie Carson.

He was badly injured in a hunting accident in 1984 but his enormous courage in face of adversity was rewarded when Petoski made it a record five "King George" successes for him a year later – just a fortnight after he had won the '85 Irish Oaks with Helen Street.

❋ ❋ ❋ ❋

"A gentleman among racing's many players, was how Simon Holt in a pre-Epsom Derby '94 feature in the *Sporting Life* described the Master of Arundel Castle, John Dunlop and went on to write that he exuded "quintessential Englishness . . . and, win or lose, retained the same politeness and dignity to the watching world."

Yes, Dunlop looking across the parkland of his spread as he smokes a cool cigarette, cutting a figure of almost detached elegance.

With the pained weariness of a Sir Laurence Olivier in one of his great dramatic roles, he talked to Simon Holt of his "delight" at escaping the "absolute circus" at Newmarket in the count-down to the '94 Epsom – "with jockeys running around riding three horses for different trainers."

Could one deduce a subtle swipe at Henry Cecil in that and the near-hysteric media attention the Master of Warren Place commanded as the fateful decision was being taken on who would ride King's Theatre?

Dunlop's Erhaab showed the acceleration of a Golden Fleece as Willie Carson brought him with a devastating late run to win the '94 Epsom Derby, form that was franked when the runner-up, King's Theatre, won the King George VI and Queen Elizabeth Stakes in the hands of Michael Kinane. Erhaab had to be good to win as he did but we shall never know just how good he really was. After he had run far below expectations in both the Coral Eclipse Stakes and in the "King George", exhaustive tests were carried out and these showed that he was suffering from serious damage to suspensory ligaments. Sheikh Hamdam Al Maktoum had no choice other than to retire the colt.

Dunlop's Mehthaaf had started favourite for the 1994 English 1,000 Guineas but was beaten into fourth place by the Tommy Stack-trained Las Meninas. However, Mehthaaf turned the tables in the Irish 1,000 Guineas, winning by one-and-a-half lengths from her Newmarket conquerer.

Dunlop's first Epsom Derby winner had been Shirley Heights in 1978 and this colt went on to win the Irish Derby at the Curragh. Dunlop had his second Irish Derby win with Salsabil in 1990 and Hamdan Al Maktoum's brilliant filly had earlier won the English 1,000 Guineas and the Oaks.

Dunlop also won the English 1,000 Guineas with Quick As Lightning (1980) and Shadayid in 1991, the English Oaks with Circus Plume in 1984 and the English St. Leger with Moon Madness in 1986. He won the Irish Leger in 1983 with Mountain Lodge.

The smart miler, Posse and Coronation Cup winner, Sea Chimes, were other good horses to be trained at Arundel but there was the great disappointment also of Snaafi Dancer, the world's most expensive yearling at 10.2m dollars, failing to even make the racecourse after being two years in training.

❋ ❋ ❋ ❋

Paul Cole, a pupil of George Todd, who started training at Lambourn in 1968 before moving to Whatcombe, finished leading trainer in Britain with £1,260,000 in prize-money in 1991 mainly through the exploits of Generous, who completed the Epsom Derby-Irish Derby-King George VI and Queen Elizabeth Stakes treble. And the previous season Snurge (who was to pass out Pebbles as the highest money-earner trained on British or Irish shores) had won the English St. Leger and Knight's Baroness took the Irish Oaks.

Highly-articulate Robert Charlton had his hour in 1990 when Quest For Fame won the Epsom Derby and Sanglamore the French Derby in his very first season as a licence holder.

Alec Stewart was dubbed the "Boy Wonder" when he hit the Classic trail at 29 through Opale winning the Irish St. Leger in 1984. And by the end of the decade his exploits, particularly with a hand of outstanding stayers, had insiders predicting that he would in time be right up there at the top of the "Premier League" with fellow Newmarket trainers like Henry Cecil, Michael Stoute and Luca Cumani.

Mtoto was "Horse of the Year" in 1988, winning the King George VI and Queen Elizabeth Stakes and taking the Eclipse Stakes that same season for the second successive year. Indeed, in the 1987-'88 seasons Mtoto recorded seven wins in all and it would have been eight had he not been so narrowly beaten by Tony Bin in the 1988 "Arc".

The world appeared to be at Stewart's feet as he won 20 Group races across Europe in four years and big handicaps too like the Ebor and Chester Cup.

375

But then it all turned sour. He was hit by a crippling virus. Soon half the boxes at his once full 100-box Clarehaven Stables were empty as frustrated owners took their horses elsewhere. Fortunately, as Rodney Masters revealed in a profile in the *Racing Post*, Stewart, who is the son of a wealthy Kinrosshire farmer and a former pupil of prestigious tradition-laden Gordonstoun, had made ample provision for the rainy days. "We had won some serious prizes and I had worked long enough in the City to know how to manage money", the canny Scot told Masters. "I didn't spend much of my percentage. I banked it."

So even though he had to rent boxes elsewhere while he waited for the virus to clear, he wasn't under the kind of intense pressure from the banks that would otherwise have been the case had he kidded himself in the good times into believing that they would keep on rolling.

He regained the winning trail on the High Plains when Wagon Master won the 1994 Princess of Wales's Stakes at Newmarket – his first Group success since Filia Ardross won the Select Stakes at Goodwood in 1991.

It had been a long four years in the wilderness for one who had drunk so deeply of the vintage wines of success. "I must get back to those heady days", he said. "I feel my career is at a critical crossroads."

The racing world would be watching to see if Stewart could regain his golden touch of the late Eighties. More important still: would he get the greater cross-section of owners he sought to provide him with the "ammunition" to hit the big targets?

❊   ❊   ❊   ❊

Clive Brittain, who came late to training, having worked for Noel Murless for 21 years, has always been admired for not being afraid to have a crack at the big prizes with horses that sometimes appeared to have little chance in such company. But his bold attacking policy has been rewarded on more than one occasion and from his Carlburg Stables in Newmarket he sent out Bold Arrangement on a trail-blazing venture for Europe in 1968 to take on America's best three-year-old colts in the Kentucky Derby. Although Bold Arrangement had to settle for runner-up position, Brittain still deserved the highest possible praise for his adventurous spirit – and the first to acknowledge that would be Dermot Weld.

Brittain's name will always be linked with the brilliant Pebbles (Sharpen Up-La Dolce, by Connaught) who won the English 1,000 Guineas for her breeder, Marcos Lemos in 1984 and, after being sold to Sheikh Mohammed in midsummer, finished second that year in his colours in the Champion Stakes. She went on the following year to become the first filly to win the Eclipse Stakes, climaxing a brilliant autumn campaign by scoring scintillating triumphs in the Champion Stakes and the Breeders' Cup Turf race in New York.

A man who has worked his way up from the bottom, Brittain was training 124 horses at his Carlburg, Newmarket stables in '94. Apart from Pebbles, he has had his share of champions in his time, his other Classic winners being Julio Mariner (1978 English St. Leger), Mystiko (1991 English 2,000 Guineas), User Friendly (1992 English Oaks, Irish Oaks and English St. Leger) and Sayyedati (1993 English 1,000 Guineas). He won the Italian Derby with Hailsham in 1991.

❈ ❈ ❈ ❈

Jack Berry has proved himself a grafter in getting the best results possible from two-year-olds bought cheaply. The policy of going after precocious yearlings that he felt would win early-season races for their owners before the big guns got going, stemmed from the time that the Cockerham (near Lancaster) trainer was forced to give up his career as a National Hunt rider in the North of England because of injury. He started training at Doncaster in 1968 with a handful of jumpers for owners of moderate enough means. The general assumption, after he had his first winners, was that he was basically a National Hunt trainer. But he became convinced that if he was to stay in business, he needed winners on the Flat as well and his best bet was to concentrate on youngsters that would pay a quick dividend to a small outlay.

In those days it was possible to purchase a yearling for £700 or £800 – "and you could hope to pick up a maiden race or a seller with it."

He graduated to the point where he was able to enlarge his stables and switch the emphasis to Flat racing in the early Eighties. By August '94 he was celebrating his fifth consecutive century of winners, though a Group One victory still eluded him as he headed for Leopardstown bidding to win the Heinz 57 Phoenix Stakes with Norfolk Stakes winner, Mind Games (this one could only finish fifth behind the brilliant Jim Bolger-trained filly, Eva Luna).

The Berry philosophy was summed up aptly in an interview in the Wiliam Hill *Action Line* magazine in the Spring of '94 when he said that to many businessmen bringing off a deal worth thousands may not really turn them on all that much – "but I've seen them shake like a leaf watching their horse win a maiden for peanuts at places like Hamilton. It's the adrenalin that racing creates . . . what owners want is winners. It doesn't have to be a big race or great prizemoney. It's just the sheer joy of seeing the horse come first past the post."

He admits to having more small owners than any other yard in Britain with all the syndicates and partnerships but, where the Sangsters and the Arab Sheikhs aim to conquer the Everests in the Classic arena, Berry is Berry and on a Bank Holiday week-end, like the August Bank Holiday week-end, his Union Jack-painted horse-boxes will head south and east from Lancashire with a raiding party maybe 20-strong and take in no less than five meetings. As he told Richard Pitman, he sees a Bank Holiday meeting as "a rich fishing ground" and invariably he will be looking for a good "catch" from the long day.

Yes, that's Barry – the grafter but a very successful one and he's happy as long as he can keep up the kind of successful buying of precocious yearlings that saw him turn out 17 first-time winners in 1993. In fact, Richard Hannon and himself have amassed a staggering total of 640 two-year-old winners between them over the last four campaigns.

❈　❈　❈　❈

Of the "Young Tigers" in Britain, three commanding a lot of headlines in recent times have been Peter Chapple-Hyam, Mark Johnston and John Hills.

By the time he was 29 Peter Chapple-Hyam had saddled three Anglo-Irish Classic winners and sent out from his Manton stables the runner-up in a fourth. His first Classic triumph came on Newmarket's Rowley Mile when Rodrigo de Triano won the 1992 English 2,000 Guineas, bringing Lester Piggott's Classic score to an unprecedented 30. Rodrigo went on to complete his Guineas double at the Curragh – and it was Irish Classic victory No. 16 for Lester.

And then he pulled off a masterly training feat in winning the Epsom Derby with Dr Devious, who had trailed home seventh in the 118th Kentucky Derby at Churchill Downs and Robert Sangster's son-in-law had every reason to believe at one stage that the American owners would not be sending the colt back to Manton.

Just imagine, Chapple-Hyam was only fourteen months into his training career and already he had three Classics under his belt. It would have been four if Dr Devious had not caught St. Jovite in awesome mood at the Curragh on Budweiser Irish Derby Day '92.

The greengrocer's son had a solid education to the racing game. He had been involved in racing for twelve years by the time he took over as Master of historic Manton, the magnificent Wiltshire establishment near Marlborough. He was only 16 when he started with the legendary Fred Rimell, then moved to Barry Hills at Lambourn and when Robert Sangster terminated his contract with Michael Dickinson and invited Hills to take over at Manton, Chapple-Hyam moved with him.

Barry Hills in turn moved back to the South Bank stables at Lambourn and Robert Sangster in what seemed to many a major gamble at the time put his faith in Peter Chapple-Hyam, who became his son-in-law when he married Jane Peacock, daugher of Sangster's second wife, Susan.

It had seemed that Manton would become racing's most expensive white elephant when a deal to dispose of it fell through. The quick Classic victories achieved by Peter Chapple-Hyam not alone vindicated Sangster's faith but restored his own fortunes on the High Plains as Rodrigo de Triano carried his colours in his Newmarket and Curragh triumphs. And they were carried again to a stunning fifteen-lengths triumph when Chapple-Hyam sent Turtle Island to win the Irish 2,000 Guineas in the hands of John Reid on Sunday, 15 May 1994.

The flags of Manton and the Swettenham Stud were flying high and proudly and deservedly so.

❊ ❊ ❊ ❊

In 25 years as a trainer Barry Hills had taken a lion's share of Europe's major prizes. Numbered among these were victories in the English 2,000 Guineas with Tap On Wood (1979), the English 1,000 Guineas with Enstone Spark (1978), the Irish Derby with Sir Harry Lewis (1987) and the Irish Oaks with Dibidale (1974). He won the Prix de l'Arc de Triomphe with Rheingold (1973) and this colt also won the Grand Prix de Saint-Cloud twice; he experienced desperate luck when Dibidale's saddle slipped when she looked certain to win the English Oaks in 1974, though she gained compensation by winning the Irish Oaks and Yorkshire Oaks.

The English Derby and Oaks have eluded Hills, though he could be forgiven for biting his nails in frustration at the so-near-and-yet-so-far Epsom Derby defeats of Rheingold by Roberto in 1972 and Hawaiian Sound by Shirley Heights in 1978. And one could understand his 33-year-old son, Johnd wanting so much to make amends for his father's ill-luck by conquering the twin peaks of the Derby and Oaks in '94 with Chester Vase winner, Broadway Flyer and the highly-rated filly, Wind In Her Hair.

But Broadway Flyer was unplaced and Wind In Her Hair had to settle for runner-up place behind Balanchine.

Where his younger brothers, the twins Michael and Richard became Flat jockeys and first-class ones at that, John seemed destined from the outset to follow in his father's footsteps, though he did make his mark at first as an amateur rider.

He advanced the learning stage in the art of training by spending time initially at the County Tipperary stables of Edward O'Grady and then moved on to Tom Jones, the Newmarket trainer and later to John Gosden when he was based in the United States and Colin Hayes in Australia. He was assistant to his father before taking out a licence seven years ago to begin training on his own in Lambourn. Today he handles 45 horses.

John Hills was able to take the defeats of Broadway Flyer and Wind In Her Hair in philosophical manner, for beforehand he had said to Greg Wood of *The Independent* that there was immense satisfaction to be derived from just "being there".

"You train away with moderate horses going here, there and everywhere, and then you have two good ones, with all the build-up and excitement. It's like a tennis player getting to the final. If you're Martina Navratilova and you get to the final and don't win, you're disappointed, but the first time you ever get to the final you're delighted just to be there", he said.

Now that he had been there, John Hills knows more fully what is required. Nothing would give him greater satisfaction in life than to turn out the winners of the Epsom Derby and the Oaks.

Lady Fortune owes it to him, for the manner in which she has failed to smile on his father at Epsom.

❀ ❀ ❀ ❀

When Mark Johnston sent over Loveyoumillions from Middleham to win the £150,000 Tattersalls Breeders Stakes (6f) at the Curragh in the hands of Jason Weaver on Saturday, 27 August 1994, and supplemented that victory by providing the first and second (Jural and Indian Wedding) in the Futurity Stakes, he was confirming all the accolades showered on him when he won the 1994 English 2,000 Guineas with Mister Baileys – Middleham's first Classic success for half a century.

No one knew Mark Johnston when as a 27-year-old Scottish-born vet he sent out his first winner in 1987 from a small 12-horse stable sited next to a live bombing practice range on the Lincolnshire coast between Grimsby and Mablethorpe and gallops were arranged around tide times. Now 34, he has long since put anonymity behind him. And with 80 horses in his beautifully-renovated Kingsley House stables, numbers among his newest patrons, Sheikh Mohammed for whom he was training five two-year-olds in 1994.

After qualifying as a vet at the University of Glasgow, he practised for a while in Northern Ireland and then in North Yorkshire and Braintree in Essex.

But it was always his long-term goal to become a trainer. Like Jim Bolger he has brought his own distinctive methods to the business of training. Rather than pouring over laboratory print-outs and over-burdening himself with blood tests – unless, of course, a horse is sick – he has based his phenomenal success story on the principle of good feeding and putting his charges through the kind of exercise regime on the high moors that ensure that they don't fold when the pressure really comes on.

The combination he has built with Paul Venner, Managing Director of Baileys Horse Feeds, ensures that there is immense nutritional value in the feed the Johnston-trained horses are given four times a day. The emphasis on these feeds is on animal fat to make good what a horse burns up when at full stretch while providing valuable glucose for the muscles at the same time.

Johnston's business partner is Brian Palmer and together they purchased in the summer of '94 the Warwick House stables, formerly the yard of Neville Crump. This means that Johnston now has boxes for 120 horses.

Everything is on the up-and-up and each season his strike rate goes on improving (he sent out 77 winners in '93 and by mid-July '94 had already passed that total). Before Mister Baileys put a new spotlight on his ability, Johnston had won the Ebor Handicap with Quick Ransom in 1992 and Marina Park gave him his first Royal Ascot success when winning the Princess Margaret Stakes the same year.

"Every indicator suggests we have seen nothing yet", predicted Brough Scott in the *Sunday Times* in July of '94.

The crumbling Middleham Castle, once the seat of Richard III, casts its shadow over the area where Johnston now has his seat.

A Lion of Middleham and Yorkshire – a Lion of the summer

season of '94. And unless Brough Scott has got it very badly wrong, we have a lot to expect in the seasons to come from the man who started out so small on the Lincolnshire coast and who has the confidence in is own ability and in his methods to build on that first Classic win of Mr Baileys.

❊ ❊ ❊ ❊

The "Young Tigers", both among the Flat jockeys of the current era and the training profession also, can never hope, of course, to emulate or surpass the records set by Lester Piggott and Vincent O'Brien. For me they remain the two incomparables.

When Piggott was in prison I wrote to him telling him that his problems with the Inland Revenue did not affect in the least his standing with the Irish as the "Daddy of them all" when it came to bringing it off in the races that really mattered, the Epsom Derby most of all. I wrote that if we were sitting having a coffee at Fouquets on the Champs Elysees around the time of the Prix de l'Arc de Triomphe and we saw him coming towards us, his sojourn in prison would not influence our rating. Every aficionado in Ireland would react the same as I did and in a way I was conveying the feelings of a nation of horse-lovers.

I know it touched a chord with Lester. We became good friends – a friendship cemented when I visited his Newmarket home more than once when I was researching my biography of Vincent O'Brien (titled *Vincent O'Brien – The Master of Ballydoyle*).

And I felt honoured when he accepted an invitation to attend the launching of the book in the Berkeley Court Hotel. I was amazed when he spontaneously – without any prior planning whatsoever – went up to the podium and took the microphone and delivered some very sincere words.

Always on my trips to Newmarket, Lester would inquire about Vincent O'Brien. And each time I visited Vincent, he would ask in turn how Lester was keeping when I told him I had been over to Newmarket. The mutual bonds between them, I could see, were deep and lasting. How could they be otherwise when you reflected on the golden era of Nijinsky, Roberto, The Minstrel and Alleged?

One Spring day in the sun lounge of Ballydoyle House I asked Vincent O'Brien over coffee if he had any idea of stepping down and he replied simply: "It is hard to break the habits of years."

He was still training – more as a hobby now as the entire operation had been scaled down to a handful of horses in his care – as he passed his 77th birthday on 9 April 1994. Amazing really when you think that he first took out a licence in 1943 and was assisting his father to land some clever coups in 1938 – a span of well over half a century.

But on Wednesday, 6 October 1994, came the dramatic announcement that Vincent O'Brien would be retiring at the end of the season. The Master of Ballydoyle issued a short statement after spending the day at Goffs Sales with his son Charles. It marked the end of an era.

He was stepping down fifty years after he had brought off the Irish Autumn double, his charge Drybob dead-heating at 20/1 in the Irish Cambridgeshire and Good Days, also a 20/1 chance, winning the Irish Cesarewitch. Both horses were ridden by the legendary Morny Wing.

The overall record reads – 16 English Classics, 27 Irish Classics and one French Classic, making a total of 44. If you add to this the three "Arcs", the three "King Georges" and the two big races on the other side of the Atlantic (the Washington DC International Stakes and the Breeders' Cup Mile Turf), you get a grand total of 52.

What "Young Tiger" of the training world can hope to equal or surpass that record?

Lester Piggott, however, found it impossible to let go – to break the habits of years. He was to be found still in the saddle as a grandfather of 58 during the 1994 season, riding all over Europe and surviving a crashing fall at Goodwood to boot. In his case we must also ask: What "Young Tiger" of the current crop of Flat riders gracing the English scene from Frankie Dettori to Jason Weaver can hope to leave the same imprint on the racing sands of time, particularly as you contemplate Piggott's eleven Jockeys' Championship wins and 46 Classic triumphs (30 in England and 16 in Ireland)?

Yes, O'Brien and Piggott stand on a pedestal apart – THE two "Tigers" supreme of their era on the Turf.

PART FOURTEEN

EPILOGUE

Closing the
Shergar File

23

Provos Shot Shergar Shortly After Kidnap

He was a real "Tiger of The Turf", a racing machine in his three-year-old season (1981), winning in turn the Epsom Derby, the Irish Derby and the King George VI and Queen Elizabeth Stakes.

His very brilliance on the racecourse and the fact that he was syndicated at stud for a record figure of £10 million made the fate of the colt who had carried the Aga Khan's colours all the more tragic. Even though his body was never found, all the evidence clearly indicates that Shergar was killed not long after his kidnap by the Provisional IRA in February, 1983.

There has been speculation that he was buried in a bog at Aughnasheelin, near Ballinamore, County Leitrim – but top Garda sources, while expressing absolutely no doubt that Shergar is dead, will not go so far as to pinpoint any particular spot in the Republic as the likely place where he was hastily buried. That must remain an open book.

The Provos in demanding a ransom of £2 million made the mistake of thinking that they could get an immediate decision from those with whom they had made contact by phone. They did not understand fully the machinations involved in the syndication of a stallion. They believed that they could get a quick "Yes" from one individual and that, under threat of Shergar being assassinated, they would be able to collect in double quick time the sum they were seeking.

The Aga Khan could have got £30 million for Shergar if he had acccepted any one of a number of offers from the United States, from breeders in Kentucky. But he decided to keep Shergar at stud in Europe. It was a tremendous tribute on his part to the Irish bloodstock industry that Shergar was earmarked to begin his stud career at the Aga Khan's own Ballymany Stud at the edge of the Curragh.

The Aga Khan was the biggest shareholder in the Syndicate, retaining six of the forty shares himself. That meant that there were 35 other shareholders who had to be contacted before any ransom could be paid. The Aga Khan could NOT act unilaterally.

Complicating matters still further was the fact that these thirty-five shareholders were scattered through nine different countries and in some instances the shares had been bought by companies rather than by individuals, so the head of a company had to be sought out to give his reaction.

And then there was the complex situation, which the Provos could never have known, that looking after the interests of the thirty-five shareholders was a Committee of Five, who in turn were drawn from four countries – Britain, Switzerland, the United States and Ireland (Ghislain Drion as manager of the Ballymany Stud, where Shergar was standing before being kidnapped, was one of the Five). The Provos were not dealing with men who could be expected to be at the end of a phone in the one location at any time of the day or night. They were men constantly on the move as they travelled widely and thus again to make contact with each one of them and expect an immediate reaction presented immense problems.

While the Aga Khan was not a member of the Committee of Five, he had to be kept informed of every move as the single biggest shareholder and owner of the stud where Shergar had been standing. Ghislain Drion experienced quite a deal of difficulty in getting in touch with the Aga Khan to acquaint him in the first place of the kidnapping. He finally reached him in Switzerland.

The kidnappers were on to the home of Ghislain Drion the morning after the kidnap, which took place at approximately 8.40 p.m. on the Tuesday night, 8 February 1983. Drion's wife took the first call and referred the caller to Ballymany Stud. A further call came at 3.45 p.m. and it was as a result of this that Ghislain Drion himself talked that afternoon to the kidnappers' representative and learned that a ransom of £2 million was being sought.

The kidnappers' representative then requested a phone number in France. This was done and confirmation was given in a call to this number that the ransom sum for the safe return of Shergar had been set at £2 million. There was never going to be any suggestion of lowering it.

There is no need to detail the further contacts between the kidnappers and those acting for the shareholders or what evolved from the efforts to get proof that Shergar was actually being held by those making the calls and that he was still alive. Suffice it to say that one evening at 5.45 p.m. a demand was made that the £2 million be delivered by Ghislain Drion in sterling notes in Paris by 12 noon the next day.

It didn't wash with the kidnappers when it was pointed out to them that this was well-nigh impossible. The contacts extended over four days. The kidnappers then made one final demand to have the money ready and when they didn't get the reply they wanted, they used the ominous words "that's it".

The rest was silence.

Later when the Committee of Five tried to restore contact, they couldn't do so – even after clear hints were made through media reports that there was a wish to recommense dialogue.

It was obvious at that point that Shergar had been killed. Time had run out on his Provo kidnappers. The theory in official circles is that he became fractious and that his minders could not control him. They had no other course open to them but to put him down and dispose of the body.

You will still get people willing to give credence to this day to reports that a horse looking like Shergar was sighted in the Channel Islands. Or to the even more bizarre theory that he was somehow spirited out of Ireland to Libya where he is still siring crops of racehorses for an unscrupulous Middle East breeder.

The Garda authorities never had any doubt that it was "a Provo job". They had no doubt either about the identity of the senior Provisional IRA figure who mastermined the kidnapping.

They are convinced he was the same man who was behind the attempt to kidnap Galen Weston, the Canadian-born supermart tycoon from his County Wicklow mansion in August, 1983 – an attempt that went very badly wrong because Weston was in England at the time playing polo and the six-man gang was confronted by members of the Special Branch and most were captured after a shoot-out.

The same gang, with new faces replacing those who had been captured, then kidnapped Don Tidy, an executive of Weston's Quinnsworth supermart chain. Tidy was rescued in Decenmber 1983 by Gardai and troops.

The Provisional IRA's kidnapping policy was aimed at getting funds for the organisation. But an even more sinister aspect of it was that there would be a "protection" approach as well – in a word, multinationals would be told that they would be immune from kidnapping if they were prepared to "cough up" the "necessary".

Naturally, top executives conscious of the ordeal that Don Tidy had gone through and very fearful for their families would be willing to meet the demands without necessarily acquainting the Gardai – and some sources claim that the Provos did extort quite sizeable sums in this manner, though it has never been proved for obvious reasons.

❊   ❊   ❊   ❊

Seán O'Callaghan, who in 1983 was a senior figure in what was dubbed the IRA's "Southern Command", made a statement while in Maghaberry Prison near Belfast in March '93 to the effect that he was told of the fate of Shergar by one of the unit that actually carried out the kidnapping and subsequent killing of the stallion.

The masked gang of six, armed and carrying walkie-talkies, had planned to keep Shergar in the Ballinamore area of

County Leitrim (where Don Tidy was held captive) while endeavouring to gain the £2 million ransom.

But, according to O'Callaghan, the gang never realised just how highly-strung a thoroughbred sire can be when taken from familiar surroundings. "The horse threw himself into a frenzy after being disturbed and since they were unable to pacify him, they had to kill him eventually", said O'Callaghan.

In a state of panic, the kidnappers quickly buried the body – never to be found again – in the area around Ballinamore.

Now it must be stressed that top Garda sources are not accepting this version as confirming beyond any shadow of doubt that Shergar's remains lie somewhere in County Leitrim.

Tom Brady, Security Editor of the *Irish Independent*, who has the best sources in his area of journalism of any newsman in Dublin and who has broken some very big stories in recent times, told me: "What the Garda authorities are certain of beyond any shadow of doubt is that Shergar is dead. They know who was the mastermind behind the kidnapping, as they know who masterminded all the other major kidnappings.

"But they are not prepared to pinpoint any one place in the country and state categorically that Shergar was buried there. So unless his remains can be uncovered and positively identified, that question must remain open – and will remain open."

The "Shergar File" can be closed then to the extent that the "wonder colt" of the 1981 season, who won the Epsom Derby by ten lengths, then pulverised the opposition in the Irish Derby, winning pulling up by four lengths in the hands of Lester Piggott (deputising for the suspended Walter Swinburn) and set the seal on his greatness by winning the King George VI and Queen Elizabeth Stakes, is definitely DEAD.

And that means that personally I will never give any credence to bizarre stories of "sightings" in various parts of the world. I accept fully the word of those who had the inside track – sources I trust and whose job it was to deal only in facts.

Shergar was not long enough at stud to establish himself on

the same level as, say, Nijinsky. In fact, he was only starting his second season at Ballymany when he was kidnapped. It must be remembered that such was the impact that he made in winning his first five races as a three-year-old (he won the Sandown Classic Trial and the Chester Vase in addition to the Epsom Derby, Irish Derby and "King George") that it was inevitable that he would be expected to sire a string of potential champions straight off at stud. The one defeat he suffered as a three-year-old when he finished fourth in the St. Leger – could not take in any way from the aura surrounding his name.

In his first crop he produced Authasl, who went through the ring for 325,000 Irish guineas as a foal and made a European record of 3.1 m. Irish guineas as a yearling when bought by Sheikh Mohammed at Goffs in 1984. He won the 1986 Irish St. leger at 8/1 for Sheikh Mohammed. He was trained by Daid O'Brien and ridden to victory by Christy Roche.

He was also the sire of Maysoon (out of Triple First by High Top), who after winning the Gainsborough Stud Fred Darling Stakes at Newbury on her three-year-old debut in 1986 went on to lose by only three-quarters-of-a-length to Midway Lady in the English 1,000 Guineas (ridden that day, incidentally, by Yves St. Martin) and then looked to have a tremendous chance of victory a furlong out in the Oaks, only to be beaten again by Midway Lady, this time into third place with Untold second. Only a length-and-three-quarters separated the first three and *Raceform Note-Book* noted that Maysoon's effort on that occasion, when she was ridden by Walter Swinburn, "would have won most Oaks".

So one can make no conclusive judgements on what kind of a lasting reputation Shergar would have forged for himself at stud if he had not been kidnapped. With the top-class mares being sent to him, everything was in his favour and in a way it was a tragedy for the Irish breeding industry that he was the cruel victim of a "Provo job" that one would never have imagined would be attempted in a country where the thoroughbred means so much to so many.

Finally, it can be revealed that Chief Superintendent James Murphy, now living in retirement in County Kildare, who was a central figure in leading the investigations into the kidnapping of Shergar and whose grey trilby and distinctive style made him known globally overnight as a result of the intense television coverage of every aspect of the case, refused a sum of at least £250,000 sterling to give his story exclusively to one British paper. All he was asked to do was sit down and speak into a tape-recorder and a "ghost" writer would do the rest.

But the day he retired he made a vow to himself that he would never give an interview about the case or ever talk to any member of the media about it, even on a non-attributable basis. All the financial inducements in the world would not make him change his mind on that.

He has been true to his word.

The man they came to know affectionately in County Kildare as "Jazzer" Murphy will carry to the grave his own conclusions on the "Shergar Affair". His file is closed.

That in itself adds another ironic twist to the story.